# HELEN

*Canada's First Lady of Folklore*

## Clary Croft

## NIMBUS
### PUBLISHING

Nimbus Publishing Limited
PO Box 9301, Station A
Halifax, NS    B3K 5N5
(902)455-4286

Design: Kate Westphal, Graphic Detail
Cover design: Heather Bryan
Author photo: Sharon Croft
Portrait of Helen Creighton by Gillian McCulloch
Transparency provided by:
University of King's College, Halifax, Nova Scotia

Printed and bound in Canada


**Canadian Cataloguing in Publication Data**

ISBN 1-55109-289-1

1. Creighton, Helen, 1899-1989.  2. Folklorists – Canada – Biography.
3. Women folklorists – Canada – Biography.  4. Folklore – Maritime Provinces.  5. Folk songs – Maritime Provinces.  I. Title.

GR55.C74C76 1999    398'.092    C99-9050143-7


Nimbus Publishing acknowledges the financial support of the Canada Council and the Department of Canadian Heritage.

# TABLE OF CONTENTS

# ACKNOWLEDGEMENTS

The writing of a book is a solo project .... I'm sure that's what every writer likes to think, but I know writing this book was made easier and more pleasant with the help of family, friends, colleagues, and staff members at various repositories. I am ever grateful for the love and support I continue to get from my family. I would also like to thank the members of Helen's family, especially Jake Creighton and Lois Harnish, who were always generous with their memories of their Aunt Helen. A special thanks to Alice and Dave Nicholl for their continued support, encouragement, and advice. Helen had many wonderful friends who offered me advice and council. Thanks to Rosemary Bauchman; Ron Caplan; Jackie Dale; Joan Gregson; Mary Kelly; Ronald Labelle; Scott McMillan and Jennyfer Brickenden; Edla Owen; Kaye Dimock Pottie; Marie-Catherine (MacNeil) Saulnier; and Ruth Holmes Whitehead. To friends, informants, and professional colleagues who gave of their time and knowledge, I offer my sincere appreciation: James Bennett; Finvola (Redden) Bower; Fanny (Sellick) Burtram; Hilda Chiasson; Peryl Daly; Edith Fowke; Donald Gallagher; Joleen Gordon; Cora Greenaway; Terry Harnish; Sandy Ives; Bill Langstroth; Pat Martin; Alice (Creighton) Nicholl; Henry Orenstein; Thomas Raddall; Sadie Redden; Mr. and Mrs. Hector Richard; Ernest Sellick; and Eunice Sircom. To those colleagues who helped me find an answer or took the time to give advice, I am also deeply grateful: Terry Eyland; Elizabeth Fraser; Ronald Labelle; Elizabeth Morash; Effie Rankin; Carolyn Thomas; Diane Tye; and Lorne White. Many thanks as well to colleagues working at repositories: Henry Bishop (Black Cultural Centre of Nova Scotia); Carmel Begin, René Landry, and Benoit Terreault (Canadian Museum of Civilization); R.B. Burn (Dartington College of Arts, Devon); Mabel Laine (Encyclopaedia of Music in Canada); Laura Barreiro (St. Christopher House); the St. Roch National Historic Museum, Vancouver; the Victoria University Archives, Toronto; and, especially, to the staff at the Spring Garden Road Branch, Halifax Regional Municipal Library, Reference Department. To the past and present board members of the Helen Creighton Folklore Society I offer my respect and sincere gratitude. The Helen Creighton Fonds is housed at the Public Archives of Nova Scotia. I have worked there off and on over the past 15 years. While working as Contract Archivist for Helen's collection I benefited greatly from the support and advice of the former Provincial Archivist, Carmen Carroll. My supervisor, Joann Watson, and co-worker, Margaret McBride, added greatly to the organization of Helen's work. I cannot properly express my gratitude to the present staff at the Public Archives of Nova Scotia. In the face of cutbacks and downsizing, they continue to offer service unparalleled in any other repository I have ever used. I owe my gratitude to Mary and Eric Vienneau for "technical support." I gratefully acknowledge funding in support of my interviews from the Dr. Helen Creighton Memorial Foundation. Additional support came from my dear friends, Martha and Robin (Robert) Creighton, whose funding enabled me to travel to Upper Canada to conduct research and interviews. I would like to offer my thanks to Dorothy Blythe and Amy Black at Nimbus Publishing and to my editor, Jennifer Lambert. They guided, argued, and advised me in the best interests of the finished work. My ultimate thanks go to my wife, Sharon. She never ceases to amaze me with her love and sustenance. She took notes, helped with interviews, and freed up her own time so that I could devote much of mine to this work. But her most cherished gift comes with her advice and counsel—and that is immeasurable. Thank you my love!

*To Helen—with love from "her boy"*

# INTRODUCTION

\* \* \*

On 1 October 1986 I sat at my desk at the Public Archives of Nova Scotia, opened up my journal to the first blank page, and wrote: "Today I begin work on the Helen Creighton Collection. It is perhaps the most important work I have been asked to do so far. I am, naturally, very excited; and not just a little bit scared—for the challenge is great. However, I feel it is a great honour to be chosen—even more so because Helen said she wanted no one else but me to get this position. I shall try to keep a log of my work, my feelings about the collection, and also record Helen's comments about the collection as we go through it together."

I would be arranging and identifying the collection of one of the world's leading pioneers in the field of folklore. I would also be working on a daily basis with the woman who had become my friend and mentor. It would be a chance for Helen to go through her collection one more time, and to offer insights and observations that she might never have shared with anyone else. For me? It was the opportunity of a lifetime.

I had been collecting my own variants of Nova Scotia's folklore and had taken a course in the discipline at St. Mary's University in Halifax. Now here I was, working with what would eventually be identified as the largest individually collected assemblage of folklore in Canada.

Coming to terms with the concept of folklore can be perplexing. Many people think of it as a collection of ancient beliefs and superstitions, sprinkled with quaint songs and traditional methods of making crafts. In fairness, the discipline of folklore is difficult to explain. *The Standard Dictionary of Folklore, Mythology and Legend* lists 21 separate definitions.

In its simplest terms, folklore is any information or material that encompasses the popular culture of a particular group of people. This knowledge is usually passed on through oral transmission or through customary example. Children's skipping rhymes, even today learned on school playgrounds, are examples of material passed on through oral transmission. Information can also be passed on without speech. If an individual crosses her fingers, most North Americans can attach at least one meaning to this gesture. It could mean "good luck," "keys" in a game of tag, or, if held behind her back, her crossed fingers might indicate that she is telling a falsehood.

By working to understand the origins of these aspects of our folk heritage—and the way in which we pass that information on today—folklore scholars are trying to determine our place in cultural history and how we use that knowledge to explain our lives. Folklore is as contemporary as the symbols used in e-mail messages—think of the sideways happy face :)—and as old as human beings' most primal beliefs.

In times gone by, the materials included in these aspects of our culture were called "popular antiquities." Then in 1846 an Englishman named William John Thoms coined the term "folklore" to distinguish the stories and information of the people. It was these examples of "folklore," the songs, stories, and beliefs of the people of Nova Scotia, that so intrigued Helen when she first heard them in 1928. She did not realize there would be so much to collect—and she certainly had no idea that the collecting would consume her life. All she knew was that these bits of popular culture had something to say about the people who passed them on to her, and that the songs and stories they shared helped to reflect and define them as a homogeneous and holistic society. Helen hoped that by collecting and publishing this material she might, in some way, earn a living. It was a long time coming, but she eventually went on to have a rewarding career in folklore that brought her, if not fortune, then at least fame. In doing so, she helped to bring the concept of Canadian folk culture to public attention.

She was in the right place at the right time. Many people fall into the same category, but few of us realize it when we see it. Helen almost immediately grasped the concept of a rich and diverse folk culture that had yet to be documented to any extent. She initially thought she might collect a few pirate songs and stories and write an article or two that she could sell to a magazine. But the work soon consumed her, even at a time when collecting old songs and beliefs was not seen as significant to the study of the evolution of our cultural heritage. Helen worked hard for decades, for little tangible reward. Yet she knew the work she was doing was important. Years later, when the major folk song revivals occurred, and collecting songs and stories became the hobby and/or vocation of people around the world, she had already amassed such a body of work that she stood heads above many of her contemporaries.

More than half a century later, the study of folklore is divided between academics and those who are seen as popularizers. And there stands the major division between folklorists and people who represent folk culture. The standard school of thought today is that one must be one or the other. Most folklorists learn to compromise, but new students are frequently encouraged to take what is perceived to be the high road. Folklorist Diane Tye alluded to this school of thought in an essay on Helen's career:

As a new student to folklore in the late 1970s, I considered the dichotomy of popular and academic folklore pursuits an important classification. I quickly learned that this was one way academics ... separated themselves from ... performers and enthusiasts not formally educated in folklore studies. I believed members of the latter group were reflexive, rather than reflective, about materials collected, and therefore, were undeserving of the title 'folklorist,' which I happily appropriated. Fellow Maritimer, Helen Creighton, provided me with a local example of such a popularist.[1]

Diane Tye's attitude eventually shifted to be more understanding (if not accepting) of Helen's methodologies, later writing that "her publications comprise an important source of information about women's roles—both as performers and supporters—in the folksong tradition of Nova Scotia, even though this was not an area of academic inquiry at the time she was collecting."[2]

It's not easy being a pioneer. Mistakes are made, one learns as one goes, and errors are always more obvious in hindsight. As Helen's friend, colleague, and recognized folklore authority, Dr. Edward D. (Sandy) Ives told me, "She should be best remembered as a collector. As someone who went out and got the data; who was very much a pioneer in the whole area here."[3] But Sandy also noted the change in attitude within folklore studies and said that Helen's style of what some consider to be "salvage" folklore is looked down on. Helen explained her own point of view to David Holt in an interview for *Atlantic Insight* in 1987: "I didn't put much analysis in my books .... I wanted to present the material as it was told to me. I wanted to show the way the people here think."[4] Although her material did omit, for the most part, certain subject matters such as bawdy songs and stories, that is what she did. Helen felt it was more important to collect than to analyze, just the opposite of current thinking in folklore research.

She left Canadians with a rich store of folklore. Future folklorists will work in differing ways but few, if any, will assemble the body of work she did. She will be judged; her work will be judged; and those judgements will change as each new phase of the folklore discipline is explored and revisited. But it is her work as a collector that will stand out, a body of work that received many accolades and much respect. Folklorist Horace Beck wrote to her, "Unlike many of your contemporaries who concentrated on one aspect of folklore to the exclusion of others you had the foresight to take folklore as it came and thereby preserved what otherwise might have been lost."[5] Pauline Greenhill maintained that "Creighton was ... remarkably flexible with respect to the material she actually collected, and though much of it is unpublished, local songs and poems are at least recorded."[6] And Herbert Halpert, one of North America's leading folklore scholars, claimed that "she has done the best job for any province in Canada. Her book on the Folklore of Lunenburg County shows her scholarship. It's a very competent book, a rich collection itself. It still hasn't been matched"[7]

Helen started her research a decade before the academic study of folklore in North America began.[8] There were no ground rules for her to follow; she was helping to create a discipline. Contemporaneous examples of similar work came from academics and visionaries who looked on folk studies as a way of establishing contact with a older, purer form of society. In the 1920s a group of Maritime Canadian poets, including Sir Charles G.D. Roberts, Bliss Carmen, Robert Norwood, and Charles Bruce, published their works in Andrew Merkel's *Song Fishermen Song Sheets*. They romanticized "the folk" and looked to them as the representatives of a naive and more holistic culture.[9]

Others saw the collection and study of folklore as a hobby for the upper classes. In 1923 Canadian journalist Beatrice Shaw wrote an article for *The Dalhousie Review* in which she pronounced that "in the Maritime Provinces and Newfoundland, all of which are extraordinarily rich in such material, practically nothing is being done to conserve this on a systematic basis.... The field for the folklorist in Nova Scotia alone is immense .... At present only a few isolated individuals are making tentative efforts to collect this lore .... This work requires an expenditure of time and money. It is essentially a work for leisured people."[10]

That attitude saw little change until the 1940s, when several universities began offering folklore studies as part of their curricula. The work being carried out by Helen in Nova Scotia had enough influence that by the 1950s the Provincial Department of Education had established the Nova Scotia Folkschool. Offered through the Adult Education Division, the program was short-lived, although it did manage to issue several newsletters. It was less a program of academic folklore study than an exercise in early cooperative learning for rural workers. A statement in the 1951 newsletter suggests its mandate:

The theme is based on rural living and working together ... to increase reading and develop an awareness and appreciation for the rural life; in some cases the folkschool was an opportunity for people to attend few classes not related to college ... the two week course provides the first experience in serious study of farm and community problems, discussion group methods, recreation and group living.[11]

This was far removed from the kind of work Helen was doing. When she began collecting, her initial search was for "old time songs." In those early years she didn't even call herself a folklorist. Others came up with labels—the media, for example, needed a title for people such as her.

The search for songs was looked upon as an adventure and the monikers attached to collectors reflected that perception. In 1942 the *Indiana Daily Student* called Helen a "feminine song-sleuth,"[12] and in 1958 the *Star Weekly* labelled Helen's friend and colleague, Edith Fowke, as "Canada's 'Come-All-Ye' Detective."[13] Frequently people writing about the kind of work Helen and her contemporaries were doing played up the quaint and unusual, sometimes to an absurd extreme. After Helen's death the *Mariposa Folk Festival Newsletter* offered a tribute to her work, and asked the question, "Can you imagine her pushing her wheel barrow along deserted dirt roads under all kinds of skies into clapboard villages along the Atlantic shore, knocking on doors and coaxing toothless old-timers to sing their guarded stories into the whirling reels of tape?"[14]

Critics have accused Helen of overplaying the rural aspect of folk culture. Perhaps she did, but the understanding of folklore as urban is a relatively recent tangent to folk studies. Moreover, she was not alone in her way of thinking. The grandfather of Canadian folklore studies, Marius Barbeau, began collecting folk songs in his native Quebec in 1915. But as late as 1956 he told a reporter for Halifax's *The Chronicle-Herald* that "folk music is almost dead ... because the folk singers themselves are dying out."[15] The English Folk Dance and Song Society, the early arbitrators of "true folk songs" for Helen and her contemporaries, regarded songs collected from the rural folk as vestigial remnants of a pre-industrial society.[16] Cecil Sharp, perhaps the preeminent folk song collector of his day, believed that folk songs were the product of people living apart from urban areas and access to education.[17] Clearly this was the school of thought to which Helen and her early companion, Doreen Senior, adhered during their mutual collecting heyday. They measured every song against the collection of ballads assembled from Britain by Professor Francis James Child. These old British ballads took precedence over local songs on topical subjects. However, despite what her critics might say, it was obvious that Helen had a keen interest in the local songs she encountered. She retained a bias towards the older ballads, but that was also a reflection of contemporary expectations among most folk song scholars.

In his 1992 article for the *Canadian Folk Music Journal*, "Lessons Learned, Questions Raised: Writing a History of Ethnomusicology in Canada," James Robbins acknowledged Helen's early recognition of the value of local songs: "When a Canadian—Creighton—began her prodigious collecting in the early 1930s, the 'Child canon' approach still dominated research. Creighton sent the songs she collected to the English Folksong Society who classified them variously as 'good and worthy of publication' and 'genuine, but better variants known elsewhere.' Nevertheless, to her everlasting credit, Creighton ignored their advice and published songs of both categories."[18]

Still, since Child Ballads made a scholar's name, they were put at the top of the wish list for most English folk song collectors. Common songs were less desirable, as Helen's 1937 diary entry illustrates: "went to Kinsac to see Mr. William Nelson ... he was interested in book, so left him mine .... When I went back he was waiting .... Started not too well, but soon slipped into real old time form and gave me *Lady Isabel and the Elf Knight* and *Three Crows*. .... We will probably get quality from him but not much quantity due to his illness. Irish songs are a dashed nuisance. The country is full of them."[19] Doreen Senior did not always share her collaborator's interest in the local songs, as Helen noted, again in 1937:

In one week we collected music of 33 songs. I had most of the words down before. What a good job I did that advance collecting. With the words all down on paper we could ask for our songs and give the words to start them off. It has saved a tremendous amount of time. However it isn't quantity we want but quality. Occasionally we get a song that isn't worth taking down. We usually spot it at the same moment, and say we have it already, or make some excuse to leave it. Sometimes where the words are poor D. wants to hear the music just in case. Still, there are not many songs that are not worth having.[20]

Often the local songs were not that good, but for the historian they remain valuable records of what people thought at the time. Helen may have been a bit too harsh in her assessment of the "Sable Island Song"[21] published in *Songs and Ballads from Nova Scotia*:

This was composed on Sable Island. Where Mr. Allan Hartlan was employed at the Main Station. In 1926 the wireless men lost some potatoes and accused the Main Station men of taking them. A fort-night later the potatoes were found in a cellar behind a barrel. This exonerated the Main Station staff, but they decided to make up a song about it, composing verse and verse to see who could do the best. The first verse is my singer's composition. The music is also original.... The song has no intrinsic value, but illustrates the song-making in-stinct is not dormant.[22]

It was an uncharitable judgement, perhaps, but one shared by many of her colleagues. In a review of *Traditional Songs from Nova Scotia*, Edith Fowke echoed Helen's sentiments, but applauded her inclusion of local songs, writing, "some will share my regret that Miss Creighton has not included a larger proportion of the songs that originated on this continent. She is undoubtedly right in deciding that most of the Nova Scotian songs are inferior musically or literal; they have not yet travelled through enough generations to acquire the polish of the ancient ballads. However, they are of interest because they are Canadian, and I hope that Miss Creighton will later publish more of them."[23] To Helen's credit, she went on to publish many more examples of indigenous songs. Even in her early collecting days she rose above normal expectations of folk song collectors and saved whatever local songs she could find.

Folklorists are supposed to remain outside of the material they collect. Detachment allows for unbiased analysis. However, as Helen was not a folklore analyst, she immersed herself in all aspects of her work. The best example of this is her interest in the supernatural. Over the years, after hearing thousands of supernatural experiences from informants, she developed an empathy for their tales of the unexplained. She couldn't claim that something didn't happen when it was told to her by such honest and unassuming people.[24] She once told me that she didn't disbelieve in the supernatural and, in certain cases, was convinced of its reality. Moreover, she felt that her own experiences were all too real to be easily dismissed.

Helen always felt a strong need to give back to her community. She had been brought up to contribute whenever and wherever possible. In her own way, she helped many people, offering letters of support for grant applications and lending her name to causes she believed to be worthy. However, she avoided public controversy as much as possible, except when it directly impacted on her professional or personal life. Neutrality and a low profile are fortunate traits for one whose job it is to seek information from others. Had she been better known for her own opinions and convictions, she might not have been as successful in getting people to talk about theirs. There was a point during the 1930s that she expressed some interest in getting involved in politics, but decided that she was probably too thin-skinned.[25] That might have been, but given her tenacity Helen probably would have made a good politician. She was not shy about offering her opinions when asked, she was feisty, and she could be aggressive in making her point. Her friend, John Robins once told her, "the notion of you doing anything *meekly* is very funny indeed, unless the leopard has changed his spots alarmingly since the last time I saw him. You have many virtues and many very nice qualities—but I should never count meekness among your virtues."[26]

If Helen could not claim meekness as a personal virtue, she did hold a deep respect for privacy. When I began work as Contract Archivist for her collection, I told Helen I was going to begin keeping a journal. I knew this would prove useful. I would be examining her entire life's work in detail and the journal would be my record of things she might tell me. She had already shared many confidences with me and, once the journal came into use, frequently she would preface her conversation with, "Here's something for your journal!" She told me once that I would eventually be able to tell of things she felt she couldn't disclose during her own lifetime. Not that this biography divulges any deep, dark secrets, but I hope that it does reveal the complexities of a farsighted woman who chose a path that brought her fame, respect, and criticism.

I was most fortunate in Helen's candour, not only in what she chose to confide in me personally, but what she wrote in her diaries. These diaries were closed to the public until 1 January 1999, but I had read them all while working with her on her collection. Helen could have destroyed her diaries and have her innermost thoughts remain private. But she included them in the repository at the Public Archives, ensuring that I—and future researchers—could be made privy to her intimate thoughts. Few of us would be so brave as to leave our inner life open to public scrutiny, but Helen elected to leave us that legacy, one that reveals her human weaknesses as well as her strengths.

I have tried, whenever possible, to allow Helen to speak on her own behalf through her diaries, my journal—which includes confidences made to me—and her letters to friends and colleagues. Because of our close relationship, many entries concerning me are embarrassingly flattering. As I did not edit any other of her comments, I chose not to exclude those in which I am mentioned. On 21 January 1989 CBC Radio aired a concert of mine recorded from the previous summer's Lunenburg Folk Harbour Festival. After the broadcast, Helen called and said she was so pleased with my performance she could hardly speak. Then she said, "Clary, I thank God every day for sending you to me— I know my work will always be in good hands."

My hope is that Helen would be equally pleased with this biography. I tried to be as fair and unbiased as one can be to a mentor and cherished friend. Her legacy has been placed in my hands. I hope to honour it with an honest portrait of "Canada's First Lady of Folklore."

# CHAPTER ONE

✳ ✳ ✳

Teh paddle dug deep into the waters of First Lake,[1] urging the canoe forward. It was time—a bit earlier than expected—but the child was in a rush to enter the world.

Alice Creighton hadn't anticipated going into labour while vacationing at Camp Retreat. But here she was being raced across the lake and portaged through the woods. They were going to make it—her seventh child would be born at home.

It was a comfortable home, a duplex on Portland Street in Dartmouth, only two doors from the house where she had married Charles Creighton in 1883, and just down the street from Evergreen, where she would live with her family for 21 years.

The doctor arrived in time. The child, so eager to come into the world, almost didn't make it. The umbilical cord was wrapped around her neck three times. But there was a good omen. Wrapped over the baby's head was a caul, a thin membrane of skin, so fine that when the doctor removed it and placed it on a piece of foolscap it looked as if someone had smeared egg white on the lined paper. Alice would save it for her daughter. Some believed it to be a sign of good fortune, an indication of second sight, protection against drowning, and the premonition of a charmed life.

The baby was named Mary Helen Creighton. Born at the end of the nineteenth century, on 5 September 1899, to her family she was to be Nellie or Helen, and she was part of one of the oldest and most distinguished families in Nova Scotia.

When Edward Cornwallis founded Halifax in 1749, one of his passengers was 16-year-old James Creighton. Family legend claims that he was the first person ashore. Born in 1733, James left Glastonbury, Somerset to seek his fortune in North America. His original land grant included a sizeable portion of Citadel Hill, which he later exchanged for $3,500, two houses, and land in the less populated north end of the fledgling town.

One of James' daughters, Lucy, married Captain Thomas Maynard of the Royal Navy. A lake in Dartmouth bears his name, and Creighton and Maynard Streets still run parallel to one another in Halifax. Another daughter, Mary, also wed a Navy man, Captain James Crichton. It must have caused some confusion—a Creighton marrying a Crichton, since at that time both names were pronounced "Cry-ton."[2] The Crichtons eventually moved away and the more common pronunciation of "Cray-ten" prevailed.

Helen's paternal grandfather was Thomas Colton Creighton. Like many Nova Scotian lads he followed the sea, and at the age of 17 undertook a three-and-a-half year whaling voyage to the South Pacific. He eventually rose to the rank of Captain, married Ann Albro, and had four children, including Helen's father Charles. When he was lost at sea in 1862 on a return trip from Puerto Rico, the widowed Ann moved her family from their home on Brunswick Street in Halifax to the

*Charles Edward Creighton and Alice Julia (Terry) Creighton on their wedding day, 1883.*

Albro homestead across the harbour at Turtle Grove. This move would firmly plant subsequent Creightons as Dartmouth natives.

Ann Albro's family had roots in Nova Scotia that could be traced back to Samuel and William Aldborough, New England settlers from Rhode Island who were given land grants in Hants County, Nova Scotia in 1761. Samuel's grandson, Edward Albro, made his fortune like numerous other Halifax merchants during the American Civil War—as a merchant agent for the Confederates. Helen and her family grew up under the watchful eyes of the portraits of Edward, his wife Elizabeth, and their son John, all painted by the English artist Herrick in 1854.

Helen's grandmother was not left destitute when her husband drowned. But whatever monies she did receive from her husband's estate and from her father were not sufficient to prevent her son Charles from leaving school at 14 to support the family. He eventually took a book-keeping course and in 1875, at the age of 18, he established his own business, C.E. Creighton: wholesale grocer, broker, and importer. Charles' business interests were in lumber, foodstuffs from the West Indies, pig iron, and flour. In 1881 Charles was joined by his cousin, H.D. Creighton, and together they formed C.E. Creighton & Company, "Commission Merchants and General Brokers." By 1883, the year of his marriage to Alice Terry, the company had offices on Upper Water Street in Halifax.[3]

Helen was to tell people that her "family has never been wealthy, but

*Creighton family, Portland Street, 1912. Helen, Sydney, Paul, Alice, Mac, Terry, Lilian, Charles.*

*Camp Retreat, c. 1907.*

has always been able to live comfortably."[4] Looking at the business ledger for 1899, the year of Helen's birth, it appears that C.E. Creighton & Company was fairly successful.[5] The business did have its ups and downs during Charles' tenure as owner; while they launched such classics as The Gold Dust Twins soap powder, they erred in letting go of a contract to handle the Converted Rice Company, which eventually became Uncle Ben's.[6] Overall, however, C.E. Creighton & Company supported the family in a manner far above most Nova Scotians, and Helen's mother was herself not without means.

*Terry and Helen Creighton. Helen aged one year and four months. January 1901.*

Alice Julia Terry was descended from Captain John Terry, who came to Cornwallis, Nova Scotia in the late 1700s. She and Charles had six children: Paul Henry, Lilian Lawless, Thomas McCully (Mac), Charles Sydney (Syd), Horace Terry (Terry), and Helen. A quintessentially Edwardian family, they were raised in a strict but loving Anglican fashion, in which so-

*"Nellie's first print." c. 1913. This may be the first print developed by Helen in the family's darkroom.*

cial duty and responsibility were paramount. The Creighton's family and business connections put them in a league with the elite of Halifax and Dartmouth, and both Alice and Charles encouraged their children to take their place in society. They were actively involved in church and community organizations.

As the baby of the family—and as a girl—Helen was certainly indulged, if not spoiled. Her sister Lilian had suffered a head injury when she was ten, and her mental development never grew beyond that of an eight-year-old. Helen and Lilian had a special relationship, and when she was older Helen became mainly responsible for her sister's care. But her childhood was happy and secure, even idyllic. With their father at the office every day and their mother at home and active in civic and charitable duties, the children enjoyed boating and swimming in summer, and skating and coasting on Dartmouth's many lakes and hills during winter.

Christmas was an exciting time for young Helen. Being the youngest, she had the privilege of leading the family procession throughout the house, shaking bells and blowing horns. They would open their Christmas stockings before breakfast and church, then come home for luncheon before scampering off to see what gifts their friends had received. After dinner the family gathered around their own tree, which was decorated with small toys and treats. Only then could they open their presents. It was a long wait for a child, but the anticipation heightened the joy of the festivities.

The Christmas of 1903 was especially memorable for Helen, as that December she had nearly died of pneumonia. By Christmas Day she was well enough to be carried downstairs, but because she was still weak, one of her brothers had led the traditional parade. Pneumonia, like tuberculosis and even measles, was a very serious illness in 1903, and it was with great relief that the family watched Helen's recovery. Helen later recalled that a few weeks after the holidays, when once again she was able to attend Sunday school, the teacher said, "And now we thank Thee for one little girl who was very sick and has been restored to us."[7] Helen recounted that moment as her first memory of being singled out in public—and confessed that she quite liked it!

In 1904 Helen's family moved further down Portland Street, closer to Dartmouth's town centre. The property had a large house, a croquet lawn, and a greenhouse where Charles and Alice grew vegetables, grapes, and roses. They furnished their new home with some fine antiques bought at auction from Admiralty House in Halifax. Keen photographers, they had a small darkroom built in the house. The photographs they took remain as valuable social records of an era that vanished with the First World War. While Halifax was the province's major business centre, Dartmouth possessed a number of industries and offered fine private and recreational properties for businessmen such as Charles Creighton, who commuted daily across the harbour by ferry.

The harbour ferries were also a social channel for adults and children alike. Helen's Sunday school would gather at the Parish Hall of Christ Church in Dartmouth, and with a brass band leading the way, parade down to the ferry terminal and embark on picnic excursions to McNab's Island. She and her family would also join the day-trip-

*"The Jolly Campers" at Creighton's wharf with Alice Creighton as chaperone, August 1912.*

pers who took the 10-mile journey to the stunning beach at Cow Bay, travelling there and back in straw-filled wagons.

But for Helen, the real magic of summer was found at Camp Retreat. Long before Helen was born, Charles had developed digestive problems for which his doctors prescribed fresh air and regular exercise. Each summer the entire family would move to their campsite on First Lake. Charles' daily commute involved rowing across the lake each morning, walking to the ferry, and crossing the harbour to Halifax and his work.

In the beginning the family roughed it in canvas tents, but by the time Helen arrived the camp had grown into a quadrangle of three sleeping huts with the forth side forming an open dining area. Their beds consisted of bolsters laid over fir boughs. Water was drawn from the lake, meals were cooked outdoors, and every night ended with a family campfire and pow-wow. When Helen turned six, her father marked the occasion by allowing her to row their big boat on the lake—she had come of age.

Helen loved the freedom of Camp Retreat. There she could romp through the woods, canoe and row on the lake, and sit for hours in a tree, reading her precious adventure stories. She had limited interest in girls' adventure books, which she considered "a little sissy."[8] By the time she was nine she had found a kindred soul in Lil Weldon, the daughter of a retired Dalhousie Law School dean. She and Lil, whose family also had a camp on First Lake, would sit in their favourite tree and pour over copies of *The Boys Own Annual* and *Chum*.

A natural adventurer, Helen used to lament the fact that she was born a girl.[9] Her brothers were all strong-willed young men and she admired them greatly. But she too had a strong will. Even as a child she could she set her mind to a task with dogged tenacity. Vivacious, but not conventionally pretty, Helen deplored her prominent jaw, which caused her lower teeth to jut out. By the time she was 10 she had determined to rectify this perceived flaw. Every night, as she lay in her bed, she would manoeuvre her lower jaw to align her teeth to where she felt they should be. Whether it was this exercise or perhaps simply that her face altered as she matured, in time her lower jaw did protrude less. Such determination would stand her in good stead throughout her life.

The year that Helen was 12, her mother invited 11 other girls, ages 12 and 13, to accompany her and Helen for a week's adventure at Camp Retreat. This youthful gang was quickly dubbed "The Infants" by an older group of girls, who in turn were nicknamed "The Grandmothers." Both sets of girls enjoyed Dartmouth's Natal Day celebrations. Especially fun were the paddling races with local boys and the romance of the decorated boats and canoes, which glided in procession across the lake, their Chinese lanterns reflecting off the night waters. The Infants were too young to go to the evening dances, but that didn't stop them from sneaking across the lake to watch couples dancing at the local boat club.

When the magic of that summer retreated, Helen and her family settled back into life on Portland Street. Helen had begun her formal education at Greenvale School, which burned in a spectacular fire early in the school year. The students were transferred to the older, more crowded Central School, another building her mother considered a firetrap. As Helen later wrote, "This fact helped my mother carry out a cherished ambition: to give me a taste of life in a boarding school."[10] And so in April of 1914 Helen began the daily ferry ride across the harbour to attend Halifax Ladies College[11] as a day scholar. Her travelling companion was Annie Carson, who was scheduled to graduate that year. It was to Annie that Helen remembers confiding: "When I grow up I want to write a book. If I could write only one book I would be so happy."[12]

As a young girl, Helen enjoyed making up stories and poems. Her earliest extant letter, written in February of 1905 on the reverse side of her father's business letterhead, shows a youthful and bold printing style.[13] A few years later she could boast of having her work published in the children's page of *The Montreal Star*, for which she was awarded prizes of a gunmetal watch and a fountain pen. At age nine, young Nellie Creighton completed a six-page story entitled "How Dot Spent Her Birthday."[14] It demonstrated a good sense of dialogue, spelling, and punctuation, showing early promise of a writing career.

She continued to work on her writing, and began to enter her thoughts and observations in a diary, chronicling her days (somewhat sporadi-

*Helen Creighton Fonds, PANS Album 11: 11:168. Photographer: unknown*

***Doris Davis, Captain Adam and Helen Creighton aboard RMSP Chignecto, West Indies, 1917.***

cally) at the Ladies College. It was at this time that she changed not only her pen name, but her common name, from Nellie to Helen. Her family and friends all knew her as Nellie, a name she detested because "everyone had a cow named Nellie."[15] Named in honour of her mother's dear friend, Miss Nellie Dustan, Helen was relieved when her mother suggested that she might mark her start at Halifax Ladies College by changing her name. And so it was Helen Creighton who crossed the harbour to begin a new phase in her life.

But even Helen could not have anticipated the changes about to happen. Ladies College closed for the summer and once more the family moved to their lakeside refuge. It was during an idyllic August afternoon at Camp Retreat that Helen's father arrived, wearing what she remembered as "an expression of fear and incredulity on his face,"[16] to tell them that the country was at war.

The war didn't stop Helen's schooling. She resumed classes at Halifax Ladies College that fall, where she boarded during the week and returned home for weekends. She and her family soon were involved in war work. Helen's four brothers would contribute to the war effort, and the family would eventually experience some great personal losses. However, the early years of World War I were heady days for a young girl in Halifax and Dartmouth. Helen was too young to date the young soldiers who sometimes visited her school, but she and her chums admired them greatly.

On 5 January 1916, Helen began to board full-time at the College. Her diary entry that day states that she "was not homesick though rather lonesome on the first night."[17] She made many friends and enjoyed life at private school. Classes were demanding, discipline was strict but not harsh, and the girls looked forward to the food parcels from home, which they shared in clandestine binges after lights out. In the vernacular of her day, Helen remembered the "crushes we had on older girls picked out as our Ideal."[18] And there was the thrill of meeting young men from Canadian college military units who came to social events at the Ladies College en route overseas.

Helen's diary from this time also illustrates her adolescent interest in slightly risqué jokes, as well as the period's tendency to lampoon various ethnicities, including blacks, Jews, Scots, and the Irish. Some of the jokes are handwritten and others are clipped from newspapers and magazines.[19] While they reflect the epoch's common currency of humour, Helen was aware that these jokes did not reflect the true nature of people. She would later recall an incident from her schooldays in Dartmouth. Halifax and Dartmouth had (and still have) a considerable black minority, many of whose ancestors predated Helen's own forebears in Nova Scotia. During a recitation contest, she tied with an African Nova Scotian girl, and it was the first time she consciously realized that a black person could be as smart as a white person—and perhaps smarter. She said the incident opened her eyes.[20]

Helen graduated from Halifax Ladies College in the spring of 1916. She wore a silk crepe de Chine dress that her brother Mac had had made for her in England, where he was stationed. After graduation she continued her studies with piano lessons and classes in domestic science and elocution. However, Helen was going through a difficult puberty; her nerves were very bad and she suffered from depression. One evening, while practising her elocution with, "To be or not to be," she burst into tears and continued to sob for nearly three weeks.[21] Whether it was stress from the war, fatigue from school, or simply the trials of her teenage years, Helen was definitely not well. Physicians were unable to offer her relief, and she remained listless and despondent for several months.

Charles Creighton had taken a "rest cure" in the West Indies after recovering from pneumonia in 1910. Remembering how uplifting he had found both the climate and visits with business and family connections, he suggested a similar trip for his daughter. She jumped at the opportunity. Chaperoned by her mother, Helen sailed for the Caribbean, stopping off at several islands including Trinidad, where she visited her cousins, the Todd Creightons. Life at sea was agreeable for a young girl. She flirted with the ships company, let her hair down (or, rather, put it up in the usual coming-of-age ritual), and basked in the undivided attention of her mother. The vacation did her some good, but after they returned Helen once again became nervous and listless.

*Helen Creighton at Pier 2 during World War I, c. 1918.*

This time she did just the opposite of relaxing, and threw herself into the war effort.

Helen worked alongside her father, who had helped establish the Halifax Citizens Reception Committee to welcome home wounded troops arriving on hospital ships. She and several other young women were chosen to greet and offer the men packages that included cigarettes, an apple, the daily newspaper, and a card printed with the message, "Welcome Home Gallant Boys." Helen carried out her duties with such enthusiasm that she was dubbed "The King's Messenger."[22] She also served as a hostess, offering refreshments to servicemen at Halifax's Tally Ho Club, a popular hospitality organization whose profits went to the Mayflower Chapter of the Imperial Order of the Daughters of the Empire.

Despite her busy volunteer schedule, Helen kept up a friendship with Doris Davis, whom she had met during her trip to the West Indies. On 5 December 1917, Doris spent the night at Helen's home. The following morning they were jolted awake by a heavy blast, and looked out the window to see a great fireball in the sky. Suddenly a huge explosion ripped through the air and Helen screamed, "Duck, Doris, duck!" Both girls slipped under the bed covers just as the glass and parts of the casing from four bedroom windows came crashing down on them. When Helen looked out from under the covers she discovered a section of window casing with exposed nails embedded in her pillow.

Helen and Doris were terrified but unhurt. They believed the Germans had bombed Halifax, and the entire household fled to the safety of the cellar. Miraculously, despite the fact that they ran in bare feet over shards of broken glass, Alice Creighton was the only one to suffer injury, with a slight abrasion over one eye.

*After the Halifax Explosion: view from Dartmouth looking toward the north end of Halifax, December 1917.*

Helen Creighton Fonds. PANS Album 11: 11-259. Photographer: unknown

When no further explosions followed, Helen and Doris dressed and began to make their way to Halifax in order to relieve Alice's mind over Charles. At the time of the blast he had been on the harbour ferry, and was thus an eyewitness to the infamous Halifax Explosion.[23] A Belgian relief ship, the *Imo*, had struck a French munitions ship, the *Mont Blanc*, causing a fire aboard the second ship. When the fire reached the munitions on board the *Mont Blanc*, the explosion sent a fireball a mile into the sky, levelling the north ends of Halifax and Dartmouth. Over 2,000 people were killed and thousands more injured or missing. Charles escaped unhurt and made his way through the rubble to his office on Bedford Row.

By the time Helen and Doris had crossed the harbour (the ferries did not cease their operations) and made their way to his office, they discovered that Charles had gone to Citadel Hill. On learning that her father was not harmed, Helen returned home and swung into action. Whether out of a sense of adventure, acting on the Creighton notion of civic duty, or a combination of both, Helen saw a job that needed doing and took control.

She commandeered the family car and headed downtown. The streets were littered with glass and her car quickly developed a flat tire. After some men had fixed the tire she was asked to take a mother and her children across to Halifax; on the return voyage she was relieved to meet her brother, Syd, who had brought a company of engineers over from McNab's Island where he was stationed.

Helen made several trips delivering the injured to hospital and driving patients to their homes. One of these journeys took her into the northern section of Dartmouth, past shattered and burning buildings and the stunned and bleeding victims of flying debris. From there she had a view of the most devastated area of Halifax, where an entire neighborhood was reduced to rubble.

Towards evening she returned home to find the grey blankets from

*Halifax Explosion: store in north end of Dartmouth, December 1917.*

Camp Retreat hanging at the windows to keep out the December air: 106 panes of glass had broken. Years later Helen would show picture frames still studded with tiny fragments of glass. They were grateful that nobody in the family had been injured, and that their property damage had been limited to the broken windows, some fallen plaster, and broken chimneys.

Survivors closer to the impact were less fortunate. Many went through the rest of their lives with telltale blue marks under their skin, reminders of glass shards buried in their flesh. The horror of the explosion increased the next morning when a snowstorm blanketed the cities, making rescue efforts even more difficult.

The day after the storm, Helen and Doris offered their services at Halifax City Hall, where relief efforts were underway. They worked for several days helping to locate clothing and delivering supplies to those houses left standing. Halifax's citizens had read about the devastation and horrors of the war, and now they bore witness to a similar tragedy. Terrible sights were seen at every turn and when Helen was offered a copy of a printed broadsheet she declined its purchase. The line she read, "There lies a little baby's hand and there an old man's head," was enough for her to realize she wanted no part in such a reminder. Later, as a ballad collector, she would regret not spending the 10 cents for the broadsheet titled *Halifax in Ruins.*[24]

After the horrors of the explosion, Helen was happy to spend more time with Guy, a handsome young beau who resembled the dashing Prince of Wales and was stationed with a cable ship in the Halifax Harbour. She also continued her work greeting the wounded troops, which turned out to be a more dangerous activity than one would have thought. On 20 December, a family friend was coming into Halifax Harbour via a steamer. Helen and her father wanted to welcome him personally, but as vessels with fewer than 50 passengers disembarking didn't tie up at the wharf, they had to go out to the ship. Usually it was possible to hitch a ride on the Immigration Boat, but Helen was too impatient to wait, and instead called on Guy, who came to her service in a small boat with a driver. Eager to show off, he remained standing with his arms folded as they made the journey out to the ship. Unable to dock directly at the wharf on their return, they tied up alongside several other small boats, then traversed across their slippery decks. Just before they reached the safety of the wharf, the boat tipped and all three fell in the harbour. Helen was wearing a large raccoon coat that helped to keep her afloat, and being an excellent swimmer, she yelled for them to save her father. But nothing would be done for the two men until the young lady was rescued. She consented to being hoisted up, with Guy pushing on her rear from the water. Neither she nor her father wanted to alarm Alice, so they sneaked in through the cellar door, had hot baths, and went to bed. About half an hour later the phone rang. It was the people from the Immigration Boat, saying they were ready! Helen was furious— fragile, delicate girl indeed![25]

# CHAPTER TWO

※ ※ ※

Helen was till seeing Guy, but socialized with other young men as well. In the early months of 1918 the US warship, *Old Colony*, was stationed at Dartmouth Cove. Thanks to her war work, Helen met many of the young officers attached to the ship, and they soon made her Portland Street home their social base. It was through them that she met a group of young American women who belonged to a wartime ambulance corp.

This sounded like just the adventure Helen was looking for. Informed that she was too young to go overseas, she applied and was accepted by the Royal Flying Corps in Toronto. Her application was strengthened with a letter of recommendation from the Honourable MacCallum Grant, Lieutenant Governor of Nova Scotia. In late August she took the train to Toronto, making her first trip outside of her home province without a chaperone. While in Toronto, she boarded at a house filled with other young people doing similar work for the war effort.

Classified as a Civilian Subordinate, Helen was issued a man's greatcoat with a badge on one shoulder that read "The Royal Flying Corps." Even the smallest regulation greatcoat was too large for Helen's tiny five-foot frame, and photographs of her in uniform make her appear as a child playing dress-up. The image was compounded by the large ambulance assigned to her, and she frequently evoked second glances.

But Helen didn't care—she was having a wonderful adventure. She was serving her country, working on her own in a big city, and making new friends and acquaintances daily. Among them was Helen's co-worker, Augusta Jarvis, whose family was prominent in Toronto's business and social community. Helen spent a good deal of time at Augusta's home and when the war ended she rode in the family car as it drove up and down Yonge Street amidst the jubilant cavalcade. Helen's telegram to her father said, "Wonderful news great rejoicing Toronto gone wild big parade today," adding, "Looks as if be home for Christmas."[1] Although her job actually required her to stay into the New Year, she would indeed get home before the holidays.

Helen's primary assignment with the Flying Corp was to chauffeur officers between their homes and offices, which frequently left her to her own devices for much of the day. A young girl driving an official

Helen Creighton Fonds, PANS Album 12: 12.151. Photographer: unknown

*Helen Creighton in uniform of the Royal Flying Corps, Toronto, 1918.*

military car naturally attracted the attention of servicemen, and Helen was a keen flirt. When an officer found her sitting in her car with young airmen draped over the hood and running board, she was hauled up before her commanding officer and told she was being sent home—in disgrace.

Once again, Helen's social connections came to the rescue. Mrs. Jarvis had a word with Helen's commanding officer, arguing that Helen was simply an innocent girl whose name should not be ruined because of a silly indiscretion. The officer agreed and Helen's record was wiped clean. But that wasn't the end to her troubles. On 11 December she received an AWOL notice, demanding that she report to authorities.[2]

Helen's nerves were quite shaken by these two incidents and instead of waiting to be reprimanded, she saved herself (and her superiors) further embarrassment and tendered her resignation: "To the Officer Commanding, Mechanical Transport Section, Royal Air Force, Canada—Sir. Owing to a nervous breakdown I have been forced to tender my resignation from the Royal Air Force. My doctor's certificate is following to that affect … December 13, 1918."[3] As she had told her father, Helen arrived home in time for Christmas.

During the following year, Helen resumed her active social life in Dartmouth, but without finding the career path she was seeking. In 1920 the Creighton family moved again. "Evergreen" was to be Alice and Charles' last home, and where Helen would live for most of her adult life. Named for the grove of evergreens that originally surrounded the house, 26 Newcastle Street was built in 1867 for Judge Alexander James. Alice purchased Evergreen from her cousin, Jean Creighton, and signed the deed on 29 June 1920. She put $2,000 down and agreed to pay the balance of $5,265.50 by August.[4]

The Creighton's new home was three storeys high with a raised stone basement. The back garden sloped down towards Halifax Harbour, and a wide bay window in the parlour offered sweeping vistas up and down the waterfront. Spacious and comfortable, Evergreen had enough bedrooms for Helen, her parents, and those brothers still living at home, as well as a room for a live-in maid.

Helen was just getting settled in her new home when she received a telephone call. Following the great explosion of 1917, the authorities had set up the Halifax Relief Fund, and by 1920 the monies had been allocated to relief work. Helen's caller, Dr. F.W. Woodbury, explained that surplus funds were being turned over to the Red Cross to organize two public health caravans that would tour the province, bringing free medical services to remote rural areas. Each caravan would consist of three ambulances, a truck carrying motion picture equipment to document the efforts, and a touring car for doctors and nurses. They were looking for one more ambulance driver, and based on her experience with the Royal Flying Corps, Helen was invited to join the team.

Her immediate answer was negative. Her Toronto experience had left Helen cold about driving for any organization, and she had already planned her summer to be one of relaxation and socializing. However, those plans changed a few days later when the morning newspaper carried a story about the upcoming caravans, featuring an item about the young girl who would be driving one of the ambulances—Miss Helen Creighton.

With only three days to get ready, she scrambled to make the necessary preparations. But when the caravan assembled in Halifax for the Pathescope newsreels to record the beginning of their journey, Helen was prepared. The early diary entries in the journal she kept during the tour note her embarrassment at being made the centre of attention merely because she was a female driver: "I'd have much rather dropped through the floor but they had to feature some oddity, and as I was the only one they chose me."[5]

Helen was assigned an old US army clunker that, like her Royal Flying Corp ambulance, dwarfed its tiny driver. Accompanying Helen in her transport was a spare driver—a man about Helen's age named Henry Davidson (Davy), and a reporter from *The Halifax Herald*, Rita Chisholm Frame. On the first day of their journey, Helen and the caravan made their way to Truro, a distance of 100 kilometres. Helen noted in her diary that they made good time—about 20 miles per hour.

Few women in 1920s Nova Scotia drove automobiles, and even an experienced driver such as Helen had to prove herself. Her first big hurdle was to convince people that she could handle the difficult roads, but she passed that test after she took her ambulance over Economy Mountain, where the shores of the Bay of Fundy climb the steep slopes into Colchester County. This route took them to their first clinic location, Five Islands. It was here that the dentist, Dr. Ritchie, asked Helen to act as his assistant for the day, a job she retained for the duration of the tour. In addition to passing instruments to Dr. Ritchie, Helen talked to children about dental hygiene. Her other task, once the caravan had arrived at its location, was to pick up and deliver patients. For some it their first ride in an automobile and the sight of such a petite—and female—driver must have given them pause.

Helen, Davy, and Rita became great companions. They were the youngest members of the caravan team and before long Helen and Davy had developed a romantic interest. This took the form of affectionate notes, evening strolls, and even a quiet twilight boat ride. Helen's pleasure in Davy's high regard for her is clear in several diary entries. At Ingonish, in Cape Breton, she wrote: "In the afternoon I pulled two teeth all myself. The patient was an old man and it didn't hurt a bit. He was so pleased [and said] it didn't hurt as much as the last dentist who had pulled his teeth. I was so proud of myself. Davy ... was watching me through the window when I did it. I was as happy as could be."[6]

Her bubble burst a few days later when the caravan had to traverse a difficult section over the top of Smokey Mountain. At 366 metres, it is one of the highest peaks in Nova Scotia and even in summer is often capped in the white mist for which it is named. In 1920 a Halifax newspaper had reported

*Helen Creighton Fonds, PANS Helen Creighton Collection #2319 Location 35.3.3*

*Original pencil sketch of Helen Creighton c. 1920 by Robert W. Chambers. Chambers went on to be Nova Scotia's most famous political cartoonist. Helen used to play bridge with his sisters in Wolfville and sat for the portrait there. When he had finished, Helen said that it was all right except for the mouth. "What do you expect?" he said, "It was never still."*

that Smokey had never been driven over by a motor truck. Helen knew this and wanted to be the first. Her wish did not come true: "Being a girl I was not allowed to drive ... but had to hand my ambulance over to Davy .... I, to my indignation, was taken the safe way by boat."[7] Years later she saw the decision in a different light. "I wasn't allowed to drive over Smokey ... because I was a girl. They weren't worried about my driving; it was the thought that there could be a breakdown and we might be out until all hours of the night. There was more protection for women in those days, not that we asked for it."[8]

Traversing Cape Smokey wasn't the only opportunity that Helen was forced to miss. On August 18 the caravan reached Baddeck on the Bras d'Or Lake, and the town's most famous residents, Alexander Graham Bell and his wife Mabel Hubbard Bell, received the caravan staff at their beautiful home. Helen forwent this treat in order to assist at an ad hoc "kitchen table" operation: the removal of a boy's tonsils. However, her diary records that she did see Bell's "water flying boat [hydrofoil], the fastest in the world."[9]

The Red Cross Caravans met at Halifax at the end of the summer

*Evergreen, c. 1955.*

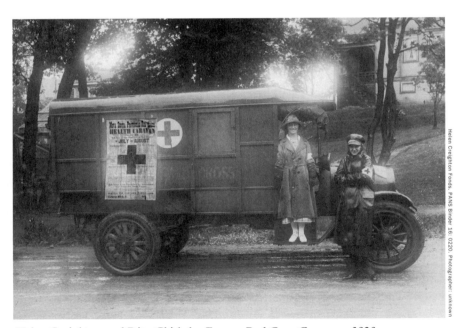

**Helen Creighton and Rita Chisholm Frame. Red Cross Caravan, 1920.**

and the staff received a tremendous reception at the base of Citadel Hill. Thousands of people turned out for the welcoming ceremonies, which marked the end of another adventure in Helen's life.

When the caravan adventure ended, so did Helen's romance with Davy. She had just turned twenty, and knew it was time to make some decisions about her future. Her 1975 autobiography describes her feelings at the time: "In the days when I grew up, it was assumed a girl would marry and set up her own home, probably with a maid to wait on her. If not, she would live with her parents and do volunteer work or enjoy the social round. The former hadn't happened, and the latter had never appealed to me as a way of life."[10]

It was then that Helen recognized the pattern her life had taken. Beginning with her wartime volunteer work; followed by the Halifax Explosion, which had hinted at her capacity to function in an emergency situation; and her work as an ambulance driver, Helen had demonstrated an ability to help others. And so it was that she decided on social work as her calling. Since Nova Scotia had no appropriate training facilities, she applied to study at the University of Toronto. Once again her application was strengthened by a letter of recommendation from the province's lieutenant governor, MacAllum Grant, who wrote that "few young ladies of my acquaintance are better qualified in every way."[11]

The University of Toronto's Social Services Course, begun in 1914, was the first such program in Canada. To give the students practical training while at the same time providing accommodation, the University allied itself with a newly formed settlement home, St. Christopher House. Of the students billeted there in 1920–1921, three of them, including Helen, were from Nova Scotia. They lived in an imposing red brick building in one of Toronto's poorest districts, and Helen certainly was given a realistic introduction to urban poverty. She found the academic courses exhausting and was not comfortable dealing with the problems and people she encountered at the settlement house.

When her brother Mac, en route from London to Mexico, invited Helen to visit him in New York City for the Christmas break, she jumped at the chance. Helen adored Mac and relished both his company and the attention he showed her. A highlight of her visit was a luncheon they had with the famous Klondyke Boyle, whose exploits with the Rumanian royal family was the stuff of legend—such legend, in fact, that it may not have been Klondyke Boyle at all, but rather his son who dined with the Creightons.[12] In any case, despite the diversion, by February Helen's strength had given out and she again had to plead illness and exhaustion, returning home in the company of her beloved and devoted father, "Faddy."

After a brief rest, Helen offered her services at the Halifax Infants Home, a refuge for unwed mothers. It was to prove another situation for which she was ill-suited. Her job was to interview prospective mothers (and sometimes fathers) and help them to decide whether to keep their child or give it up for adoption. One adopted child was named in her honour, but by her own admission Helen was "too immature"[13] for the job, and so once more was in search of her life's direction.

*"My Angels". Helen and her students in Guadalajara, Mexico, 1923. L-R: Helen McNab, Dora——, Josie ——, Helen Creighton, Fanny Howard, Estelle ——, Ema Howard.*

She came closer to finding it in 1923, in what she would later recall as "the happiest, most carefree days" of her life.[14] Having completed his medical studies in England, her brother Mac had taken up a post in Mexico, serving British and Canadians foreign workers in Mexico City. Mac invited Helen to join his wife and him. It was a long journey for a young woman alone, but Helen's travel experiences had given her confidence.

In Mexico, Helen hit her stride. She was vivacious, a bit flirtatious, and safely under the watchful eye of the brother she adored and respected. She was popular at dances and social gatherings, courted by a number of eligible men, including a dashing young man named Charlie, who came calling on horseback several times but was always rebuffed.[15] In recalling those happy days, she wrote that "I should have been looking for a husband ...[but] no young man could stand comparison with Mac."[16]

Helen set her standard for men by the two most important male figures in her life—her father Charles and her brother Mac. Her father was kind, wise, and always a gentleman. Her brother Mac was a Lothario, a dashing and handsome self-made man. Helen either did not understand or chose to ignore his faults, and placed him on a pedestal. Later on she came to understand how people might have misread their relationship. She destroyed letters she had sent home from Mexico, worried that someone might misconstrue their relationship as incestuous due to her mentions of kissing him and telling him how she loved him. While they were simply the enthusiastic utterances of a devoted younger sister, the letters and memories were too personal to risk anyone reading them out of context.[17]

Mac was generous to Helen while she was in Mexico. He made sure she was invited to the evening festivities celebrating the 1810 Mexican

Revolution. Massive crowds surrounded the National Palace and at 11 o'clock the Cathedral bells rang out and every man in the square took out his revolver and fired celebratory shots into the air. Returning from a trip to see the great Temple of the Sun, the driver was speeding and put the car in a ditch. Everyone but Helen thought it very amusing. She was furious and told them so. Perhaps the driver had good reason for his haste, as their car was later chased by a group of bandits. Recalling the incident some 60 years later, Helen's anger had obviously abated, as she casually remarked, "but we outran them!"[18]

Her whirlwind social scene of dinner parties, dances, and picnics finally came to an end when the high altitude of Mexico City began to have an impact on Helen's health. Realizing that she didn't want to go home to Nova Scotia, Mac suggested Helen apply for a teaching position at the American School at Guadalajara. Helen knew she had few qualifications, but sent a resumé detailing what credentials she did—and did not—have. She was offered the post.

Leaving the security of her brother's circle of family and friends, Helen journeyed alone to Guadalajara. Her six-month contract obliged her to teach six girls, daughters of both Mexican and foreign parents. When she reported for duty with her bobbed, curled hair and daringly short skirts, she was mistaken for one of her students. She was only a few years older than her charges and had to admit that she barely kept ahead of them in their lessons. But she managed, and at the end of each month received her salary, which was paid out in silver dollars poured into a cotton handkerchief.

Helen maintained a formal teacher/student relationship with the girls during classes, but in their leisure time they became comrades in arms. She grew quite close to two sisters named Howard and maintained a relationship with them long after she left Mexico. Fanny Howard wrote several poems to Helen, expressing love and admiration for her teacher. As with Helen's letters about her brother, the language of the period could be misinterpreted by the modern reader. The poems are very loving, describing Helen's nature and physical beauty in an intimate manner. Helen always thought of them as simply touching and sweet.[19]

Along with her teaching duties, Helen resumed her writing, working on short stories about her experiences and observations in a foreign land. She aimed her material at a Canadian audience and pitched several stories to *Maclean's*, writing to the editor: "Being a Canadian myself I have chosen your magazine in hopes that these descriptions may interest other Canadians."[20] The story she sent was titled "Have You Ever Seen A Bull Fight?" "Have you ever seen a bullfight? No? Then come, leave your cozy fire, your winter winds and snow, and in this land of sunshine we will see our first bull fight together."[21] The twist in the tale is that the proceeds from the gate went to the SPCA.

During this period Helen was using a pseudonym. As she told the magazine's editor, "The name 'Golliwog' though perhaps a bit absurd, is the one under which I wish to write."[22] She freely borrowed her pen name from the title character of the American children's books by Bertha Upton,[23] illustrated by her daughter Florence. Florence's creation of a black rag doll with fly-away hair was assumed by many to be an image of an African, but her illustrations of Africans showed brown skins, rather than the black body of the Golliwog.[24] In retrospect, Helen might have chosen a less controversial name as a pseudonym, as—despite his creator's intentions—the Golliwog came to represent the degradation of people of African heritage, and the Upton books are now out of favour. However, the Golliwog's adventures took him to the far corners of the world, and the character was so popular at the time that Helen's readers would have known the significance of her pseudonym.[25]

Helen was successful in attracting the interest of several publishers, and at the end of her teaching contract in Guadalajara she returned home to Dartmouth to begin a serious writing career. She concentrated her efforts on poetry, and many of her early poems seem naive and sweet today. Her ode to her native province, "Nova Scotia," ends with the lines: "Oh I've been far away o'er the face of the globe / And I've seen many sights wondrous fair / But down in my heart is the thought firmly sown / Nova Scotia had none to compare."[26] But by the time *The Sunday Leader* published her first poem in 1925—a lampoon of the golfing fad titled "Unseasonable Golf"[27]— Helen had switched from poetry to prose. She began with a book-length story featuring the Golliwog character, which was never published.[28]

Helen was not alone in her ignorance regarding copyright laws. The newly established Halifax radio station CHNS saw no difficulties when Helen proposed reading bedtime stories to children, including her Golliwog tales. Helen later wrote to various station managers across the country, trying to interest them in her Golliwog adventure stories, but while she received plenty of rejections, no one advised her that she was infringing on someone else's intellectual property.[29] Perhaps Upton's character had become so popular that it was thought of as within the public domain.

During 1926 Helen continued her radio work, reading from her unpublished Golliwog book on a children's program sponsored by *The Halifax Herald*. It paid the princely sum of two dollars for each half-hour broadcast. Billed as "Aunt Helen," she became "the first station 'aunt' in Halifax and probably in Canada."[30] Apart from reading her stories, she also chose the show's recorded music and wrote all the dialogue. On her own initiative, she knitted little woolen Golliwog dolls to send to children who wrote into the station.

It was because of her writing for radio that Helen was invited to join the Canadian Authors' Association. Founded just five years earlier, the Association was especially significant in the recognition and encouragement it gave to fledgling women authors. In fact, by the early 1930s the majority of its members were women.[31] Additional support for Canadian writers came by way of John Murray Gibbon, Chief Publicity Agent for the Canadian Pacific Railways (CPR), who joined forces with the Canadian National Railway (CNR) in providing free transportation to enable Canadian writers to attend Association conventions.

With her new membership and the offer of free transportation, Helen decided to attend the CAA convention being held in Ottawa. She met many leading Canadian writers of the day, including Douglas MacKay of the Parliamentary Press Gallery and his wife

*Helen Creighton in gown for presentation to the Governor General and his wife, Lord and Lady Willington, Ottawa, 1927.*

Alice. The MacKays encouraged her to stay in Ottawa, where she could move in larger literary circles and have better commercial opportunities for being published. They promised to help her hone her writing skills and oversee her manuscripts. Moreover, they would see that Helen was formally presented to Canada's Governor General, a great coup for any young woman making her entrance into society.

With her parents' emotional and financial support, Helen moved to Ottawa and gave herself a year to establish a writing career. The year away would also give her distance from her sister Lilian, for whom Helen continued to feel a great responsibility. On her own, pursuing her chosen career, and able to take advantage of important social and work connections, Helen's health improved. That didn't stop her father from worrying, and in July he wrote to express his concerns: "I know you will do your level best to make a success this time but you will have to be careful and not do more than your strength will allow."[32]

Helen found many exciting things to write about in Ottawa, but it was her stories about Nova Scotia that were getting her published. In one week she had three pieces accepted by leading Canadian publishers, including the prestigious Toronto paper, *Saturday Night*. Her proud Faddy wrote his congratulations: "how thrilling. I don't wonder you are bucked up. Three accepted in one week. Whew! You have arrived. Keep it up my dear. Your staying in Ottawa is certainly justifying itself.... You have been so brave and persistent in face of all refusals that you certainly are entitled to congratulations now."[33]

However, by the year's end Helen was ready to move back to Dartmouth and resume her career from home. With the success of her Nova Scotia stories, she was sure there would be an endless supply of things to write about in her own familiar territory. Yet once home, she found that subjects which had seemed so exotic and romantic from a distance did not shine so brightly. By the spring of 1928 she was, once again, in need of advice.

Helen made a fortuitous choice in the person she asked for guidance. Henry Munroe was the Superintendent of Education for Nova Scotia. At around the same time Helen called on him, he had developed an experimental school program that was broadcast over CHNS, the radio station that had launched "Aunt Helen."[34] One of his primary reasons for establishing these broadcasts was to "keep alive the local and national songs of the people of Nova Scotia."[35] He showed Helen a copy of a newly released book called *Ballads and Sea Songs of Nova Scotia*, by Dr. W. Roy Mackenzie.[36] It was a collection of songs that Dr. Mackenzie had located near his home at River John, on the Northumberland Strait.

Henry Munroe saw a young writer in need of direction. He suggested that Helen do for the rest of Nova Scotia what Mackenzie had done in his small part of the province. He also advised that she borrow Mackenzie's book and study the style. And he told her, "If you could find only one ballad your fortune would be made."[37] Helen would later freely admit that "at that time I didn't know what a folk song was."[38]

# CHAPTER THREE

### ✳ ✳ ✳

Helen was not alone in her ignorance of the folk music of her native province. While Dr. Mackenzie's song collections were respected among ballad scholars, they had received little popular recognition. The folk songs taught in schools and at music education facilities were gleaned almost exclusively from published sources in Great Britain, with a smattering of French Canadian songs added for regional flavour. One of the best known translations of French Canadian folk songs, J. Murray Gibbon's *Canadian Folk Songs*,[1] had only been released a year earlier in 1927.

That same year Helen had written an article about the carillon, whose bells rang out from Canada's Parliament Buildings. It was published in 1928 under the title "Are We Truly Musical?" She lauded the new instrument in lavish terms: "Canadians have stood the test to an amazing degree, qualifying themselves now to take their place among the great music-loving nations of the world."[2] Establishing a set of bells in the nation's capital hardly qualified a burst of national pride in Canada's emergence as a music-loving nation; Helen was simply a young author seeking a literary hook.

It was thus to her credit that she took Henry Munroe's advice to consider Mackenzie's collections and how she might use them to find ideas for future articles. An opportunity would arise sooner than she might have anticipated. A few days after her meeting with Mr. Munroe, Helen and a group of friends were having a picnic on the beach at Eastern Passage, a fishing community near her home in Dartmouth. Returning to their bonfire after an evening stroll, they met Mike Matthews, a local resident. Their conversation led to local history, and Mr. Matthews mentioned several people who told stories of buried treasure and tales of oxen speaking in human voices. Asked if he thought they might share the stories with her, Mr. Matthews replied, "They'll tell you stories and sing songs as well."[3] Tales and songs of buried treasure—and of pirates! Even if the stories proved too fantastical, Helen thought she could always write about the storytellers and singers themselves. She asked Mr. Matthews were she could find these singers and was directed further down the road to a point at the eastern side of the mouth of Halifax Harbour—a place later known as Hartlan's Point. On that spring evening in 1928 Mike Matthews pointed Helen Creighton down what she would come to call her "path of destiny."[4]

Having enquired of Mr. Matthews as to the best singers and storytellers, several days later Helen and her author friend, Helen O'Connor, made their first song-collecting foray. It was to the home of Mr. and Mrs. Thomas Osborne.[5] It turned out that Mrs. Osborne was the singer in the family. She said she would sing for them at a later date and also agreed to write down the lyrics to some of her songs. Continuing down towards the point, over roads so rutted that they were forced to walk the last half mile, they found a cluster of houses surrounding an abandoned dwelling. They were seeking Mr. and Mrs. Enos Hartlan.

Helen was already acquainted with Mrs. Hartlan, who used to bring

*"Enos Hartlan, my first folk singer,"* c. 1929.

market produce to the Creighton family in Dartmouth. Mrs. Hartlan explained that it was the local men who sang and, as they were out fishing, the song collectors would have to return when the men were ashore. When she noticed her guests' interest in the deserted house, she offered the explanation, "That's our Ghost House."[6] Built from the wood of wrecked ships, the building was believed to be haunted. Mrs. Hartlan, along with others, had experienced ghostly knocks and the sound of spectral footsteps coming down the stairs. Someone lived in a new addition built on to the house, but the old section remained vacant.

The house inhabited by the Enos Hartlans had its own point of interest. Helen would eventually use their home as her temporary location office, setting up her notebooks on their kitchen table. But during this first visit she noticed something peculiar. Above the door was a board on which were written nine letters—UDWWFUWUU—which in German stood for *Und das Wort ward fleisch und wohnte unter uns.* Translated from John 1:14, the verse is "And the Word was made flesh and dwelt among us." Enos later explained to Helen that with these holy letters above the door a witch could not enter their house.[7]

As the collectors were leaving, they met Mrs. Hartlan's brother-in-law, Richard. Helen enquired about pirate songs. Yes, he did know some and would sing for her when she returned. It had been a remarkable day. Although she heard no folk songs that first visit, she had discovered a source for them and, moreover, had been introduced to aspects of traditional culture of which she previously had been unaware.

A few evenings later, when Helen visited Enos Hartlan with her companions Helen O'Connor and Dr. Stanley Walker (later to become president of the University of King's College), she heard her first folk song. To her query about old-time songs, Enos replied, "We don't sing nothin' else … see them stars in the sky? As many stars as there are up there is as many songs as I used to sing."[8] Then he sang "When I Was a Young Man I Took Delight in Love."[9] Helen had found her first folk song.

Hearing a song was one thing, but preserving it was another. She could get the words down easily enough, as she wrote a quick longhand. However, while Helen had taken rudimentary piano and music theory lessons, her training was not sufficient to enable her to transcribe melody lines as presented by the singers. Dr. Walker suggested that she use a series of dots to indicate where the melody rose and fell, and then have someone transcribe the music later. This solution proved highly ineffectual. She would need to find a way to capture the music if she were going to collect folk songs. Recording equipment was known and used in Nova Scotia by 1928, but since most of the houses she visited on her early collecting trips were without electricity, machines such as Dictaphones were useless. While Helen continued to visit the people of Eastern Passage and Hartlan's Point collecting song lyrics, her dilemma regarding the music itself remained.

The initial answer came in the form of a small melodeon, or hand organ, which was given to Helen by a friend, Judge R.H. Murray. It measured less than three feet in length and had a keyboard. The melodeon's sound came from air pumped through its reeds using the left hand, while the right hand played the melody. The instrument was cumbersome and heavy, but Helen would eventually use it to help collect the tunes that appeared in *Songs and Ballads from Nova Scotia*. She was originally told that it was used by Judge Murray's father in his missionary work with Nova Scotia's indigenous people, the Mi'kmaq. But when Helen published this statement in her introduction to *Songs and Ballads*, it caused the Murray family considerable embarrassment. It seems the Judge, tongue in cheek, had made up the missionary story. In truth, he had spied the melodeon in a Halifax shop window and purchased it to play hymns at his dying father's bedside.[10] Regardless of its provenance, the melodeon would become an icon in the Helen Creighton legend.

Helen carried on with her song collecting, buoyed by her new-found solution to the problem of transcribing the music sung by her informants. She was brought up short when she played "The Turkish Lady" for Mr. Hartlan. When asked if he liked her melodeon rendition of the tune she had collected from him, he replied, "It's a fine tune, a fine tune, but it's not 'The Turkish Lady'."[11] Transcribing the melody for a traditional folk song can be a difficult process. It can alter drastically from one verse to the next, and from one singing to another. Helen had much to learn.[12] But she felt confident that she was on to something and realized she would have to make a decision—pursue what she believed might be her "path of destiny," or continue with the limited success she was having with her children's stories and magazine articles.

A number of factors guided her decision. Foremost was the aid she received from her parents, who continued to offer encouragement and financial support. While they had the means to indulge her pursuits, their concerns for Helen's health also led them to encourage their youngest daughter to find a job that could bring her happiness and stability.

Helen had suffered a bout of nervous exhaustion a few years before, over what she later called "a disappointment in love."[13] Her relationship with Guy during 1917–18 had been intense, and she was devastated when duty called him away. She felt she would never see him again.[14] This was followed by a second heartbreak; one of the officers stationed with the American warship, *Old Colony,* had shown an interest in her, but was shipped out before they had an opportunity to really get involved. Helen was left with a broken heart and a despondence that alarmed her parents. A heart specialist was consulted, who advised Helen to find an occupation that she enjoyed but was not too taxing; to rest when she tired and then continue with her work. The folk-song collecting seemed to be the one thing that helped bring Helen out of her depression, so Charles and Alice threw their support behind these efforts.

Another mitigating factor in her decision to pursue folk songs came from a more ambiguous source. Helen had always looked for signs to tell her what to do. While she had a firm faith in prayer, she also took stock in less orthodox activities. Earlier that year she had had her handwriting analyzed by F. Oland, Dominion Graphologist.[15] His appraisal suggested that:

The outstanding features here are the intellectual and critical temperament shown, the big control of mind that won't let the emotions run as they want & the queer extent of the telepathy that exists and may not be used in any way as yet. Here is a lady that certainly does know her own mind and likes to set the daily programs of everyone likely. The t-bar is full of argument and is positive in talking, could show just a bit of temper I expect in some righteous cause or her plans happened to get a trifle blocked. I don't know if marriage has been entered into but if so then the mate won't get his affections treated properly all the time though there is enough love tucked away to thaw

*Helen Creighton and children at Devil's Island with melodeon in wheelbarrow. c. 1929.*

a Labrador iceberg .... Sex demand should not play too big a part in his life.[16] There is enough intuition here to get into fortune-telling, investment house, diagnose disease. It's the investigative type & researcher, checker of accounts, teacher Introvert type that is shown chiefly but also one could go out and mingle well with the crowd.[17]

Was this the sign she was looking for? We can assume so, as Helen included the appraisal in her autobiography as one reason for ending her relationship with Guy and for pursuing her work collecting folk songs. At any rate, her path was set once more—and she would continue on along this particular road for the rest of her life.

During those early weeks of collecting songs from the Osbournes and Hartlans, Helen kept hearing the name of Ben Henneberry, who lived on Devil's Island.[18] The island sits near the mouth of Halifax Harbour, half a mile from the eastern shore. One mile in circumference, the island lies low in the water like a shale-blue turtle, barely rising 11 feet above sea level at its highest point, on which a lighthouse perches. These days the lighthouse is automated and the island remains uninhabited. Most of its former residents were relocated to Eastern Passage during World War II due to a fear of enemy attack. However, when Helen visited Devil's Island in 1928, a number of fishing families still lived there. The island had two lighthouses back then, and was also a base for one of the government's harbour lifeboat stations. Ben Henneberry served as the lifeboat's coxswain. He was the man she wanted to see. His reputation as a singer was legendary among the locals. But how was she supposed to meet him? Enos

Hartlan told her to go to the end of the point and holler.

It was a fine day in June that she and Helen O'Conner made their way to the point, where they soon saw a boat being rowed to meet them. On the island, Helen felt as if she had stepped into another world. Over a dozen families made their livelihood from the sea, enjoying a relatively isolated life within view of the largest city in eastern Canada. The girls were greeted on the wharf by several women and children, including Mrs. Ken Faulkner, wife of the lightkeeper, who recognized Helen as "Aunt Helen," the radio storyteller. (In fact, for years after that first meeting, islanders continued to address her as "Aunt Helen," until "one day Mr. Henneberry shocked his family by just saying Helen."[19])

Helen and her companion spent the day at the Faulkner's home. The men were out fishing, but she was hoping to meet Ben Henneberry before they had to take the boat back to the mainland. In the early evening they took a stroll to a small artificial harbour formed by two breakwaters, where the residents seemed to congregate. There were a few men sitting on a log, and when Helen asked about Ben Henneberry and his songs, a short, powerful man with a bushy moustache and his mouth twisted on an angle stood up. She had found her singer. As the sun set over Citadel Hill, some ten miles in the distance, Mr. Ben (as the islanders called him) sang a song of two little girls lost in the woods of Dartmouth.[20] The ballad tells a tragic tale, and the tune is haunting. The locals had heard the song countless times before, but nonetheless sat enraptured. To Helen it was almost surreal.

Other islanders also sang that evening, and Helen realized that if she wanted to get their songs she would have to stay on Devil's Island for several days. She made arrangements to board with Mrs. Faulkner and a few weeks later crossed to the island for a week's collecting trip. It proved to be one of the most strenuous weeks of her life.

Her primary goal was to collect as much of Ben Henneberry's repertoire as she could. Each morning she would sit in the doorway of his fish shed with her notebook and melodeon, and document his singing while he mended his nets. After he went off to his day's fishing she collected songs from the island's women and children. By late afternoon her informant would be back, ready to sing some more. In the evening practically the entire island would gather at the Faulkners to hear Ben sing—and to offer their own songs. Sometimes the singing would go on until three o'clock in the morning, with Helen taking down the songs entirely by hand. By the end of that week she had collected 100 songs.

Helen's melodeon was too heavy to lug back and forth by hand, so she borrowed the Faulkner's wheelbarrow to transport her instrument between Ben's fish shed and the various singers' homes. It was to be one of the most famous and misrepresented images of folklore collecting in North America. Even today people remember Helen Creighton as the woman who collected songs while pushing her recorder in a wheelbarrow around Nova Scotia: "How writers love that wheelbarrow. It was only on Devil's Island that I used it.... I doubt if I could have carried it in my car although in later years I used a grocery cart for the same reason."[21]

After several more trips to Devil's Island that summer and into the fall of 1928, Helen had an impressive collection of songs. She remembered Henry Munroe's comment about making one's fortune with just one ballad, but she had no idea where to find a market for the material she had collected. In July 1929 Helen wrote to John Murray Gibbon, the publicity agent for the CPR. Gibbon had been instrumental in helping to provide Canadian authors with free train travel to their conventions and in 1927 had inaugurated the Sea Music Festival in Victoria, British Columbia.[22] Helen sent him examples of her work in the hopes that the Festival might want to buy some of the songs, adding, "There is no difficulty in getting pirate songs, ballads and ditties."[23]

His reply was not as encouraging as she had hoped. "The market for this picking up of folksongs is, I fear, not remunerative in itself, but if you can weave a good story round it, you can sell anything. If I could get half a dozen real pirate songs of fairly good tunes, I could pay something for these out of our festival appropriation—about ten dollars apiece."[24] It was not the fortune Henry Munroe had hinted at, but she did sell the festival six songs at ten dollars each. It would be a long time before she made much money from folk songs.[25]

Six pirate songs had brought her sixty dollars—not a large sum for a year's work. What was she to do with the remainder of her collection? She turned for advice to Dr. Archibald MacMechan, who headed the English department at Dalhousie University, and whom Helen knew from his past role as president of the Canadian Authors Association. Dr. MacMechan consulted a colleague, a ballad scholar named Dr. McOdrum, and suggested to Helen that he was the man to prepare the scholarly notes required if she were serious about having her collection published.

With her manuscript in the hands of a man who had received his doctorate in ballads in Scotland, Helen felt confident that the research notes explaining the origins of the songs would be done properly. She had far less faith in her own transcriptions of the songs' melodies. Her father used a Dictaphone at his office, and she wondered if this machine could help her capture the music, which in turn could be transcribed by someone trained in notation. Helen's initial reluctance to use a recording device was due to the fact that few of her informants had electricity in their houses. However, as Ben Henneberry proved willing to come to her, and Richard Hartlan and others offered her the use of their homes, she was eventually able to record a number of the melodies that had originally been documented only though her melodeon.

Helen also enlisted the aid of a childhood friend, Peryl Daly, who had formal music training and worked as a music teacher. Helen asked Peryl to accompany her on a collecting trip to Devil's Island. Peryl remembered this trip as taking place in the fall of 1930, recalling that Helen "really didn't have much musical training ... she wanted someone who knew about music."[26]

By this time Devil's Island had telephone connection, and Helen arranged for herself and Peryl to make their base of operations at the Faulkner's home. Peryl fondly recalled that Ken Faulkner caught some sea ducks, which his wife roasted for their supper that first evening on the island. After dinner the song collecting began and by six o'clock, when it was beginning to get dark, Helen and Peryl decided to stay the night. Helen stayed up collecting songs long after Peryl grew tired and went upstairs to bed.

Peryl accompanied Helen on several more collecting forays, but while she did transcribe a few songs to manuscript paper, she didn't relish working on folk songs and soon told Helen she was no longer interested. In any event, Helen had no money to pay herself, let alone hire someone to transcribe music.

It was a frustrating time for Helen. She had a wonderful collection of songs but only her own weak attempts at notation for the melodies. She was also becoming frustrated by the delay in the scholarly notes she had arranged for her manuscript. Dr. McOdrum was having his own problems, dealing with the loss of his wife and establishing himself at Queen's University in Kingston, Ontario. Helen began seeking advice and direction from others. She wrote to Marius Barbeau, the dean of Canadian folklore scholars, and to Maud Karpeles of the English Folk Dance and Song Society. Maud, who would eventually publish important folk song collections from Newfoundland, asked Helen to "keep in touch with what you are doing, and if you ever find that the field of research is bigger that you can tackle, let me know, and I will try to come along and do what I can."[27]

Dr. Barbeau supported Murray Gibbon's suggestion that Helen forget about Dr. McOdrum and do the notes herself. As a result, Helen went to Kingston to retrieve her manuscript and continued on to Toronto, hoping to find a solution. Once again her contacts with the Canadian Authors Association proved helpful. The national president suggested a contact at the University of Toronto, who in turn sent her to see Dr. John Robins, a professor of English at Victoria College. Dr. Robins was a respected ballad scholar and he immediately saw the value of Helen's song collection. He secured for Helen a room at Victoria

College as well as the use of the university library, and augmented that source with his own private collection. He taught her how to do research and every few days would go over her notes and offer encouragement or make corrections. Recognizing that Helen didn't have the academic credentials to write a scholarly treatise, he allowed her natural enthusiasm and keen sense of observation to come through in the notes she wrote to accompany her songs. His appreciation for her style was manifest in the introduction he wrote for her book: "There is an academic, clinical approach to folk-songs, and there is a sentimental approach, maudlin or mocking, as the case may be, but the ideal is a combination of the scientific and the sympathetic, and that is the one Miss Creighton has shown."[28]

Fortune smiled upon Helen the day she met John Robins. She had found a supporter and a teacher. She was equally fortunate in finding a solution to the problem of her music transcription when she met Dr. Healey Willan at the Toronto Conservatory of Music, who also realized the significance of her folk song collection. With the aid of Campbell McInnes and Sir Ernest MacMillan, Healey Willan transcribed Helen's amateur music notations. The finished manuscript was sent to J.M. Dent & Sons, whom Helen had contacted earlier. They agreed to publish it and pay Willan up front for his music transcriptions as well as initial artwork costs, on the condition that these expenses would eventually come out of any author royalties.[29] One of the primary incentives for J.M. Dents & Sons to publish the manuscript of a relatively unknown author was that Henry Munroe had already contracted to purchase 250 copies for the Nova Scotia School Board.

With her manuscript out of her hands, Helen began to seek other outlets for her writing. Despite the considerable time and effort she had spent collecting folk songs and preparing her manuscript for publication, she was still pursuing other avenues.

# CHAPTER FOUR

## ✳ ✳ ✳

In February 1931 Helen began writing a children's column for the Anglican magazine *Church Work*, featuring stories she had broadcast on her radio series, along with new poems and tales centred around her nieces and nephew. Her inaugural piece set the tone: "My dear children, are you surprised to find a column in "Church Work" this month written especially for children? I hope you are pleased, because every month now we are going to have a story for the tiny tots, the not-so-tiny-tots, and the bigger brothers and sisters, and any of the grown-up people who would like to be children again."[1] The stories were typically adventure or moral tales with didactic titles such as "David and the Christmas Canary," "Chico" (the adventures of a monkey living in Nova Scotia), "Alice at the Party," and a 22-stanza poem called "The Elf."[2]

She would continue contributing to *Church Work* well into the mid 1930s, despite that its publishers were not always able to afford her negligible fee of one dollar per column. These were the Depression years, and in 1932 the magazine's editor, Charles C. Rand, advised Helen that her column might be cancelled due to falling subscription levels: "We are owing you for several months, and our funds are so low that I do not see how we can pay for a time at least."[3] Helen offered to continue her column without payment. An active member of the Anglican community, she saw the children's column as a way of making a contribution to her church.

In the meantime, she tried to interest other publishers in longer stories such as "A Gift at the Feet of the Christ Child," "Roly the Frog," and "Stubby Tail." She also made attempts to publish two book-length stories, "Adventures of the Little White Hen and Princess Edith" and "Prince of Stone."[4] Her efforts as a children's author were only mildly successful, but she did make some money as the Maritimes' social columnist for *Mayfair*, a society magazine published in Toronto. She reported on social visits, weddings, classical music programs at the hotels, and the various comings and goings of the elite in New Brunswick, Prince Edward Island, and Nova Scotia. Helen was acquainted with many of the people she included in her *Mayfair* articles, but didn't always appreciate their aggressive efforts to appear

*Doreen H. Senior, c. 1933.*

in her column. One woman called her at home and tried to direct her as to how her daughter's wedding should be covered, exhorting Helen to make sure it appeared on the front page.[5]

Helen did enjoy some national success with an article she wrote about Sable Island, which was published by *Macleans* in December 1931. Although she had never visited the island, the piece was highly descriptive, waxing poetically on the rugged beauty and dangers surrounding the "Graveyard of the Atlantic." There was one jarring flaw—she placed its location west of Halifax instead of east. In a letter to the magazine's assistant editor, Helen acknowledged the error as hers alone: "in the copy I saw that it was my mistake indeed. I felt shrunken to the size of a three-penny bit. To prevent any little technical error I took the precaution of having the article scrutinized by the agent of Marine and Fisheries from who I have since received a very congratulatory letter. My father, who is also a careful reader perused it. I hope the writers of brickbats will not deal too unkindly with me."[6]

With her folk song manuscript at the publishers, Helen continued her various writing endeavours while adding to her ballad collection with periodic trips close to home. On 14 July she was invited to meet a woman brought from England to teach English folk songs and dances at the Nova Scotia Summer School.[7] Doreen Senior was about Helen's age, a quick, wiry woman with round, dark-rimmed glasses. She was a member of the English Folk Dance and Song Society,[8] possessed perfect musical pitch, and had a keen interest in folk songs. Helen had found a kindred spirit.

Doreen was a great admirer of the English folk song collector Cecil Sharp and had attended functions at the Society's club in London, the Cecil Sharp House. She was acquainted with many of the current publications on English folk songs, but had never experienced the field-work of song collecting. When Helen suggested a trip together at the end of her teaching term, Doreen jumped at the opportunity. Helen would seek out the informants and record the lyrics and relevant data about songs and singers while Doreen transcribed the music. Helen made it clear that the probability of making money from the venture would be slim at best, but that they would share authorship if the material warranted publication.

The current assumption on how best to find folk songs was to seek them in remote areas, so they decided on a two-week excursion to Cape Breton. Prior to their journey Helen wrote to Marius Barbeau asking his opinion about buying an Edison recording machine she had discovered for 25 dollars.[9] There is no evidence of his reply, but she did make the purchase, and on 15 August she and Doreen packed up her father's car—which they named Cecil in honour of Cecil Sharp—and headed off.

*Joseph Crampton at* **Evergreen,** *c. 1933.*

Separated from mainland Nova Scotia by Canso Strait, Cape Breton Island was settled primarily by people of French and Scottish heritage. Helen remembered her sojourn there during the Red Cross Caravan trip of 1920 and felt that its many isolated communities would be ideal places in which to find traditional singers.

The collectors made no appointments, but simply began driving, expecting to find singers along the way. Their plan was to stay at guest homes, and picnic as much as possible. The people of Cape Breton have a deserved reputation for fine hospitality and Helen and Doreen were treated kindly, although in the first few days of their journey they found no folksingers. Eventually they were led to the home of D.B. MacLeod of Breton Cove. They were in luck. Not only did the MacLeods run a delightful tourist home, but Mr. MacLeod would sing for them. A further surprise was that most of the songs in his repertoire were in Gaelic. However, as Mr. MacLeod could also write out the lyrics for Helen, they took the opportunity of collecting his songs and set aside the issue of what they would do with them. As it turned out, John D. Robins later advised Helen to "by all means collect those Gaelic songs. They may not make your fortune, but they will certainly make your name."[10]

Helen and Doreen had a wonderful time with the MacLeods, establishing a friendship that would continue for years to come. They met many of the MacLeod's friends and collected songs from them in both Gaelic and English. Every day brought a new experience. Their hosts took them to a Gaelic church service where the singing was led by precentors; they made the requisite pilgrimage to the grave of Cape Breton's giant, Angus McAskill; and they met and photographed a woman working her magic with homespun—wool from the sheep's back to the man's! It was with reluctance that they turned Cecil towards Halifax

*Helen Creighton and Ben Henneberry holding* Songs and Ballads from Nova Scotia, *c. 1933.*

and home in order for Doreen to board the *Westmoreland* for England. They had collected a number of songs and, more important, formed an effective working relationship and a warm and genuine mutual affection. With plans to continue their collecting adventures the following summer, Doreen sailed for England and Helen continued her own collecting between rest periods and writing.

J.M. Dent & Sons hoped to release Helen's book of folk songs early in 1933. But as late as September the previous year Helen was requesting changes to the manuscript. Her concern was centered around a song entitled "Hatfield Boys," and she wrote to her publishers: "I should be most obliged if you would change the name of Hatfield to Hanstead. I am asking it for personal reasons, having lately met some of the Hatfield family who are charming people. The song is not complimentary, and I should hate to hurt their feelings."[11]

Helen also took the time to write an account of her Cape Breton trip to Marius Barbeau. She and Doreen had used the Edison to record some of their informants, and Doreen had transcribed from the discs. However, like the melodeon, it proved a short-lived solution. "Our trip to Cape Breton is over ... The little gramophone was not, I regret to say, altogether successful. It recorded all right, but after the second or third playing of a record the sound was worn off."[12]

The poor result with the recording machine was only a minor setback for Helen. She'd had a very productive year, publishing several articles and a chalking up a rewarding trip to Cape Breton with her new friend and colleague. She was also nurturing a relationship with W. Joseph (Joe) Crampton, whom she later referred to as "sort of a beau." Joe worked in the Halifax office of the CPR. By the end of 1932 he and Helen were seeing quite a bit of each other. He spent many late evenings at Evergreen with Helen and her family—so late, in fact, that Helen frequently had to usher him out with reminders of the last ferry back to Halifax.

Her financial picture had turned slightly brighter as well. She earned a small fee for her regular *Mayfair* column and inherited some money from her uncle, Jonathan Terry, who died earlier in the year. The legacy was not large, but would provide her with a modest income, and although she still had to rely on her parents, she hoped to make some additional money when her book was released the following year.

On 11 February 1933 Helen made the following entry in her diary:

> At 12:45 mother and I were sitting by fire when bell rang and I went to find express man with parcel. Seeing red lettering on label I knew at once what it was. My book a last! As it was so near time for father to come home I thought of waiting but was too impatient. Was wonderful moment, but far more wonderful when I saw the books.... I was pleased, and I am not always easily pleased.... Such kind expressions of pleasure from Joe.[13]

The first order of the day was to plan a book launching party, and she telephoned her friends to come and share in her joy. She had every right to be proud. *Songs and Ballads from Nova Scotia* was a beautifully produced volume containing 150 of the songs she had collected since 1928. The slate blue cover and end papers were designed by Reginald Knowles, one of the most sought after illustrators of the day. The musical notation was inscribed by hand, with the titles of each song printed in flowing calligraphy. Helen couldn't put it down, later writing, "I felt as a mother must when she holds her first child in her arms."[14] And so she hosted the christening party for her progeny the following day. It was a grand event with many congratulations and accolades for both author and book. Two weeks later Helen travelled to Devil's Island and presented Ben Henneberry with a copy.

Reviews for *Songs and Ballads* were favourable and occasionally glowing. Some reviewers weren't qualified to judge the content and opted to direct their praise towards the presentation, including the critic for Toronto's *Evening Telegram*, who wrote almost exclusively about Reginald Knowles' artwork.[15] Helen was particularly pleased with a review that appeared in a Nova Scotia trade publication, *Port and Province*. It wasn't published until April, but on 22 March its author allowed Helen an advanced reading. Joe Crampton—not surprisingly—had written a very positive review, concluding with a suggestion that he and Helen had no doubt discussed at length:

> A review of a work so important to Nova Scotia should not be concluded without an expression of hope that at some not distant date a series of concerts will be arranged to present songs from Miss Creighton's collections to audiences not only in this province but throughout Canada.[16]

It was a heady time for Helen. She was basking in the recognition and praise for her work—and she was falling deeply in love with Joe Crampton. They spent as much time together as they could, despite Helen's preoccupation with her book promotion and rehearsals for an amateur theatrical production. She and Joe made frequent trips to Devil's Island and Eastern Passage to visit the singers and hear more songs and stories. Her diary entry for 26 March recounts her pleasure in being with Joe: "Heavenly day. Joe and I went to Devil's Island ... Was midnight when we got home. The family anxious but mother very sporting and father angelic as always. Joe stayed the night."[17]

In fact, Joe stayed at Evergreen for the next three days, taking Helen to theatre rehearsals and spending hours talking and getting to know her better. On the third morning they had a late breakfast together and he "left reluctantly at eleven, badly in need of shave."[18] They had become a couple. When Joe had Easter dinner with the extended Creighton family that weekend, Helen's young niece, Lois, innocently told Joe he'd soon be a Creighton by the looks of things. Helen's diary entry notes that there was an awkward silence, but added: "All the children like him. All ages, Old folks too."[19]

It was only four days later when they learned that Joe was being transferred. That evening they dined together at the Queen Hotel in Halifax, but Helen notes it was "not exactly a success. Both feeling pretty down."[20] Unfortunately, her diary doesn't indicate whether they planned to try and maintain their relationship from a distance. Events indicate that they came to a mutual agreement and parted as friends. Once again Helen would find ways to occupy her time and move forward with her life and career.

In late spring she took several trips near Dartmouth to find more folk singers. Her mother frequently accompanied her on these reconnaissance missions and Helen soon had a growing list of potential informants. She received a much-needed lift in early June when she travelled to the Annapolis Valley to attend Nova Scotia's first Apple Blossom Festival. There, true to Joe's suggestion that concerts be held using songs from Helen's book, she heard a chorus of 1,300 school children singing "Caroline and Her Young Sailor Bold."[21]

Helen and Joe kept up a correspondence and in late June they had an opportunity to be together again. The Canadian Authors Association had organized a trip to England and Scotland. The tour would leave from Montreal after the Association's annual meeting. Not only would Helen go to the Montreal meeting as a published book author, but her mother paid for her to join the overseas tour. On 28 June Helen boarded the train for Montreal, having received a telegram from Joe saying he would meet her at the Empress Hotel. They met up on the second day of the convention and Joe joined Helen on the *Empress of Britain*, which was to be her floating hotel until it sailed for England two days later. Joe was covering the convention, but he and Helen still managed occasional snatches of private conversation. She notes that it was "awfully nice to be together again. Joe has arranged for chief officer to have me to tea, and wants me to show him my book."[22]

Despite her enthusiasm on seeing Joe again, they seem to have come to a final understanding on Helen's last night in Montreal. The ship sailed on 2 July and Helen's diary entry for the day reads: "[the] purser wanted to know if I stayed up til Joe left at three. Even thought I'd be hanging over rail when he left, weeping copious tears. Funny ideas people have. Wouldn't he loved it if I had."[23] Whether or not she wept for Joe, she was very excited to be part of this great literary adventure, and threw herself into shipboard life with enthusiasm. Their first evening at sea featured a play and other entertainments prepared during the Association's two days docked in Montreal. Helen played the part of a boy (wearing one of Joe's ties) and was thrilled when a baritone from the ship's orchestra performed "Green Bushes" from her *Songs and Ballads.*

Helen was one of a contingency of seventy Canadian authors, including the folk song translators J. Murray Gibbon and Charles G.D. Roberts. The party was to visit the major historic, literary, and cultural sites of Britain, and meet some its most famous writers. When they landed on 7 July the Canadians were greeted by the press and civic officials, a courtesy that would be routine throughout their tour. They were treated as celebrities, even if most of them were virtually unknown in Great Britain. Helen's diary describes an exhausting schedule of luncheons, civic receptions, and dinners followed by speeches. On the first day they met with the widow of Thomas Hardy, had tea with the mayor of Dorchester, and attended a reception at Salsbury's Guildhall, where Helen met and talked with the Earl of Pembroke and his wife.[24]

Helen held great regard for the monarchy and all things royal. So she was very pleased when the group was invited to Sunday tea at the home of Lady Pentland, whose parents, Lord and Lady Aberdeen, had strong ties to Canada—he as a former governor general and she as the founder of the Victorian Order of Nurses of Canada. Helen was even more honoured when she was introduced to Canada's prime minister, R.B. Bennett, who astonished her by saying, "I was just telling Lady Pentland about your book of songs and ballads."[25] She was brought down a peg or two later in the day when she met the sister of the late Cecil Sharp, the famous folk song collector for whom Helen and Doreen had named their car. She was not impressed by the complement of having her brother's name bequeathed to an automobile, but Helen was more amused than dismayed by the snub.

The following day brought a genuine thrill for Helen, when she was introduced to Rudyard Kipling and his wife. He was her favourite author and she later wrote in her diary that her "pleasure in meeting them [was] more than realized."[26] Three days later she witnessed what was perhaps the most infamous encounter of the Association's tour. A grand party had been arranged at the Forum Club in London, where

**Nova Scotia Song** *manuscript, original writing, c. 1933.*

the guest speaker was none other than the great playwright and wit, George Bernard Shaw. The guest of honour arrived more than fashionably late—and lived up to his controversial reputation by announcing that "He'd never heard of a Canadian author ... He'd like to know what Canadians thought of England and of him but he had no desire to visit so wild and uncivilized a country lest he be mobbed or blindly idolised."[27] As he had no doubt anticipated, his audience was stunned. However, Howard Kennedy, the Association's national secretary, quickly assured Mr. Shaw that he would be neither mobbed nor idolized but treated as a distinguished British citizen.

Touring through Scotland provided a pleasant antidote to Mr. Shaw's acid wit. Helen took the time to write to her family and send notes to the Faulkners and Henneberrys on Devil's Island. But by the tour's end on 23 July she was feeling homesick and depressed. She rested at the home of her brother, who had set up a successful medical practice treating London's upper classes. And soon she and Mac boarded the *Empress of Britain* to arrive home in time to celebrate their parents' golden wedding anniversary.

Helen had another reason for returning to Nova Scotia. Doreen Senior had been invited back to teach at the Summer School, and the friends had planned another collecting session. Because they were both tired and wanted to keep travel costs to a minimum, they decided to concentrate their efforts within driving distance of Helen's home.

They spent most of their time searching for songs along Nova Scotia's eastern shore—a rugged and beautiful stretch of inlets and small villages and communities. They visited many of the informants Helen had lined up on her earlier trips with her mother. Their first stop was in the Petpeswick Harbour area, where they called on 83-year-old Thomas Young. Helen had already collected the lyrics for many of his songs, but she wanted Doreen to transcribe the music. It was a successful collaboration and it was at West Petpeswick that Helen and Doreen came across what eventually would become their most recognized song.

The morning of 4 August 1933 dawned grey and by late afternoon the skies had opened, soaking the two collectors as they ate their picnic supper. In the early evening they walked up a steep hill through the wet grass to visit Mrs. Ann Greenough. Showing true and typical Maritime hospitality, Mrs. Greenough invited the strangers into her warm kitchen and told them to remove their shoes and stockings and dry their feet near the open oven. She couldn't understand why the two young women would want to picnic in the rain. "Why didn't you use our kitchen?" she enquired. "You're perfectly welcome to it."[28]

After chatting for a while, Helen asked Mrs. Greenough if she knew any of the old-time songs. Ann Grennough obliged them by singing "The Nova Scotia Song."[29] It was the ballad of a sailor saying farewell to Nova Scotia's sea-bound coast. A local song perhaps? They had never heard it before. It wasn't one of the "lovelies" Helen and Doreen were searching for—versions of ancient ballads from Britain. Nonetheless, Helen wrote down the lyrics and Doreen transcribed the music to manuscript paper—and they thought little of it. As Helen later wrote: "Doreen and I had been so steeped in the English tradition that we didn't realize anything locally composed could have that much value, and anyhow Doreen didn't consider it a folk song."[30] They still had much to learn.[31]

They collected in the Petpeswick area for several more days before Helen had to return home for her parents' anniversary party. The celebrations were bittersweet because her family knew that Alice had developed diabetes, news they kept from her until after the festivities.

It would be the last family celebration the Creightons would have together. At the end of the month Terry and his family moved to Toronto, Mac sailed back to England, and Helen was left to shoulder the growing responsibilities of providing comfort and care to her mother. As Alice's illness progressed, Helen was obliged to take over caring for her sister Lilian as well. Alice was hospitalized for observation for two weeks in October and by the end of January 1934 had become very weak. Her diabetes worsened and she had to be given daily injections of insulin. On 5 March Helen wrote in her diary: "Started insulin. 10cc twice daily, morning and evening."[32] For the time being, Helen's writing and folk song collecting would take a backseat to caring for her mother and sister.

# CHAPTER FIVE

### * * *

For the next two years Helen's career was put on hold as she devoted herself almost entirely to her mother's care. She did, however, continue to write for *Church Work and Mayfair* and, when her mother felt well enough, the two took short excursions in search of more folk singers.

In March 1934 Helen enjoyed a brief reunion with Joe Crampton when he attended a Halifax meeting of the Canadian Authors Association, which Helen chaired. They had but an hour together. Helen's diary noted that he looked well, but tired, and that it was good to see him.[1] The other brief break in her routine that year was when Doreen returned for sessions at the Nova Scotia Summer School. The school's student recital of traditional English music and folk dancing included two pieces from Helen's collection. As Doreen was tired and Helen's heart wasn't in it, the two did little collecting, although they did manage to work on material found earlier.

1935 proved no more eventful. Helen tried to get caught up in the social life of bridge parties and teas. She made the rounds among the elite of Halifax and Dartmouth and had recently been elected president of the Halifax Ladies College Alumnae.[2] However, while she enjoyed both the activities and the company, she longed for a productive work life. With the recent success of her collection of folk songs and regular columns in two national publications, at 34 years of age she was too young to retire. Moreover, she was broke. There were no book royalties. She did receive the occasional small cheque from *Mayfair* and dividends from her uncle's estate and the few stocks she'd acquired. And she did have a fine roof over her head as well as a weekly allowance of ten dollars from her father. However, none of this would further her career or give her independent means.

Meanwhile, Alice's arteriosclerosis and diabetes were getting worse and her illness was beginning to affect Helen's health as well. When Helen did manage to get away for a break, her mother became moody and angry on her return. Witnessing the change in her mother's gentle disposition was as heartbreaking as the progress of her physical deterioration.

Helen rallied herself for the Christmas holidays, realizing it might be the last one spent with her mother. The extended Creighton family gathered at Evergreen for the traditional Christmas Day dinner. Two days later, Helen asked her family for help. She told her brother Syd that she wanted a permanent housekeeper. She was tired and didn't like the job.[3] She was frequently exhausted to the point of tears.

Her parents had long retained domestic help and Helen was probably given additional support with her mother as her diary indicates increased activity outside the home in early 1936. She joined a skating club and participated in badminton games. But as Alice's condition worsened—by February she was crying every night and becoming increasingly depressed[4]—Helen began to show signs of exhaustion and stress. Concerned about her heart, Helen consulted the family doctor in April. He told her that she was in good shape, but needed rest. Once again she sought support from her brothers, asking for the means to take time off from caring for her mother and help in establishing a better financial future for herself.

Mac came home for a visit in August. Helen was elated. He was her knight in shining armour—the man she hoped would make everything right again. Her diary records her renewed infatuation with her favourite brother: "Fell in love all over again. I must be a one man girl. There's only one Mac for me!"[5] But Mac would not prove himself as her saviour. On 1 September Helen met with her brothers at Terry's office in Halifax to discuss the logistics of caring for their mother. Since Helen was giving up her work to provide that care, she was anticipating that her brothers would offer her physical and financial support. She was especially counting on Mac, whose London medical practice had proved financially rewarding. Her diary entry after the meeting was far from positive: "Gist of communication. Mac will never do anything for me financially, even when I'm left. Wants me to get job. Terribly hurt. Terry very understanding and agrees job is here at present."[6] Her knight had let her down. She would have to make her own way in the world.

Accepting the reality of her situation, Helen took action. She thought that her work collecting folk songs, backed up by the publication of her book, might interest government officials in hiring her as a provincial folklorist. Her first application was turned down by the minister in charge of highways on 28 September. She persevered. On 27 October she enlisted the aid of the provincial archivist, D.C. Harvey, who supported her aspirations, and the very next day she met with Premier Angus L. Macdonald. "Did not waste time over preliminaries, but went straight to subject. Was definitely interested. Meeting of gov't next week. Will hear from him."[7] The answer would again be negative. There would be no official provincial folklorist for Nova Scotia. However, at the end of the month Helen made a decision to try her luck further afield.

Earlier that summer she had met Rosalind Reimer and Helena Oppenheimer. Rosalind had a keen interest in folk culture and Helena was an executive with the Girl Scouts of America. The pair had discovered Helen's book on their travels through Nova Scotia and was anxious to meet its author. Helen not only met with them, but entertained them for several days, even taking them to meet some of her informants. At the end of their visit the women suggested that Helen join them in New York, where they would put her up and arrange for her to give lectures on folklore. Would she consider it? Only if she were paid, replied Helen. Rosalind and Helena returned home to make the arrangements. They were true to their word—in a manner. They did arrange speaking engagements, but they were all without fees. Rosalind's letter to Helen emphasized the opportunities that would present themselves despite the lack of up-front renumeration.[8]

As usual, Helen turned to her father, who advised, "If you don't go you'll be no further ahead; if you do, there's no telling what may come of it."[9] The family would make arrangements for additional help with Alice and Helen started another journey, which was to prove "the beginning of a ball that started rolling and has never stopped."[10] On 24 November 1936 she sailed from Halifax for New York. In the spirit of quid pro quo, similar to that of the Canadian Authors Association and the railways, Helen had applied to the Furness Withy Steamship Company, who offered complimentary passage to writers in exchange for mention in forthcoming articles and lectures.

Once in New York, Helen engaged the services of Bert Davis, a Welsh tenor and madrigal singer. He would sing selections from *Songs and Ballads* to accompany her lectures. Her first engagement was with the Canadian Women's Club. She recounted her folk song experiences, especially those of collecting on Devil's Island and meeting Ben Henneberry. At the end of her talk Bert Davis sang to Rosalind Reimer's piano accompaniment. A few evenings later Helen made her own singing debut on the New York stage when she joined Mr. Davis in singing "The Quaker's Courtship." The response from her audiences was enthusiastic—more for her lectures than her singing. On 6 December she sent off a telegram to her parents: "Enos amuses, Benny amazes, singer delights & lecturer rejoices."[11]

During her stay in New York Helen made the rounds to several literary agents and booking agents. She had several thousand brochures printed and sent out by one agent—who failed to find her any successful bookings. She also met with film companies, including Paramount and Fox News, trying to interest them in coming to Nova Scotia to film the land of folk songs. Her ideas were met with encouragement but not success. No one knew quite what to do with either Helen or her folk songs. As she later wrote in her autobiography, "I was in advance of my time and folk songs as a subject created little interest."[12]

Aside from her attempts to drum up work, New York provided Helen with a welcome holiday. Her hostesses ensured her a busy social calendar, including a trip to the theatre to see Noel Coward on Broadway. When King Edward announced his abdication on 10 December, Helen's status as a member of the British Commonwealth made her opinions much sought after. Whatever comments Helen offered her American acquaintances, her diary entry leaves no doubt as to how she felt about the king's renouncement of duty for love: "King Edward abdicated. Feel dreadfully ashamed of him, but pity him too. As for Mrs. Simpson, may she get what she deserves."[13]

Her lecture tour was not lucrative, but it did increase Helen's resolve to put her folk song work at the centre of her life. She sailed for Nova Scotia on 19 December, enduring a terrible storm at sea but arriving home determined to find a way to begin active collecting again.

In January 1937 Helen began searching for more songs close to home. Her mother was able to accompany her on day trips and they found several good informants near Dartmouth. One of her discoveries was the sister of Enos and Richard Hartlan. Mrs. R.W. Duncan was a kind, motherly woman whose folk song repertoire included many of the old-style ballads Helen was seeking. During this period she also collected from Mrs. William McNab in Halifax. In this instance she used a dictaphone to record six of Mrs. McNab's songs, which she would later transcribe to paper.

Aside from the weekly allowance she received from her father, Helen's parents must have provided additional funds that enabled her to make a collecting trip to Lunenburg County in February. It is unclear why she selected Lunenburg, but it was a wise choice, for the area proved rich in folklore and would eventually provide her with enough material for a book.[14]

The town of Lunenburg was founded in the mid-eighteenth century by German and other northern European immigrants, "foreign Protestants" encouraged by the English crown to provide a stable settlement to counter Catholic Acadian interests. Many of these first- and second-generation settlers retained their native languages and folk traditions. By the time Helen began collecting there in 1937, the language remained only in a few pockets (and even then was spoken phonetically). Perhaps she was looking for German folk songs, but it is more likely that she went to Lunenburg County to find sea songs. The area was well known for producing excellent shipwrights and sailors. Only 16 years earlier Nova Scotia's famous fishing schooner, *Bluenose*, was built and launched from the slips of Lunenburg Harbour.[15]

On 15 February Helen took the train to Lunenburg and established her base of operations at the home of Captain and Mrs. Ammon Zink. Her brief diary entries from this period paint an intriguing picture of both her early collecting techniques and of the people she met and the environment in which she collected:

At the Z's was only p.g. [paying guest]. Ate alone at round table which was covered with white cloth and doily in centre. Set for four people all the time. They must have been ghosts! Family ate in kitchen. ... Only heat from pipeless furnace. Took hot water bottle fortunately. ... On first day said to Mrs. Z. "What is the best time (meaning of the day) for me to take my bath?" "Well, " she said, "we all have one on Saturday, but if you want yours then we can change the day." ... Capt. Nice old salt. Spoke very slowly and deliberately. Very kind too. Went to much trouble trying to find singers. Best bet the village sot, but he developed flu.... On Sunday Mrs. Lohnes of Sea Breeze Hotel—called by us Mrs. Sea Breeze Lohnes—took me to Blue Rocks.... Went to home of Mrs. Eddy Knickle pronounced k-nickle. Old woman of 80 getting ready for church. Spry as a kitten.... Daughter Ollie gave us tea. Very kind of her as no payment expected, but awful tea, strong as lye.... Spent morning with Captain Berringer and listened for half hour to how his weight varied from 150 to 210 pounds. One needs infinite patience in collecting.[16]

Helen was learning as she went along. Her experiences in Cape Breton and closer to home had taught her that one didn't simply go out and find folk singers in every house. She also realized that even if people had no songs, she should at least record the beliefs, customs, and other aspects of traditional life they shared with her. It was a fortuitous observation, for eventually her work would take her beyond the scope of traditional music to include almost all aspects of folk life. Her eight days in Lunenburg County showed her that there was abundant material at hand—even if she would need the patience of Job to find it.

Her choice of Lunenburg County, with its strong German-based folk heritage, was also interesting when one considers the times in which she was living. The troubles developing in Europe were certainly being discussed in Nova Scotia and soon the Nazi presence would be right at her own back door. She had already recorded her thrill at seeing the famous Zeppelin, *Hindenburg*,[17] flying almost directly over her house in Dartmouth the previous summer: "Some people fearful of time when it might come bearing bombs. Personally it looked beautiful to me floating so easily through the air."[18]

Shortly after she returned from her collecting trip to Lunenburg, she became acquainted with several officers attached to a German warship visiting Halifax. Her diary entry for 11 March reads: "Saw Nazi salute for 1st time, four men off German warship. Looks silly done individually. Not nearly as smart as our salute."[19] Her contemporaries frequently invited visiting officers to tea, and Helen had the opportunity to speak with some of them: "Aft. Tea at Gerry's for German officers. Very interesting young man ready and anxious to tell about his country. Questioned him from 6 to 8:30. Evidently anxious to understand our mentality. Gave impression would willingly die for ideal. Nation comes first. Nice chap and very much in earnest."[20] The Germans, in return, hosted a tea dance aboard ship, which Helen attended. Thinking that the visit of a German warship to Halifax would make an interesting—and marketable—article, she wrote her observations and sent the manuscript to *Maclean's*. They promptly returned it and so she offered it to *The Star Weekly*, who also rejected it. Perhaps the subject matter was too controversial, or maybe Helen's perspectives did not jibe with editorial policies. Unfortunately her files do not contain a copy of the manuscript.[21]

Helen was still trying to develop her lecture career. Recognizing that she could not always afford a professional singer to illustrate songs from her collection, she enrolled in singing lessons.[22] It may have been a wise decision; a week after her first lesson she received a letter from the premier advising that there were no funds available to pay her to collect folk songs for Nova Scotia.[23] If she wanted to make any money from her work, she would need to find alternative applications for it. To date the folk songs she had collected and published had not brought the fortune Henry Munroe had hinted at. From January 1936 to April 1937 her entire income, aside from her father's allowance, amounted to $250.[24]

Throughout spring and early summer Helen made scouting trips to find singers. Her mother was her frequent companion. She was supportive of Helen's work and took great interest in the people they met. Several times they stayed away overnight, boarding with informants, which allowed Helen intimate contact with their everyday lives. For the most part she was visiting rural areas where people lived fairly quietly. Since the majority of her informants were middle-aged or older, her efforts to collect songs were concentrated on that generation. However, she did occasionally encounter children who sang traditional songs when adults were not present. While driving with her mother they passed three boys on the road, one of whom was singing what Helen recognized to be a traditional folk song—"Spanish Ladies." She noted later that she was sorry she hadn't stopped and talked to them.[25]

Helen also had encounters that she found disturbing. It was common at that time for families to provide home care for physically and mentally challenged relatives, and Helen's diary entry for April mentions one such household: "In carriage beside hot stove boy asleep breathing so heavily his little chest heaved. Head too big. Idiot I think. Pale face. Mother nice, woman ... Talked for a while, but unpleasant smell probably from child, so got away as soon as possible. Will return some warm day when we can sit outside."[26] She certainly had empathy for their situation, as her own sister had a mental disability. Nevertheless, she knew it would be difficult to collect songs with someone present who required the informant's attention—and she was uncomfortable in situations where she might encounter a person whom she thought had the potential to become physically aggressive.

Collecting could also pose health risks. Helen and her mother were collecting in West Chezzetcook and made arrangements to stay overnight with a local family:

> Mother and I congratulated ourselves on clenliness [sic] of house but in eve. Mr. R. Told how they had lost two sons of t.b. and I judge they slept in room we were to occupy.... Realized we all used same cups so planned to go home soon as possible.... All meals in kitchen because dining room too cold. Spotlessly clean, but no serving spoons or forks. Everybody helps self with own utensils.[27]

Helen Creighton Fonds, PANS Album 14: 14-28. Photographer: unknown

*Walter Roast, East Chezzetcook, c. 1930.*

Despite her misgivings, it was a successful trip. She collected 25 songs and 3 singing games, with an outlay of only $4.00 for their food and board.

It was during this same spring quest that Helen met Dennis Smith and his wife. She had been picnicking at West Chezzetcook with her mother and sister and left to follow up a lead. Her diary records the significance she attached to finding such an important singer: "had name of Dennis Smith on list. Was not in collecting mood, but it seemed dreadful to be in the gold mine and not take out any gold, so I looked him up. Found dear old man of 87 sitting with his wife in very clean kitchen. These people are amazing in the way they accept the quest for songs without question, and try at once to satisfy my need.... He seems like a second Benny Henneberry."[28] The Smiths took Helen into their hearts and she in turn grew very fond of them. Dennis Smith had worked on the sea for 15 years and when he came ashore had operated a general store in Musquodoboit Harbour. His folk song repertoire was large and included many of the older songs Helen was seeking at the time.

Another exciting find was Walter Roast. He was a tall, thin bachelor about Helen's age, who operated a small farm at Lower East Chezzetcook and also delivered the local mail. He had the lyrics to his songs written in a scribbler, which he permitted Helen to take home and type out the words. She was most anxious for Doreen to return later in the summer so that they could get the music from both these singers.

Helen made return visits to the Smiths throughout that summer, also seeking out other informants. Alice continued to be a frequent companion on these collecting forays, but when Doreen arrived Alice would need more care at home. In early June the Creightons hired a new maid named Gertrude.[29] Helen's diary doesn't give Gertrude's last name, which indicates the social position of domestic workers at that time. Years later Helen would describe two incidents that illustrated the relationship between her family and the maids they hired.

One woman, remembered by Helen as being very nice, refused to wear a uniform because it reminded her of a previous employer, whom she had disliked. She was also "a bit too free with gentlemen" and so had to be dismissed.[30] Annie was later hired and turned out to be a good worker, but the Creightons were concerned because she repeatedly "received phone calls from men with cultured voices." Annie was near Helen's age and, according to custom, addressed her as "Miss Helen." When Annie's brother died, the Creightons loaned her the fare to Newfoundland for his funeral—something in the region of 17 dollars. Two weeks after she returned she announced that she was quitting and tried to leave without paying her debt. Helen informed Annie that the Creightons would keep her trunk until she had paid off the loan. Annie left and came back a few days later accompanied by a policeman, who chastized Helen for her illegal seizure of the trunk. Helen reminded him that her side of the story should be heard as well, adding, "unlike you—I am unswayed by a pretty face." An agreement was reached whereby Annie would take her trunk, but repay the loan in instalments. She was good to her word and sent regular payments, beginning her enclosure with "Dear Miss Helen" and ending with "Yours sincerely, Annie." Her final payment was attached to a note addressed to "Dear Helen," and was signed "Miss Annie." Helen was very amused by the story and liked Annie all the more for her spunk.[31]

With a new maid to help with her mother's care, Helen was able to devote more time to leisure. She began to play golf, frequently joining her father on a course near their home in Dartmouth. She also took on a few speaking engagements, which she rounded out with her own singing. Most important, she persisted in her search for singers. Doreen arrived on 9 July and Helen continued to follow up leads until such time as they were both free to collect the songs.

Things had changed since they had first started to collect. Many past informants knew Doreen to be an accomplished musician and frequently requested that she play for them on their home organs. Something of a musical snob, Doreen disliked the small country organs, but realized the value of giving something back to the people who were offering their songs. She and Helen also encountered a reluctance from some singers to share their songs, lest they be exploited. "Doreen and I went to Tom Conrod's. Had to assure Mr. Conrod we were not making a fortune out of this business or exploiting him in any way. He was perfectly nice about it, but evidently people have been talking."[32]

While it was natural for people to assume that Helen and Doreen were profiting from their songs, there was no truth in it. Helen's book had yet to earn her a penny in royalties, and the collectors' travelling expenses all came out their own pockets. What's more, the advanced age of many of their informants necessitated frequent return visits— as was the case with Dennis Smith: "When Doreen arrived that summer of 1937, we found that two songs were enough for one sitting, as he tended to mix his tunes if one followed another too quickly. To reach him was a distance of thirty-three miles. Suppose he sang fifty songs— you can see the time and milage it would take to get the lot."[33]

Helen and Doreen continued collecting along the eastern shore and in July they made a trip to Devil's Island. Helen had recorded the lyrics for nine songs from Ben Henneberry and was anxious for Doreen to transcribe his melodies. But after working for two and a half hours Doreen became visibly ill. When Helen suggested they stop and come back at a later date, Doreen replied, "If I don't finish now I'll never come back."[34] They concluded their work and while waiting for their dinner at the Faulkners, Doreen went for a walk along the rocky coast. It was there that Helen found her weeping uncontrollably.

Doreen told her that she was experiencing an overwhelming premonition that the island "was literally possessed by the devil.... She liked Mr. Ben tremendously, but she felt that the island was bad.... She felt there was incest."[35] The sensation vanished as soon as they left Devil's Island.

Helen's autobiography doesn't identify Doreen in the incident. When she asked Doreen's permission to tell the story, her friend had emphatically requested that she not.

Now as to our personal difference of opinion about your use of my experience on Devil's Island.... E.S.P. is part of the "make up" of my Mother's side of our family, & I have it in full measure ... But you are now writing your Autobiography, which should be a factual document about the happenings in your life. What you record about your *own* experiences on Devil's Island is, of course, your own business. But when you propose to put down what happened to *me* I would much prefer that you did not.... I have more happy recollections that frightening ones, & can still recall to mind the faces of Ben Henneberry & his wife, & the peace of the lighthouse. I would go there again tomorrow if I were on your side of the Atlantic![36]

Doreen was not alone in experiencing inexplicably uncomfortable feelings on Devil's Island. Helen said that others she took to the island frequently had similar experiences.[37]

Because Doreen wouldn't return to Devil's Island, the women decided to explore a whole new region. But first they needed to find transportation. "Cecil" was no longer at their service, as Helen's parents needed the car for their own use. On 20 July Helen and Doreen went to visit Nova Scotia's premier in the hopes that the province would lend them a car. They explained their situation, and since Angus L. Macdonald was a Cape Bretoner, Doreen sang some of the songs she and Helen had collected there. They got their car, which within a week was taken away with the promise of a replacement. However, Helen was far from pleased with the substitute: "Old model gone 28,000 miles and filthy dirty inside. Never saw such a dirty

*Helen Creighton recording the Gallagher family, c. 1950. L-R: Edmund, Catherine, Donald and Mac Gallagher. Seated: Helen*

car. Refused absolutely to drive it."[38] They badly needed a car, but Helen sent it back. She expected the government to offer a better form of transportation to someone carrying out what she perceived to be valuable work. She had an altercation with an official from the premier's office assigned to look after the incident:

I have heard he is a rough diamond. Saw no evidence of the diamond, but a lot of the rough. Said he, "What is N.S. going to get out of this? You're publishing a book in the fall, aren't you?" Said I, "I don't see that it's necessary for me to discuss that with you. The premier knows. But—I go to New York and talk to people who have never heard a speaker from N.S. before? Is that nothing? I've just had an invitation to go to Montreal to speak? Is that nothing?" He looked somewhat abashed at this, but my mad was up for he had tol[d] me I had looked a gift horse in the mouth. I told him if that was the best gift the gov't could do it was a pretty poor best.[39]

It was Helen's mother who came up with a solution for both transportation and accomodation. She rented a Layfayette automobile with a compartment that folded out to form a sleeping platform. Mobile at last, Helen and Doreen decided to explore the area on the opposite side of Halifax Harbour from Eastern Passage. They had been told about a fine singer named Gallagher, the lightkeeper at Chebecto Head, overlooking the mouth of the harbour. Their anticipation was short lived, as they discovered that the man they were seeking had died and it was his son who tended the light. But Mr. Gallagher the younger told the collectors that his wife was a fine singer. Assuming she would be too young to know the old songs, they were pleasantly surprised to meet a delightful woman who proved to hold a wonderful repertoire of traditional songs. Turning the pages of Helen's book, she began to hum the many tunes she knew.

Catherine Gallagher possessed a light, sweet voice. A school teacher before her marriage, she and Edward had three small sons and the entire family loved music. Edward played the accordion and harmonica, and the boys all played musical instruments when they grew older. But it was their mother who was the musical star of the family. Writing of that first meeting, Helen noted how Catherine Gallagher's talent was not thought of in the context of performance, but rather as a natural and integral part of everyday life:

When Mrs. Gallagher sang "Seven Long Years" she did it while scrubbing her kitchen floor. It was amazing to hear this beautiful song sung to the accompaniment of a homely task. One delightful feature about these people is the way they take you in and make no fuss over you while at the same time they do all they can to help you. The floor had to be scrubbed, and the song must be sung for the "ladies." What more sensible then than combining the two?"[40]

Later that evening, after the children had been put to bed, the Gallaghers sat in their lighthouse parlour with Helen and Doreen, and Catherine astounded the collectors with her enchanting voice and amazing recall of the old songs. When they finally left to sleep in their car beside the lighthouse, Helen and Doreen felt they had experienced their best single day yet."[41]

After the climax of their collecting trip, both women were exhausted. Doreen's schedule at the summer school had been draining and Helen was having difficulties coping with thoughts about her financial problems and the ever increasing difficulties at home with her mother. On 26 August one of Helen's favourite aunts died. Given her emotional state, the stress became too much for her. They returned to Halifax that afternoon in order for Doreen to get packed for London. On the ferry ride home Helen broke down, "started crying and couldn't stop."[42] The next morning she and Charles saw Doreen off at the train station. Then she told her father she wanted to go shopping for a new mattress, "because I'm going to spend a lot of time on it in the next few months."[43]

# CHAPTER SIX

*** * ***

In early January 1938 Helen travelled to Montreal to address the Maritime Women's Club. By now she was comfortable with lecturing, but still had some trouble singing: "Didn't mind singing the silly songs, but nearly died over *Broken Ring* and *Peggy Gordon*."[1] After her speaking engagement she took a pleasure trip to Ottawa to visit old friends, also attending a meeting of the Canadian Author's Association. Gladstone Murray, head of the Canadian Broadcasting Corporation, was the guest speaker. During the discussion and question period following his talk, Helen volunteered that she had an idea for a radio series. Mr. Murray immediately consulted his appointment book and made a date with her for Saturday morning.

At their meeting, Helen sketched out her rather vague concept for a radio series featuring folk songs from her collection. Mr. Murray offered her a national series on the spot. He also suggested that she audition for a position as a radio announcer, advising her to make an appointment with the Halifax CBC director, Frank Willis, who would also be her series producer. Helen left his office walking on air. That afternoon some of her writer friends gave her a luncheon at the Ottawa Press Club, where she spoke of her work and sang from her collection. Too excited to plan her talk in any detail, the adrenaline from the morning's triumph nonetheless helped her to make the event a success.

She returned to Nova Scotia primed for working hard on her new project. The radio series would be breaking new ground. Programs of folk music were common, but ones that featured traditional singers performing unaccompanied were not. Helen would write the scripts and provide the narrative sections that tied the programs together. Each program would also include professional singers and would open and close with a selection of folk tunes arranged for string quartet by Doreen Senior. Helen worked directly with the series' producer, Robert Anderson, who helped to guide her in writing for radio. Friendly and young, he and Helen got along well together.[2]

The radio series was an opportunity for Helen and Doreen to make some money from their collection. Helen received 50 dollars for each of the 10 programs; Doreen was paid for writing arrangements for the string quartet. The professional musicians and singers were paid the

Helen Creighton Fonds, PANS Binder 17, 0445. Photographer: unknown

*CBC Radio Shows staff and principle performers, c.1938. L-R: back row: one of the first two people is Connie Inglis, Julias Silverman, Oscar Wette, Edmund Henneberry, Terry Creighton, Doris Baker, Carl Ritchie, Catherine Gallagher. Front row: producer, Robert Anderson, Helen Creighton.*

usual CBC rate for their services and the traditional singers (Walter Roast, Edmund Henneberry, and Catherine Gallagher) each received 10 dollars per broadcast. The shows were broadcast live from the CBC studios at the Nova Scotia Hotel.[3] Rehearsals began at four and they went live-to-air at six o'clock. The program received a large amount of fan mail, some telling of people listening with tears streaming down their faces. Alice Henneberry, wife of Edmund Henneberry of Devil's Island, wrote with a not too subtle (or perhaps tongue-in-cheek) request to hear more songs from Edmund: "I am writing to let you know what I think of your 'Broadcast.' I think it was just grand ... especially Edmund Henneberry.... He has such a sweet voice ... I think he can be called a Radio Starr."[4]

Whether or not the series was making radio stars, it was certainly producing innovative programming. After the fourth week of broadcasts, when Helen and the local producers still hadn't received any feedback from the national executives, they began to worry. However, Frank Willis contacted Ottawa and to everyone's relief was told that they loved the program. Several weeks later Gladstone Murray offered Helen another 10-week series, telling her, "Your program was magnificent; it gave distinction to the whole network."[5]

Helen would continue working on the radio series until the end of June. It took so much of her time that in February she wrote to

*Mayfair* offering her resignation as the Maritimes' social editor. It was during this period that she auditioned for the job of CBC staff announcer, as had been suggested by Gladstone Murray. Her work as a narrator for her own folk song series was acceptable, but could she pass the strict tests for becoming a national staff announcer? Her diary records the outcome: "It was horrible. I was put in a room all by my lonesome and given a paper to read over. There were various and different types of announcements to read and questions to be answered.... It was a horrible experience. Went off to my singing lesson feeling like a sucked orange."[6] Told that her reading needed to be more conversational, Helen was not offered a permanent position.

She was more successful with her announcing work on the radio series, receiving positive responses from across the country. But perhaps the people most affected by the broadcasts were the traditional singers. They and their songs shared airtime with trained singers and professional musicians—and they held their own with honour. The recognition and prestige Walter Roast received helped to change his life. When some of his acquaintances suggested that the CBC would never allow him to sing on the air, he proved them wrong. After the broadcasts many people began to request that he repeat his songs at each house where he delivered mail. His stature in his own community rose. He told Helen, "You've done a big thing for me and a big thing for Chezzetcook."[7] He also garnered respect from the trained performers on the program. Earle Spicer, a baritone hired to sing on the series, told Walter, "You know us fellows can learn a lot from you fellows about singing."[8]

But not everyone appreciated hearing untrained and unaccompanied singers.[9] After one broadcast, Robert Anderson told Helen that two people had called asking to have Walter Roast taken off the air. On the other hand, the traditional singers and their families did not always approve of the treatment given their songs by the trained performers. Some told Helen that after listening to the broadcasts they would turn to the singers and ask them to "sing it right."

Regardless of opinions as to who was best suited to interpreting folk songs, the radio series was a success. It brought the traditional music of Nova Scotia to a large national audience; it offered recognition and remuneration to the tradition bearers; and it gave Helen national exposure for her work. When the series ended she took a well-deserved rest. Doreen was not coming over for the Nova Scotia Summer School sessions that year, but Helen was making plans for a fall trip with her mother.

On the first of September Helen and Alice embarked on a collecting trip in the eastern end of mainland Nova Scotia. Because Doreen was not with her, Helen took along a Dictaphone. She and her mother began their search near Antigonish, where they made their base at the guest home of John and Hattie MacNeill. The MacNeills advised Helen to seek out the well-known bagpiper Angus MacDonald—known locally as "Angus the Ridge." Angus received his moniker as a way of distinguishing him from other MacDonalds who lived nearby,[10] a form of folk-naming once common in specific areas of the province, especially among people of Scottish ancestry. If Angus had had red hair, he might have been called "Angus the Red" or "Red Angus"; in turn, his wife Mary might have been called "Mary Red Angus" or even "Mary Red," to distinguish her

*"Angus the Ridge MacDonald, piper and Gaelic singer," c. 1938.*

from another Mary MacDonald. Helen tried her hand at attaching a folk name to Donald MacNeill, the son of her hosts. A young man who spent a good deal of time chopping wood, Helen suggested that he be called "Donald the Woodpiler." However, the locals soon shortened this to "Donald the Woodpile"—a nickname young Donald carried for the rest of his life.

Angus the Ridge—so called because he lived on the slope of a hill, was a respected piper, fiddler, and Gaelic singer. As the MacDonalds' home didn't have electricity, Helen couldn't use her Dictaphone to record his repertoire.[11] She did, however, take photographs of him, and when she suggested that he wear his kilt, he simply hauled it on over his trousers and told her to take his picture from the knees up.

Helen and her mother spent several days collecting in Antigonish and Guysborough Counties. It was a beautiful area and they found the people most friendly. However, what affected Helen most were the difficult circumstances under which many of the poorer residents lived. She encountered several families barely eking a living out of the limited natural resources. Accompanying her host on a visit to an acquaintance, John MacNeill told Helen that he had once called on this friend and been offered a meal of pancakes, accompanied by tea served in a tomato can—there were no cups in the house.[12] This was a world far removed from the one she and Alice knew in Dartmouth. Helen was later to write: "We enjoyed the ... people ... but the poverty and hopelessness of many farms where soil seemed unyielding and the future unpromising was depressing."[13] She was also unprepared to find that some informants were willing to show their frustration and discontent by offering their opinions on political and social issues. She was there to collect songs, but one man insisted on giving his thoughts on socialism before he would sing for her.[14]

Helen and Alice eventually journeyed to Sherbrooke and the surrounding area before it was time for Helen to take her mother home. After a brief rest she returned alone to Country Harbour, Guysborough County, where she met up with the local school inspector, Mr. Coldwell. School inspectors were required to travel throughout their district during the spring and fall terms; during her early collecting years Helen accompanied several of these inspectors along their routes. It gave her the opportunity to travel with a government representative, someone who knew the local area and could direct her to possible informants. Sometimes these local officials brought Helen in contact with people and events to which she might otherwise not have access. Such was the case when they came across a wedding party at Giant's Lake. Going in to offer his compliments to the newlyweds, Mr. Coldweels returned to the car and told Helen that they were both invited to join the festivities. It was Helen's first opportunity to see what was known as an old-style Scotch wedding. Duncan MacIsaac had married Catherine MacDonald and, true to tradition, had begun the reception by leading the dancing of an eight-hand reel. The music was provided by Angus the Ridge, who later led a Gaelic singsong and then played his pipes while some of the men danced.[15]

Helen returned home in October to begin assembling her research notes. She was anxiously awaiting an international radio broadcast on 23 October. Three of her songs had been chosen for inclusion in a program of folk music from around the world. It was a coupe for both her and the CBC, but Helen was disappointed with the treatment given her selections.[16] However, the following month she would chance to hear another international broadcast, one that would cause her much excitement and bring a new champion of folk song interpretation into her life:

In 1938 the usual way to hear folk-song programs was by short wave radio from England since we had few, if any here. These were listed in our papers, and when I read that Canadian songs would be on I thought, "I wish they knew ours." My radio was upstairs where I heard it announced that there would be songs in English, French, "and finally from Nova Scotia where Helen Creighton has discovered." I didn't wait for the rest but ran downstairs to tell the exciting news, for this had never happened before. We crowded around the radio. The voice would fade and static interfered but we heard enough to realize this was a lovely voice and the choice of songs was to my liking. The singer was Eve Maxwell-Lyte and the next day I wrote her the first fan letter she ever received.[17]

Helen's brother Mac had been in attendance at Miss Maxwell-Lyte's recital in London and sent a cable to Helen the next day: "Lyte says your songs greatest success of all. [When I Was In My] Prime one of loveliest songs ever collected. Hall full. Am very proud."[18] Helen began a correspondence with Eve, and when she discovered that the singer was coming to Canada for a concert tour beginning in Montreal, she made arrangements with the Halifax Ladies Musical Club to sponsor a performance. On 7 January 1939 Helen met her new idol at the pier in Halifax. Eve was Helen's houseguest at Evergreen and presented her with a record of "When I Was In My Prime" and "Broken Ring Song." After a brief visit, Eve went on to fulfil her concert engagements and returned to Nova Scotia for her recital on 16 March. Helen had worked hard to procure Eve as much publicity as possible and her performance was received with great enthusiasm.

Eve Maxwell-Lyte was the great granddaughter of Reverend Henry Francis Lyte, author of the well-known hymn "Abide with Me." She was an accomplished singer, but her penchant for dramatizing songs annoyed some folk-song purists, who didn't appreciate her use of costumes to create characters or her penchant for acting out the ballads' story lines. However, it was a style that appealed to general audiences, and her Canadian tour received many favourable reviews. Helen was thrilled to have such a distinguished artist include several songs from *Songs and Ballads* in her repertoire.

Having her songs performed was wonderful, but they were still not providing Helen with a stable income. To all appearances, Helen seemed as if she were able to live easily off her radio work and book royalties. (One informant even wrote asking to borrow money, a request that she politely refused.[19]) Her radio work did pay well, but was done on short-term contracts. However, it was her family who provided her with a comfortable home and helped her to finance her collecting endeavours. She had obviously discussed her financial situation with Doreen Senior, who offered her little encouragement: "It disturbs me just a little where you so obviously rely on the sale of your volume to secure your financial position! Do bear in mind that Folk Songs have a very limited appeal, & I've never heard of anyone making a fortune over them, not even the Sharps!" Doreen also pointed out Helen's advantage of having family resources to fall back upon: "I laugh at your 'floor scrubbing' fear; I guess I'm nearer that than you—I, who have *no* money or business in the family at all."[20]

Although her collecting work was hardly lucrative, it did bring her to the attention of people working in similar fields. In April 1939 Professor Henry Alexander of Queen's University came to Nova Scotia to collect dialects.[21] He was interested in meeting both literate and illiterate informants and contacted Helen to help him locate people with

Helen Creighton Fonds, PANS Album 14: 50. Photographer: unknown

*Mrs. Enos Roast, Doreen Senior, Nina Bartley Finn, East Chezzetcook, c. 1932.*

distinct and interesting speech patterns. He interviewed a wide range of people, including Helen's father and several of her informants—Enos Roast, Dennis Smith, and some of the residents of Devil's Island. Professor Alexander's research provoked Helen to think that she too should be examining more of the non-musical aspects of her informants' lives. In assisting him, she was able to demonstrate her own collecting techniques:

Went to Eastern Passage with Alexanders…. Prof. A. was shy and wanted me there for initial contact…. Had planned call on Mr. Willie Hartlan. Expected it to be very short, so started in alone. Then thought Prof. might be interested so extended invitation and he jumped at it. We went in kitchen and saw man lying down. Went in and asked about song, Famous Flower. Was very disappointed when he recognized it but couldn't help fill in any gaps…. When we got back to car Prof. A said, "I don't know how you do it. It's a gift. You go into a house and wake a man up and he sings for you. A man couldn't do it."[22]

Things became hectic in the month of May. Helen had been waiting for the go-ahead to begin the second radio series for CBC. It came at the last minute and so she informed the cast and began writing scripts. She would use the same traditional singers and professional musicians, but asked Nina Bartley Finn to be the featured professional soloist for this 10-week series.[23] Helen had met Nina the year before. Her husband

*Helen Creighton, Betty Raynor, Dennis Smith, Mrs. Smith, Joan Raynor, East Chezzetcook, 1938.*

was a naval officer stationed in Halifax and Nina had impressed Helen with her beautiful, clear singing voice and her enthusiasm for folk songs—and the fact that traditional singers liked the way Nina interpreted their songs.

The first of the broadcasts went to air on 21 May. During the following weeks Helen was kept busy with production work and making preparations for the annual meeting of the Canadian Authors Association, to be held in Halifax. She was asked to present a program for the meeting and assembled her cast from the radio series. While busy and happy in her work, conditions at home were becoming more difficult. Alice Creighton's health was in steady decline and as it grew worse so did the problems between mother and caregiver/daughter. However, the following months would bring some respite for Helen, who was planning a collecting trip for when Doreen returned for her usual stint at the summer school. She also had a new project to look forward to in the fall.

Her long-time friend, Stanley Walker (who had witnessed the collection of Helen's first folk song in 1928), had been appointed President of the University of King's College, in Halifax. He invited Helen to take up the position of Dean of Women, beginning in the fall term. It seemed the perfect opportunity for her to live away from her mother but be close enough to visit frequently. It also offered some financial stability, at least for the university term. The money she was currently receiving from her father could go towards paying for additional help for Alice. Helen saw it as a win-win situation.

In June Helen was visited by two professional entertainers who called themselves "The Troubadours." Joan and Betty Rayner were sisters who travelled the world seeking folk songs that they in turn interpreted for use in their stage and school programs.[24] They were working out of New York when they learned of Helen's *Songs and Ballads,* and came to Nova Scotia to meet the author and some of the original singers.

Helen liked the Raynors immediately and kept up a correspondence with the sisters for many years. She took them to visit Dennis Smith and his wife, who also took a liking to "the troubadours," often asking after "the little girls" in later years. The Raynors liked to perform dressed in the traditional costumes of the regions in which they found their songs. When they first met the Smiths, Dennis was wearing a waistcoat with brass buttons—part of a uniform he had worn at sea. Mrs. Smith was wearing a long cotton dress, boots, a small shawl, and the ubiquitous dust cap that was still a fairly common headdress among older rural women. On a return visit to photograph the elderly couple, the Raynors asked them to dress in this fashion, despite Mrs. Smith's suggestion that she wear something more appropriate for having her photograph taken. But the Raynors wanted them as they had first appeared, and they used that model for the costumes they would eventually wear when singing folk songs from Nova Scotia. The costumes were far from typical of clothing worn by the average Nova Scotian in the late 1930s, but they did fit the quaint and old-fashioned image the Raynors thought suitable to accompany traditional ballads.

Although Helen enjoyed the Raynor sisters' company, she did have strong reservations about their use of songs from her collection. She had to come to terms with the possibility that people other than herself and Doreen were interested in making money from Nova Scotia folk songs; and she realized that she couldn't very well stop others from collecting. However, she was clearly relieved when the Raynors assured her that they would not infringe upon what Helen perceived to be her territory: "They do collect, but won't here since this is my territory, bless 'em."[25] Nonetheless, she took precautions to ensure they would not use her collected material outside of their performances: "They had copied down words of songs they want to use, and I'd asked for statement saying wouldn't publish or let anybody else use. Had it beautifully typed out and signed."[26]

On 5 August Doreen and Helen started out on their summer's collecting trip. They worked with many of the informants gleaned from Helen's reconnaissance of the past few months. They took extended trips to an area on the Bay of Fundy known as the Noel Shore, then along the Northumberland Strait and down to their familiar territory on the eastern shore. It must have been an especially difficult time for Doreen. The probability of war in Europe was becoming all too real and she knew that she might be called home at any moment. Employed as a music teacher, she had been informed that all school employees would be required to evacuate children from London if the need arose.

Doreen and Helen had learned a great deal about traditional folk songs since their first forays, but they still chose to seek out the old ballads, giving them preference over local songs. They were particularly interested in finding variants of Child Ballads. These were examples of songs assembled in a collection by Professor Francis James Child and published in five volumes between 1882 and 1898 as *The English and Scottish Popular Ballads*.[27] They were the song standards that collectors of the day were working towards. The 305 titles in Professor Child's publications were considered the *crème de la crème* of English-language ballads. To find a variant outside of Great Britain was considered a great coupe, and Helen and Doreen eagerly sought out Nova Scotian variants. But the traditional singers didn't know their songs as Child Ballads. When making enquiries, Helen would frequently ask about "old-time songs," hoping to find an ancient ballad about Robin Hood or a version of "The Golden Vanity."

Many of the Child Ballads contained stock phrases—e.g., "rings on her fingers, gold in her ears"—and it was during this collecting trip that Helen stumbled upon an idea to get her informants thinking about the older ballads. She and Doreen were trying to collect songs from a group of men at Ostrea Lake, near Musquodoboit Harbour. The men had been drinking and Helen kept trying to steer them towards the kinds of songs she and Doreen were interested in. She couldn't come out and ask them for Child Ballads, so she asked instead if they knew the one about the "milk white steed." This could be one of several Child Ballads, as it was a stock phrase referring to any horse belonging to a nobleman, but chances were if a song contained the expression it was what Helen was looking for. Her autobiography tells what happened next. "They nodded negatively, but the seed had been sown. A face brightened and a voice said, 'I know one about a little page boy,' and away he went."[28]

As their collecting trip grew to a close, Helen and Doreen were conscious of the ever present possibility of war. On 24 August, as they rested in their guest home after a day's work collecting songs from

Catherine Gallagher, Nina Bartley Finn telephoned to say that Doreen had received word to return to England. She would have to be on the morning train to catch the *Empress of Britain* at Quebec. The women rushed back home and had a late dinner with Nina at the Hotel Nova Scotian. The next day Doreen caught the train at Halifax. Sixteen days later Canada entered the Second World War.

The war—and later work—would keep Helen and Doreen apart for many years, but they had established a relationship that would endure all their lives. Neither knew what the war years would bring. Helen would be starting her new job at King's College, and Doreen, arriving in London, would find her world turned upside down. A letter from Doreen, written en route to Quebec, vividly illustrates the anxiety and uncertainty of the moment. But it also shows hope and an appreciation of what they had shared together:

I shall always be thankful that I spent my last afternoon collecting with Mrs. Gallagher—even if the world goes up in smoke ageless things like "The Broken Ring" & "The Bailiff's Daughter" will still go on, & perhaps our chief cause for thankfulness may be that we have collected them up.[29]

# CHAPTER SEVEN

## ✳ ✳ ✳

In September 1939 Helen moved to Halifax to begin her new job as Dean of Women at King's College.[1] In 1923 the college had moved from Windsor, Nova Scotia to its present location beside Dalhousie University, where its grey and red stone buildings form a quadrangle. Helen lived in the women's residence, Alexandra Hall. Her rooms were small, but she gave them a personal touch with a new sofa and matching curtains. It was the first time she'd had the opportunity to have a place of her own and she relished the experience. She took her meals in the dining hall with the students, and during dinner she and the other officials were required to wear academic gowns, which were also worn in Chapel each Sunday morning.

College life was new to Helen. Her primary task was to monitor the 15 women housed at Alexandra Hall and to be on hand to offer advice or support if the need arose. However, she didn't always understand the rules and protocol and frequently had to ask the college president, Stanley Walker, for help. She developed a good rapport with the residents who obeyed the rules, but had difficulty with those who broke curfew and didn't abide by other college regulations. She wasn't a natural disciplinarian, and Dr. Walker occasionally had to remind her to enforce the rules. She worried that the women wouldn't like her if she were too harsh. It would take a full term until she hit her stride and felt on top of her job.

In the meanwhile, she had a fair amount of free time—time she needed after the strain of caring for her mother. Her father had hired live-in help—nurses who went home on their off-shifts—and Lilian had moved back home after spending the summer at West Gore, Colchester County, in a special needs facility. Helen went home to Evergreen as much as possible. She was there on 5 October and watched with her family as one of the first convoys of ships carrying supplies to Europe left Halifax Harbour.

The war had turned Halifax into a boomtown, filled with service personnel. Helen's autobiography doesn't provide much detail of the war efforts going on around her, but she was certainly aware of what was happening, at least in her own world.[2] In fact, because of her experience as a writer, she was requested by the War Information Board to submit written reports on daily life, morale, and conditions in Halifax and Dartmouth.[3]

Helen went home to have Christmas with her family and returned to

Helen Creighton Fonds. PANS Album 14: 14-206. Photographer: unknown

*Helen Creighton and William "Bill" Gilkie, Sambro, with unidentified children, c. 1950.*

King's right after the New Year. She was determined to get the upper hand on the discipline situation, in particular with some of the residents who were openly "petting" with their visiting boyfriends. She called the women in question into the lounge and reminded them of the college's rules against that behaviour. Her diary notes that she "felt silly but saw it through."[4] The success of her lecture was doubtful, as the next day one of her resident's dates turned up at the door to Alexandra Hall and tried to give Helen a kiss.

However, the new Dean of Women faced more serious problems than sophomoric flirtation. One of the more privileged residents was treating everyone around her, including Helen, as if they were her personal servants, and blatantly disobeying college rules. Helen recorded one occasion when, having been late for breakfast and turned out of the dining hall, the young woman admonished the cook by informing her that she was only a servant and couldn't tell her when she could and could not eat. The matter was taken out of Helen's hands and the problem went straight to the college president. Dr. Walker in turn told Helen he didn't want to have to deal with such matters and admonished her for not being more severe in enforcing discipline. By the end of January the miscreant had apologized and tensions lessened on all sides. Still, Helen was happy when the spring term ended in mid May.

Henry Alexander returned to Nova Scotia that summer to collect further examples of folk speech, and Helen took him to meet more of her informants during the month of July. He particularly wanted to pay a visit to the fishing community of Sambro to interview William (Sandy) Gilkie, but on his initial foray he encountered an unexpected obstacle. Sambro lies on the coast at the tip of the large peninsula leading into Halifax Harbour, and the Sambro Light was a main navigational aid for ships entering and leaving Halifax. The point held a strategic position in the war effort. Somewhat naively, Professor Alexander didn't think about the consequences of asking to meet people who were very sensitive to the dangers that could be brought their way by land and sea. Word quickly spread throughout the village that a strange man who spoke with an accent was asking questions. The professor was promptly arrested as a spy.[5]

Of course, once he had explained his story and received the proper papers, he was free to pursue his research. He asked Helen to accompany him to Sambro, where she was pleased to meet Mr. Gilkie and discover another interesting informant. But, once again, her old fears about others encroaching on her territory would come back to haunt her. Ten days later, she returned alone to interview Mr. Gilkie and was told that he was across the "crick" singing for another lady. Helen's diary indicates her concerns:

Was rather floored for a moment, until they told me she was with Prof. A. Thought I'd seen his car, so knew then was just someone who wanted to hear folk singer. Thought first someone from Ont. Was collecting in N.S. First experience of that. Only hoped she hadn't paid for songs as I have no funds to do that. After all, no reason why I should have monopoly, but was relieved all the same.[6]

The war continued to be the catalyst for new adventures. Helen had recently met Anna Mill, an Associate Professor at Mount Holyoke University in Massachusetts. Professor Mill was from Scotland, but because of wartime restrictions on travel she was unable to book passage back to her homeland. And so it was that during her holidays she decided to come to the next best place—New Scotland, or Nova Scotia. She taught a class in balladry at Holyoke, but had never heard a traditional singer. When Helen offered to take her to see Mrs. Gallagher, she was elated.

They stood on the cliff beside the lighthouse at Chebucto Head and looked down at the mouth of Halifax Harbour, which was shrouded in fog. Suddenly, gliding through the haze, they saw the tops of masts from ships leaving in a convoy. As they gazed down into the mist, Mrs. Gallagher began to sing an ancient Scottish ballad—"The Bonny House o'Airlie."[7] The poignancy of the moment had an emotional impact on all three women that would remain with them forever.[8]

On 10 August Helen travelled to North Sydney, Cape Breton, to catch the ferry for Newfoundland. Her friends, Fred Emerson and his wife, had been to stay with her and suggested that she accompany them home for a visit. This was just the break Helen had been looking for. Yet in the back of her mind she felt that something would stop her from taking the journey. At the ferry terminal, she directed the ship's purser not to load her luggage until after she'd returned from dinner at a local restaurant. Her intuition proved correct. During dinner she received a telephone call from her brother Paul. Their mother had had a cerebral stroke. Helen left her friends and rushed home expecting the worse. When she arrived at Evergreen, she found that her mother had indeed suffered a massive stroke affecting the right side of her body. But what Alice Creighton had lost in physical ability, she'd gained in her mental outlook. Helen wrote in her diary, "Mother very jolly, like old self."[9]

With her mother well cared for at home by live-in help, Helen was able to resume her duties at King's in September. She was rather dreading the anticipated altercations with her residents, but was pleasantly surprised to find the situation much improved:"To great amazement and delight found entirely different spirit. Everybody seems keen to play the game."[10] Helen's primary disciplinary problem was partially solved by having the residents elect house seniors. Some of these seniors had been troublemakers the previous year, and their attitudes quickly turned around when faced with enforcing the rules themselves. Helen also made things easier by relaxing some of the rules and making life at Alexandra Hall less structured. She encouraged the women to bring their dates back to the resident lounge, and even chaperoned evening dances, including a Halloween bash where she came dressed as an old folk singer.

In January 1941 Helen saw the release of her second book.[11] Co-authored with Doreen Senior, *Twelve Folk Songs from Nova Scotia* was published in London by Novello.[12] It was a plain, no-frills volume featuring a dozen of the songs collected by her and Doreen. But although Helen's name appeared on the title, she'd had very little to do with the actual manuscript preparation, which Doreen had carried out in London.

Publishing in Britain during that period was no easy feat, as many of the necessary materials were reserved for the war effort. That a book of traditional folk songs from Nova Scotia was produced by a British publisher during the war was quite astonishing. But Doreen's efforts to promote the work that she and Helen had done together in Canada had created enough interest to attract the attention of some influential people. In February 1940 Doreen had given a recital at Cecil Sharp House. She described the collecting experiences she and Helen had shared and sang some of the songs they'd found. Writing Helen about the talk she had given, she recounted: "I made them laugh by telling them how sceptical you were when I proposed trying to take down tunes—but how you accepted me as a travelling companion; I then admitted that I had no idea myself whether I could do it."[13] Among those in attendance was the famed Danish folk song interpreter, Engel Lund. She was enthralled by the songs and was so anxious to add them to her repertoire that she lobbied Novello to publish them.

Helen handed over the responsibility for negotiating the publication to Doreen. She was comfortable with Novello's reputation as a well-respected publisher of folk songs. She wrote the introductory notes and added some research on each song, but Doreen altered the manuscript to suit her own agenda, which resulted in a stronger emphasis on the piano accompaniment for each of the songs. It was important for Doreen to make her mark in her own territory—and distance and time made it difficult for Helen to do anything but acquiesce.[14]

*Twelve Folk Songs from Nova Scotia* didn't attract the attention that Helen's first book had garnered. It was a much smaller volume and, to be fair, people were less inclined to purchase books of folk songs in the midst of wartime. Still, the reviewer for *English Dance and Song*, the journal of the English Folk Dance and Song Society—and the organization that Doreen wanted most to impress—called it "an attractive collection; well turned out and sure of a welcome."[15]

With the release of a new book and improved conditions at King's, it should have been a more restful time for Helen. However, things at home were getting worse. Alice had begun to show signs of developing her old animosities toward her absentee daughter. Helen went home to Evergreen in March to celebrate her mother's birthday, but Alice grew upset and jealous when Helen also spent time with her father. She wasn't looking forward to the end of the college term when she would have to move home once again. Alexandra Hall was being taken over by the navy and would be renamed HMCS King's. To prepare herself for what she thought would be a difficult summer taking care of her mother, Helen took a vacation trip to Bear River, Annapolis County, with her cousin, Belle Albro. While she was there she received the news that Alice had died.[16]

The last few years with her mother had been difficult for Helen. She didn't want the bad times caused by Alice's illness to cloud her memories; she wanted to remember Alice as a "truly wonderful and beloved mother."[17] So she set her mind to forgetting the troublesome years and "in time the lovely memories came back."[18]

Helen moved home to Evergreen to help care for her father. They retained a full-time maid for domestic work, but the personal caregivers they'd employed for Alice were no longer needed. After Alice's death, Helen and Charles decided to have Lilian remain year round at the home in West Gore. She seemed to function best without the interruption of moving home every summer—and it was certainly easier for

Helen not to have the added responsibilities of her care. And so Helen, Charles, and one maid were left alone in their large house in Dartmouth.[19]

The war brought an extreme housing shortage to Halifax and Dartmouth and many people with rooms to spare rented them out, especially to service personnel and their families. It was an obvious way to contribute to the war effort and provide extra income. Helen suggested turning a section of their upstairs into an apartment. Charles was reluctant at first, saying that he didn't want his home turned into a rabbit warren.[20] But once he came around to Helen's way of thinking, he gave up his personal space to move downstairs with Helen and the maid and, with a minimum of alterations, they turned the upper floor into two apartments.

*"Laura Bolton, Judy Crawley of Crawley Films at Florenceville,"* 1941.

Most of the summer was taken up with preparing Evergreen for tenants. Helen carried out some collecting near home, but for the most part she took it easy, enjoying the company of her father and her friends, and getting her strength back after the two years at King's and the stress of losing her mother. However, in September she received a letter from Marius Barbeau that brought her an opportunity to go out into the collecting field again. He wrote from lower Quebec, where he was escorting a filmmaker named Laura Bolton. Barbeau was most impressed with her work—calling it remarkable—and asked Helen if she would take Mrs. Bolton around Nova Scotia.[21] He had helped to secure a contract for Laura Bolton to film rural life in eastern Canada for the National Film Board, with an emphasis on filming folk music performances.

A recommendation from Marius Barbeau carried a great deal of weight, and so on 21 September, accompanied by her father, Helen eagerly met Laura at her hotel in Halifax. Laura told them she was in need of a guide to find informants whom she could film in their natural environment. Helen was the obvious choice and she came with Dr. Barbeau's recommendation. Laura offered to pay Helen three dollars per day, plus a small travel per diem,[22] and four days later Helen took Laura and her camera operator to Devil's Island to begin work with Ben and Edmund Henneberry.

Helen jumped into the project too quickly. She wasn't comfortable with the fact that Laura would be making film and audio recordings of material she considered to be hers—or at least from her collection. Her old fears of losing control over the material surfaced yet again.

When she voiced these concerns to Laura, she was told that the material would be deposited with the National Film Board authorities in Ottawa as being recorded by Laura Bolton. Marius Barbeau and Helen Creighton would be listed as research assistants. Despite her misgivings, Helen continued working, perhaps out of loyalty to Dr. Barbeau or because she wanted to stay by Laura and see what she was up to. Things grew worse a few days later when Laura said she couldn't afford to pay Helen's fee and per diem to have her accompany the film crew to any locations outside the Halifax/Dartmouth area. The best she could offer was three cents per mile for car expenses. But Helen was in too deep to quit. She was not about to have Laura Bolton going off into "her" territory filming folk singers without being present to monitor the situation.

Their first stop was to film a reenactment of the Scotch wedding Helen had witnessed in 1938. Helen had orchestrated the attendance of some of the original members of the reception and enlisted other locals to act as the wedding party.[23] Next they moved on to Cape Breton, where Laura had made arrangements to film miners at Florenceville. On the drive out to the mines Laura dropped another bombshell on Helen:

On way she suggested hoped to come back here and spend six months collecting songs. I so horrified at her thinking of doing that in my territory completely put off for morning. Probably only technique of buttering up.... Had spent my morning blowing off steam to Doreen ... can't help thinking how Doreen and I kept out of Pictou County as point of honour as Prof. MacKenzie found it first.[24]

Helen's patience hit breaking point at Baddeck. She rose at 7:30 in the morning to drive into the country and bring singers back for the filming. The clay roads were very slippery and she got lost. The gears in her car were not working properly and she was worried that they wouldn't make it. By the time she returned with the singers she knew she had to have the car serviced, which meant withdrawing 20 dollars of her own money from the bank to pay for repairs. Not surprisingly, by the time she got back to the location shoot she was tired and frustrated:

When I came back from having car serviced ... they were all ready to sing. Three men faced microphone, and another was ready to write words down for Mrs. B. Suddenly I couldn't take any more. Here she was with everything I had wanted so badly to work with, taking songs down in my territory while I wore myself out driving her around for nothing but my own generosity, The position was intolerable, so I pleaded fatigue and fled.... told Mrs. B both car and I getting too tired and in no condition to go on. Said couldn't afford expense or strength. She was horrified. Finally on trip home she asked me why I hadn't stayed for singing, so thought I might as well tell her. [She] as perfectly sweet and certainly understands. Told her I was glad records being made. Mind could reason all it liked, but am only human. Mightn't even ever do it myself, but couldn't bear to stand aside and watch someone else do it. She didn't fuss or plead or do anything silly, but buttered me up in her charming way and faced the problem sensibly. She couldn't have been nicer about it. Then having discussed it we talked of other things. She felt her work and mine should be correlated and not conflicting.[25]

In spite of this flare-up, Helen continued with Laura for the rest of the day, which they spent filming a milling frolic until after midnight. Two days later Helen would discover that she was not alone in her frustrations with Laura Bolton. Judy Crawley, the camera operator on the shoot, came to Helen's room in tears. She and her husband operated Crawley Films, the company in charge of production. She had earlier called her husband to make arrangements to have another camera operator brought down in her place. None was available and Judy would have to remain. She told Helen that Laura was constantly dissatisfied with her camera work; that everyone who worked with Laura ran into the same problems. (In fact, the very next day the still photographer also told Helen he was unhappy working with Laura).[26] Helen was relieved to discover an ally, and in a more jovial mood, she put her frustrations into verse: "Once I had thunder / To-day I have none / I used to be happy / And have lots of fun / I want to swear roundly / Profane I not am / So please say it for me / A thundering damn."[27]

However, she realized that the situation required more action than to pen bad poetry. She called home and discussed her predicament with Mac, who had joined the Canadian army and was stationed in Halifax. He advised her to insist on a written affidavit stating that everything Laura Bolton collected as a result of Helen assistance with informants be considered theirs jointly, and any of Helen's previously collected songs used by Laura would remain Helen's exclusively. He also reminded Helen that her reputation was known internationally and that she needn't put up with such treatment. Helen took his advice and drew up an agreement. She called Laura to her room:

Felt like Dean of Women with Co-ed. This one very clever. Explained my position again, and that I was talking to Mac and what he thought. Said she would sign anything. Had no idea I had this possessive feeling, but I gave her paper all typed out, said she had no rights to anything, and wouldn't sign. She very nearly lost her temper but controlled herself with effort. Instead got very nice and understanding and kissed me most affectionately. But of course I was no further ahead.[28]

Helen had finally had enough. The following day she returned to Dartmouth where she found a letter from Marius Barbeau. She had written him her concerns and his reply assured her that Laura Bolton was working for the Dominion government and that all records would be safely housed at the National Archives. However, a telegram from the National Film Board suggested a different scenario—the Film Board had the rights to the material in Canada; Laura Bolton retained the international rights.[29]

Helen met with the film crew for a final meeting on 11 October when they came over to Evergreen to pick up their luggage and say goodbye. Laura stayed to tie up loose business ends before Helen drove her to the ferry terminal, where Laura kissed her goodbye. Helen later noted: "Extraordinary person.... Poor Laura, she is a curious mixture. So much good, but—."[30]

If Laura Bolton were out of Helen's life, her impact would be felt for some time. Judy Crawley wrote to Helen in November, confiding that she was not happy with the attention Laura was getting in film circles. She was also not pleased that neither Helen's nor her own name would be appearing in the film credits: "The main point I want to express is 'What the Hell—toujours gai.' Laura is insuperable. But she is not a folklore collector, nor a musician, nor a film producer, and for us, who like to consider ourselves in one of the foregoing categories the only thing to do is to stick to our own jobs, love it for its own sake, and let Laura have her superficial success."[31]

# CHAPTER EIGHT

✳ ✳ ✳

The unpleasant affair with Laura Bolton left Helen drained. She had even lost interest in collecting.[1] She continued to write her reports for the Wartime Information Board and did some volunteer work at the various service canteens that had been set up to provide R & R for the large numbers of military personnel moving through Halifax. But most of her activities revolved around caring for her father and making Evergreen a comfortable place for him. However, once again, fate intervened and Helen was offered a new path to travel.

In May 1942 she received a telephone call from Carleton W. Stanley, the president of Dalhousie University. He wanted her to meet John Marshall of the Rockefeller Foundation, which was interested in promoting cultural cooperation between Canada and the United States. Helen's work had been brought to their attention as fitting their mandate. After discussing her achievements with collecting folklore in Nova Scotia, Mr. Marshall asked Helen if she would be attending the Institute of Folklore that summer at Indiana University. Helen had seen the literature on the course and told him that the curriculum looked more scholarly than anything she had done before. When he asked again if she would be going, she replied, "Going? I wouldn't think of going. There's a war on."[2] However, she did think to request that her name be kept in mind if the Foundation ever wanted to award a grant to allow work to be carried out in Nova Scotia.

Dr. Stanley called the next day to enquire how her meeting had gone. It was only then that Helen realized that John Marshall had been making her an offer to go to Indiana. This was a tremendous opportunity, but how could she leave her responsibilities at home? Her father was requiring greater attention as his health was beginning to fail. She discussed the possibilities with her family. Mac was stationed in Halifax and could attend to his father's medical needs. Helen was confident in the maid's ability to run the daily operations of the house, and her tenants, the Garrets, had become good friends and would help out wherever they could. Satisfied that things wouldn't fall apart in her absence, she called John Marshall to accept the grant. The Rockefeller Foundation would pay her tuition, registration, and four dollars a day for living and travelling expenses.[3]

Indiana University was prominent in the field of folklore in the United States, and the 1942 summer session was attended by most of the major players in academic folklore studies. Although she had no formal training in folklore studies, based on her books and status as a Rockefeller award holder, Helen was accepted for registration in the graduate courses. Her reputation as a collector preceded her. Many of her fellow students had more academic credentials, but few had two important folk song publications to their credit. They told Helen that her books were not only in their libraries, but many of them used them in their course material when teaching.

The list of lecturers at the 1942 summer session included Dr. Stith Thompson, who had assembled much of the known folk literature in an index of their various motifs. He and his wife took an instant liking to Helen and they became fast friends. Another instructor was the flamboyant folk song collector and teacher, John Jacob Niles. During lectures he would frequently compare songs he had collected in the Appalachian Mountains of the United States to those found in Helen's collection. He would turn to her and enquire, "Sister Creighton, what do you think of that?"[4] Then, to Helen's embarrassment, he would demand that she sing her version. Other lecturers—who later became friends— were Alan Lomax and Herbert Halpert. Alan was following his father's footsteps; John A. Lomax had been one of the first folk song collectors in the United States to compile indigenous material. Herbert Halpert was a folklore researcher whose reputation as a respected bibliographer was well deserved. The combined credentials and experience these academics brought to the summer session went beyond anything Helen could be exposed to in any one undergraduate program anywhere else.

She was being introduced to a whole new world. She'd had no idea that the study of folklore encompassed so many aspects of human culture and areas of study: "Friday morning's class was the first one I didn't enjoy. Alan [Lomax] talked and played the type of music known as blues. I tried to look politely interested, but it was an effort."[5] Alan Lomax also introduced Helen to the music of African Americans and the possibility of collecting songs from African Nova Scotians, which would later open up a whole new area of work for her. For the most part she kept private her thoughts concerning those genres of folklore she didn't understand. But her opinions concerning her collecting techniques were sought, even if she and the instructor didn't always agree: "Today Herbert [Halpert] was our lecturer on folk song collecting. We argue at length and he is painfully conscious of my presence in class as a successful collector who probably has theories quite at variance with his. I have, actually, but discussion is encouraged and by this means we help one another. There is no hard feelings as Herbert proved by leaving his table to sit beside me at lunch."[6]

Helen's reputation at Indiana University spread beyond the class-room. The student newspaper requested an interview with her, which Helen had to decline in accordance with her agreement with the Rockefeller Foundation to refrain from making public information concerning her funding. However, the newspaper did run an article titled "Miss Creighton, Folklorist, Knows Plenty of Songs and Folkways but She Can't Give Out Interviews."[7]

At the end of term Helen wrote her father with the favourable re-sults of her exams: "two A's and one B. Not bad for an undergradu-ate."[8] The paper that earned her a B was about her personal collecting experiences. It points out the importance she placed on what she per-ceived as the proper clothing to wear while conducting interviews.

The matter of dress is important, but in Nova Scotia where tailored clothes are the most comfortable and are always in good taste, the problem is fairly simple. A well made suit, not my best, with sweaters of differ-ent weights ... medium heeled shoes ... summer print dresses ... The folk miss no detail of appearance ... Extremes of fashion are to be avoided.[9]

However, it is her statements concerning offering payment for songs that perhaps are most revealing. By today's standards they appear pa-tronizing and condescending, but in the 1940s it was common to refer to informants as "the folk" and to view their lives as being quaintly foreign from those of the collector.

We realize that we who lead very full busy lives are a grea[t] event in the lives of humble fisherfolk. We bring them something of an-other world. We therefore look out for the thoughtful little things that will give them something to remember.... We send them cards at Christmas. They usually send them to us. No cards I receive give me the pleasure that those do which come from the folk. They treas-ure these things so much more than money. The friendship is mutu-ally agreeable.... I love to think of these kindly, simple, and gener-ous folk.[10]

At one point during the summer session Alan Lomax asked Helen if she would consider using a recording machine to collect songs in Nova Scotia on behalf of the Library of Congress. He was in charge of the library's archive of American folk song division and was able to arrange for her to borrow one of their machines if she would collect songs from members of the armed services stationed in—or passing through—her province. The Library of Congress was inter-ested in adding to their international song collection and Helen's work would compliment their existing materials. Helen saw this as a golden opportunity. The facilities and support of a respected institution would enable her to collect material documenting the war effort in Canada, as well as to resume her own collecting work. The problem of her financial support was solved when the Rockefeller Foundation came forward with another grant.[11]

Instead of going straight home to Nova Scotia after the summer folklore session, Helen went on to Washington to learn how to use the recording equipment she would borrowfrom the Library of Congress. While there she met Charles Seeger, head of the music division of the Pan American Union. Dr. Seeger was a noted musicologist and Helen was delighted to be invited to dine with him and his family in their home. After dinner Dr. Seeger played the piano while his three children danced. Years later Helen would meet the two boys again when they visited Halifax. By then both Michael Seeger and his brother Pete were international folk music stars.

After several days in Washington Helen went to New York to visit the offices of the Rockefeller Foundation and finalize the arrangements for her grant. She returned to Nova Scotia ready and eager to resume her collecting. She was especially interested in songs from African Nova Scotians and immediately set about finding possible informants, beginning her search near her home in Dartmouth. Until her introduction to (what was then called) "Negro" music at Indiana University, she had given no thought to the possibility of collecting songs from people of African heritage living in her native province. Her first informant, Mrs. Bundy, told her about traditional church services at Preston. Helen also asked the Dartmouth ferry captain whether he knew of any singers who used the ferry. She wrote to John Marshall of the Rockefeller Foundation about her excitement at finding such a ready source of folk singers: "I have found that our negroes, always spoken of here as coloured people, sing spirituals, adding verses of their own. This opens up an entirely new field. I have a date with an old coachman for Monday morning. He is going to sing while he works in the garden of a friend of ours."[12]

Early in October Helen drove out to Preston with Charles Dunn, who was on his way to Cape Breton to study Gaelic folklore. He wanted to see how Helen approached a new collecting area and so she took him along, although to her it was also an "entirely new and fascinating field."[13]

Dartmouth was close to the communities of Preston, North Preston, and Cherry Brook—all three almost exclusively populated by African Nova Scotians—and Helen was just now learning of the potential for collecting folklore from these residents.[14] Other nearby communities, including Lucasville and Africville, offered the potential for finding even more informants. But these communities were worlds apart from that of Helen and her social circle. Although Helen had attended public school with African Nova Scotian children, beyond those early years the most social contact she would have had with black people was when she encountered them as domestic help. She illustrated the common prejudices of the day with comments in a letter to Alan Lomax: "On the whole they are very nice people to work with. I've always liked our coloured people here. We have often employed them in the house."[15] On the same day she wrote to Lomax she made a note in her diary that she had offered the elderly coachman, John Tynes, the position of handyman at Evergreen.[16]

This was the world in which Helen grew up. Divergent cultures rarely crossed paths and she would be breaking new ground merely by collecting from this ethnic group. The only other important study directed at African Nova Scotians had been conducted almost 20 years earlier by Arthur Huff Fauset, whose heritage was partially African American.[17] Helen didn't understand African Nova Scotian culture and she brought with her long established biases, but she was willing to learn and grow.

The lack of cultural understanding went both ways. Few African Nova Scotian families would have received unannounced visits from whites, let alone from a woman asking about their social customs and songs. It demonstrated a considerable sensibility for the collector and the informants to open up to each other. Helen was particularly fortunate in this regard with William Riley, the patriarch of Cherry Brook, where he was esteemed for his large repertoire of African Nova Scotian songs. Helen made several trips to collect information concerning his repertoire, as she hadn't yet received the recorder from the Library of Congress and was still collecting song titles and lyrics.

Mr. Riley was happy to share his songs with Helen, but had reasonable concerns as to why she was collecting them. He asked Helen if she were going to make a lot of money out of his songs. When she explained what she was doing, he understood and heartily approved.[18] On a later visit, after a two-and-a-half-hour collecting session, Mr. Riley thanked Helen for coming and asked, "You like coloured people?"[19]

Helen also made inroads into finding sources for future recording sessions among the military. She made enquiries at local branches of the Canadian Legion and was successful in finding at least one song— "La Malbie"—about a Corvette, one of the fleet that accompanied convoys across the Atlantic. She also continued her volunteer work at the military canteens, now asking many questions about songs. Alan Lomax had particularly requested that she look for war songs. For one such as Helen, who disliked collecting bawdy songs, this petition would present a problem. In November a military friend wrote out the words to the infamous "North Atlantic Squadron," a song filled with bravado and containing enough raw language to make a sailor blush. Helen dutifully retyped the lyrics to send along to Alan, but it was obvious that there were a few words she didn't understand. While she modestly typed bum as b— and shit as s—, where one might have expected her to type f—, she wrote out the entire word.[20]

While waiting for the recording equipment to be sent from the Library of Congress, Helen continued to seek out informants. But most of her attention was given over to her father, whose health was steadily deteriorating. In order to allow her time to pursue her work, the Rockefeller Foundation not only provided her with a grant-in-aid, but paid 45 dollars a month for the services of a private caregiver for Charles.[21] By the time the recording machine arrived in July, Helen had made many contacts and was ready to begin recording.

The recording equipment arrived in seven large boxes. It consisted of a Presto Model "K" Recorder, blank acetate discs, a microphone fitted to a stand, sapphire needles (some for cutting the groove into the discs and others specifically for playback), and an electronic converter for use with batteries. The machine was worked by placing a blank disc on the turntable, with the cutting needle at its centre. As the sound was recorded, the needle moved towards the outer edge of the disc, cutting grooves into its shiny acetate surface. While this was happening, the tiny filaments of acetate being cut away were drawn by static electricity towards the central brass spindle. Helen used a small brush to whisk away these threads to prevent them from entangling the machinery. If she aligned the cutting needle to cut either too deep or too shallow, the disc would be ruined. She had received operating instructions in Washington, but now—without the help of the library's technicians—she was on her own. Unfortunately, the equipment itself was in poor working condition and Helen eventually had to rely on technicians at CHNS radio station to help her keep it in running order. She made several practice records at home before calling on her first informant, Mrs. Duncan. Helen was very pleased with the results.

Once familiar with her recording equipment, she devoted her time to finding military songs. Unhappily for her, most of the military songs she found were not the kind she was comfortable collecting. She had also enlisted several high-ranking military officials to locate songs, and they too came up with the same conclusion: "Stewart Robertson called in the aft. To say he was definitely discouraged. He had enquired in the mess and none of the officers had heard anything but lewd songs."[22] She did eventually find and record some material more to her liking, including the Fusilier's pipe band, but that is not to say that Helen wouldn't collect bawdy songs when she found them. On a visit to Camp Debert she recorded a young member of the Sherbrooke Fusiliers. He "sang a French folk-song and two of his own composition ... He was a little worried about singing the second song because it had damn in it. It turned out to have bastard and an even more vulgar expression, but we took it because it was the story of the regiment's moves from Sherbrooke to Debert."[23]

Making a successful recording was only the first step towards having a permanent record of songs for herself. After she cut the records they had to be packed carefully in crates and sent back to the Library of Congress in Washington. The dulled recording needles also had to be returned for sharpening. The discs were duplicated in Washington and Helen was sent a copy. This meant filling out customs forms for sending and receiving the materials and, if an acetate disc was broken in transit, the recording session would be lost. Thus it was only natural that after she had sent off her first shipment, Helen opened a letter from the Library of Congress with some trepidation. Her apprehension turned to delight: "They are very pleased, and the engineer con-

*William Riley and Rose Mann, Cherrybrook, 1948.*

siders the bagpipe records the finest he has ever heard. Greatly encouraged now, and looking forward to arrival of duplicates."[24] She was not always so fortunate. Several weeks later her diary notes a less welcome message from Washington: "Joy taken out of I when telegram came saying last shipment ... arrived broken. This included Richard Hartlan's Flying Cloud ... One redeeming feature was that these may have bad echo. But in any case it was a nasty jolt."[25]

Whenever possible Helen had informants come to Evergreen to record. Only at home could she be certain of a reliable source of electricity, not have to tote heavy equipment about, and, most important, be close to her father. Conducting her work and providing care for her father could not have been easy, but a diary entry shows us how she got it all done.

Walter Roast arrived at eleven.... In order to sing he first went to doctor to have ears blown out so could hear. It cost him $2.00 which I am sure he could ill afford.... father became very weak and thought he was passing away. His pulse was strong, so I didn't think he was, but had to stand by. Was uncertain what to do, but after tbsp. of whiskey, he went to sleep. Was difficult recording. Would take last look at him and then record, going back as soon as finished each number.... Gave him [Walter] $5.50 for his expenses and then remembered ears and of course paid him for that. If I had taken it out of my own pocket he wouldn't have accepted it, but when I told him I had a fund for expenses he was willing enough.... Told him we would go over duplicates when they come back and I would make him a present of his choice.[26]

Sometimes an informant's advanced age made it necessary for Helen to travel to him or her. At 92, Dennis Smith was still able to sing but not likely to make the journey to Dartmouth to record. So Helen packed her equipment, including a newly charged battery, and went to him. Few people would have seen a disc recorder in 1943, and the arrival of Helen and her new machine was a novelty. In fact, although it was a Saturday and the busiest day of the week for a storekeeper, Dennis Williams closed shop and he—and his customers—all crowded into his house while Helen captured his voice on disc.

Helen had made several recordings with William Riley at his home in Cherry Brook. On previous visits he was being cared for by his daughter-in-law, Cassie Downey, but when Helen and Nina Bartley Finn took the recorder to his house on 25 August, they also found his daughter, Rose Mann, who was visiting from New York. Rose was a bright, inquisitive woman who wanted to know what Helen would do with her father's songs. It was a natural, daughterly concern, but Helen's old insecurities about provenance rose to the fore. She and Rose were about the same age and Helen was stung by Rose's challenge of her integrity as a collector. Helen assured her that Mr. Riley had already agreed to share his songs with her, and made arrangements to return another day to record him.

Two weeks later Helen and two companions, Nina Bartley Finn and Mrs, Coffin, went back to record more of Mr. Riley's songs. Helen's diary entry for that day gives a vivid account of her thoughts on the subsequent events.

What a day! 'Phoned Nina, and she and Mrs. Coffin came over early to go to Cherry Brook. Hoped Rose had gone, but arrived to find her sitting with father in doorway. Gave us pleasant enough welcome, but didn't think her father well enough to sing. However he looked better than ever, so put things together. Wanted Blessings of Mary. Had got to 5th [verse] when Rose said Here comes George. Then trouble began. George said he didn't want his father to sing. Was bad for him. Went stalking off. Nina and Mrs. C. Wanted to pack right up, but I didn't want to run away just like that. George came back presently, so I went up to him and told him I didn't want him to think was taking anything from his father shouldn't take, and wouldn't tire him for anything. What did Rose say about it? Said had been necessary to stop him one night because was bad for him. Mr. Riley himself kept saying to come back another day and would sing whole song through. Told Geo. I expected he could sing too. Said yes, he could sing all kinds of songs, but didn't give his stuff away. Wanted $5.00 a song. Also mentioned something about a drink, but I told him how Enos always hints for a drink but that of course it wouldn't do for me to carry it around to singers. Noticed Geo. going in house and closing door of front room. Then he called companion. Evidently he was starting a binge. Knew then it was time we left. However asked first if all right to take picture of Mr. Riley. Nina helped him up and he was very feeble. Rose seemed interested. Then I told Rose off politely but firmly. Said I wasn't coming out again. Had honoured her father by letting him sing, but were too many people wanting to do it to put up with being talked to that way. Therefore would not return unless they asked me to. She said she knew it was difficult, but that her father hadn't been well after last time we were there, but story doubtful because she had said nothing of that before. Whole thing was they wanted us away so the party could go on. Was sorry for the old man who seemed disappointed to have us go, but Mrs. C. had seen the bottles go in and had counted 6. Poor people, spending $25.00 on drink. What a state they will be in tonight.[27]

This incident shows Helen at a stage in her career where she allowed fear and prejudice to override her professional judgment. In an earlier diary entry she referred to Rose as "a typical Harlem negress."[28] However, it is more than likely that Rose Mann was the first resident of Harlem whom Helen ever met (in fact, Rose lived in Brooklyn). She was concerned for her 87-year-old father's health and George wasn't the first informant to suggest payment for songs—and he certainly wouldn't be the last. It was presumptuous of Helen to arrive unannounced to collect from an informant and expect everyone in the household to change their plans. Moreover, she demonstrated a disregard for the integrity of the informant by suggesting that it was an honour for him to contribute to her collection. It was an event that marred her usual understanding and compassionate method of collecting.[29] On the other hand, it did reveal the gap that separated many African Nova Scotians from mainstream society.

Helen grew up in a world in which people were not comfortable when others overstepped perceived boundaries. Another occasion on which Helen overreacted involved her father and his practical nurse, Miss A. Gordon Etter. Miss Etter was quite elderly and grew very fond of Charles, telling Helen that he was such a dear man that she felt like giving him a hug and a kiss. Sure enough, Helen returned from collecting one day to have her father complain, "What is wrong with that woman—she hugged and kissed me and I won't have it."[30] Helen dismissed her outright and drove her home.

Charles's health was in steady decline and Helen took over his primary care, assisted by her brothers, Ruth (the maid), and Ruth's husband. On 3 October Charles refused his food for the first time. Four days later he was confined to bed and taking only liquids. But despite her father's condition, Helen kept an appointment to record a special military showcase at the Capital Theatre in Halifax.

*Meet the Navy* was a musical extravaganza featuring orchestra, bands, chorus, soloists, and comedians in a show designed to boost morale and showcase naval talent. Helen had received a tentative go-ahead from military authorities to record the performance on 7 October. That evening, she and her friend Marjorie Sircom (Simmie) set up the Presto recorder in the centre aisle of the theatre. Panic struck when it was realized that Helen didn't have formal permission to record the show. A few calls were made and—two minutes before curtain—Helen was given the green light, provided she give a copy of the recordings to the naval authorities. As the show progressed, Simmie would hand Helen blank records and hold a flashlight so that she could see to brush away the filaments gathering around the spindle. Two of Helen's friends were in the audience and when she drove them home after the show they told Helen that her recordings were "irreplaceable and precious." Helen entered their comments in her diary and added, "That is the way I felt about them too."[31]

Once the *Meet the Navy* recording was done, she could devote herself entirely to her father's care. Charles lived only one more week. He died, with Helen by his side, at eight o'clock in the morning on 14 October. She was now truly on her own.

# CHAPTER NINE

\* \* \*

Although Helen had the love and support of her brothers, the responsibility for Lilian's care and the upkeep of Evergreen fell on her shoulders. Charles had left Evergreen to his daughters. Helen received $2,000; Terry and Syd each received $100; and the remainder of Charles Creighton's estate was turned over to executors.[1] Helen and Lilian shared a monthly income of approximately $100 from their father's estate, Lilian's half being paid in trust to Helen. Unfortunately, no one advised Helen that the money was being withdrawn from capital, and so in a few years this income was exhausted.[2]

Helen's immediate concern was for her sister. Lilian's mental abilities had never progressed beyond that of an eight-year-old. She suffered from mood swings—sometimes happy and carefree, at others sullen and silent. She was particularly fond of Helen and of her brother Paul, who might have had a special empathy with Lilian because he stuttered and had been sent to an American school to overcome his impediment.[3] Lilian was happy at her home in West Gore, but Helen was responsible for her maintenance and had to make decisions about her care and well being.

Helen was also now a homeowner. The occasional funds she still received from her uncle's estate helped to maintain Evergreen, but she needed to keep tenants if she were going to hold on to her home. She did receive help from her brother Mac, who provided an allowance for hair appointments and clothing. And as she continued to be supported in her work by the Rockefeller Foundation, she was not without means.

When Charles became ill and Helen had been faced with the reality of being left alone, she had seriously entertained the notion of adopting two children. Whether she feared loneliness or assumed she might never marry, some time after Charles died she concluded that she wanted a career in folklore more than she wanted a family of her own. If anything could have challenged that decision, it was a visit she received shortly after her father's death. Guy, her old love from the First World War, stepped back into her life.

After he was shipped out in 1918, Guy initially corresponded with Helen. When after a while his letters and occasional gifts stopped coming, Helen assumed he had been torpedoed or perhaps found someone else. So it was truly out of the blue when she heard Guy's voice on the telephone. He was back in Halifax—once again on a warship—and wanting to see her. She was unsure how to react, but asked Guy to dinner, inviting her neighbours along for support. The old spark was still there—on both sides. Guy explained that he had always intended to come back to Helen, but was prevented by various circumstances. He now wanted to pick up where they had left off. Older and wiser now, Helen told him that she couldn't wait for another war to bring him back again. Despite her feelings for him, she wouldn't wait for his return. Shortly after that meeting, Guy sailed with a convoy and Helen never heard from him again. She threw herself back into her work.

In November she paid a visit to the naval base at HMCS Cornwallis, in Annapolis County, where she befriended a young writer named Henry Sherman. Henry wrote a regular fiction column for the navy's newspaper, *The Crows Nest*, featuring a mermaid called Miranda who wanted to become a Wren. She also met and recorded Clifford Clark, a naval pianist originally from Toronto. After she left Cornwallis she continued along the coast to Yarmouth to keep an appointment with a retired seaman, Captain Arthur Hilton.

At Helen's request, Captain Hilton had gathered together a group of his contemporaries—all former sea captains—to sing shanties. Helen made the rounds to visit them individually and confirm the evening appointment. She found them to be bright, relaxed men, of an average age of 75, dressed informally for their daily chores. When she met them again that evening, they all wore navy blue suits and sat stiffly in straight-backed chairs in the Hilton's parlour. Helen set up her recorder and for half an hour collected the songs they had sung aboard the tall ships that sailed out of Yarmouth Harbour. They were good songs, albeit delivered with a formality Helen knew was not usual for shanty singing. Eventually their host announced that they would stop for refreshment. Sweet, dark rum was frequently the beverage of choice among sailors, and Helen felt that perhaps a glass of "rusty water" might be just the thing to make the singers more relaxed. As she recorded in her diary, "I thought it was a grand idea, and that a little something would loosen them up and help them to forget themselves. I was too busy to wonder much about what it would be, but when seven tumblers came in on a tray, the liquid was white. Could it be gin? No. It was water, and nobody but me was surprised."[4] It seemed the captains were all members of the local Temperance Society!

Helen recorded several shanties from the Yarmouth captains and would have stayed in the area longer had her supply of blank discs not run out. She would have to return home to retrieve a new batch through customs. In any case, she was expecting a weekend visit from

Clifford Clark, the pianist she had met at HMCS Cornwallis.[5] She made a recording of his playing while he was at Evergreen and then drove him to see Stadacona, the naval base in Halifax. He left with an invitation to return on his next leave.

The following day Helen had an exciting visit from Portia White and her singing coach, Ernesto Vinci. Portia was an African Nova Scotian singer who was well on her way to becoming an international star. Her warm contralto voice so enthralled those who heard it that the government of Nova Scotia eventually established the Nova Scotia Talent Trust to provide funds for her formal musical training. Helen hoped that their meeting might lead to Portia recording songs from her collection, thus introducing them to an international audience. She played her guests some examples of William Riley's music and had them listen to the same songs as sung by her friend, Nina Bartley Finn, to illustrate their potential when interpreted by a trained singer. The meeting clearly demonstrated that Helen was still interested in having the songs from her collection performed by trained singers, who could bring them to a larger audience. Although her guests didn't choose songs from Helen's African Nova Scotian collection, they did select two unrecorded songs to add to Portia's repertoire. Then Helen diplomatically broached the idea of making a recording using her equipment. She was overjoyed when Portia replied that she had a blank disc of her own and would return to sing one of the songs from Helen's collection: "The whole aft. was like a dream come true, because it looks as though my research will bear fruit."[6]

Aside from her personal research interests, Helen continued to make recordings with military personnel and other groups involved in the war effort. Late in 1943 she had visited the Merchant Seamen's Home in Halifax in search of songs or stories. These men worked on the ships carrying goods and supplies across the Atlantic. Helen was told that she couldn't come and record them as they were generally too exhausted by their harrowing work and just wanted to be left alone. Moreover, even if they did consent to talk with her, the Board of Censors forbade them to tell of their experiences.[7]

She ran into a different censorship obstacle in trying to record another interesting informant in March 1944. One of her tenants at Evergreen, Lieutenant Commander E.O. (Stocky) Stockman, came home one day and told her that the Royal Canadian Mounted Police schooner, *St. Roch*, was berthed at the Dartmouth Shipyards. Under the command of Staff Sergeant Henry Asbjorn Larsen, the *St. Roch* had just completed a trip through Canada's arctic waters, from Vancouver to Halifax—a great feat of seamanship and presumably intended to establish Canada's sovereignty in northern waters.[8] Staff Sergeant Larsen was a national hero and Stocky suggested that Helen ask him to record his account of the *St. Roch*'s adventures. The sergeant refused at first, but then seemed to change his mind, and called Helen back. However, he was still hesitant; they would need permission from the RCMP and, besides, he didn't think that he could find her house. Helen told him that she would seek the proper permission and, laughing, added, "If you could find your way from Vancouver to Halifax by way of the Arctic, you can easily find my house because you can see it from where you are."[9]

Several days later she set up the recording machine in her bay window, which looked down on the harbour and offered a splendid view of the *St. Roch*. Staff Sergeant Larsen arrived accompanied by an RCMP Inspector, who granted permission for the interview. When Helen asked if there were any subjects off limit, the Inspector told her that Sergeant Larsen knew how far to allow a conversation to go without breaching security.

Although Henry Larsen could handle a ship through the Arctic Strait, he was less comfortable talking into a microphone. Perhaps he was simply hesitant of slipping up and revealing classified information, but in any event his voice was so shaky that the recordings were useless. Helen suggested that he try writing out what he wanted to say and then read it aloud. This proved a good solution, as he relaxed somewhat and she was able to record his adventures through the Northwest Passage. Once he became comfortable with the recording machine, he settled into it and filled six records with tales of his time spent among the Inuit.[10]

In the last week of March Clifford Clark came back to visit Helen, bearing a rather romantic gift: "Clifford went to Hfx. bought Shakespeare for himself, and lovely bottle of toilet water for me. Had tried everywhere for a certain perfume which he couldn't get. Soon after lunch Mrs. Tilley [who came to record a talk on life on the Isle of Jersey] arrived, so she and I sat in sun room and went over mms. to accompaniment of Clifford's playing."[11] They spent two days together, but despite the poetry and perfume, the relationship never developed into a romance. Perhaps Helen's work got in the way, as she was once again branching into new territory.

Shortly after Clifford's visit Helen began to seek out informants among Nova Scotia's indigenous peoples. In February she had written to the Department of Indian Affairs for advice and permission to record with the Mi'kmaq, and in April she wrote to Stith Thompson in Indiana seeking counsel about what kinds of material she should try and find. Her initial search took her to the Halifax City Market, where she met basket maker John Knockwood. A week later she invited Mr. Knockwood and his son Noel to come to Evergreen to record. At the end of the month she took her recorder to the Shubenacadie Indian Reserve, in Colchester County. Her companion was Staff Sergeant Larsen, who was interested in meeting members of the native community and eagerly

*Mi'kmaq singers at Shubenacadie reserve, 1948. William Paul (in feathered band).*

accepted Helen's invitation to join her for the day.

Once again Helen was entering a world unfamiliar to her. She knew little of the customs and traditions of the Mi'kmaq people and seemed to expect a more primitive lifestyle than that which she encountered. She had already learned from John Knockwood that much of the traditional music had been subjugated by the Catholic Church. Stith Thompson had advised Helen to collect myths and legends, so she sought out examples of tales concerning Kluskap [Glooscap], the Mi'kmaq's cultural hero.[12]

Just as she had been guided in her introduction to African-Nova Scotian music by William Riley, Helen was tutored in Mi'kmaq narratives and music by Chief William Paul. He and his friend, Martin Sack, recorded numerous legends, beliefs, and ancient songs. As the following diary entry illustrates, rather than living in a remote and antiquated world, these men moved comfortably between their sphere of beliefs and modern society. Many times, the two were interchangeable.

Was surprised not to get more of Glooscap whom they called a great man but not a chief nor a god. All they could say was that he was such a great man he might have been God. Also noted they never spoke of

*Mi'kmaq singer, Nyanza, 1948.*

squaw, but called the woman in the story the lady.... Women not round at all, but younger men kept coming in and out quietly.... one of nicest collecting experiences yet. Just before leaving I suggested taking picture. So the four old men came out to front of house, and Mr. Paul put on cap with Micmac on it. Just a cheap commercial cap, but it had feathers. A far cry from the ancient feathered ceremonial headgear.... There was little to photograph that was picturesque. Everything was entirely modern, and on wall of Mr. Sack's house was even a pennant from Princeton University.[13]

A month later Helen took another trip to Lunenburg County. She was fascinated by the unique folk culture she had found there and wanted to make audio recordings of material she had only written down on previous trips. This time her travelling companion was her brother Terry, who was making business calls throughout the county. Helen's own sense of the wonder of the place led her make a recording of a rather unusual group of informants. Driving home after a day of collecting, she and Terry experienced one of Nova Scotia's spring rituals—the singing of the peeper frogs. On that particular evening, in that special place, the sound of the frogs was so loud that she got out her Presto recorder and cut a disc, capturing their music forever. It must have seemed a strange scene to the two young girls who came walking down the road and—lest they think that she and Terry were German spies—Helen let them listen to the sound of the recording through her earphones.

At the end of May Helen picked up her friend Isabel Dimock and headed for Cape Breton, where she recorded some fine Gaelic singers, including Neil Gillis of Gillisdale. He was home on leave and considered to be one of the finest Gaelic singers in the district. From there the women moved on to Cheticamp to collect Acadian songs. They met Peter Chiasson, Helen's guide to finding additional informants, who helped to set up an evening of music with his family and friends: "there were twenty-five in the little kitchen and ten or fifteen outside.... I recorded from seven until ten, filling the ends of the discs with short songs and lullabies.... when I took Peter home and offered to pay for the beer he wouldn't hear of it."[14] The next day Helen recorded school children at the Petit Étang school and then drove down through the Margaree Valley to the Indian reservation at Whycocogmagh on the shores of the Bras d'Or Lakes.[15]

At Whycocogmagh Helen met John Goo Goo, who informed her that a local chief had died a few days before and that there would be a funeral service for him at nearby Nyanza that Saturday. Mr. Goo Goo advised her to go to Nyanza, as natives from all over Cape Breton Island would be there and he was sure no one would mind. His advice was ill-founded and Helen's decision to go to Nyanza would prove misguided and inappropriate. When the women arrived at the church the service had just ended, and Helen felt uncomfortable intruding. However, she met the priest, Father Rankin, who took them in his car to the chief's home, where his mourners had assembled. Her diary entry records the subsequent events:

Father R. asked for old woman who was in house. She came out and talked for a little while. Said she knew many stories her father used to tell, but she didn't feel like telling them that day. Captain had been her brother. We sympathized of course, and didn't press her. However chief said he would do a record in Micmac. So we decided to set up there where all could see, as I thought it would interest them.... Father R. said his oration at the funeral was masterful, and he wished I could get it. However he did talk on arrival of Scots and how they made peace with the Indians; all told in Micmac. But he didn't feel like repeating oration, and I felt he considered it a private matter. Then Father R. got a young man to sing, and he did it very nicely. Then another one spoke a few words. Haven't any idea what they were about, and Frank Bernard sang again to finish the record. Then to please them I suggested he sing a few lines and I would play it back, and he sang whole long song. Thought I might as well take all he was willing to give. Had just begun when young Indian came up to me looking angry and said with fire in his eyes, This is the last, see. We want to get on with our business. I suppose he meant prayers, and anyway I felt uncomfortable about putting on a show just after a funeral, especially in the yard of the man who had died. Although I asked the daughter if she minded, and she had turned her back on me and laughed like everything. But this was menacing. So I packed up at once, and by the time the song was over I had most of the equipment packed up. Then Father Rankin said to me, They'll be able to buy these records I suppose. And Bernard looked simply horrified. He said, Buy them! I expect to be paid for singing. So I told him I had no funds for paying singers, but I would send him a record for a present, and Father Rankin slipped him a dollar which I paid back to him as soon as we were out of sight. Must say that most of them looked friendly enough as we left, but I wasn't happy about it at all. We left

Father R. at hall, hoping we would all meet again at Iona, and I feeling very thankful he had been there as I would have hated tackling Indians without his help. Then as we started back Isabel told me that what they had been unhappy about was not our intrusion in this time of mourning, but the fact that we were holding up the taking of the collection. Apparently there is a way of going about it, and they expected it to take until three in the afternoon. Our usurping of their time meant that they wouldn't get their money and that was why they were so angry. What a relief to find that out. So I gave Isabel two dollars which she gave to the men as we passed, and they looked very pleased. So I trust they did not think ill of us any more.... Can see no point in pursuing Indians further in Cape Breton, although I would like to get the old woman talking.[16]

This was field research at its most intrusive. Helen made a major blunder in deciding to collect during such an important rite of passage. John Goo Goo and Father Rankin should have counselled her against it, but instead they encouraged her. She obviously felt uneasy being there and realized that she had overstepped the boundaries of good taste, but her ignorance of Mi'kmaq culture left her vulnerable to mistake. The incident would later be recognized as the low point in her collecting career.[17]

After a few more days of collecting in Cape Breton, it was time to return to Dartmouth. It was also time for the recording equipment to be sent back to the Library of Congress. Helen would once again have to rely on her shorthand to take down information. She had tried earlier to purchase a recording machine for herself, but without success. In the midst of war, even the Library of Congress wasn't able to acquire more machines.[18] Helen had also made attempts to persuade the province to buy a recorder for her use. Her long-time advisor, Henry Munroe, supported this idea, but as late as November 1944 she was meeting with government officials and being rejected in both her requests for funding and equipment.[19] The only way the province contributed towards her work was to provide extra ration coupons for gasoline.[20]

When peace came in September, Helen no longer had to concentrate on collecting war-related materials. Her last official duty was to send in her final report to the Wartime Information Board. Twelve days after Japan surrendered, she received a telegram requesting one final overview of consumer opinion on meat rationing.[21] With that report filed, she was free to pursue her own agenda.

Before attending the summer session at Indiana University, Helen had been primarily a collector of songs. Since then her interests had widened to include all aspects of folkways, and she began a concerted effort to incorporate folk tales, superstitions, examples of folk medicine and material culture—e.g., crafts and folk architecture—oral history, and more in her field research. In October she went back down to the South Shore looking for examples of transplanted New England folklore in Nova Scotia. One of the first places she visited was Tancook Island, eight kilometres off the coast near Chester. The island's cultural base was firmly rooted in its German heritage, and the residents' livelihoods came primarily from either fishing or growing cabbages to produce the famous Lunenburg County sauerkraut. Helen arrived unannounced and found accommodation with Mrs. Ralph Cross. She also met Reverend Bezanson, who was himself collecting folklore on the island. He and Helen worked together for three days, comparing notes and sharing suggestions. When it was time to leave, her collecting journal was full—so full, in fact, that Helen abandoned her previous idea of looking for transplanted New England folklore. Tancook proved so rich in folklore, and the rest of Lunenburg County looked so promising, that she decided to concentrate her efforts exclusively in Lunenburg County. She established two collecting bases, at the respective homes of Mr. and Mrs. Eleazer Nauss in Mahone Bay and the Norman Veinottes in Lunenburg. For transportation to some of the smaller communities, Helen relied once more on the local school inspector. At the end of six weeks she had a sizeable collection—enough to begin working on a book of Lunenburg County folklore.

During the winter of 1945 Helen worked on the research notes for her manuscript. She had neither a publisher nor a firm direction for her book, but persisted nonetheless, hoping that something would come about. And it did—courtesy of the Rockefeller Foundation. Having received a questionnaire regarding the usefulness of the grants awarded her, she wrote to John Marshall expressing her gratitude and telling of her work with the Lunenburg County material. She also asked if there were any funding available to provide her with access to a folklore library. In due course she was awarded a grant to work on her manuscript at Indiana University, under the direction of her friend, Stith Thompson. In December 1945 she went to Chicago to attend the meetings of the American Folklore Society, and then accompanied Dr. Thompson to Bloomington. At the university, he helped Helen to formulate the major components of her manuscript and fine-tune her research notes. On her way home to Halifax she stopped off at the Rockefeller Foundation office in New York and was able to show John Marshall an almost completed manuscript. But there was still no publisher.

Helen was also working on research notes for the songs she had collected with Doreen, in the hopes of producing another volume of folk songs. In late September she drove to Ottawa with one of her tenants. She sought out Marius Barbeau at the National Museum to solicit his advice about finding publishers for her research. She was also interested to learn whether there were any way she could work under the umbrella of the Museum. Her timing couldn't have been better. They were not hiring full-time researchers, but did have limited funding for research projects. Helen's work fit the bill perfectly. As the Museum couldn't access a recording machine, Dr. Barbeau wrote to the Library of Congress and brokered a deal whereby Washington would continue to provide Helen with the Presto recorder while the Museum would pay her research stipend.[22] In April she was offered a four-month contract and in May she was officially welcomed by her friend Marius Barbeau, who wrote, "I am delighted to know that you will be doing folklore for us this Summer. I hope that this will prove the beginning of closer relations and support between the Museum and yourself. This I had hoped for a long time."[23]

It was the beginning of a 20-year relationship. It was one that would have its ups and downs, but the recognition and support the Museum afforded Helen would give her the credibility and financial stability she needed to continue her work. Finally her folk songs had found a way to pay for themselves.

# CHAPTER TEN

✳ ✳ ✳

On 1 May 1947 Helen began a four-month contract with the National Museum. Marius Barbeau would act as her advisor, but she would deal directly with the Museum's director, F.J. Alcock. Her scope of possible research topics was very wide. She was to concentrate on songs, but could collect any aspects of folklore she found. This was in stark contrast to some of her American colleagues, who were sent into the research field looking for specific genres—e.g., traditional log cabin construction methods or folk narratives among cowboys. The leeway given her by the National Museum suited Helen's collecting methods, whose style was more "sweep and cull" than "target and find."

Transportation would be a problem. The Museum provided her with a salary and per diem, but no car. Her brother Paul advised her to purchase a car, even if she had to return it in the fall. But there were few cars for sale in postwar Nova Scotia, so Helen renewed her arrangements through the province's Department of Education to accompany the school inspectors on their rounds.

After consulting with Dr. Barbeau, Helen decided to concentrate her initial efforts in southwestern Nova Scotia. She had already collected some Acadian material in Cape Breton, but wanted to explore the region known as the "French Shore," which included Francophone communities between Digby and Cape Sable Island. It was during one of her early trips to Digby County that Helen met Laura Irene McNeil. Mrs. McNeil was a teacher at the Little Brook school, but lived in Yarmouth County at West Pubnico.[1] Born a Pothier, both she and her husband came from long established Acadian families. She would not only become Helen's friend, but her guide to Acadian songs and folktales.

Mrs. McNeil already had a good idea of what Helen was seeking. Several years earlier she'd had her own collection of folktales published in the province's only French-language newspaper, *Le Petit Courrier*. The editor, Desiré D'eon, had embellished the texts to make them longer, but Helen was eager to collect them in their original form. Mrs. McNeil also had experience as an informant, having sung a lullaby and several other songs for the Quebec collector, Juliette Gaultier. She recounted to Helen that when another collector came looking for songs, she had been concerned that Miss Gaultier might not be happy about sharing material, so she wrote to her. Juliette Gaultier replied that "if she sang

*West Pubnico children playing singing game "See the Robbers Passing Through." Teacher, Laura Irene McNeil, c. 1955.*

it to anybody else she would be liable for a heavy lawsuit!"[2] Helen was horrified, later noting that "Mrs. McNeil was far too intelligent to pay much attention."[3]

By the middle of June Helen had moved her collecting base to Victoria Beach in Digby County. It is a beautiful location overlooking the area known as Digby Gut, a narrow channel connecting the Annapolis Basin with the Bay of Fundy. Helen stayed in a guest cottage at a tourist complex run by Mr. and Mrs. Joseph Casey and their son Joe. Helen relished the atmosphere at Victoria Beach. The other cottages were rented out to artists and writers, including the American writer, Martha Banning Thomas,[4] who

*Martha Banning Thomas in front of Fundy House, Victoria Beach, c. 1947.*

became a close friend of Helen. Her days soon developed a routine. She would type out her research notes in the morning and collect in the afternoon and early evening. There was also time for relaxation, and she delighted in hearing the Casey's stories told at lobster-boils and clambakes.

Helen made several extended forays away from Victoria Beach during her summer collecting, but most of her time was spent in and around the immediate region. In fact, she was later to write that she disovered "more ghost stories from Annapolis Royal to Victoria Beach than in any other part of the province."[5] However, she found one of her most unusual tales of the supernatural while visiting with well-known author Thomas Raddall[6] near his home in Liverpool, Queens County. Thomas Raddall's use of folklore and local history in his writing intrigued Helen and she sought his advice in finding informants. He had written earlier to tell her about an informant he thought she should meet—a woman reputedly having the powers of a witch. He recalled their meeting 43 years later:

*Mrs. Alma Joudrey and Captain Erlin Colp, Eagle Head, 1947.*

Helen Creighton Fonds, PANS Album 14: 14-148. Photographer: unknown

Well, my wife was pregnant and there was danger of miscarriage, and we had to get somebody in here who could take charge of the house ... and Dr. Wickwire recommended this woman from the La Have, and she was a great big woman ... I found that she was full of the hex business ... So on one occasion Helen called here; she was chasing down the same sort of thing.... I said now, Mrs. Jourdey is now keeping house for an old retired sea cook, down at Eagle Head. And he won't let her talk about witchcraft at all. So we'll have to do a little strategy here. We'll go in and I'll introduce you. And then I will get the old fellow to go out in the kitchen and talk about his adventures on the Banks. And all you got to do is say the word hex and she'll be away. And that's what we did.[7]

The story, which Helen later published in *Bluenose Magic*, and the circumstances under which it was told, was one of her most unnerving folklore experiences. On 21 June she and Tom Raddall visited the home of Mr. Colp to interview Tom's former housekeeper, Alma Joudrey. Mrs. Joudrey was a large, kind-faced woman, dressed in overalls and a man's plaid shirt. She was eager to tell her story. When Helen was left alone with her in the dark parlour facing a funeral wreath of pressed flowers, the atmosphere was set. Mrs. Joudrey told of how she

*Joseph Raben, 1947.*

was brought up in Lunenburg County and of how she could tell if a person were a witch. One winter, when her husband had gone into the woods to work, a local man—a witch—began to bother her. He would change into a cat and sneak through a hole into her room and press himself upon her chest. He continued to torment her in various ways until she confronted him. He then transferred his torments to her pig. When the pig died, she took drastic action. She removed the pig's heart, stuck it full of pins, and roasted it slowly in the oven for six days—until the witch died.[8]

When Helen asked Mrs. Joudrey if she felt any remorse in thinking that she had taken a life, the woman replied, "He deserved to die. It says in the Bible, 'thou shalt not suffer a witch to live.'"[9] Helen sat awestruck and not a little uneasy. Later that day she noted in her diary: "thought I would have liked to go to the bathroom, if any, I wouldn't have for anything, knowing how a witch can torture if they get some of one's water!"[10]

Towards the end of June Helen returned to Dartmouth and cashed in four government bonds to buy a used car. The school term was over for the summer and she could no longer rely on the school inspectors for transportation. It was the first car she ever bought. A few days later she returned to Victoria Beach and purchased another "first"—a pair of slacks. It was still uncommon to see women wearing trousers in Nova Scotia, but Helen felt they might be comfortable on collecting trips. Wearing them was certainly a novelty for her. She wore them for the first time at the Casey's: "Put slacks on and felt as though I was stepping out in my pyjamas ... took my courage in my hands and went into the dining room. I saw Co. Eaton's eyes pop, and later his wife told me he had said he'd have to get her a pyjama suit like it. Anyhow they were quite a success."[11]

In the last week of August Helen received a visit from Joseph Raben, a folklore student from New York who had written to ask if he could tag along with Helen to look for regional dance styles. He knew much that she didn't, and she hoped to learn from him as well as to teach him about collecting in the field. His visit would mean more than she ever expected.

He arrived at the Casey's on 26 August and Helen was surprised by both his worldliness and his age. He was tall, slim, and good looking, not the young student she'd been expecting. He was still more than a decade younger than Helen, but she was instantly infatuated. She introduced him to her territory by taking him to hear a local singer. Joe had brought his banjo and soon joined in. Four days later they went to a dance at Kemp in nearby Queens County and Helen was able to see Joe in his element.

This was the highlight, for I saw dancing as I've never seen it before. They do what is called an 8, but Joe says is a mixture of an 8 and the running set which Cecil Sharp had found in the Kentucky Mts. It was dignified and stately, and when the couples promenaded with a polka step in a circle I felt I was living in another world. Joe took notes and then joined in, and I looked on and loved it. Most square dancing I had seen had been very fast, but while they twirled quickly, the rest of the dance was unhurried. Nobody calls because they all know the steps so well. Music, fiddle and guitar, with the musicians on a platform at the side front of the room. In the intermission they played what the local people called a waltz, but Joe says is a polka. The men didn't dance it, but the girls danced together.[12]

The next day they continued through to Liverpool so that Helen could introduce Joe to Tom Raddall. She secretly purchased a book from Tom for Joe's upcoming birthday, and they attended another dance that evening. Helen's diary mentions that Joe took notes and then they danced together: "Wonderful happy day."[13]

By week's end they were collecting at Pubnico. As Joe spoke French he was able to help Helen with her work. They made their way back up the coast to Victoria Beach and spent their last day together at the Casey's. That evening they dined with friends, whom Helen later wrote were quite taken with "my Joe."[14] In the morning Joe caught the ferry at Digby and Helen was left alone: "I felt very lonely when the boat pulled out, for we'd had a wonderful three weeks together. Understatement!"[15]

Helen was despondent for the next three days. She felt tired, lonely, and was constantly thinking of Joe. He shared so many of her interests. He loved to laugh and brought out Helen's playful side. But did he ever know how deeply she felt for him? Probably not. If he did Helen never mentioned it. Nine months after their collecting trip he was married in New York. Helen marked the day with a brief entry in her diary: "This is Joe's wedding day. I do hope he will always be happy."[16]

She continued collecting in southwestern Nova Scotia until the end of September, then returned to Evergreen to work on her notes. Her Museum salary ended in December and she worked through the winter on her Lunenburg manuscript and the collection of songs from her collecting trips with Doreen Senior.

By June 1948 she had another contract with the National Museum and began visiting informants to record what she had previously only taken down in writing. Her first trip was to visit the people from Devil's Island, who had been moved to Eastern Passage during the war. Her old friends made her feel very welcome: "So nice to be working with these people again and to go back after all these years, twenty of 'em. They all told me I hadn't changed from the time I first went down there. Nice to hear, although the mirror says differently."[17]

Time had taken its toll on some of her friends as well. She felt sorry for Ben Henneberry. He had been such a vibrant singer in his day and now he relegated his songs to his son, Edmund. But the tradition was being passed on. The next day Edmund and his young daughter recorded his father's song, "The Gay Spanish Maid."[18] Helen continued to record with Edmund for several more days. He went through his father's repertoire, much of which was published in *Songs and Ballads from Nova Scotia*, singing most of them from memory.

What was left of June and early July Helen spent collecting in Lunenburg County and visiting with her cousin Belle Albro, who was dying. When Belle died in Windsor on 19 July a rift developed among her family over which funeral home should handle the arrangements. Helen was fond of her cousin and it dismayed her to see the family divided at such a tragic time. At the end of the month she was only too happy to head for West Pubnico and a warm welcome from Laura Irene McNeil. She spent two weeks collecting Acadian folktales and songs. Her poor command of the French language hindered her, but Mrs. McNeil proved invaluable. In one week she filled 29 records. She was constantly reminded of the three happy weeks she'd spent collecting with Joe the previous year, especially when she heard from his new wife: "Had letter from Joe's Marie who sounds nice. How I miss him this year, but wish we could have had as much luck in getting material when he was here.... Was ready to drop, and came home to very quiet house. Couldn't settle down, but a cigarette helped ... I have much to thank Mrs. McN. for."[19]

In mid August Helen drove down to Liverpool to collect sea shanties from William Smith. From there she moved on to Hubbards to attend the wedding of her niece, Alice, to David Nicholl. She finished her collecting season at Victoria Beach and West Pubnico. It had been a good summer for work, but one filled with mixed emotions and bitter-sweet memories. She filled her winter with making plans to convert her basement into another apartment and preparing her next two books for publication.

It had been 10 years since she'd last collected folk songs with Doreen Senior. Helen had been picking away at the research notes and by the time she resumed work on her Museum contract in June, the manuscript for *Traditional Songs from Nova Scotia* was sent off to The Ryerson Press.[20] She had also found a publisher for her Lunenburg County research—the National Museum. Her scholarly notes had been much improved under the influence of Stith Thompson, so the Museum's editor had little work to do. But given the postwar sensitivity concerning German material and Helen's inclusion of some bawdy and racist material, there was discussion about certain sections that the Museum advised be excised.[21] It is interesting to note that the Museum brought out not one, but two important monographs on German-Canadian folklore just five years after the end of the war. The other, which complimented Helen's research in Lunenburg County, was by W.J. Wintemberg and looked at the German-based folklore from Waterloo County, Ontario.[22] It too, was under examination. The exclusion of the bawdy and racist material in Helen's manuscript was a different story. Today it would be considered poor scholarship to exclude material collected from an informant that illustrated assumptions about his or her personal environment. It is understood that the inclusion of such material does not reflect the opinions of the collector. Ironically, the omission of the very items that critics would fault Helen for in later years were the things she tried to include in her first serious study of a given area. Stith Thompson's influence probably had a considerable impact on the argument for inclusion, but public sentiment and the position of the National Museum held sway. In any case, given Helen's own predisposition against such material, she was probably not too concerned when the Museum's editor made these few changes. She was more likely perturbed at having to relinquish the book's dedication to her brothers, a convention not allowed in government publications.

At any rate, by 1 June her manuscripts were in the hands of their respective publishers and Helen was ready to begin the 1949 collecting season. Her first priority was to learn how to operate her new recording machine. The old Presto disc recorder had been returned to the Library of Congress and the National Museum now provided her with a Revere tape recorder. She thought she had "died and gone to heaven"[23]: no more cumbersome equipment to haul in and out of the car; no more broken and ruined discs; no more running out of supplies and waiting for replenishments to clear customs. She could now record as much as she could find, play back the material to make sure it was to her liking, and allow the informants to hear themselves without fear of ruining a fragile disc.

One of her first recording sessions with the new Revere was with the Armstrong brothers at Sherwood in Lunenburg County. Identical twins in their late sixties, they sang a number of beautiful songs for her. Her diary suggests that they offered Helen more than songs: Alistair "came out and we introduced ourselves. He asked me if I was married, said he wasn't and how about it. Quick work."[24] Later that day she met his brother, Judson, and he too hinted at marriage. Helen attributed the proposals to the enthusiasm she projected due to her new tape recorder!

After continued work around Lunenburg County she returned to Halifax to attend the Canadian Authors Association convention. Then she was back down to the south shore to Clark's Harbour and Cape Sable Island, the southernmost point in Atlantic Canada.[25] The island had recently been joined to the rest of the province by a causeway and Helen was eager to collect samples of the inhabitants' New England-based folklore before they became too assimilated with the mainland. At her base in Clark's Harbour she met the Toronto author Maida Parlow French.[26] Together they journeyed to Bon Portage Island to spend the day with Evelyn Richardson, whose book on her family's life at the Bon Portage Island lighthouse had captured the imaginations of many Canadian readers.[27]

Several days later Helen returned alone for three more days on the island. It was an idyllic summer spot. The Richardsons were delightful hosts and Evelyn was a marvelous cook. Helen's autobiography recalls:

> We picnicked in the lee of the lighthouse with a gentle summer mist caressing our brows. She gave us macaroni and cheese, lobster salad, wonderful homemade bread, the best peas I've ever tasted fresh from the garden, and for dessert bake apple, a local small fruit that grows in a few places along the coast. She told us that when her eldest daughter was married she threw her bouquet not from the steps of the house, but from the lighthouse.[28]

Helen had a choice of sleeping in a cabin on the property or in the lighthouse proper. She chose the lighthouse and "slept there like a top."[29]

By the first of August Helen was back at Clark's Harbour collecting folktales from Carolyn Murphy. Mrs. Murphy was the local telephone operator and although she never attended school, she taught herself to read and write so well that she would frequently pick up her receiver to find someone asking her how to spell a word.

Helen's reputation as a collector was becoming so well known that after working in the area for a few days, Mrs. Murphy composed a 13-verse poem about her:

Miss Creighton

A story I will tell you now
of a Lady I have met
The day she came to call on me
I never will forget...

The lady came from Halifax
To learn of our folk-lore
She has learned from different folks
And is still looking for more...

Miss Creighton said she'd call again
I hope she will I'm sure
For I would like her company
If me she can endure.[30]

Today this poem about the folklorist has become folklore itself. In 1977 students under the direction of Dr. Martin Lovelace of the folklore department at Memorial University in Newfoundland, collected a variant of it on Cape Sable Island. A similar experience happened to Helen in 1947: "Called at Community Centre [at Annapolis Royal] to get ballad from Mr. Potts. Read it and found it so like Ben Henneberry's version it made me suspicious. Asked what the tune was like. "It's got a wonderful tune," he said, and hummed Benny's tune exactly, only much too slowly. So here was I collecting my own song back again, and very happy to find it being used."[31]

On 5 August the causeway linking Cape Sable Island to the mainland was officially opened. Helen made arrangements to record the opening speeches and hoped to meet many of the locals who might eventually share their folklore with her. The night before the big event she joined a group of local women—professional lobster processors from the nearby factory—to shell lobsters for the following day's banquet. She enjoyed the comradeship and felt it helped to bridge the gap between collector and informant. She was making more of an effort to learn about the daily lives of her informants and it seemed to be working to her advantage.

Although it had been two full years since the summer of Joe Raben, he still occupied her thoughts: "Wonder if all well with Joe. Felt his presence near me all eve."[32] Two weeks later she was glad to receive some "mail ... long one from Joe, so very welcome. Went later to record dance in high spirits."[33] Helen continued collecting in the old spots where she and Joe had worked together—West Pubnico and Victoria Beach—and on 5 September she celebrated her fiftieth birthday with

Martha Banning Thomas and her friends at the Casey's. Two days earlier her diary carefully noted "Joe's birthday; may it be a happy one."[34] Her own birthday entry showed her personal feelings about the last ten years: "A new decade is such a step. Of all life, the first 17 years and the roarin' forties have been the best."[35]

Helen ended her 1949 collecting sessions closer to home, with Mrs. Gallagher and William Gilkie. When Helen told Catherine Gallagher of her visit to the Bon Portage Island lighthouse, Catherine confided that she too had a manuscript, which she had begun before Mrs. Richardson's book came out. Helen found her friend in failing health, but Mrs. Gallagher still managed several recording sessions and allowed Helen to use her home to record William Gilkie. But this time he was reluctant to sing certain songs. It was all right when Helen was just writing down the words, but now she was asking him to make a permanent record, and he was hesitant to sing one song in particular. His reservations about "The Baffled Knight"[36] were due to it containing what he called "something of the blue in it."[37] He eventually compromised, stopping throughout the song to censor what he felt to be indelicate. Helen later wrote: "Most fishermen have definite ideas about what to sing to a lady."[38]

# CHAPTER ELEVEN

✳ ✳ ✳

Helen celebrated the beginning of a new collecting season for the National Museum by buying a new car. It was an Austin, much easier to operate and more powerful than her previous car. She had plans to visit various locations around the province, but ended up spending most of her time closer to home.

It was the beginning of a new decade and a new era. Nova Scotia was moving ahead with the times and Helen saw some of the older folkways disappear and new traditions being introduced. In early June she accompanied her friends to a dance at Peggy's Cove, hoping to collect traditional dances. She found the people dancing not to a local orchestra, but to a group playing Hawaiian-style music.[1] At the end of the month she moved slightly further down the coast to Seabright, a small settlement situated halfway between Peggy's Cove and the popular beach community of Hubbards, where her niece Lois Harnish and her family lived. She expected to stay in the area for a week, but found so much to collect that she was still there when school resumed again in the fall.

In the middle of July the first of her two new books arrived. She didn't want to open the package alone so she drove to her brother Terry's home and shared the unveiling with his wife Rita and their children. *Folklore of Lunenburg County* was a modest looking publication with a plain cover and bindings, but it marked Helen's debut as an author of a folklore genre other than songs. Several reviewers commented on the wide range of subjects and commended the detailed notes that accompanied the text. Perhaps one of the most interesting reviews, if only from a personal perspective, came from Joseph Raben. He praised Helen's meticulous note-taking and references, but made no mention of his collecting experiences with her.[2]

Throughout the summer Helen worked on a series of drills to improve her eyesight. She was trying to get by without using her glasses and began studying a handbook that taught the Bates method of strengthening the eyes through physical exercises. By 23 July she was able to record some success in her diary: "Near vision still very bad, and still almost impossible to read without glasses.... Drove home still without glasses, blinking quietly all the way. Later sitting on verandah, suddenly felt eyes relaxed. Distant vision perfectly clear as it hasn't been for years ... still can't read."[3] But her success was limited. Five days later she wrote:

"Eyes certainly no good for reading yet. Got magnifying glass from house."[4]

Seabright provided Helen with some interesting informants. At the end of the month she met Sydney Pete Boutilier. Her initial assessment was that he was a dour looking old man, but she soon realized that he had suffered a paralytic stroke and was very ill and in constant pain. He knew some good songs, but told Helen his singing days were over. She tried to coax him out of his reticence by playing songs she had previously recorded from local friends of his. He rose to the challenge and offered several of his own. For the first time in months he was happy and laughing again, telling Helen, "You've got a way with you, you'd bewitch the devil."[5]

Two weeks later, she had a similar affect on Edward Deal. He was a fisherman and farmer and Helen made her first visit to him to collect ghost tales. His wife told Helen he never sang for anyone else in his life. But Helen felt he was a good prospect and kept working on him. Finally he sang—and continued to do so for the rest of his life. In fact, towards the end of the summer he surprised Helen with an original composition describing the local people and ending with verses about her.

> Now here is Miss Creighton, she feels rather sore,
> I don't think she'll come down to Seabright no more,
> She came down to Seabright a-looking for tales
> And all that she found was six fish without scales.
> Now her heart it is heavy and her feet they are sore,
> The sea gulls goes loudly and the billows they roar,
> And when she gets back to the old Dartmouth shore
> I don't think she'll make a recording no more.
> Chorus:
> Right torrel, right torrel, right torrel oh dey,
> For to see those queer sights Miss Creighton came a long way,
> And it cost her from one to two dollars a day,
> Right torrel, right torrel, Paddy wack fol the dey.[6]

At the end of August Helen saw her work being used in a novel way. The Adult Education Department at Hubbards put on an evening concert, with one of the featured acts being a dramatization of a song from her collection. As a choir sang "The Farmer's Curst Wife" a group of actors mimed the actions of the farmer who sends his wife to the devil, only to find the devil won't have her and sends her back. It seemed that the singers and the public alike were eager to participate in saving and performing the local folk songs.

Earlier in the year the National Film Board of Canada had produced *The Rising Tide* and asked composer Eugene Kash to provide the musical score. He requested permission to use five songs from Helen's collection and she, in turn, asked that the user fee go to the original informants from whom she had collected. She was able to pay Ben Henneberry $40. She also paid money to some of her informants out of her Museum per diem. Mrs. Gallagher received $24 a week as payment for Helen's room and board while she was there collecting.[7]

But not everyone was as pleased with how the accumulation of songs—and they way they were being used—was handled. A few of her informants told Helen they had heard one of "their" songs on the radio and wondered if any money were being made from it. Helen explained that only in special circumstances, such as the money from the National Film Board for Ben Henneberry, did she receive a fee to pass on to singers. She wrote in her diary, "Their hospitality left nothing to be desired, but there was something holding singing back."[8]

In October Helen's second book of the year was released. *Traditional Songs from Nova Scotia*[9] was the culmination of years of collecting, alone and with Doreen Senior. This time she didn't wait to share the unwrapping of her long awaited publication: "opened it alone and immediately loved it.... Just wanted to sit and hold it all day; couldn't let it out of my hands."[10] A week later she was able to share her joy with Catherine Gallagher, who came to Evergreen to record more songs: "Had great joy of being with her when she saw book for first time. Like me, could hardly keep her hands off it. And she was so amused at artist's conception of her on jacket sitting beside lighthouse singing."[11] Her friend was also able to offer Helen comfort. Lilian had recently been diagnosed with a heart disturbance and Catherine's concern touched Helen deeply.

In a reversal of their first joint publication, Twelve Folk Songs, while Doreen Senior's name appeared on the title page of *Traditional Songs from Nova Scotia*, the structure of their second volume was entirely Helen's doing. Doreen had been instrumental in transcribing the tunes, but the initial scouting for informants and accompanying research notes were Helen's. Distance would have made a joint preparation of such a detailed manuscript difficult, but not impossible. Doreen was displeased to have been ignored in the manuscript's treatment and retaliated in the best way she knew. A year later she published an article about their songs in the *Journal of the English Folk Dance and Song Society*, and listed her name first in all the variants.[12]

Helen certainly acknowledged Doreen's contribution to the book, but even John D. Robins, who wrote the preface for the book, focused on Helen's contributions: "In this volume Helen Creighton has consolidated her position as the outstanding collector of folk songs in English-speaking Canada."[13] In Toronto, *The Globe and Mail* said that Helen had "succeeded in capturing between covers a splendid selection for the use of both professional musicians and for those who enjoy these quaint old songs for their own sake."[14] And the one publication that reached the homes of many of Helen's informants gave the book a glowing acclamation. *The Family Herald and Weekly Star* wrote: "It is a rare occasion indeed when this page takes time out to tell its readers of a book, but then it is an equally rare occasion when one can herald a book with the character and quality of .... And certainly no other part of the Canadian reading public could be more interested in this type of book than the followers of the Old Favorites page."[15] The paper not only recommended the book but reproduced several of its songs.

Helen worked throughout the winter on her research notes, but enjoyed more free time than the previous winter, when she had been preparing two manuscripts for publication. Things were running smoothly at home. All the apartments in Evergreen were rented out and she was on the best financial footing in years.

Her new books continued to bring requests for interviews and speaking engagements and when she began her 1951 collecting season, they were all the talk with most of her informants. Most, but not all. After a 10-year absence she returned to Chezzetcook to visit Walter Roast. She noted the visit in her diary: "Walter had never acknowledged the book, so I asked him if he'd received it. Oh yes he said, and looked pleased, and said he had taken it around for people to see. Expect it has been much gone through. No superlatives from these people, but a quiet satisfaction that is much better."[16]

Once again Helen returned to Seabright. She stayed in the area until the middle of July and then went home to attend to Lilian. Her sister needed new eyeglasses and was suffering from various ailments, so Helen made arrangements for her to stay at Evergreen while she kept her doctors' appointments. The visit proved distressing to both of them. "Things look very strange to her at such times, and I had to guide her in to house. Went to bed and cried and groaned, poor thing. Would like to stay here with me, but realized I must get on with my job. Wasn't long before she felt better and the unpleasant feeling left her."[17] Helen was also concerned that Lilian was becoming attached to a male patient at the care facility in West Gore. She didn't want her vulnerable sister hurt and felt it best to remove her from what might be a difficult situation.[18] Her concerns haunted her even as she drove Lilian back home:

Before leaving, Lil had another weak feeling and cried and said she didn't want to go back. But she really didn't mean it, and after a little rest felt better. Drove at moderate speed and she was all right. But at the house felt they expect too much of Lil and don't sympathize enough with her limited mentality, or perhaps it was my imagination when I am worried and tired. Anyhow must look for a place nearer home, as that is such a long lonely drive and she is so remote up there.[19]

*Freeman Young, Bernard Young, Grace Clergy and Helen Creighton,*
*Petpeswick, 1951.*

Once Lilian was settled at West Gore, Helen continued on to Petpeswick, renewing some old acquaintances and making new contacts. One of her new informants was a large, heavyset fisherman named Grace Clergy. He suffered from crippling arthritis but was a willing singer, and Helen's diary entry after their first meeting illustrates her excitement in finding him: "What surprise[d] me was his voice which is one of the best I've recorded in a long time. How did we miss him before?"[20]

She was anxious to share the news of her latest discovery with her National Museum boss when he came to visit at the end of July. Dr. Alcock and his family had been planning a trip to Nova Scotia, and when Helen heard they were coming she offered them the use of one of her temporarily vacant apartments. It was a successful visit and helped to form a cordial friendship between folklorist and Museum director.

In August Helen received two more visitors. Earlier in the summer Edith Fowke had written to say that she and her husband Frank were coming to Nova Scotia on holidays and would like to meet with her.[21] Edith had a keen interest in folklore and although she had never conducted field research, she was hoping to meet Helen and see how she carried out her work. They couldn't have chosen a better time or place. Helen's new informant, Grace Clergy, was only too eager to sing, and in the area around Petpeswick and Musquodoboit Harbour lived many others whom Helen could take the Fowkes to meet. The three-day visit would open up a brand new world for Edith and she would go on to become one of Canada's finest folklore scholars. It was

Helen Creighton Fonds, PANS Album 14: 212. Photographer: unknown

*Edith and Frank Fowke with John Roast, Lower Chezzetcook, 1951.*

also the beginning of a lifelong friendship—one fraught with disagree-ments and rivalry, but also filled with genuine affection and regard. Helen's diary paints a vivid picture of Edith's introduction to field research.

On 6 August Helen returned from a recording session to find the Fowkes waiting for her at the Lazy Tide Inn in Musquodoboit Harbour:

> She rather small and dark and quiet of manner and he tall and agree-able and interested in her research. Liked them both. [August 7] Mrs. Fowke appeared for breakfast in adorable grey dress with tiny pattern in it and beautifully stitched collar. Wore dainty shoes that matched, and even her glasses rims blended. We spent all morning on the veran-dah playing tapes ... right after dinner we went down to East P. and I went into Bernard Young's. House full of children. Could see Mr. Young didn't want to sing at the moment. I told him about the people from Toronto who wanted to hear him, and he asked me to come back after I'd seen Mr. Clergy. No suggestion now of not singing before stran-gers. Was just getting machine from car at the Clergy's when saw Mr. Young walking toward car. Had decided to come there and sing which was unexpected cooperation. Think both men were flattered by atten-tion of people from Toronto. They sat quietly by and let us do most of the talking which was wise. Both men did their best and it was a good show, though both apologized a lot for their voices not being what the used to be, esp. Mr. Clergy. Everybody was happy.... The Fowkes had

never before heard folk singing in the original. At one point there was a dispute over the words, and it got quite tense for a moment. Tom Foley dropped in before it was over in the quiet way people do, and sat down without a word to anyone lest he interrupt. The whole aft. was a good introduction to people interested in the subject. [August 8] The Fowkes still wanted to hear more singers ... we drove to ... [Eastern] Passage ... and they saw Devil's Island ... drove in to Passage and called at Edmund's. He out fishing, and Mr. Ben ill with heart. I went over to other house and they asked me to go in. He was in bed and looking so white but seemed pleased. I told him of the Toronto people being here who wanted to meet him and they said to bring them in. We did, and they were kind but left most of the talking to the rest of us. Didn't stay awfully long.... would love to know what they made of it all, as they were quietly taking everything in and making own conclusions. Was pleasant interlude all through.[22]

After Edith and Frank Fowke left, Helen drove down to Pubnico to represent the National Museum at the tercentenary celebrations of Acadian settlement in the region. She was treated as a guest of honour. She accompanied Mrs. McNeil to the banquet and was invited to be a judge for the parade. On the final evening of the festivities the entire community put on a pageant illustrating their long history. Helen set up her tape recorder and captured the celebrations for posterity.

Following the celebrations she continued around the coast to Lunenburg County. It was her first visit to the region since the release of *Folklore of Lunenburg County* and she was eager—and a bit anxious—to find out how it was being received on its home ground. Her fears were allayed when people told her they thought it was the best thing ever published about their county.[23]

Helen returned to Dartmouth ready to write up her summer's research notes and participate in a pleasant social life of club meetings and gatherings with friends. In October a group of 18 women were invited to meet in Halifax to discuss the formation of a branch of the Zonta Club. This was an organization of executive and professional women and Helen's name was put forward as its charter president. She accepted the challenge, later saying, "At this time I hadn't the assurance that people probably thought I had and this has helped me more than any of the many offices I have held."[24]

The night of the banquet she dreamed about a fluffy white mouse that appeared in her bedroom. Despite her usual terror of all rodents, she was captivated by the dream mouse's purity and beauty. A few days later she heard Ben Henneberry had died. She thought there might be some connection between her dream and the loss of her treasured informant, whom she wrote about in her autobiography: "Mr. Ben was not perfect, and certainly not beautiful, but his soul may well have been because nobody without sterling qualities could have been as beloved as Grandfather Ben."[25] Helen went to his funeral with her friend Peryl Daly, who had visited Devil's Island with her many years before. Helen's flowers were given a place of honour at the head of Ben's casket. She recorded her sense of loss in her diary: "Mr. H. looked white lying there; I always think of him as rugged. His death had quite upset me; after all he had made me, and I him. The family were quite touching in their welcome ... For the first time they all spoke to me as Helen."[26]

She set out on her 1952 collecting season with mixed emotions. Her books had been well received and she was at last gaining attention for the years she had worked without financial gain or professional recognition. But the death of Ben Henneberry marked the passing of an era. Gone were the days when she could move into a community unknown. The folklore collector herself was becoming such an important visitor that her presence sometimes overshadowed her reason for being there. Helen had become a public persona. She had to find a way to turn that to her advantage. She also had to come to terms with the new focus in folklore research.

Helen still had the notion of folklore as old and quaint. While some of her contemporaries were collecting songs of the labour movement, she avoided any hint of radicalism. She had made a conscious decision not to collect these types of songs the previous summer. Dan Livingston and his family, all originally from Cape Breton, had come to Evergreen to record traditional songs. After Helen collected what she wanted, Dan suggested singing a few union songs. She later wrote in her diary: "They made me shiver, for they were all very red. Apparently he had belonged to a youth movement in Toronto. Could see how these songs would pierce deeply into the consciousness of dissatisfied people. They frightened me."[27]

Helen was searching for songs from an era that had passed. The songs she had collected so far were important to the understanding of Maritime culture. The songs she would continue to collect would also be important in helping to place history in context. But she was finding it increasingly difficult to get what she and Doreen used to call their "lovelies." Five years earlier, in her report to the National Museum, she had lamented their demise: "I was forced to conclude that the singing of folk-songs is a lost art in Nova Scotia. Nearly all the old people who used to sing them have passed away, and those who are left have, like the younger rural people, been so influenced by the radio that they are no longer interested in the old songs. I kept saying to myself, 'Crumbs; crumbs. These are no more than crumbs,' as incomplete versions would with difficulty be recalled."[28] Fortunately her appreciation and understanding of local songs had grown and she willingly collected these,

*Nathat Hatt and his daughter, Mrs. McInnes, 1954.*

but she longed to find another singer with a repertoire similar to Ben Henneberry's. If she needed any encouragement at this stage in her career, she was certainly given it by the first informant she visited in 1952.

Helen had received a letter from Dr. B.C. Woodroffe of Chester, telling her about an elderly patient who was always singing while waiting in his reception area. Dr. Woodroffe thought the songs sounded old and suggested that Helen make a trip to visit the singer. On 16 May Helen made the journey to Middle River, Lunenburg County, near Chester. She drove up a dirt road to find a small house nestled on the top of a hill. As she knocked on the door she could smell the aroma of fresh-baked cookies. Ushered in, she introduced herself to a man in perhaps his eighties sitting in a rocking chair. His name was Nathan Hatt, but his friends called him "Chippy" because he used to work cutting wood. Nathan and his wife were being cared for by their daughter, Nellie McInnes. Dr. Woodroffe had forewarned Nathan that Helen might pay a visit so he knew what she was looking for. In no time at all he had launched into his first song, a variant of "The Gay Spanish Maid." He told Helen how on summer evenings he used to sit on the back steps and sing into the night, while the neighbours would listen in. He recalled one song after the next, many of them "lovelies." He was just the type of singer she was looking for. Helen knew it was best to record elderly singers in their own environment and that she would get the best results from Mr. Hatt if she could set up her tape recorder in his home. But there was a technical hitch—they had no electricity.

Since Nathan Hatt's repertoire appeared to be large, Helen realized that it was worth going to a bit of trouble. She contacted the power company and made arrangements to have a cable run from the main road, over a field, and through a window into their kitchen. For two weeks she worked with Nathan, collecting ancient ballads, local tunes of adventurous deeds, and beautiful love songs. He sang with his hands covering his face, peeking out through his fingers. When his throat grew raspy from singing he would shake salt on his tongue, saying,

"I've got a toad in me troat. Do you know how to get rid of a toad? Put salt on him. That'll make his toes turn up."[29] Nathan had a strong bond with his music; his songs told wonderful stories and the characters in them were his friends. After singing an ancient ballad he would say of the heroine and her lover, "She was a good girl. She didn't go out on the roads on Saturday nights but stayed home with her parents, and he was a fine young man."[30] He could neither read nor write, and his songs were his literature.

When he first heard himself on tape a "look of wonder came over his face."[31] He greatly enjoyed the recording sessions, but Helen was initially concerned that he might not understand what the tape recorder was doing and she didn't want to confuse him. "Mr. Hatt is the most willing and cooperative person imaginable, and Mrs. McInnes says he watches for me and keeps asking the time. Am still uncertain what he makes of machine. Said of voice coming back in conversation 'He heard me say it.' And 'There's where I made a mistake; now he does it.'"[32] Her concerns were allayed when his daughter told Helen, "He's just playing a game."[33]

Helen had to leave at the end of the month but told Mr. Hatt she would like to return. She prepared to settle her bill with the power company—five dollars for running a cable, connecting it every morning, and disconnecting it every night. She also discovered the reason for a cable shorting out during one rainy-day recording session. The cause was not the fault of the power company: "Mrs. McInnes had asked if would be safe to put cow in pasture. They've kept the poor thing in all week since she stepped on the cable."[34]

At the end of her recording session with Nathan Hatt, Helen returned home to keep an appointment with a writer from *Maclean's* magazine. Ian Sclanders had phoned to say he was writing an in-depth article on Helen and wanted to observe her in the collecting field. Meeting him at his Halifax hotel, she was disturbed to realize that he had been drinking. When he ordered a bottle of champagne she curtly advised him that it would be wasted on her. At a nearby table sat two other members of the *Maclean's* staff, Jack Brayley and Pierre Berton. Ian took Helen to their table and made the introductions. When Ian left them briefly, Helen told Jack and Pierre that she was disappointed with their colleague's behaviour. They rose to his defence and assured her that he would be fine by the next day.[35]

When Helen met Ian the following morning she made her feelings about his previous behaviour emphatically clear. She wouldn't tolerate drunkenness from an informant and removed herself from situations in which she felt uncomfortable. And she certainly wouldn't stand for it from an interviewer. She wrote in her diary: "He must have been in agony.... plans to see me at Kennetcook next week and swears will be sober. Was perfectly honest about how I felt, but didn't rub it in."[36]

By the time Ian met up with her at Kennetcook, a small farming community in Hants County, the incident was behind them. He observed her collecting songs from an informant she had know before, and at the end of the day they had dinner together and became better acquainted. That evening Helen was able to write a far more favourable note in her diary: "He is devoted to his wife and family, and I liked him very much."[37]

On the second day Ian got to observe Helen meeting a singer for the first time. She had been given the name of Jack Turple, and Helen and Ian found him sitting at the side of the road with his neighbour. Helen stopped the car and enquired, "Are you the famous Mr. Turple who sings songs?" and he acknowledged without embarrassment that he was.[38] He was well known in the area, a fine practitioner of the style known as "dunning," in which the lyrics tell of someone who has crossed the songwriter in some way—perhaps owing him money. If a song were good enough it would move into the popular local repertoire and forever haunt the ill-doer.[39]

Ian spent two more days accompanying Helen around the countryside as she collected songs. Although their initial meeting had suggested a short relationship, they parted as friends. "The past few days have been entirely delightful although I haven't talked about myself so much for a very long time, if ever. But there were long breaks when we talked of everything else. Last week was mentioned occasionally, and always by Ian. We didn't dwell on it, but he was obviously sorry, and asked if he'd been forgiven. So we parted excellent friends, and hope to meet again."[40]

They did meet again in August. Ian was accompanying famed photographer Yousuf Karsh and his wife on a photography assignment for *Maclean's*. Solange Karsh had read Helen's *Songs and Ballads* and asked Ian to arrange a meeting. On 17 August Helen met with Ian and the Karshes at their hotel. She was immediately impressed with Karsh's artistic qualities and with the easy way he had with people. "He's 44 but looks older. She 51. Were easy to make friends with.... Child at next table had wanted an autograph, so Karsh told her he would take her picture if she would take his. All done with child's own camera in dining room."[41] From Halifax they drove down to Peggy's Cove where Karsh was intrigued by the way the morning light played upon the small white church at the entrance to the village. He wanted to capture the scene but needed to set a mood. Helen's autobiography describes him at work:

He declared, "The light on the church is just right," and although we showed him the great boulders and lighthouse, nothing else would do. For a congregation he recruited from a tourist home a New York singer, a Toronto professor named Tait, an artist named Paton, a Texan and so forth. Women, recognizing him, came out hatted and gloved, and some carried prayer books. As cars stopped with sightseers they too joined the procession of worshippers, and I looked on fascinated as he got in all sort of contortions, taking one picture from a space underneath one of Peggy's Cove's huge rocks. Passing tourists either recognized him or realized this was no ordinary photographer and stopped to photograph him and he would flash a smile toward them for their picture.[42]

After his impromptu session at the church, Karsh took photographs of two of Helen's informants and then they moved on to Lunenburg, where he had an assignment to photograph Thomas Raddall for an upcoming piece in *Maclean's*. From there they went to the home of the Ralph Bells. They had scheduled their visit with the Bells for four in the afternoon, but didn't arrive until after six. By then they were all tired and hungry.

*Thomas Raddall, Yousuf Karsh, Ian Sclanders, Lunenburg, 1953.*

The Bells had been expecting them for cocktails and crackers and made no offer of dinner. As they were leaving, Helen quietly whispered to Solange, "This is the difference between the rich and poor. In a poor home we'd have been fed."[43] They left, still hungry, and at ten o'clock found a roadside spot known as The Bizzee Centre, where they sat on stools and enjoyed bacon and eggs.

Ian Sclander's article about Helen appeared in *Maclean's* that September[44] "She's Collecting Long Lost Songs" told of Helen's adventures collecting from various informants and featured several photographs taken earlier in July by Nova Scotian photographer Edward Bollinger. Helen didn't comment on the article's contents in her diary, but did say she was disappointed in the photographs of herself, Mrs. Gallagher, and Grace Clergy. However, the article did give her greater exposure and was another step towards establishing a national reputation for herself. One of her comments that made it into Sclander's article was how she was happy to see her songs being used for purposes other than strictly in the folk vein. She cited a recent CBC radio broadcast on Thomas Haliburton's famous Yankee peddlar known as "Sam Slick," which used melodies from her publications as incidental background music.

After the appearance of the article, the writer of the "Sam Slick" program, Joseph Schull, telephoned Helen with a request to dine. He wanted to discuss other possible projects. Her diary records a successful meeting: "Most good looking, and liked him. Drove to Hartlan's Pt. so he could see where songs collected and also get view. Sat there overlooking water and heard Alan Mills sing 2 of my songs. Drove slowly back and dined at Belmont. Never had such attentive service; must have been handsome escort. Came back to house and looked at my manuscript. Surprise ending; another Joe."[45]

First there was Joseph Crampton, then Joseph Raben, and now Joseph Schull. Helen lost her heart to a third Joe. Four days later they dined out again: "Joe and I had dinner at Belmont. Talked with great animation and ate nothing.... Joe most thoughtful and considerate man I've ever met, and mind very quick and direct. Also very sweet to me."[46] The next day her diary entry was full of her impressions of what Joe thought of her work: "Head in clouds this week ... By the way, Joe tremendously impressed by article. Asked how it impressed him and he said the importance of the work, the way it being done and the honours I'd received of which he had no idea. His tone of respect was terrific."[47]

Joe Schull was a man who met Helen on an equal footing. He understood her need for a career and offered her the respect she required. He too was a hard worker and Helen worried that he might be overdoing it. She invited him on a picnic to get him away from his work—and to allow him to see her in her element. Once again, her diary received a lengthy account of the day's events, with its bittersweet ending:

Drove to West Jeddore and in looking for place to picnic got stuck in grass. But men came from nearby house with bags and pushed him out. Wonderful disposition, Joe never seems to get fussed. He found two flat rocks that weren't, beside lake back of beach, a lovely spot. Had good food, soup, lamb chops, sandwiches, fruit salad, little cakes and coffee. He was very appreciative of effort I'd made. Interrupted eating to go to his car and listen to Alan Mills singing Maid Wrapt in Wether Skin. Just sat for quite a while and it was perfect. No was hard to say. Were both tense when we arrived at the Doyles, and it was hard for both of us to do an interview. We bungled through somehow. Drove home in sweet content at about 20 miles per hour and this time listened to Joe's play on the radio C.B.C. A sharing of the fruits of the labour, each having great respect for the talent of the other, and both of very hard workers. Came in and had tea and sandwiches. Good-bye very difficult for us both. But again this age discrepancy. Were it not so—but there it is. "A Maid I am in love" and four pounds lighter at the end of the week![48]

# CHAPTER TWELVE

*** 

Helen's brief encounter with yet "another Joe" was over. What went wrong? Was it simply, as her diary suggests, the age difference again? Was it she who called it off when it began to get serious? The answer is unclear, but by the time Joseph Schull wrote to her a year later, his correspondence was cordial but certainly not personal: "I hope you're still getting as much fun as ever out of the work and meeting interesting people."[1]

She was certainly meeting interesting people. In the late fall she flew to Vermont to attend a meeting of Zonta International and arranged for her flight to stop over in Montreal in order to meet Alan Mills and his wife Bernie. Alan was a well-known folk song interpreter who championed Helen's material on his national radio show. Born Alan Miller in Quebec, he was a jovial man who'd worked hard at gaining a reputation as one of Canada's foremost bilingual folk singers. Their meeting at the airport was brief, but they instantly took a liking to each other. It was to be a friendship for life.

When Helen returned from her Zonta meeting she immediately began work on a CBC national radio broadcast about her collecting experiences. She was asked to describe the approach she used to get singers to open up to her. Attempting to interject a little humour into her narrative, she was horrified when Toronto rejected the script because they thought it appeared as if she were boasting about her ability to manipulate people. Her local producer didn't see it in the same light, but asked her to redo the script anyway. After the initial shock Helen came around to seeing their point of view. If the CBC executives had missed her point of humour, so might the listeners and she didn't want to insult her informants. She revised the script and it aired on 23 November. It must have met with approval because the *CBC Times* made a request to publish her talk, and shortly after that *The Star Weekly* telephoned, wanting to do a feature article about her work collecting witchcraft.

With more interviews, meetings, and her field research preparation, Helen had another busy and productive winter. She continued her collecting in 1953, visiting several communities around the province. But for Helen, the year's highlight was the presentation of a folk opera based on songs from her collection. Although much had been done to

*Helen Creighton, Dr. W. Roy Mackenzie and Mrs. Mackenzie, c. 1951.*

make use of her material, she still felt that the music could have a wider appeal if it were brought into the popular and classical fields. She had attended the Halifax Music Festival the previous spring, and was delighted that some of her songs had been arranged by a local musician, Trevor Jones, but lamented the fact that many of the additional folk songs performed were from other collections. She believed that her variants were just as good, if not better, but noted that "so many of the songs heard during the evening were in my collections but quite unknown to local singers since they have not been arranged for singing groups. Vaughan Williams' Dark Eyed Sailor is word for word and note for note the same.... When will people wake up to all we have here, and why aren't there more Trevor Jones."[2]

Trevor Jones had been captivated by many of the beautiful melodies in Helen's books and on 15 July he and librettist Donald Wetmore premiered their folk opera, *The Broken Ring*, which was based on a well-known folk song motif. The opera's storyline is ageless. When two young lovers are forced to part, they exchange tokens of their devotion. According to the thousands of versions found in folk songs, the token is usually a ring, broken in two. Each lover keeps half of the ring until they meet again and join the band, bringing their love full circle. After a time apart (usually seven years) they meet again, only this time the young man is in disguise because he wants to test his lover's fidelity. Once he establishes that she has been true, he

Helen Creighton Fonds, PANS Binder 17, 0762. Photographer: unknown

*Alan Mills and Peter Chiasson, Grand Etang, 1954.*

reveals his half of the ring and they fall into each other's arms. It was perfect melodrama for an opera and—as performed in Halifax by the Nova Scotia Opera Association—it pleased both collector and audience.[3]

In June 1954 Helen began another collecting season at Seabright. She wanted to record more songs with Nathan Hatt, but didn't like to disturb his family with the previous year's solution of passing an electrical cord through the kitchen window. So she took Nathan and his daughter to a local garage and, with an extension cord leading to the car, set up her recorder in the back seat. Mrs. McInnes held the microphone for her father and sat with him in the front seat while he added to his list of recordings.

Helen was delighted to be back with Mr. Hatt, but found it difficult to concentrate on the project. He brother Paul had recently been diagnosed with a cancerous tumour and the prognosis for recovery was not good. However, as was her wont, she rallied her strength and kept on with her work.

In July she flew to Indianapolis to lecture at a folklore conference at the Indiana University Institute, stopping off in Toronto for a visit with Edith Fowke. They had kept up a correspondence and were developing their friendship. At Indiana U, Helen presented papers and attended lectures. She also received the acknowledgement of many of her peers. When Stith Thompson introduced her to the eminent Finnish folklore scholar, Otto Anderson, he surprised her by saying, "Oh yes, we have one of her books in our library in Finland."[4]

Back home Helen prepared for a visit from Alan and Bernie Mills. They wanted a holiday in Nova Scotia and Alan wanted to see Helen at work, so they combined the two interests and planned a collecting tour together. Their first stop was to visit Dr. W. Roy Mackenzie, whose work had inspired Helen's career back in 1928. Alan was excited to meet the great folk song collector and Dr. Mackenzie was equally taken with Alan, who could illustrate a folk song by singing it at a moment's notice. Helen then

*Angelo Dornan, Elgin, 1954.*

took the Mills to Cape Breton, back home by way of Sherbrooke, where Alan serenaded Helen and his wife in a cabin by the St. Mary's River. Then they were off to visit with Mrs. Gallagher and Nathan Hatt. Most of the singers knew Alan from his program on the radio and were a bit reluctant to sing for him. But with his easy manner he soon not only had them singing for him, but he was sharing songs with them. On the other hand, at times just being in the company of a tradition bearer made him most humble, as Helen noted: "One of highlights was their reaction to Nathan Hatt's singing. They listened with tears in their eyes and looked positively enchanted."[5]

When the Mills left towards the end of August, Helen drove to Tatamagouche, a fishing and farming community on the Northumberland Strait. Her friend Betty Murray had developed a School of Community Arts[6] and was featuring Helen's work throughout the sessions. Helen made good use of her time there, seeking out informants. One man, named McQueen, asked her to set up her recorder at a local restaurant so his friends could see him. Before he began to record he removed his dentures and, as he sang, he used them to keep time on the counter.

At the end of the summer Helen made her first collecting foray outside Nova Scotia. She drove to New Brunswick to meet Angelo Dornan. She had been reluctant to infringe upon what she felt to be the territory of another collector. Louise Manny, who lived in Newcastle, had her own radio program that featured local singers. She didn't go into the field to record but brought the singers to the radio station. She and Helen had been corresponding and Louise assured her that she didn't feel Helen would be doing any work she eventually hoped to do herself.

Angelo Dornan lived with his family at Elgin, a farming centre in Albert County, in southern New Brunswick. He had written to Helen the year before, telling her that he knew many songs and assuring her, "Can put you up over night, have a fine wife and six boys so will not annoy you with proposals of marriage."[7] In the past she had heard from— or about—several singers who claimed prodigious repertoires, only to discover on meeting them that the number of songs they knew had been greatly exaggerated. Angelo Dornan would make good on his boast. Helen would later claim that "it is the most extraordinary story in my 40 year's experience as a folklorist."[8]

Angelo grew up in a house filled with music. His father was well known locally as a fine traditional singer and young Angelo absorbed a good deal of his repertoire. When he was 19 years old Angelo left for Western Canada and the songs lay dormant for 45 years—his own wife having no idea that he knew any folk songs. In his mid sixties he grew homesick and bought a farm in New Brunswick, sight unseen. Back in his childhood environment the songs began to return to him. When he read about Helen's publications he decided to write and invite her to visit. It proved to be a momentous decision for both of them.

Helen arrived at the Dornans on 31 August. By the end of the following day she was able to write in her diary, "25 songs in two days is a lot of songs."[9] Helen stayed with the Dornans for 10 days, collecting dozens of songs from Angelo. Each day he would attend to his chores in the morning and then come into the house, wash up, and put on a clean shirt before beginning a session. On several evenings the Dornans took Helen to visit other singers in the area. It was a pleasant way to collect songs and Angelo's supply appeared to be inexhaustible. The family went out of their way to make her feel at home, even surprising her with a cake on her birthday. But Helen was having difficulties sharing their house for such an extended period. She was concerned because the cows had not been tested for tuberculosis. She avoided milk and drank pop instead. She also had another concern: "Such a pleasant house with everything pleasing to the eye, so important to me. Is a pity to be so fastidious on a job like mine. Digestion had gone bad from outside convenience on farm."[10] To keep herself happy, inside and out, for the remainder of the collecting visit she stayed at the Marshland's Inn in Sackville. Before she left she paid the Dornans $37.50 for her room and board, who "were quite taken aback. He had been going to ask $1.50."[11]

At the end of her marathon session with Angelo Dornan, Helen returned home to spend some time with her ailing brother and his family. She noted sadly in her diary, "He is slowly slipping away."[12] On 9 November she wrote simply: "Paul died peacefully after long illness."[13]

It was a sad ending to her year, although professionally it had been "one of the best season[s], if *not* the best yet."[14] She summed up her thoughts in her annual report to the National Museum.

I would like to begin my report where most people end them. That is by saying that my eight years spent in part time work with the National Museum have been among the happiest I have ever known. I say that in spite of the fact that my work has completely taken over my life and absorbed it ... But that is all right. Before joining the Museum staff I collected folklore as a hobby, fitting it in as best I could. Now I am relieved of financial worry and I have the proper equipment so necessary if this work is to be done properly.[15]

Helen's winter was, once again, filled with labouring over her previous summer's research. It always amused her when people thought that all she had to do was go out and collect the material. They didn't realize the time it took to transcribe and annotate everything. She also took on a number of speaking engagements. These brought little financial remuneration, but she looked upon them as promotion for her work and this inevitably resulted in names of informants for future contact.

As she planned on being away from Evergreen for most of the 1955 collecting season, Helen turned her own apartment and spare bedroom over to Eunice and Richard Sircom. Richard's mother was Marjorie (Simmie), one of Helen's dearest friends, and she was happy to have the young couple staying at Evergreen. It meant that during the few days she did return home she wouldn't have to catch up on household chores. Her summer was free for work.

She began her contract for the National Museum in June and headed directly to the south shore. Much had changed since her first visits to the area in the 1930s. She noticed, for instance, that several informants had acquired televisions.

At the end of the month she took the train to Montreal and met up with Bernie and Alan Mills. They were joined by folk singer Helène Baillargeon Coté[16] and her husband, and the group travelled to the music festival at Ile aux Coudres. From Quebec, Helen continued on to Kingston, Ontario for a meeting of the Canadian Authors Association. She was delighted with the reception she received and had offers from three publishers wanting to promote her work. After the convention, she returned to Montreal and joined the Mills at their vacation cottage at Lake Memphramegog.

It was time to get back to work. She returned to New Brunswick to collect again from Angelo Dornan. The Dornans had made several changes to their house. Angelo had been ill over the winter and his sons had made arrangements to have indoor plumbing installed. They had also purchased a television. Nonetheless, Helen opted to stay in a motel in Moncton and each day Angelo came into town and recorded at the home of his cousin.

In July Helen moved her base of operations to the Annapolis Valley, but had to take several days off to bring Lilian to Dartmouth for medical attention. She was diagnosed with digestive problems and soon returned to West Gore, but Helen was discouraged that she'd had to take time from her collecting season:

*Sadie and Fred Redden, Middle Musquodoboit, 1955.*

"Lil much better....Family all want to know about her but as usual offer no help. This always depresses me greatly."[17]

At the end of August Helen travelled to Middle Musquodoboit to visit Fred Redden. Like Angelo Dornan, Fred had contacted Helen himself. He had a large repertoire of folk tunes—mainly Irish songs he had learned as a boy. He was a rugged, handsome man who possessed a beautiful lilting voice. He also played the bagpipes and had recently been amongst the 100 pipers who played for the opening of the Canso Causeway connecting Cape Breton to mainland Nova Scotia. He worked his farm, tended a woodlot, and did occasional mining and construction work. In his spare time, he and his family made music.

On her second day collecting with Fred, his daughter Finvola[18] returned home and Helen was delighted to find she had an extraordinary talent. "At 14 she shows unusual promise and could go far singing her father's, and even as far back as her great grandfather's, songs."[19] Two wonderful singers in one family—it had been a visit well worth making. She didn't know it then, but Helen's relationship with Fred Redden, his wife Sadie, and their children (especially Finvola), would eventually develop into the strongest bond she would ever make with informants.

After her collecting season was over in the fall, Helen took the train to Ottawa. She had been asked by Moses Asch of Folkways Records to select recordings for an album they wanted to produce featuring field recordings from her collection. The National Museum gave their blessing

Helen Creighton Fonds, PANS Binder 18: 0960. Photographer: unknown

*Finvola Redden, Helen Creighton, Louise Manny, Alan Mills at Queen Elizabeth High School, Halifax Festival of the Arts, 1958.*

and provided funds for Helen to work there while she made her selections. While in Ottawa, Helen had a pleasant luncheon with Solange Karsh and several meetings with Marius Barbeau, who brought up an old wound on their last day together: "Funniest thing was my last visit when he escorted me to elevator and I had been asking him about other collectors. As I disappeared down the shaft could hear his gentle voice saying, 'Laura Bolton is the greatest collector of folksongs in the world to-day'."[20] She soothed her bruised ego by relaxing with Alan and Bernie Mills on her way back to Nova Scotia.

Whether Marius Barbeau was speaking in jest is open to conjecture. Helen knew that others felt her own status was very high in folklore circles. In September she had received a letter from Horace Beck, inviting her to speak at the December meeting of the American Folklore Society in Washington. Helen quoted from his letter in her diary: "'Certainly you are the greatest collector in the world to-day.' That astonished me."[21]

While the National Museum found the funds for Helen to go to Ottawa and work on her selections for Folkways, they wouldn't support her trip to Washington to attend the convention. So Helen asked the provincial government for help and was pleasantly surprised to be both given the funding and requested to officially represent Nova Scotia. On the way to and from Washington she made a stopover in New York, where she had a meeting with Moses Asch concerning her record. She also visited an old friend—Joseph Raben. She met his wife and "liked her at once."[22] The Rabens invited Helen to stay with them and she spent two nights in their New York apartment. She noted in her diary that when she left, Joe "must have been surprised at warmth of leave taking."[23]

January 1956 began on a very positive note. The previous November Helen had taped a CBC television program called Roving Reporter, where she spoke of her collection of ghost stories with host Ken Homer. After the program aired in January she received a letter from Ryerson Press asking if she would like to bring out a collection of her ghost stories and supernatural tales. She thought this was an excellent idea. Ever since she'd started collecting folk songs, informants would also tell her ghostly tales. She had hundreds of them, and while it would take a great deal of work to assemble them from her notes, it would be an income-earning project for her spare time. The small legacy she had been receiving from her uncle's estate had expired the previous year, and Helen was looking to her own resources to establish a source of steady income. If the book were a success the royalties might offset the loss of the legacy. She set herself the task of working on her ghost stories for an hour each morning.

However, this plan was put on the back burner in February when Frank Willis telephoned from Toronto to offer her two half-hour CBC radio programs on folk songs from Nova Scotia. She would go to Toronto to record the narration. As the producers insisted on using professional singers, they needed proper musical arrangements for voice and orchestra. Helen thought she had the ideal solution.

Two years earlier she had begun to do some work with a local arranger named Gertrude Innes. Helen had written in her diary that Gertrude "transcribes directly on paper ... very easy to work with and no fuss."[24] Helen sent off several of her arrangements and told Gertrude that Edith Fowke would be giving her some advice over song selections for the show. But Gertrude was furious when she found out, writing, "How could you have been so utterly stupid as to send the songs off without consulting me, and since when is Edith Fowke such an authority? Now, I'm asking that every song I arranged be returned to me immediately, and I mean *everyone*. I'll bill you for my services as a musicologist and consider that I've wasted time I could have used to better advantage."[25]

Helen was shocked. She didn't see the problem. Gertrude had recently sent a local festival an arrangement of a song from Helen's collection without seeking her permission, and Helen had thought she would be happy to have her worked used and paid for by the CBC. Moreover, she felt Gertrude had ruined her chances at having the CBC use any of her work if she were going to be difficult. "Well, I did my best for her, but she probably ruined her chances.... This unexpected opposition took the jam out of the gingerbread for a while."[26]

When she arrived in Toronto Helen found that Gertrude's arrangements had not been what the producers were looking for.

Gertrude's work was declared unpublishable with technical errors, slapdash, and singers like Joyce [Sullivan] wouldn't use it. Mr. Waddington gave his opinion by simple shaking his head negatively ... [her arrangements] ... had been returned by three publishers ... Arranged for CBC to pay her for tunes transcribed from tapes, and to return all manuscripts ... She had agreed to try, and had lost, but took defeat badly. Is bitter ... Later she wrote she had heard programs and was glad not to be identified with them. No lilt etc. That only jarring note. Otherwise everything wonderful beyond belief.[27]

Aside from the unfortunate incident with Gertrude Innes, the experience in Toronto was pleasant and productive. When she arrived Helen was pleased to find that well-known arranger Richard Johnston had been given the assignment of preparing her songs for broadcast. She liked Richard's arrangements and asked him to have a look at Finvola Redden's own composition to see if he might arrange that. Helen believed Finvola to be a promising songwriter and hoped her published music might earn some money for her education.

Helen went to Edith Fowke's home to use her typewriter and asked Edith for some help in preparing her script: "She made a few suggestions about linking songs up, but mainly the script was mine, though her help made all the difference . . . I had a tidy script to take to Frank [Willis] and sat anxiously while he read it over and heaved a great sigh of relief when he pronounced it excellent."[28] During the taping session Helen was nervous, but managed to get through part of the script without showing her apprehension. Then suddenly she felt she might not be able to carry on: "In middle of broadcast felt a little weak and suddenly was aware of Ben Henneberry ... there with me saying, 'You're doing very well; keep it up'."[29]

When she returned to Nova Scotia Helen hoped she might have extra time to work on her ghost tales. It was not to be. By the time she began her summer sessions for the National Museum, she was already in pre-production for *Marine Highway*, a promotional film for tourism along Nova Scotia's eastern shore. The filmmaker was Margaret Perry, who wanted to use folk music from the eastern shore to accompany the rural scenes she would be shooting. After several meetings with Helen it was decided to focus the film on the traditional folk singers and their environment. Helen took Margaret to visit with several singers and accompanied her on several shoots throughout the summer.

Helen's own collecting work got off to a slow start in June. She was suffering from neuralgia and had a cyst removed from one eye. She was also busy getting Lilian moved down to a home in Westphall, near Dartmouth. But by 2 June she was able to drive down to Seabright to hear Edward Deal's new composition. The folk singer who had earlier been inspired to write verses about Helen's visit now had new inspiration. He had seen a television program about Adam and Eve and was anxious to have Helen hear his new work, "Waiting for the Leaves to Start to Fall."[30]

Television was making its impact. Two days later she tried to collect the words to a song from an informant she had visited on a previous occasion, but he had the television on and made no move to turn it off. The rules of hospitality were changing. In Cape Breton, however, Helen would find them stretched to the extreme in the opposite direction.

In July she recorded several informants in Cape Breton. She spent most of her time in Glace Bay and around the Sydney area, but on 1 August went with the Alex Morrisons to the home of Lauchie Gillis at Grand Mira South. Mr. Gillis was a respected Gaelic singer and Helen spent an enjoyable evening with him, his eight children, and his charming and very pregnant wife. As Mr. Gillis sang, his wife perched on the piano stool and when the recording session finally ended at 10 o'clock she offered her guests tea. However, the Morrisons suggested that since their hosts had so many children to put to bed, they had better forego the tea. They said their goodbyes and left, Helen taking her time driving home along the country road. Two days later Mr. Gillis visited the Morrisons and joked, "You nearly had a picnic on your hands the other night.... Just before you came my wife said she was ready for the hospital. When you left we followed you to Marion Bridge but didn't like to pass in case you'd think you'd kept us from something. Then we raced to Sydney and an hour later the baby was born."[31]

Back in Dartmouth Helen recorded 43 songs with Charles Cates, the mayor of North Vancouver. He was visiting family in Nova Scotia and eager to record the songs he had learned from his father. In September Helen caught the ferry to Prince Edward Island. It was her first collecting trip to the Island so she went to Charlottetown radio station CFCY to seek advice on finding informants. She also had an appointment to meet a regional radio celebrity and his band of musicians—Don Messer and his Islanders. Although they were very friendly, the band seemed not to know any of the types of songs Helen was looking for. But individual members did and she made appointments to meet with them separately. She visited Julius "Duke" Neilsen at his home and recorded some of his own compositions, and was pleasantly surprised to discover that he knew some folk songs. From Charlie Chamberlain she collected folk songs from his native New Brunswick. Don Messer and his Islanders had not yet become Canadian television stars and Helen had to work around the busy schedules of various band members. Duke and his wife tuned pianos and organs, and Charlie had to put off an appointment because he had a job waxing a car. But in the end they not only gave her good songs, they steered her to a local traditional singer.

It was through them that Helen met Edward Sellick, who surprised her by singing an English/Gaelic song about a cow named "Drimindown."[32] The song was not the surprise. What she found so intriguing was that she had never heard it until the previous month when Charles Cates of North Vancouver had recorded his father's version.

Helen returned home at the end of September, making a brief stop to collect songs from Fred Redden, and ended her collecting season with a positive diary entry: "Home very thankfully after happiest season yet."[33] However, the next day she would be saddened when she paid a visit to her cherished friend, Catherine Gallagher. Helen had visited the Gallaghers in July and been shocked to learn that Catherine had been ill since Easter and showed no signs of making a recovery. As soon as she got home from her field trip she drove to Ketch Harbour and approached the Gallagher's house with apprehension. When Edward Gallagher saw her, he was so relieved he threw his arms around her and kissed her soundly. Catherine had been in hospital for 11 weeks and had been constantly asking for Helen. She drove straight to the hospital in Halifax and when Mrs. Gallagher saw her she cried, "It's you at last."[34] Her friend was dying. Helen knew they had a strong bond, but hadn't appreciated the extent of Catherine's feelings for her. She later wrote in her diary, "Frightens me to mean so much to so many people. Hadn't quite realized it."[35]

Helen was pleased to be able to send Catherine a copy of the Folkways record when it was released in November.[36] She also took a copy to Edmund Henneberry. A month later, a young soprano from Nova Scotia named Diane Oxner released an album titled *Traditional Folksongs of Nova Scotia*.[37] Helen had helped Diane to choose songs for her recording and the dust jacket advertised that all the selections were from the Helen Creighton collection. Helen was pleased with both the Folkways traditional field recordings and Diane's contemporary interpretations of her songs.

It had been a good year for work—a productive collecting season, national radio and television programs, a film, and two albums. But if 1956 seemed busy, 1957 would stand out as what Helen would later call her "banner year."[38]

# CHAPTER THIRTEEN

✳ ✳ ✳

"**S**tarted typing book of ghost stories. Important day."[1] Helen's diary entry for 7 January kicked off the beginning of a very exciting, busy, and rewarding year. She had been culling her research notes for several months, selecting tales of the supernatural, and now it was time to assemble them in manuscript form. Her work on the ghost tales was interrupted in January by the taping of a national CBC television program for the "Graphic" series. The producers wanted to illustrate her collecting work and Helen arranged for Fred and Finvola Redden to be included as prime examples of the quality of informants to be found in Nova Scotia. It was also important to show the audience how the traditional songs were being passed down from one generation to the next. Helen had grown fond of the Reddens and was especially eager to help young Finvola pursue her interests in music.

By the last week in March the television show had been filmed and Helen was able to write, "Except for one story from the furnace man that needs to be completed, the book is finished, and the time 8:30 Saturday night.... Will spend next week revising then to Nassau and a well earned rest and holiday."[2] Her cousin, Ralph Creighton, lived and worked in the Bahamas and had invited Helen down for a vacation. A few days later her plans were changed drastically. Her physician discovered a fibrous tumour and sent her immediately to the Victoria General Hospital in Halifax. The tumour turned out to be benign, but it was serious enough for her to undergo a partial hysterectomy and the removal of her uterus. She spent 10 days recovering in the hospital—the trip to Nassau was out of the question.

While she recuperated, her mail had accumulated on her bedside table. When she got around to opening it, she discovered an invitation from Dr. Ross Flemington, President of Mount Allison University. The university was offering her an honorary Doctor of Laws degree. She was overjoyed. Not only was she being honoured by the academic community for her work in folklore, but she was being asked to give the convocation address. Anxious to accept the degree in person, for six weeks she obeyed every instruction from her doctors and made a successful recovery. She still worried that she might be too tired to enjoy the ceremony if she went up to Sackville alone, so she asked her niece Lois Harnish to drive her.

In her convocation address Helen advised the graduates to make the most of their opportunities, but be ready for change in their lives.

To you who are graduating and have your whole adult life before you, may I suggest that you select an occupation that you will enjoy, and then give it everything you've got. We get out of life what we put into it, so the measurement of your enjoyment is largely up to you. That is what I did, and what happened? My health broke down and I had to give up the fine university course I was taking. I hope you will all go ahead along your chosen paths to great accomplishments unhindered but, if misfortune should come your way, don't let it worry you too much. It may be that in the divine plan something much better is awaiting you, as it was for me in folklore.[3]

Her folklore work had brought her the distinction of an honorary doctorate and the privilege of being addressed as Dr. Creighton. But should she use the title?

She realized that one of the primary reasons her name had been put forward was to draw attention to the university's fine folk music library. However, it was also bringing attention to her and, in turn, to the informants who contributed to her collection. She also knew the title would help lend credibility to her acceptance as a serious folklorist.

And so the newly designated Dr. Creighton began her 1957 field research for the National Museum in June, and one of her first stops was to visit Catherine Gallagher. Catherine had at last finished her manuscript for the book she had based loosely around her family's life at the light at Chebucto Head. Helen sat by Catherine's sickbed and read aloud from her manuscript. Although the story was better than Helen had anticipated, she still felt it wasn't ready for publication. She didn't want to offend her friend and so said nothing of these thoughts, but took the draft and told Catherine that she would ask several people to have a look at it. It was never published.[4]

In mid June the CBC television program "Graphic" went to air. Helen had made a few television appearances before, but they had all been live. This was the first time she saw herself on television and her diary entry reveals her opinion: "Was strange to see myself. Had no idea mouth goes up at one side ... the Reddens added a nice touch although we could have had more of them.... Treated myself to two glasses of sherry and had 1st good sleep in ages."[5] Appearing on television was a big event in 1957. There was only one TV channel in Nova Scotia and a great many people saw Helen's appearance. She thought that the broadcast made people more familiar with her work and brought her a few new contacts for possible informants.

Helen began work on another film project in July, *Songs of Nova Scotia*. The National Film Board wanted to make a film showing Helen collecting folk songs throughout Nova Scotia. The director was Grant Crabtree and shooting took place over the summer as and when Helen's collecting schedule permitted. For 21 days they filmed Helen collecting from various informants, including the Reddens and Peter Chaisson and his family at Cheticamp. One of the film's most charming scenes came about when Helen and Grant Crabtree drove up to the Chaisson's house and saw the angelic faces of his children peering out through the windows. They were so enthralled with the image that they incorporated a reenactment of the scene into the film. Other aspects of the film shoot were even less realistic. The director wanted to shoot a scene where Sadie Redden came out of the door of her house to welcome home Finvola and Fred. However, the Reddens had lost their old home in a fire a few years back and were currently living in a contemporary farm home similar to many in rural Nova Scotia. This wasn't what the production staff had in mind, so they filmed the Reddens at a neighbour's old-style home nearby.

Helen had some changes of her own to make: "Grant had arranged to have the "rushes" of the film shown to us at the theatre, so we hastened there and just got it done before the evening's show started. This was the first time I'd seen myself on a theatre's screen, and my first impression was that I was very fat. The boys explained that the camera does that, and this is why film stars keep so slim. Otherwise it wasn't bad."[6] Film star or not, the next day she was ready for the camera: "got set up for Peter Chaisson. This time sure I was wearing a slimming girdle."[7]

It was an exhausting schedule, but between filming Helen was able to fit in several collecting sessions around the province. One such session involved a trip to Cape Breton with Agnes Metcalf. Mrs. Metcalf, a widow who operated a nursing home in Ontario, had been carrying on a correspondence with Helen for several years. She knew many songs and had contacts to meet informants in the area around Louisbourg and Gabarus. When she wrote telling Helen of her plans for a trip to her birthplace, Helen offered to drive her around if Mrs. Metcalf would lead her to informants. They spent several days travelling together and Agnes was able to steer Helen to some interesting people. Toward the end of July the two women were in a coffee shop in Louisbourg when Helen picked up a newspaper and read of Catherine Gallagher's death. Although it had been expected, it was still a great shock. Helen made plans to leave immediately for home, but received a message from Grant Crabtree saying he needed her for an upcoming film shoot. She sent a telegram to Edward Gallagher and his boys, with her sympathy and regrets.

Over the previous five months she had lost two cherished informants. Nathan Hatt had died in March, but Helen didn't hear of his
death until June. She knew that Catherine Gallagher was dying, but
she still felt the loss deeply. Mrs. Gallagher had perhaps been her finest
traditional female singer. Her gentle singing voice and her fondness for
the old "lovelies" that Helen and Doreen had cut their teeth on gave
her a paramount place in Helen's heart. Catherine shared Helen's sentiments about the songs and felt protective over them. But it was the
fact that they'd grown up together in the folklore field that made their
bond so strong. Helen frequently took visitors to the lighthouse at
Chebucto Head to meet Catherine, who always obliged with a song or
two. Several years earlier, when famed folk singer Ed McCurdy[8] visited
with Helen, he particularly requested an introduction to Mrs. Gallagher.
Just as their relationship had moved beyond collector and informant to
one of friendship and affection, Catherine's reputation as a singer had
moved beyond the scope of being Helen's protegé. Only a year earlier
Catherine had written to Helen about an upcoming appearance they
would be making together on CBC television with Max Ferguson: "Wasn't
it a happy day, that day you first visited us at Chebucto Head? A happy
day for you and for me, and many more."[9] Helen would later advise
other folklore collectors, "Remember, the informants are the teachers,
you are the student."[10]

She was developing a different kind of relationship with Finvola Redden,
who looked to Helen as an advisor and mentor. Throughout the year
Helen worked to get funding to enable Finvola to pursue vocal training. She made requests through the Imperial Order of the Daughters'
of the Empire and various University Women's organizations, but was
unsuccessful. She even considered funding Finvola herself, "if only I
could do it myself without putting myself too far back."[11] In late August she was finally successful in obtaining a $1,000 grant from the
Nova Scotia Talent Trust to enable Finvola to enroll at Mount Allison
University's music program.[12]

Her relationship with Finvola wasn't a one-way street. Finvola was a
bright, intelligent young woman who had a winning personality and
charmed everyone who heard her sing. She and Helen got along well
and Helen began taking Finvola with her on speaking engagements to
illustrate songs from her collection. In August she took Finvola to the
Canada/West Indies Federation Summer Institute held at Mount Allison
University, where she had been asked to present an evening of Maritime folk songs. Two days later they travelled together to Tatamagouche
for another of Betty Murray's Arts Festivals, where Finvola was joined
by her father, who also performed.

At the end of August Helen returned to Dartmouth for a few more
days filming with Grant Crabtree. She accompanied the crew down to

Eastern Passage and when she waved a cheery greeting to Alice Henneberry, she met with an unexpected reaction.

*The Star Weekly* had a story by Mr. Belliveau about the house at Devil's Island, and she had received a letter from the daughter of the former occupant. She said the facts were all wrong, but, on checking, they were right enough, but she ascribed to the wrong people. Her anger soon cooled, but she said she had been trying for weeks to get me on the telephone.... Actually I didn't like his sensational style, and I'm sure he had stories I didn't give him permission to use. Thank goodness I had refused the Star Weekly the right to publish my book. The main cover design was of a haunted castle, supposed to be the Henneberry's house.... the handling of the whole thing was not in the style I wanted. ... No reflection is cast in either story on the family.[13]

This was an interesting twist of circumstance. In July *The Star Weekly* had published an article by J.E. Belliveau called "Tales of Phantoms," which told of supernatural events at Eastern Passage and Devil's Island.[14] Helen had given the author some background information, but he had also interviewed several members from the communities themselves. Mrs. Henneberry had assumed the misrepresentation was Helen's doing, but if a magazine editor decided that a ghost story needed an image of a haunted Victorian-style mansion to represent a ghost house at Eastern Passage, that was the way they would present it. The informants themselves were becoming the subjects for outside interviews and they had yet to learn about the vagrancy of the press.

In late September Helen accompanied Finvola Redden to Mount Allison University to assist in arranging her music courses and registering for classes. She had taken a big step in offering to help with Finvola's career. It was the first time she got so involved with an informant's personal life. But she cared for Finvola and wanted the best for her. Helen felt that she had the potential to be a world-class singer, and her protegé was even generating some press of her own. *Maclean's* ran a piece under the caption "Items To Watch For": "In a province where folk singing is traditional Finvola Redden is right now the sweetest singer of all. She's 16, composes and sings her songs (unaccompanied), is a promising painter, stars at folk festivals and will sing two of her compositions in a National film Board movie."[15] Helen had some doubts, which she confided to her diary: "Hope I haven't built Finvola up too much, and hope she won't get hurt with all she has to learn in so many ways. She is old fashioned by to-days standards in speech and way of life. It has been a rich experience."[16]

On 4 October Helen's eagerly anticipated book of ghost stories arrived. It was appropriately titled *Bluenose Ghosts*.[17] When she had been asked to write the book she thought it an excellent idea. But by the time the manuscript was completed she had misgivings. She worried how the public would receive a book on ghosts, witches, and strange supernatural events. She didn't recall hearing any ghost stories at home, but she certainly had developed an affinity for things supernatural, writing in her autobiography, "Having had a number of strange things happen in my own life, I suppose I am in tune with the subject."[18]

The book was released in time for Christmas. The public loved the stories of hauntings and phantom ships, and critics were impressed by the range of material collected. American folklorist Horace Beck said it was "perhaps one of the most worthwhile studies of the occult and its effects upon a people that has been done in some time."[19]

But Helen's big year wasn't over yet. The Canadian government had recently established the Canada Council, a new funding agency that offered substantial grants for work in the arts and cultural fields. This was exactly what Helen had been waiting for. She had been storing her tapes and much of her research material at the Public Archives of Nova Scotia as well as at home, but constantly worried that if the original material were lost or destroyed, years of research would be gone forever. She applied to the Canada Council for funding to have duplicates made of the audio portion of her collection and to have the melodies of the tunes transcribed to manuscript paper by a professional musicologist. This would give her working copies to use in Halifax and allow the originals to be stored at the National Museum in Ottawa. Given the national recognition she had been receiving and a strong letter of support from her National Museum colleagues,[20] she applied and in October received a letter confirming her award for an unspecified amount. How much did she want? She consulted with Marius Barbeau and he suggested $10,000.[21] That is what she requested—and that is what she got.

Hearing of her award, musicologist and folk music scholar Kenneth Peacock contacted Helen to ask if she might consider him to work on the project of transcribing the audio material. Ken came highly recommended by the National Museum and Helen gave her consent. In October she travelled to Ottawa to make the arrangements. She was receiving one of the first Canada Council grants ever awarded and it couldn't have come at a better time in her career. As she wrote in her autobiography, "Crawley Films would duplicate a set on tape to be kept in the Public Archives in Halifax, and ... Radio Station CBO offered to make another set for the Museum if I would provide the tapes. What a blessing this was because I discovered a few years later that the sound had faded on some of the originals."[22]

The year was capped with a glowing tribute from Marius Barbeau at a Canadian Authors Association meeting where Helen was the guest speaker. "Dr. Barbeau gave vote of thanks ... he gave me most beautiful tribute have ever heard given any speaker, dwelling on lifetime devoted to folklore and so on. Was deeply touched and, as it turned out, his stroke followed in a few weeks and that may have been last appearance as speaker."[23]

# CHAPTER FOURTEEN

✳ ✳ ✳

Helen returned to Ottawa in January 1958 to oversee the duplication of her audio recordings by Crawley Films. Each day, as the tapes were being copied, she sat in the control room and made notes. The dubbing took all month and at the end of the session 250 tapes had been copied.

In May she went to Toronto to narrate two half-hour programs on folk songs. CBC radio had developed a two-part dramatization—written by Joseph Schull—on the life of the great nineteenth-century Nova Scotia statesman, Joseph Howe. The producers wanted to set the stage for the drama with Helen's folk song program. She was asked to select the songs and was able to send copies of Ken Peacock's music transcriptions to Richard Johnston, who arranged them for a choir.

Richard in turn was able to give Helen a copy of his arrangement of Finvola Redden's "Boat Song," so when she returned to Nova Scotia at the end of May Helen immediately went to see the Reddens and placed the manuscript in Finvola's hands. Helen was also eager to meet the newest addition to the Redden family. In February Sadie had written her with exciting news: "Jan 30th I had to go to the Musq[uodoboit] Hospital, and we have another little girl … as bright as a button and very sweet. We have named her "Helen Kathleen" Helen after the kindest and dearest person I know."[1]

Helen's work in Ottawa had been stimulating but tiring. Her operation and the excitement of the previous year had drained her, but the rewards had been many. She had released a popular book on ghosts, been granted an honorary degree, and awarded one of the largest Canada Council grants ever given an individual. But when the Dartmouth Choral Society put on a concert of folk songs and didn't include a single one from her collection, Helen was hurt. She wrote in her diary, "Down in the Valley, and a group of folk songs, all from other places. No Broken Ring, and not one N.S. song. That could happen only in one's home town."[2] Her disappointment at being excluded from the Dartmouth concert was a discouraging note on which to begin her new collecting season.

However, as she continued throughout the summer, her spirits rose and she found renewed energies. In June she travelled to St. Andrews, New Brunswick, to give a talk at a home economics convention. On the way she stopped off at Sussex to see a Danish family who were

*Helen Creighton and Wilmot MacDonald, Miramichi Folk Song Festival, 1961.*

becoming well-known for their unique pottery. Kjeld and Erica Deichmann, and their daughter Anneka, produced a range of clay products decorated in designs from nature. Their friendly personalities and warm reception drew Helen in and she stayed with them over the weekend and even collected some Danish songs.

In August she went to Tatamagouche to oversee the second annual meeting of the newly formed Canadian Folk Music Society. She had been elected vice president and arranged for the delegates to hold their meeting at the United Church's Christian Training Centre, just outside the town. It was an important meeting with some of the heavyweights in Canadian folk music in attendance. They drew up a constitution and made plans to host the International Folk Music Council in Quebec in three years time.

As soon as that meeting was over, Helen took Finvola Redden and flew to Lennoxville, Quebec, where she had been invited to give lectures to the National Assembly of the YWCA. After the conference they returned to Montreal with Alan Mills, who had also been in attendance. Alan and Helen had been discussing the possibility of having Finvola study with a vocal coach. They had no one in mind, but someone suggested that they contact Bernard Diamant, who worked with the famed Canadian singer Maureen Forrester. Mr. Diamant was out of town, but Alan took Helen and Finvola to visit Maureen and her husband, Eugene Kash, who were entertaining a group of well-known musicians. Finvola was asked to sing and did so with such aplomb that she utterly charmed her audience. Helen was delighted and very proud. When they returned to Nova Scotia Helen discussed the prospect of Finvola's vocal training with her parents. They agreed that if that was what their daughter wanted, they would help make it happen. And so it was decided that Finvola would go to Montreal in November and study voice.

In early September Helen attended the first Miramichi Folk Song Festival in Newcastle. The festival was the brainchild of Louise Manny, the town librarian and a folk song enthusiast. Louise had been at the Canadian Folk Music Society's meeting at Tatamagouche and had invited Helen to be one of the judges. The second judge was Edward D. (Sandy) Ives, a young folklore professor from the University of Orono, in Maine.

Newcastle is a pretty town on the shores of the Miramichi River. Several of its major buildings, including the Town Hall where the festival was held, owed their existence to the largess of Lord Beaverbrook, who was born in the area. Lord Beaverbrook was interested in the traditional songs native to his birthplace and had funded Louise Manny's search for these melodies. But he wouldn't support her collecting of non-local songs. Seven years earlier she had written to Helen expressing her frustrations: "Lord Beaverbrook won't be one bit interested in the traditional songs—he takes the stand that they are sung much better in

England, and he will send me all the records I want of them. He doesn't realize I want ours, not the old country singers, however beautiful."[3]

Louise had been collecting and broadcasting folk songs for several years. She brought the singers into the local radio station where she made recordings of their songs. She thought a festival might be a good way of bringing together many of the traditional singers under one roof to share songs and celebrate their mutual love of the genre. Since it was an untried concept, no one had any idea how it would turn out. Most of the singers had never performed on stage before an audience. And what would the two judges look for? Louise was emphatic over what she would allow. The singers had to submit the title of their song to the judges before the event, and if it were not deemed a true folk song, the singers were asked to make another selection. This wasn't difficult, for the Miramichi region was home to some of the finest traditional folk singers around. At any rate, Helen and Sandy Ives offered Solomon-like decisions. They made certain that everyone who entered received some sort of recognition—e.g., oldest singer, singer who travelled the furthest to attend, and singer who performed the song with the most verses. Everyone was pleased and the festival was a rousing success.[4] When it was over, Helen stayed in the Miramichi area with Louise and finished her collecting season there.

She returned home to a quiet fall and was able to do some work on two new projects: a collection of folk songs from the three Maritime provinces, and assembling her Gaelic material for possible publication by the National Museum. She also took time to catch up on her summer's research notes. In December the National Film Board's *Songs of Nova Scotia* was premiered at the Capital Theatre in Halifax, featured on the same bill with a film starring Spencer Tracy. It would have a long life as a tourism promotional film aboard the ferry travelling between Yarmouth, Nova Scotia and Bar Harbor, Maine.

1958 didn't live up to the banner events of its predecessor, but Helen was confident that it had been productive. She had been able to work for a number of years with little guidance or interference from the National Museum. Many of the activities she undertook were not part of her regular Musuem contract, but she was given the flexibility to take them on as she saw fit. But changes were underway.

Dr. Barbeau and Dr. Alcock had retired and the new director, Dr. Jacques Rousseau, asked Carmen Roy in the folklore department to be the Museum's primary contact with Helen. Dr. Roy was a collector herself and had several years of field research experience in Quebec. She brought a strong academic background to her work and tried to get Helen to keep up with the current trends in folklore study. She also questioned Helen's many extracurricular activities. Helen responded to her concerns in a long letter:

You ask why I tire myself with speaking and so forth. There are several very good reasons. One is that last year I asked Dr. Rousseau what his policy was [in] this regard and he wants me to do it. It is a very good way of letting the public know what the Museum is doing. Also I am much more valuable to the museum when I can travel about and speak of our work than I would be if I kept my little nose in my typewriter all the time. Then there is the question of money. As you know I work for a distressingly small fee. I've always felt that if the Museum could, they would increase it and do the right thing by me. I hope I'm right. In the meantime I'd lead a pretty confined life on what I make. As a speaker I get around and see the world. Speaking has taken me as far afield as New York, Washington and Indiana University. Last summer it took me to St. Andrews, Lennoxville, Montreal, and New Castle [sic], and it put me on television in Montreal, Sydney, and Halifax. I always get soft hearted, or soft headed, when it comes to taking fees from organizations, and usually give my services, but small organizations serve the purpose of giving the speaker experience and assurance, and from their reactions one learns what an audience finds most interesting. Then when a big assignment comes up like t.v. or radio, or something that can afford to pay, I am ready for it. Some day I might do a Canadian Club tour; the speaking end wouldn't worry me, but I might find it too fatiguing. It's a nice thing to keep in mind though. Or the Museum might want to send me somewhere. Then of course, there is the fact of sharing. I was brought up in the belief that if I had a talent which would give people pleasure it was my duty to share it. And except when I get carried away telling ghost stories and frighten timid women out of their wits, my audiences do seem to enjoy what I have to say to them.[5]

For the first time Helen's priorities were being questioned by the Museum. Was her public persona overriding her field research? Helen had arguably become the most well publicized folklorist working in Canada.[6] She had been given a free rein with her research in the past, but now Carmen Roy was trying to make sure the Museum got value for the research time and money they contracted with her. But that issue got swept under the table thanks to a far larger problem that had arisen within the Museum's hierarchy.

In January 1959 Helen went to Ottawa for a meeting of the Canadian Folk Music Society. They were in the planning stages of the Quebec conference to be held in 1961, but most of their time was spent dealing with a conflict that was a direct reflection of what was happening between key players at the National Museum. As vice president, Helen found herself thrust into the fray.

It all came about when Jacques Rousseau took over from F.J. Alcock as director of the National Museum. Dr. Rousseau was recommended for the job by Marius Barbeau, but the Civil Service Commission had wanted L.S. Russell, so the responsibilities were divided and two distinct branches of the museum were created. Dr. Rousseau was offered the Natural History Division and Dr. Russell headed the Human History Branch. Although he had retired, Dr. Barbeau still retained an office at the Museum and Dr. Rousseau accused him of abusing his ex-officio position. He also claimed that various staff members were misusing their influence—among other things, to have Museum stenographers type election campaign material for the Liberal party in 1957. Several individuals were named as miscreants and the atmosphere throughout the Museum was filled with tension.

By the time Helen attended the Canadian Folk Music Society meeting on 31 January, the rift was reaching its apex. She recorded her frustrations in her diary: "Much confusion at Museum where there have been clashes between Dr. Barbeau & Dr. Rousseau and others. Stayed to give Carmen Roy moral support and made her my first interest.... Before meeting Carmen had letter from Dr. Barbeau saying he did not wish her, for personal reasons, to attend the meeting. She sent in her resignation as member of council, and he omitted her name in everything. Meeting largely attended as so much unfavourable publicity about Dr. B."[7]

A month later, the dispute reached a further climax. As reported by *The Ottawa Citizen*, "Rousseau, dismissed as director of the Natural Museum's human history branch, has charged there was immorality and drunkenness there and has demanded an investigation. [He was] ... fired from his post by the government on February 28.... Dr. Rousseau added the comment someone had made to him that—'if you were not a French-Canadian you would still be the museum director'."[8]

As if tension and dispute among her employers were not bad enough, Helen ran into a conflict concerning the use of her unpublished material housed at the National Museum. In January she heard a broadcast from Max Ferguson's Rawhide radio program that featured a cut from the new William McCauley Choir's *Canadian Folk Songs* album.[9] The song Max played was called "Phoebe." It was definitely from Helen's collection but was not part of her published work. She believed the only place the record company could have obtained a copy of the song was from her unpublished collection at the National Museum. To add insult to injury, Helen received no credit and the song's provenance was ascribed to Prince Edward Island. Since Edith Fowke was responsible for some of the research behind the album, Helen mistakenly blamed her for obtaining the song and passing it along to William McCauley.

Edith had been working hard over the years to make a name for herself in Canadian folklore. She had developed a successful national radio show, "Folk Song Time," and was being recognized as a credible researcher, especially in the folk song field. But some people, including

Helen, perceived her as aggressively ambitious. Helen expressed her frustrations to Carmen Roy:

I have realized for some time that Edith is ambitious and craves publicity, but I never dreamed she was underhanded or dishonest. Fortunately the Crawley Films sent me a copy, which they did with great pride, and I feel sorry Edith has got them in this mess. If Louis Applebaum or Neil Chotem were to go to the Museum I would want them to be shown the tunes Ken has done, but I wouldn't expect them to take anything without my permission. After all, these tunes are mine, paid for by the Canada Council. I want composers to use them, but with the proper credits such as you would expect from any honourable person. But this is beyond the pale. And then to take it out of this province and give it to P.E.I. Moreover she has seen at the end that the Waterloo Press is given credit for the songs taken from her *Folk Songs of Canada*, but my poor Phoebe looks like a motherless child.[10]

Helen must also have expressed her concerns to Richard Johnston. He had worked with Edith before and wrote back with his own strong opinions about both his colleague and the incident in question:

I know that woman very well—too well for her own good.... she is very aggressive and will stop at nothing until she is stopped.... I must remind myself, from time to time, that when we were working on our first book together she was most insistent that any materials which we took from your books be acknowledged and that you be paid because she said many times that she didn't want to have bad relations with such a good friend to her as you were ... I must tell you again (I think I have told you this before) that when I first suggested to her that we both ought to do at least a little collecting if only for the experience, she scoffed at me, and tried to dissuade me from beginning. However, she now has the bug herself and has done quite well in her collecting. But his is all fodder for the publicity mill, too, and don't forget that. She has never offered one note of her collection to the Museum but she has tried to sell parts of it to various people.... Edith figures that she has built herself sufficiently to be unquestioned in her opinions. This is a dangerous thing, and, because of her fearful personality and ungainly conceit, it is fitting and proper that she be clipped because if she gets away with this kind of thing once she will try it again, and eventually can do some very real harm ... Your suggestion that Edith be given a fright is very good, and I'll tell you how this can be managed.[11]

Richard was obviously hurting from his relationship with Edith. He wanted more revenge than Helen was prepared to seek. She was trying to protect her collection, not ruin a career. She still had affection for Edith—she just didn't like the way she handled some of her business. Richard suggested that Helen expose Edith's misuse of her song, deny her access to unpublished material at the Museum, and make a formal complaint to Edith's publishers. But it was more Richard's fight now than Helen's and she acted on none of his recommendations.

In fact, eventually Helen was able to clear up the mystery of how William McCauley got hold of the song in the first place. As she explained to Carmen: "A letter from Ken [Peacock] partly clears up the Phoebe misadventure. It was Ken who supplied the songs, and that was all right. We wanted them to be used by our composers, and it was to Bill MacCaulay that he gave them. Bill has never been a collector and therefore I suppose he would think one maritime province much the same as another."[12]

In April Helen once again wrote to Carmen Roy concerning her feelings toward Edith's fate. "I'm afraid Edith Fowke has had a poor winter. Her radio program, Folk Song Time has been off the air which must have been hard for her. However I think it has probably given her time to think and to realize how much the C.B.C. was responsible for her success. Actually she is a very good collector, but I think she needed a little set-back to get her values straight."[13]

But the spring wasn't filled solely with misadventure. In April CBC radio began an eight-part series of stories dramatized from *Bluenose Ghosts.* Helen acted as script consultant, but the actual writing was done by professional dramatists. That same month she flew to Montreal for the premier performance of *Sea Gallows,* a ballet based on melodies from her collection.

When she was visiting with Alan and Bernie Mills the previous spring she had met a young Quebec composer named Michel Perrault. He had been commissioned by Les Grands Ballet Canadiens to produce a ballet based on a sea theme and was inspired by Helen's collection. He invited her to the premier the following April and she successfully applied to the Nova Scotia government for travel funds. Helen attended the premiere performance and took Finvola Redden, who was studying in Montreal, as her guest the second night. The ballet was a great critical success.

The ballet told the story of the murder of a man in a seaside village. One year later the killer seeks out the victim's wife at a dance and she, not knowing his true identity, forgets her mourning and dances with him. They become betrothed and shortly after their marriage she finds a picture of herself in her new husband's possession. It is an image her former husband had carried with him, and so she discovers the guilty secret. When the murderer finds out he tries to push her into the sea, but

Helen Creighton Fonds, PANS Album 15: 15-8. Photographer: unknown

*Rumanian Folklore Conference, 1959. In front of Foisher House, King Carol's Palace. L-R: Helen Creighton, Mr. Sabin, V. Dragoi, A.E.Charbuliez, Helène Bailargeon, Jean Harris.*

she jumps in before he reaches her. Then a bolt of lightning strikes the rocky crag on which he stands and he too plunges into the sea to his death.

Helen recorded in her diary that when the curtain came down there was loud applause and cries of Bravo! She was thrilled with the performance and with Michel's score, but was not pleased at the lack of credit to her for the original music: "No credit to us for music on program or anywhere else.... When I appeared backstage he [Michel Perrault] and Mr. Decarie the manager, full of apologies, but I just said it was not too late."[14] She later wrote in her autobiography, "If I hadn't gone up, my province would have received no publicity, for the ballet was advertised simply as based on Canadian folklore, which I felt was a mistake."[15]

Helen returned to Nova Scotia and began her summer field research. She spent most of her time in New Brunswick and was eager to get as much work done as possible as she would be away for the month of August and the first part of September. The International Folk Music Council was holding their annual meeting in Rumania. As president of the Canadian Folk Music Society, the privilege of attending the conference was Marius Barbeau's. Since he was unable to attend, Helen, as vice president, requested that she represent the Museum in his stead. The Canada Council awarded her $700 and the National Museum paid her living expenses. She would present a paper and be the official representative for the National Museum. To better represent the bilingual aspect of the Museum's mandate, she began using language records to study French. An International Folk Tale Congress was being held in Germany immediately after the Rumanian event, so Helen decided to take in both. And since she was going to Europe, she made plans to stop in England to spend some time with Mac, meet Maud Karpeles, and visit with Doreen Senior, whom she hadn't seen in 20 years.

In early August she flew to London and was greeted at the airport by her brother. The following day she met up with Maud Karpeles. Maud was now well known as a folk song collector and she and Helen had kept up a regular correspondence. During the war and even into the early 1950s, Helen had sent Maud relief packages of food and other treats for which Maud was most grateful. Maud would also be attending the conference, but since they were unable to travel together, she gave Helen the names of four other delegates whom she could befriend. Helen was reluctant to travel to a communist country in the middle of the Cold War, but her new acquaintances made her feel more relaxed. On 8 August they flew to Rumania via Brussels, Vienna, and an overnight stop in Bucharest. The next day they were driven to the conference site at Sinaia in the Carpathian Mountains, where they discovered their accommodations to be in the former summer palace of the royal family. Helen's room had been the Queen's salon. It was a magical environment, but Helen later wrote "to be in this extraordinary setting was like living in a fairy tale until we were brought to reality by the sound of soldiers drilling outside and occasional gun practice in the distance."[16]

Other things too were quite different than what the delegates had anticipated in a communist country. The dinners were especially lavish affairs lasting late into the evening. The delegates were taken on a bus tour to visit a selected village, but any possibility of meeting locals was out of the question. Performers were brought to the conference site and delegates were not permitted any further than the village of Sinaia itself. The conference sessions were held in a huge hall equipped with instantaneous translation facilities for six languages. Helen presented a paper on her work and showed the National Film Board's *Songs of Nova Scotia*. Her friend, Helène Baillargeon, sang several Acadian folk songs from her collection.

When the conference was over Helen flew to Kiel, Germany by way of East Berlin. She had hoped to fly into West Berlin with an American delegate, but the authorities refused the request. They offered no explanation, so Helen was forced to land in the communist controlled area of Germany. She recorded her apprehensions in her autobiography, but was able to add, "I can only speak kindly of these people .... The wall wasn't up then, but there were signs of devastation ... it was a great relief when that part of my trip was over."[17] Exhausted by the time she arrived in Kiel, she was dismayed to find herself billeted in a youth hostel run by nuns, and required to share a room. She must have looked as bedraggled as she felt, for her hosts gave her a private room and a bottle of beer. After a day's rest she was back in form.

Helen was much more relaxed in Kiel. She was no longer responsible for presenting a paper and she knew many of the delegates who were attending from North America. There were opportunities for getting better acquainted and several evenings ended very late. But it was much more than a social occasion. She later wrote that the "real benefit came from meeting the world's great folklore scholars, and it was no small satisfaction to hear renowned professors from Norway and France quoting from [her] books."[18] Her own work with Acadian folk tales was represented in a paper given by her Quebec colleague Luc Lacourcière.[19]

At the end of the Folk Tale Congress Helen and several other delegates took a sojourn to nearby Copenhagen and by 27 August Helen was back in England and on her way to Devon to see Doreen Senior. Their meeting was warm and cordial, but their disagreement over their publications had put a wall up between them. Helen noted in her diary that Doreen "looked much the same but a great deal heavier. Lives in beautiful old rectory with wash basin in room, but very lovely setting."[20] Following her meeting with Doreen, Helen spent several days with her brother, who had established himself with an affluent clientele in London. After the greyness of communist Rumania and East Berlin, London, in the company of a wealthy and influential brother, must have been a welcome change.

She returned to Nova Scotia elated over the reception she had received in Europe. She'd made many new contacts and the trip had opened her eyes to the direction in which world folklore scholarship was moving. The Folk Music Conference had been a great success and she was determined to help make the upcoming sequel in Quebec as good, if not better.

One of the aspects that had most impressed her with the Rumanian conference was that the organizers had arranged for the delegates to hear local tradition bearers and not just trained singers illustrating traditional songs. Helen had been an early advocate for using original performers where possible and she lobbied hard to make her point with members of the Canadian Folk Music Society's steering committee. But after their fall meeting she recorded her frustrations: "I talked too much, but it was necessary, trying to prevent a lot of professional entertainment for 1961 in place of live folklore."[21] She still had her work cut out for her. Even Marius Barbeau lobbied for professional singers over tradition bearers and had made up a tentative program, to which Helen took exception. In March 1960 she wrote to him, "You will not expect me to be pleased with your program. For yourself I feel that you have missed one of the great opportunities of your life, dwelling as you are upon concerts and other sophisticated entertainments, all very fine in their place. It seems strange for me to be reminding you that the most impressive things in life are those that are simple (with taste) and sincere. One of the first things we learn about folklore is that through it we see the soul of a people, and that is what our visitors, who are scholars, will look for when they come to Canada."[22]

She was not alone in championing tradition bearers. Luc Lacourcière echoed her sentiments: "Your reactions are mine and that of my colleagues of Laval. Today I just want to assure you that we are preparing another tentative program in the very spirit of an international folk music conference. The first place will be given to living folklore representatives of the whole country."[23]

Helen and her colleagues were making a stand for what they felt best represented the real folk culture of Canada. Many of her sympathizers were also collectors and they saw the need to use some of the older tradition bearers while they were still able to perform. International visitors couldn't hope to cover several specific areas in a country as large as Canada, so Helen was trying to ensure that each region's folk-cultural elements were represented at the conference site. It wasn't easy for her to take a stand against Marius Barbeau. He was considered the dean of Canadian folklorists and she had been his student 20 years earlier. However, she made what she believed to be a professional decision and stuck by it.

Helen took a strong personal stance in another matter concerning a folklore colleague. Her reaction to Edith's latest publication would find the two sparring once again. Edith and Joe Glazer had recently published a book of songs from the labour movement called *Songs of Work and Protest*.[24] As a professional courtesy, and out of friendship, Edith sent Helen a copy. Helen was shocked at its contents. These were the kinds of songs she refused to collect. They frightened her. She was vehemently anticommunist and looked upon this genre as an instrument to incite trouble. Recently returned from several communist countries, her sentiments must have been on high alert. Her reaction, in a letter to Carmen Roy at the National Museum, illustrates just how fearful she was:

A few days ago I received a copy of Edith Fowke's new book ... It is very well done, but what a subject, for these are communist songs. I am embarrassed to know how to thank her. She does this documentary type of study very well; I would say it is her forte. But why is it that people like Alan Lomax, Pete Seegar [sic], Peggy Seegar [sic], and now Edith, apply folk songs to communist propaganda? She doesn't call this book folk songs, but it is her interest in folk songs that had led her along this path. I remember years ago recording the song Solidarity

Forever from a very nice young professor, and it made me shiver. Evangelist songs stir people do good, but trade union songs stir people to hate and to seek their own advancement. I'm glad I don't have to review it, which would be hard to so as a friend. I expect it has many things to commend it, and I'll be most curious to know what the critics have to say. She may have sent you a copy too; if so I would be most interested in your opinion.[25]

Two days later, she wrote to Edith:

Knowing me as you do, I wonder how you expected me to react to such a subject as you have chosen. If this were a document on the type of song sung by a certain section of the people at a certain time in our history, then I could find much to commend it. But you encourage people here to sing these songs. I will never forget my feeling of horror when a young professor who had sung me Cape Breton songs asked if I would like to hear Solidarity Forever. He had heard it as a communist meeting during his college days in Toronto where he went in the process of growing up. As I listened I could understand what that song would do to a group of workers. I have always understood that this is a communist song, and that raises the question in my mind as it does in the minds of my friends—where do you stand in this? It looks as though you had lined yourself up on their side. If I am wrong, and I sincerely hope I am, please wire me collect. I would be a great relief.... I know nothing of your religious convictions—it is something we have never talked about. It is love we want in the world today above all else.... These things mean a great deal to me. I don't usually let myself go like this. But you have shared your book with me and it is only right that you should know where I stand.... I hope you will forgive me for being so outspoken, but I would be a poor friend otherwise.[26]

Edith was equally quick to respond:

Apparently I made a mistake in sending you a copy of *Songs of Work and Protest*. I realized, of course, that these songs were not the type of songs in which you were interested, but I thought you'd like to see the book because I had written it, and because it is, I think, a fairly important historical document ... I am surprised that you should feel it necessary to ask me where I stand in relation to communism. If it needs to be said, I assure you that I regard communism as a totalitarian doctrine as antithetic to freedom as fascism. I thought you knew that one of the things that has bothered me about the folk-song movement is the tendency of Communists to take it over. In fact, one of the reasons Joe and I produced this book is that we wanted to supplant the existing books put out by Communist-front groups in which they mixed genuine labour songs with many sympathetic propaganda songs.... I am sorry if sending you this book has served merely to divide us further. I had really intended it as a gesture of friendship.... P.S. You might be interested to know that Dr. Barbeau does not share your concern about the book. He wrote: 'I was delighted to receive your admirable *Songs of Work and Protest*. Now I am reading them with great pleasure. You have achieved a fine piece of work, both in content and form. Let me congratulate you warmly.'[27]

Helen was comforted to hear Edith's sentiments regarding communism and wrote back to her colleague expressing her relief. Two weeks later she received another note from Edith: "I'm glad to know that my letter cleared up your misconceptions about *Songs of Work and Protest*, and that you're now more or less reconciled to it."[28]

But Helen's fears were far from allayed. When she had written to Carmen Roy she mentioned Pete Seeger's name as one of those singers she felt promoted labour songs for the communist cause. She had known Pete as a young boy, dancing to his father's piano playing in Washington, but no longer recognized the child in the man. Pete was one of the world's major folk song interpreters and a leader in the fledgling folk song revival that would peak in the 1960s. But he also had a reputation for working with songs that frightened authorities fearful of the "red menace" promoted so heavily by McCarthyism in the United States.[29]

Helen, too, was fearful of his political leanings and when Carmen told her he had made inquiries about forming a working liaison with the National Museum, she became more concerned. She wrote back:

I have been thinking about Pete Seegar [sic] and your doubt about whether I am right. I didn't know he wanted anything from the Museum, so I would like to make a suggestion. It can do him no harm, and indeed would be fairest to all of us, including yourself. It should be a simple matter for the Museum to make a confidential enquiry through the RCMP and the FBI, asking if he is known to have leanings towards the left, and what his record is. I think you will find that he is on a list of people they keep their eye on, but they must think he is keeping within the law because he seems to move freely between the two countries. Others have asked him the same question you have, and with the same result. I have met him only once, and was sorry our time was so short. He struck me as something of an idealist, and I should think he wants sincerely to help the oppressed. I found him quite charming, but even in that short time he told me that his sister was then behind the iron curtain. He must have an amazing way with a crowd, and an ability to organize group singing, that is quite phenomenal. If you could analyse his programs you would understand the use to which he puts folk songs. However why not settle the matter and put us at our ease as I suggest?[30]

Carmen's response indicated that she was less concerned about Pete Seeger's political activities than Helen, but she left the door open for further investigation by the National Museum. "It would be indeed interesting to have the RCMP making inquiries in Pete Seeger's case. But I am hesitating to do so ... I do not know why. Maybe because he is a charming (illuminated, surely) man ... but also because we are not so closely concerned with his career to undertake such investigations. It remains that anything that you could discover (as a proof) in his case and in the one of Mrs. Fowke would be mostly welcomed here."[31]

Helen's paranoia eventually lessened and she dropped the issue. She was acting out of a common fear held by many people of her generation. Communism was seen as the ultimate threat and people espousing its ideals were perceived as the enemy. It's doubtful whether Edith Fowke or Pete Seeger ever knew of Helen's wish to have them investigated. Neither ever mentioned it to her, nor she to them.[32] And in fairness to Helen, it must be remembered that while many people were interested in songs of protest to help further a cause, there were many others, like Helen, who were not. As John O'Donnell points out in his work, *Contribution of American Folklorists to Research on Canadian Coal-Mining Songs*, "Even the great Cecil Sharp, in his unparalleled collection, English Folk Songs from the Southern Appalachians, excluded occupational songs of miners and other workers. His fellow collector, Maud Karpeles, wrote of their search for traditional material in West Virginia, where 'owing to the disturbances of rural life by the big coal industry ... [songs and ballads] did not lie so ready to hand as in other states.' Canadian folklorists have simply followed the same pattern."[33] That is not to say the songs didn't exist. In many cases they were abundant. Again, John O'Donnell notes, "Years of suppression and unsuccessful attempts to obtain decent wages and working conditions made the 1920s ripe for Communist recruitment among Canadian miners, 'Arise Ye Nova Scotia Slaves,' collected by George Korson from Bob Stewart of Glace Bay, served as a call to arms in a movement that was to see the United Mine Workers of America take a firm root in the coal fields of Nova Scotia."[34]

Some people tried to sing these songs for Helen. She chose to ignore most of them. She did, however, collect a few. Even then, it was sometimes the informant who chose to remain anonymous for fear of reprisals. "Dennis Williams at Musquodoboit ... keeps a country store, so Saturday afternoon is the worst possible time to go there. However, he didn't hesitate to close the shop up while he and his wife, their daughter and her children all came to the house. One of the women could have looked after the store, but I suppose they didn't want to miss anything. ... He wouldn't let his name go with his singing of the Honest Working Man in case some Cape Bretoner heard it on the radio from New York and came and beat him up."[35]

In later years Helen developed a friendly relationship with Pete Seeger. He wrote to her in 1963 expressing great admiration for her work.[36] And she wrote glowingly about him in her autobiography, when he came to Halifax to give a concert. After his third encore he told his audience that he hadn't sung songs from the area because he didn't know any. He called Helen the next day and apologized for omitting folk songs from Nova Scotia. She responded, "You belittled our heritage to students, and that's unforgivable. I had to get that off my chest, Pete, but now I've said it, what can I do for you?"[37] She invited him to visit her at Evergreen the following afternoon to show him some of the songs she had collected. Several months after his visit his agent wrote to Helen requesting permission to include one of her songs on Pete's newest album. She replied that she would be happy to share royalties with Pete Seeger.

In retrospect, Helen's reaction to both Edith's book and Pete Seeger's activities were unfounded. She was steeped in the sensibilities of another era and was finding it difficult to make adjustments. She was also having problems coming to terms with the new direction in which the National Museum was trying to lead her. Her usual research method was to go into a collecting field and retrieve as much information as she could find—within the guidelines she set for herself, which excluded both bawdy songs and those that she felt promoted political instability.

She had not embraced the analytical approach most of her professional colleagues now used in their work. Carmen Roy tried to steer her towards this received approach in February, when they were discussing Helen's work for her upcoming season.

Folklore, as a science, should not have as an aim only the collect of material.... What appears to me the most clearly actually is that it is not the science of folklore which is regressing in our 20th century, but the folklorist's methods of research. Part of us are still looking to find the old versions, the survivals, while a new folklore is operating in our field and does not awake our curiosity or ambitions to prove that he is born.... All that has been said, dear Helen, to prepare the ground for next summer field work. Please do not get anxious or anguish.[38]

With the shift in focus from collection to analysis, Helen was unsure what the Museum now expected of her. Carmen suggested that she take the question "Is Canada suffering from an inferiority complex?" and conduct a series of prepared interviews as supplied by the Museum.

This was not the kind of folklore research with which Helen was familiar. Carmen knew that Helen was neither comfortable with nor trained to conduct such a survey, so she wrote her, "I prefer to leave you your entire freedom as to find your personal way of reaching to a conclusion."[39]

What Helen wanted was direction. She had suggested a trip to New Brunswick's Grand Manan Island to conduct her normal style of collecting. She made plans to go there in late June, but didn't know what her employers wanted her to do in the interim. She continued to search for folklore in Nova Scotia, but as late as 25 May had heard nothing from Carmen beyond a note saying not to work too hard and an advance per diem cheque for $400. Finally, on 1 June Carmen wrote to tell Helen to spend most of her season on Grand Manan conducting her usual research.

In the meantime Helen was also working on another television show for CBC's "Graphic," as well as a program for CBC Open House with host Anna Cameron. However, on 22 June she found herself on the car ferry to Grand Manan. The island, which is less than 19 kilometres long, is located near the mouth of the Bay of Fundy, past Campobello Island. The residents' primary occupation was fishing and Helen hoped that the island's geographic isolation would enable her to collect folklore specific to the inhabitants. What she found instead was people living a life based around the traditional herring fishery, but with their feet firmly planted in modern society. In fact, the women working in the local herring factory were reluctant to speak with her lest they be portrayed—as they had been by another writer—as people who lived on nothing but herring and lived in houses perched on stilts. Helen discovered an island community with a diverse mixture of people—year-round residents mixed with summer artists and writers. She collected a sizeable body of research and eventually worked it into a monograph of folklore from Grand Manan, but it was never published.

Helen left Grand Manan at the end of July and returned home to tape her contribution to "Graphic's" show, which was titled *Land of the Old Songs*. The producers had travelled around Nova Scotia doing location shoots and now assembled a cast in the Halifax studio to finish their film. The format was simple. Helen was interviewed by host Ken Homer, and Joyce Sullivan and Ed McCurdy would sing songs from her collection. Helen came across as friendly but nervous, and the outdoor scenes interspersed between studio shots added to its regional flavour. In fact, when the program went to air on 2 August, *The Winnipeg Free Press* wrote, "Watching Land of the Old Songs was like sniffing a deep breath of salt air in the middle of the prairies. It was an enchanting, compelling, Canadian experience."[40]

With the taping of the television show finished, Helen went to Tatamagouche for the annual Arts Festival. She had been invited to give a talk and this time brought five singers to illustrate her songs: Ed McCurdy, Fred Redden, and his daughters Finvola, Maureen, and Lynn. Helen also asked Joyce Sullivan to sing a few songs. The response from the audience was very good, but later she learned that some of the local organizers were less than pleased because Helen had used some professional singers. Helen was very disappointed. Joyce Sullivan was a major Canadian television star who also happened to know many songs from Helen's collection, and Helen had asked her to sing because she was her favourite female artist.[41] The Arts Festival was not a showcase for tradition bearers, so Helen had thought the mix of the Reddens with Ed McCurdy and Joyce Sullivan would be a good combination.

Perhaps she was also anxious to show Finvola that a professional singer such as Joyce Sullivan could move in both worlds. She was concerned that Finvola was not happy in her music studies. Was it wrong to have encouraged Finvola's desire to study a vocal technique that was foreign to traditional singers? Finvola's teacher, Bernard Diamant, had certainly not made any attempt to turn her into something she was not. As he had written to Helen earlier in the year, "I don't want her sweet natural quality of her voice get to much involved in vocal technique and kind of tricks."[42] But Helen was concerned that Finvola might feel she was being pushed in a direction she wasn't comfortable with. In turn, Finvola had confided to Helen that she didn't believe that she possessed the great talent her mother seemed to think, and that she wasn't even sure that she wanted a career in music. She had written to Helen in the spring to tell her she wasn't going to study voice the following year, and added, "I have absolutely no regrets about any years of study I have learned many things ... What I will do or where I will go I do not know yet."[43] Helen wanted what was best for her young friend and acceded to her wishes. And perhaps Finvola's decision was for the best from a financial perspective as well. By July Helen had received a letter from the Nova Scotia Talent Trust advising her they were no longer able to fund Finvola's training.

The past two years had been long and difficult, but frequently rewarding. Helen needed a rest. She was mentally drained and her orthopaedic doctor had advised that the newly developed soreness in her right hand would only be relieved with a month to six weeks of rest. She willingly accepted the opportunity to relax.

# CHAPTER FIFTEEN

✳ ✳ ✳

Ever since her youth Helen had had to cope with the physical and emotional trauma that followed when she became overtired. Over the years she had learned that the best way for her to get through these difficult periods was to back off and rest as much as possible. She would prepare for strenuous events with extended bedrest, lying perfectly still and conserving her energy. The six-week recovery period needed to mend her hand gave her the opportunity to rejuvenate after two exhausting years. However, this didn't mean that she remained idle. Her manuscript of folk songs from the Maritime provinces had to be completed and sent off to the publisher, and she still had work to do on her collection of Gaelic songs. She was also entering her sixtieth decade, a time when many people think of slowing down their regular activities. Not so for Helen—if anything, the 1960s would be one of her most strenuous and productive times.

In January Helen and Finvola Redden travelled to Michigan State University to present a program at the Canadian-American Seminar. Their invitation came as the result of one of the organizers, Dr. Alvin. C. Gluek, seeing the film *Land of the Old Songs*. But Dr. Gluek was also interested in discussing the possibility of a joint publication of Helen's upcoming collection of songs from the Maritimes. Helen's Canadian publisher, Ryerson Press, was anxious to find a US publisher to give her more access to the American folklore market. At the same time Folkways Records wanted to bring out another collection of field recordings, so it was agreed by all parties that a simultaneous publication of book and record would be in the best interest of the three publishers—not to mention the author/collector. When they finished in Michigan Helen and Finvola moved on to Indiana University.

Helen had written her friend Richard Dorson and suggested that as they were so close, she and Finvola could be available for a concert and lecture. They promptly received an invitation. Helen found that her own work was still being studied and the National Film Board's *Songs of Nova Scotia* was being shown as an example of how a folklorist conducts field research. It would be interesting to know how some of the students to whom she lectured would have reacted to her advice on personal appearance when meeting an informant, as she later wrote: "One or two were dressed as beatniks, for it was that era, and they must have been surprised when I stated that a collector should never dress down while working; that informants are flattered when you arrive clean and neatly dressed and are therefore more prone to make friends."[1]

When she returned to Nova Scotia, Helen began a very different collecting season for the National Museum. As usual, part of her work involved seeking out various examples of folklore from informants, but this year it would also involve being paid for her time in preparing her manuscript of Gaelic songs for publication by the Museum. However, as she didn't "have the Gaelic" she had to find a co-worker who did. Once again her timing was just right. Calum MacLeod, a specialist in Celtic languages, was a Scottish-born graduate of Glasgow and Edinburgh Universities, and had recently been brought to Antigonish to teach at the Celtic Studies Program at St. Francis Xavier University. He agreed to take on the task of translating the Gaelic lyrics to English and provide the scholarly notes to accompany Helen's own comments on provenance and informants. Ken Peacock's musical transcriptions would provide the text for the melodies.

Calum MacLeod was, as Helen wrote in her autobiography, "a poet, piper, and scholar."[2] Between her collecting sessions and his teaching duties, they worked together at his home in Antigonish throughout June and much of July. Some of the songs had been in Helen's collection since she and Doreen Senior first went to Cape Breton almost 30 years before. But for Helen it was the first time she knew what many of the songs were about. She found the English translations from the Gaelic to have a poetic beauty not always found in English songs of a similar genre.

In mid June Helen took a break from working on her Gaelic songs. She flew to Toronto to attend the annual meeting of the Canadian Authors Association, where she had been invited to be the keynote speaker. She had been active in the Association since she joined in the 1930s, but was surprised when on the final day of the convention the current president, Don Thomson, asked if she would allow her name be put forward for the job in the upcoming election. Fortunately she didn't have to give an answer right away. She would need to discuss this offer with her supervisors at the National Museum and she needed time too to mull it over in her own head.

Between working with Calum MacLeod and attending the Canadian Authors Association meeting, Helen managed to squeeze in a little collecting. She put less emphasis on finding songs and more on other aspects of folklore. The primary reason for this was the shrinking existence of traditional singers. Radio and television had made their mark on the kinds of entertainment people had in their homes. Don Messer and His Islanders broadcast their own CBC television series out of Halifax and a new summer replacement show called "Singalong Jubilee"[3] was bringing American-style folk singing into vogue. Even the traditional singers were being influenced by the new media. A close listen to audio recordings of Edmund Henneberry produced 10 years apart illustrates how he developed more of a country and western twang to his interpretation of the traditional songs he had learned from his father. Contemporary folklorists look at this kind of neo-cultural assimilation as a natural progression of the tradition bearer's art. Helen simply viewed it as a loss. But every once in a while she would find a true original—a tradition bearer of the old school.

In July she went to Meat Cove at the tip of Cape Breton Island to record the bagpipe music of Rory MacKinnon. Mr. MacKinnon was a well respected traditional piper and knew many old melodies. He was also a good storyteller. But perhaps his most unique feature was that he made his own bagpipes. He made his chanter (the section with the finger holes) by reaming out a length of wood using an old bayonet. The foreleg bone of a steer was cut into circles to manufacture mounts, which would normally be made of ivory. The reeds were made from birch bark and cane.[4] It was a classic case of making do with what is at hand.

On the way back from recording with Rory MacKinnon, Helen stopped off at the Alexander Graham Bell Museum in Baddeck, where she met a friend who invited her to his home for coffee. There were several other guests there, including Jim Bennet, one of the hosts of the new television program, "Singalong Jubilee." Helen liked the way Jim sang folk songs. In fact, she had extolled his praises to Carmen Roy in 1958:

You asked about a singer in English for next year. At present Omar Blondahl is singing for five minutes on television every evening just before the news. One evening I thought I ought to listen, but was doing it from a distance and so was surprised to find him so good. Well, it was a substitute, one of the announcers who I think sings folk songs much better than Omar. He plays a guitar accompaniment, is young, and the son of a professor of English at Dalhousie University. I should think he could give a very nice programme if he had plenty of time to think about it, and I would do anything I can to help him and add to his repertoire.[5]

However, her attitude had changed towards Jim in the intervening years. The reason was "Singalong Jubilee": "Kept carefully off subject of Singalong Jubilee, although Jim asked how Finvola was getting along with her guitar. He may have found me a bit short in my replies, since CBC has not given her a chance. But this was no place for an argument."[6]

There was more to Helen's rancour than just Finvola's lack of work with the CBC. Jim Bennet was a staff announcer and had little, if anything, to do with who got to perform on television. In fact, Finvola and her father Fred would both be unsuccessful in their bids to be part of the program's cast known as The Jubilee Singers. What was really bothering Helen was the show's lack of regional content. She first saw the program on 10 July and made the following note in her diary:

In eve. foolishly watched Jubilee Singers from Hfx. Sang from U.S.A., Nfld., everywhere but N.S. So disloyal to province's heritage and discouraging to me. What use is it if our own people disregard it? Must not watch again, as can't sleep afterwards."[7] Years later, Helen recalled that moment in answer to a question of whether there was ever a time she thought of giving up her work. "Only once, I think ... and that was when Singalong Jubilee was singing the sort of folk songs that I was collecting and publishing, and completely ignoring them. I would come home ... and I would be tired and I'd rush to turn the [television] on to listen to their program and they would sing songs that I had published but it was not my variant, it would come from somewhere else, and I did have moments of despair. However ... that was the only time I really would have thrown it all up.[8]

"Singalong Jubilee" never did champion Helen's material. It was a national program and had to reflect a diversity of folk music. They never put an emphasis on regional, or even Canadian, content. In hindsight, they could have had access to one of the great folk song collections in the world, but because of their desire to promote good regional song writers and the program's aim to appeal to as broad an audience as possible, the producers never narrowed their musical options to one particular collection or region. However, in fairness to Helen, this was a new show and they could have at least looked to her collection for a few selections. When they did eventually look at her collection, they chose a song that would not only become the show's musical theme, but would help to make a star out of its featured female singer, Catherine McKinnon. The song was "The Nova Scotia Song," more commonly known as "Farewell to Nova Scotia." In 1963 the producer, Manny Pittson, wrote Helen, "I was gratified to learn that our efforts pleased you and, for that reason, I am forwarding a tape of that song, along with "The Cherry Tree Carol." The later, Miss McKinnon will sing on our Christmas Day show."[9]

Helen's summers had by now developed somewhat of a routine. She made her usual visit to the Festival of the Arts in Tatamagouche and then proceeded to New Brunswick for the Miramichi Folk Song Festival. Escorting her to the events that year were her friends Alan and Bernie Mills, and at the Folk Song Festival she was joined by Dr. Russell from the National Museum. It gave her the opportunity to speak to her boss about the possibility of her taking on the role of president of the Canadian Authors Association. His response, as recorded in her diary,

*Laval University, taken before Helen received her honorary degree, 1961. Dr. B.H. Bronson, Helen Creighton, Francois Brassard, Maud Karpeles, Maurice Roy, Marius Barbeau, Louis A Vachon, Claudia Marcel-Dubois.*

was positive: "said at once to take it, as they like to think nationally."[10] There was more to her diary entry that day. She also wrote with great excitement that "Laval is to give me honorary degree. Letter beautifully expressed, and I so excited, showed it to everybody.... What a time to receive it, at an international conference."[11] The letter she received from Laval University in Quebec expressed their wish to bestow an honorary degree of Doctor of Letters. The reasons cited by the university authorities included "a testimony of their high esteem and to emphasize your brilliant achievements in the field of Folklore."[12]

This was a major feather in an already distinguished cap. Helen and her colleagues in the Canadian Folk Music Society had been working on the plans for the International Folk Music Council's meeting in Quebec since 1959. Helen had arranged for Calum MacLeod to bring a group of Gaelic singers and Cape Breton dancers and musicians to be part of the regional representation from tradition bearers that Helen had fought so hard to have represented. They even orchestrated an old-fashioned milling frolic where homespun cloth was fulled by beating it on a table while the workers sang traditional Gaelic songs. To top it all off, she was being honoured by her peers before the eyes of the international folklore community. On 1 September she stepped onto the podium and proudly accepted her second honorary degree.

Back at home she completed her fragmented collecting season and then recorded the voice-over for an animated short film based on one of her ghost tales. Produced by CBC Halifax staff artist Henry Orenstein, with script development by his wife, Joan Orenstein, it was an avant-garde animation in black and white called *The Box*.

In 1962 Helen released three publications. *Maritime Folk Songs* [13] was published jointly by Ryerson Press and Michigan State University Press. The book didn't contain the range of scholarly notes of some of her previous work, but placed an emphasis on the music as transcribed by Kenneth Peacock. His preface illustrates how highly he regarded some of the tunes: "With so much third-rate folkmusic bombarding us from mass media, it is refreshing to find so much quality in so small a package. Dr. Creighton is to be congratulated not only for her tireless efforts to save this material but for her perspicacity in bringing only the best of it to public attention." [14] But the publication wasn't intended to be elitist and it included piano or guitar chords so that budding folk singers could add these new old-time songs to their repertoire.

However, this emphasis on the technical aspect of the music did not please everyone. *The Fredericton Gleaner* claimed that "Mr. Peacock's foreword about the music in the book is perhaps too technical for the average reader. Certainly it would mean nothing to the people who have sung and preserved these songs over the years. It is however, a valuable part of the book for the serious collector ... interesting and valuable addition to anyone's music library." [15] And The Vancouver Sun was even more critical: "Unfortunately, nearly one fifth of the songs are textually incomplete, or so corrupt as to be useless to performers. The singer, trying to learn the songs in this book, will be baffled at times by grotesque textual errors which seem to result from thoughtless transcription of field recordings. On the whole, though, this book will be of lasting interest and of considerable use to the music-lover." [16]

The criticisms revealed a classic misunderstanding of what Helen and her publishers were trying to do. She had been censured in the past for not making the music more accessible to the amateur musician, so they added piano and guitar chords but still retained the analytical notations important to trained musicians. Raymond Hull, the reviewer for *The Vancouver Sun*, missed the point entirely when he suggested that the songs were incomplete. Helen transcribed the lyrics as they were presented to her, neither adding nor removing words, regardless of how obscure they might seem. To alter the text in any way would be poor scholarship. It seemed she was being damned if she did and damned if she didn't.

As an adjunct to *Maritime Folk Songs* Folkways Records released another collection of Helen's field recordings. It too was titled *Maritime Folk Songs*[17] and featured an eclectic mix of songs from Anglo-Saxon,

Acadian, Celtic, and African-Nova Scotian sources, which illustrated the diversity of Helen's collecting work. Folkways Records were an excellent source for field recordings. Their albums frequently provided the only way modern folk singers could hear tradition bearers. But the operation was run on a shoestring budget and at 25 cents a copy for each record sold, Helen couldn't expect to get rich on the deal.

Her third publication in 1961 was co-authored with Edward D. (Sandy) Ives, whom she'd first met at the Miramichi Folk Song Festival three years earlier. Sandy was a true folklore scholar and he and Helen published a few of the folk tales they had collected in New Brunswick in a small book called *Eight Folk Tales from Miramichi.*[18]

With the release of a new long-playing record and two books, Helen's list of publications was expanding rapidly. *Bluenose Ghosts* was a consistent seller and her other publications had earned her nationwide recognition.[19] She was a natural choice for the role of president of the Canadian Authors Association. Having given the suggestion more thought, she was ready to accept the job if elected at the upcoming annual meeting. But it was more than her work as a writer that led the Association to offer Helen the position. She had a reputation as a tireless worker and someone who could get the job done. She also enjoyed a high national profile, which the Association hoped to make use of. In July she travelled to Edmonton and was elected to a two-year term. Her election carried with it the responsibility of visiting each local branch at least once during her tenure and it would prove to consume an enormous amount of her time. Although Helen's new job had received the blessing of the National Museum's director, over the next two years her work for them would be so limited that their relations strained to the point of breaking.

Despite her hectic schedule she tried to collect whenever she could. Later that summer she returned to Prince Edward Island and spent most of her time looking for material at the western tip of the province. It was mid August and, not having any great leads on informants, she decided to visit the local Saturday fair being held outside the Legion Hall at Tignish. A small truck drove up and a correspondingly petite woman stepped out. She introduced herself as Mrs. Hector Richard. In typically friendly Island fashion, she struck up a conversation and when Helen asked if she knew any singers, her new acquaintance replied, "my husband if he is in good humour."[20]

The next day Helen drove to their tiny home. Hector Richard was indeed in good humour and Helen recorded several Acadian songs from him and his wife, who also played the fiddle. Helen was pleased with her day; it was tripping along smoothly and she was getting some unique old French songs. But experience had taught her that Sunday wasn't always the best day to collect from informants living in the country, being the traditional day for drop-in visits from family and friends. And that's exactly what happened. A car pulled into the Richard's driveway and five young men staggered out. They had been drinking—one was in such rough shape that he had to be carried into the house, where he sat beside Mr. Richard with his head on his shoulder. Helen later re-called that "what interested me was that no remark or apology was made. I never knew whether this was a son of the house or a friend, but immediately after this interruption singing was resumed. Unknown to Mr. Richard, the young man's snorts can be heard on the ... record-ings, although not recognizable as such unless you knew the circum-stances. Was it a sense of loyalty that made them so protective? No fuss, just a dignified acceptance of the situation. The Island can be proud of them."[21]

This was not an isolated event. Helen had encountered similar inci-dents several times before. She was a stranger in their home and, per-haps because the Richards were embarrassed, they offered no explana-tion. Some 30 years later, at the respective ages of 89 and 85, Mr. and Mrs. Richard spoke of Helen's visit fondly, Mrs. Richard remarking, "She was a lovely person, yes she was."[22]

But for Helen, it was a pivotal moment. She remembered thinking at the time, "What a way to spend a nice Sunday afternoon."[23] The Richards had shown her the usual warm Maritime hospitality and weren't to blame for the appearance of the youths. And while Helen had been in similar circumstances before, she was tired of the chase. She had been collecting folklore for 34 of her 63 years. She had nothing more to prove as a collector and her position at the Museum was now being treated as a formality. She needed a change. The Richards were the last informants she would visit.

# CHAPTER SIXTEEN

*** ***

elen's life changed dramatically over the next two years. She was now National President of the 900-member Canadian Authors Association and the first woman to hold the office for almost 20 years. Much of that first year was taken up with work directly for the Association and she found herself travelling from one city to the next, chairing meetings and speaking out on the organization's concerns. In Ottawa at the Annual General Meeting, she castigated the Canada Council for refusing to fund the Association's official magazine, *Canadian Author and Bookman*, saying, "I am bewildered, for it seems a very foolish country that refuses to foster its authors."[1] She spoke out in defence of government subsidies for developing Canadian writers, telling *The Victoria Daily Times*, "I believe authors write better and more deeply when they are relieved of immediate financial care and anxiety."[2] She didn't clarify whether this was simply her personal opinion or if she was speaking on behalf of the Canadian Authors Association. But state funding for the arts has always been a bone of contention with the general public and her remarks must not have been popular with many readers.

Later in the year she would face even more public controversy. As the spokesperson for the Association she received national exposure for something that began as an innocent contest to change a song.

Canada was anticipating its centennial celebrations in four years time and people had already begun to look for projects that would reflect— or at least try and identify—the Canadian cultural identity. For an older Anglo-based generation one of the keys to national identity had been the song "The Maple Leaf Forever," composed in the year of Canada's birth, 1867, by Alexander Muir, a Scottish-born school principal in Toronto. For years English Canadian school children had stood at attention and sang this ode to the brave General Wolf, who fought the decisive battle on the Plains of Abraham in Quebec and united the country under the unifying symbol of a maple leaf. But given the political climate in a nation that was attempting to move towards bilingual symbiosis, the song had gone out of favour. In any case, for obvious reasons it had never been popular in French Canada. And so it was that Gordon V. Thompson approached the Canadian Authors Association to organize a contest to find new, more politically sensitive lyrics. His publishing company would put forward a prize of $1,000 and publish the winning entry. The judges would be Dr. Roy Fenwick, Sir Ernest MacMillan, Alan Sangster, Helmut Blume, and Helen.

There were more than 1,200 legitimate entries and dozens of lampoons from the press, who seized upon the contest with zeal. *The Globe and Mail's* Maggie Grant suggested the dandelion replace the maple leaf as Canada's floral emblem, while writer Bruce West recommended that Canadians learn the newest dance craze, "The Maple Leaf Twist."[3] A few days later the paper ran an interview with Helen, who defended the contest by saying, "Times have changed. The maple leaf remains our emblem, but no one sings the old lyrics any more."[4]

*Helen Creighton, in full make-up for television appearance on Front Page Challenge, Toronto, February, 1964.*

Helen Creighton Fonds, PANS Binder 18:1082. Photographer: unknown

But not all of the response to the contest was lighthearted. Some people saw no need to change the lyrics and at least one organization, the Alexander Muir Old Girls Association, voiced strong opposition to the contest: "Surely the Canadian Authors Association can find a more suitable project with which to approach the Confederation Centennial than the emasculation of this old song which nears its own centennial."[5]

The crowning moment in all the press hoopla came with an appearance by Helen on the popular television show "Front Page Challenge." The program featured well-known Canadian newspaper columnists as panel members who tried to identify the topical headline or subject matter in question by asking a mystery guest a series of questions. Helen was invited to represent the Authors Association and the song contest. She flew to Toronto and pre-taped the program. Her old acquaintance from *Maclean's*, Pierre Berton, guessed the topic just before the buzzer rang, and then sang his own revised version of "The Maple Leaf Forever." Helen watched the broadcast later at home. She was pleased with the national exposure for the song contest, but thought that her personal appearance had been greatly altered by the heavy makeup and bouffant hairstyle given her by the CBC makeup department. In fact, she wrote in her diary, "Mrs. Moore, my char said, 'If I didn't know you were going to be on I wouldn't have known you, you looked so lovely'."[6]

From a promotional point of view, the Canadian Authors Association couldn't have invented a better press opportunity. The song contest had put them in the limelight for several months and Helen's personal recognition factor was greatly increased. The contest was eventually won by an Ottawa printer named Victor Cowley. His new lyrics made no reference to any ethnic group or particular ancestry, but they did mention the Queen. Neither the old song nor the revised-text version is popular today.

Along with her Association work Helen had taken on a new folklore project. An old friend from her Indiana University days, Dr. Wayland Hand, was trying to compile a continent-wide dictionary of popular beliefs and superstitions. He suggested that Helen work on a Nova Scotian version, which could later be incorporated into the larger project. Helen discussed the project with her Museum supervisor and got the green light to make it part of her work-term session for them. However, she didn't want the National Museum to publish the project, explaining her reasons in a letter to Carmen Roy: "Yes, of course, the entire credit will be given to the National Museum. After the manuscript has been approved by you and the Director, I would however ask that I may have it published privately. Ryersons are anxious to do it, and I need any royalties I may receive from it. Since I am not pensionable, I must provide as best I can for the future."[7]

Helen was nearing retirement age and was trying to secure some sort of financial stability. She received no royalties from her publications through the National Museum and, even worse, she found herself in a constant battle to receive her contracted salary. In September 1963 she wrote to Jeanne Monette, an assistant to Carmen in the Canadian Centre for Folk Culture Studies: "My work for the Museum and the Authors is suffering from the delay with my salary cheques. Mr. Russell has assured me that he is attending to it, but the days and weeks go on, and how is one supposed to live? I know this is not your field of worry, but if the spark has gone out of my work it is due to this uncalled for strain. I hope they will soon get it settled, because if they don't, I feel I shall be ill."[8]

By October she still hadn't received satisfaction. She got a raise—but no money. In frustration, she wrote Carmen, "I understand that from today my rate of pay has been raised from six to twenty dollars. I know they have been working on that, but has it gone through?"[9] By November her frustration had been replaced with desperation:

Every time something comes from the Museum about my position there I say, "Hooray, it's all nicely settled now;" then I go out and make some extravagant purchase, and in a few days realize I'm no further ahead than I was before. Now, though, it looks as though the difficulties might be over ... I suppose this means I will receive no money until some time in January. What a shocking way to treat an employee after 17 years of service as I have rendered. I realize, of course, that this is none of your doing ... Tres affectuessant à vous, cher Carmen.[10]

Perhaps the financial difficulties Helen encountered with the Museum stemmed from continuing problems within Museum management. In the fall of 1963 *The Ottawa Citizen* reported on the desperate situation: "In 1963 four of the five directors of the "National Museum of Canada resigned, citing dissatisfaction with aspects of government policy as laid down for the [proposed new] museum."[11]

But the more logical explanation is that the Museum had not budgeted for Helen's salary. When Dr. Russell approved Helen's acceptance of the presidency of the Canadian Authors Association, he had also assured her that the Museum would continue to honour its financial commitment to her, even though she was no longer really doing field research. This put Carmen Roy in a difficult situation:

If everybody is managing with one of my Museum Advisors or contractors, I lose control and give up. This is what happened in your case when Dr. Russell accepted that you give a lot of lectures, going in the west, being President of Canadian Authors, etc., I knew that in paying you (salary and part of the expenses) for going to Edmonton, etc., would put us short of money at the end of the fiscal year.... You see, Helen, I have Museum Advisers here in our Department; if one is sick or loses a day or half a day of work, the Administration cuts the salary. For Museum Advisors in the field, they always told me that it should be the same.[12]

Helen responded by forwarding a copy of the letter she had received from Dr. Russell two years before. He had written: "At this time I merely want to go on record as approving the idea of you accepting the office of President of the Canadian Authors' Association. This is an important honour and the Museum should benefit by its privilege of having the holder of the office associated with us."[13]

Did Helen interpret his letter incorrectly? Had Dr. Russell given her the blessing of the Museum but expected her to find alternative funding? Probably not. Helen was too dependent on her Museum salary not to have questioned him thoroughly when they first discussed the matter in person at the Miramichi Folk Song Festival. At any rate, she emphasized her point to Carmen by adding, "when things like this come to you from the highest level, you expect them to be honoured. I quite agree that when Dr. Russell encouraged me in these matters he should have made financial provisions and not left the rest of you in an embarrassing position. Nor should I, having been encouraged to accept these heavy outside responsibilities, suddenly find myself subject to financial worry."[14]

Helen eventually did receive her back pay early in 1964. She continued with her busy schedule for the Association, travelling across the country, including a trip to Newfoundland in March to launch their provincial branch. She also took a brief vacation in England to see Mac and to return a visit to Mac's son Peter and his family, who had stayed with her the previous summer.

In April she was relieved to hear that the Museum would continue to fund her involvement with the Association and her ongoing work preparing her manuscript of popular beliefs and superstitions. Her pay scale was $15 per day for 192 working days, for a total fee of $2,880. On top of this she could claim $10 per day for room and board and up to 2,000 miles of travel to be reimbursed at the rate of 10 cents a mile.[15]

Helen relinquished the presidency of the Canadian Authors Association at the annual meeting held in Halifax that June. She had served the membership well. She had successfully manoeuvred through the media circus surrounding the song contest and had been a vocal advocate for arts funding. She later wrote: "I would like to be remembered as an inspiring president, but have been cited for my success with public relations. Perhaps that is not so different after all."[16]

With the Association convention over and the reins handed over to the new president, Helen turned to face her task of compiling her popular beliefs and superstitions manuscript with renewed zeal. But only a week later she was presented with one of the biggest hurdles of her life. She was diagnosed with breast cancer. Strangely enough, the diagnosis didn't come as a complete surprise. She believed that she'd received a forewarning. She had been writing out a cheque to send to Sandy Ives for her Northeast Folklore Society dues when she remembered that she would be seeing him in August at the Miramichi Folk Song Festival. But something told her to go ahead and send the cheque: "a voice inside me objected and said, 'You won't be alive by then' ... I knew then that something bad in a physical sense would happen before the middle of August."[17]

From an early age, Helen had great faith in her own intuition. How else could she explain why she had ducked under the bed covers just seconds before the Halifax Explosion sent shattered glass flying on to her pillow? As she collected—and tried to understand—tales of the supernatural shared by her informants, she began to pay closer attention to what she perceived as an affinity with the unexplained in her own life.

In 1952, after her cousin's funeral in Wolfville, she wrote in her diary, "Just after the service when the others were leaving the room, my wreath fell down. An omen, or had it become dislodged in moving?

Wouldn't have thought about it if a figure of death hadn't appeared on my sitting room window in February, etched on pane in no way that I can possibly describe."[18]

Helen believed strongly in the power of prayer and positive thinking. In the 1950s she suffered from neuralgia in her left cheek. While visiting her friends, the Reverend Kennedy Wainwright and his wife, she complained of her condition, and Mrs. Wainwright suggested that her husband lay his hands on Helen's face. She later noted the incident in her autobiography: "He did this and, I suppose, said a short prayer. The pain didn't stop immediately but began shortly afterwards to decrease, and in a week or two it was gone. A few years later it returned so I asked him to do it again.... The pain failed to develop further, and I've never had it since."[19] Helen was fascinated to think someone might have healing powers. She asked Kennedy Wainwright's brother, the Reverend Hastings Wainwright, whether he could explain his brother's ability.[20] No one was able to offer her an explanation. She told me that she thought she might have been able to develop her own capacity for healing. On one occasion, when her tenants Peggy and Stan Wood were living at Evergreen with their two children, the little boy fell and struck his head. Helen and the Stan prayed very hard and projected a great deal of "positive thought" into his recovery. Helen passed her hands over the boy's forehead, later saying that she felt it just might have helped, adding, "We will never know."[21]

She never did try to develop her healing energies. Most of her supernatural experiences came about involuntarily— she rarely sought them until later in life. In 1960 she wrote to Carmen Roy about an incident in which she believed her late father had visited her:

I had gone to a side wall in my sitting room where a picture of him, is hanging, but he was far from my thoughts. I leaned over to place something on the floor and whether I heard a sound or what forced me to look up I can't say. Anyhow it was as though the electricity were switched on and I found myself looking straight at his picture, but it was framed in a filmy cloud about four or five inches thick and in an oval shape. Then as suddenly it was as if the switch had been turned off and everything was normal, but I felt I had made contact with my father.... It was not something I imagined, but was as real as it was unexpected.[22]

During the last years of her life, Helen tried to communicate with the spirit of her brother Mac. She once accompanied her niece, Terry Harnish, to consult a psychic named Tehuella.[23] The psychic advised Helen to post a chalkboard up in her apartment, saying that Mac would communicate with her through this medium. I remember seeing the chalkboard in Helen's kitchen, and once asked her if she had ever had any messages from Mac. The answer was no.[24]

She was not necessarily interested in the sensational aspect of the unexplained. She merely tried to keep an open mind when feelings she couldn't understand came her way. This was the case with her premonition that she might not be alive to see Sandy Ives at the upcoming festival at Miramichi. It wasn't the first time she'd had such an experience. A few years earlier, en route from Dartmouth to Newcastle to attend the Festival, she had stopped in Sackville to rest overnight at the Marshlands Inn. Waking from an evening nap, she saw an amazing vision. It was herself, as a child of 10, walking towards her with an expression of welcome. She put up her hands to push the vision away. It faded and then reappeared, fainter this time. Again she pushed the vision away and it appeared one more time, more faintly still. Helen tried to put the incident out of her mind and went downstairs to join the other guests for hot chocolate. After a while she returned to her room and enjoyed a restful sleep.

She remembered the incident the next morning and it began to bother her. She felt the vision had been some kind of warning and that she should drive with extra caution. The road from Sackville to Newcastle passes through some heavily wooded areas and in one of these sections a deer leaped out in front of her car. Realizing that she was going to hit it, and believing her fate was in God's hands, she took her hands off the steering wheel. She felt the deer hit and then the car rolled to a gentle stop. The deer was nowhere in sight and the right headlight was broken, but as no other damage was apparent she drove on, shaken yet relieved.

She was later told that the vision she experienced is known as a doppelganger (from the German for double-goer)—a non-physical double. Because she had seen herself as a child rather than an adult, it meant she was being warned not of her death, but of an accident.

Just as Helen had faith in the power of positive thinking, she set great store in premonitions. When the message came from her doppelganger— and then the one in March suggesting that she wouldn't be alive in August—she heeded their warnings. The doppelganger had warned her of danger. The March incident foretold possible death—a malignant growth in her breast. She had faith in the possibility of recovery but also prepared for the worse.

She submitted her season-end report early to the National Museum:

During the past few months I have probably worked harder than I have ever done, alternating between my time between typing notes for my book of Popular Beliefs and Superstitions, and preparing and carrying out the duties of national president of the Canadian Authors Association, both of which projects have been approved by the Museum.

Indeed, I have worked full time and over. Since I expect within the next week or two to undergo a major operation, I would like to report also for July. While awaiting hospitalization I am making the most of every possible moment and getting as much work done as I can. Although my condition is thought to be serious, I am feeling very well, so I have been able to carry on in a normal fashion. It is possible that I may be about again in two weeks but that is unlikely; the expectation is that it will be from six to eight weeks. I would appreciate receiving my salary for June at the earliest possible moment, it has been well earned.[25]

Helen entered the Victoria General Hospital in Halifax to undergo preoperative tests. As she lay in her hospital bed she envisioned her doppelganger again. This time she saw herself as she had been in her late thirties. She was holding a board at waist height and paddling through water, making slow but steady progress. She later described the vision in her autobiography, writing, "The important thing was that I paid no attention to myself but passed by without so much as a glance. 'I've had a reprieve,' I thought, and so it turned out."[26]

On 20 July Helen's brother Terry wrote to Jeanne Monette at the National Museum.

"My sister, Dr. Helen Creighton, asked me to write to you. She had a successful operation this morning. Dr. Ross did a 'radical,' i.e. he removed as much of the breast as possible, and although it was malignant he assures me that with treatment she will be all right."[27]

Helen set herself to the task of getting better with her usual determination. She was glad that her responsibilities with the Authors Association were over, and was pragmatic in setting aside her manuscript of popular beliefs and superstitions. Her family and friends gave her tremendous support. She also had the empathy of Carmen Roy, who had been absent when Terry wrote her of Helen's operation. The moment she received it she wrote to Helen: "Only upon my return at the Museum, I have heard of your sickness. I have been so sad that I nearly became sick myself.... It is not only my friendship who makes me sad, it is also because I have known these experiences the last year. ... love, Carmen."[28]

Helen immediately replied with reassuring confidence: "It was a grim experience, particularly as I'd had a forewarning last March and thought the end was near. Perhaps on that account I acted very quickly when I realized a lump had grown and then in the hospital I had another vision which told me I'd had a reprieve and would get better. Being a folklorist has its advantages sometimes. However the main thing is that the growth hasn't spread and, as long as I don't overdo, I should be all right."[29]

Helen's radical mastectomy resulted in a positive prognosis. And in the midst of it she was greatly cheered by the Museum's publication of the book she and Calum MacLeod had co-authored. *Gaelic Songs in Nova Scotia*[30] contained 93 Gaelic songs with English translations. The text was interspersed with photographs from Helen's personal collection and promotional tourist images provided by the Nova Scotia Information Service.

Reviews were mixed. Helen's contribution received the most favourable mentions. *Canadian Poetry* noted that "although she could not understand the Gaelic, she took meticulous care to record and preserve. All honour to her for it."[31] However, Kenneth Peacock's music transcriptions were occasionally questioned. In a review for *Folk Music Journal*, the voice of The English Folk Dance and Song Society, Ethel Bassin pointed out over 30 errors in timing, but added, "there is interesting material in this volume ... the printing of them requires better editing."[32] Her comments perhaps reflect a bias against "colonial" writers presuming to interpret songs originally from the old country. For indeed, how could Ethel Bassin possible have recognized timing errors without having heard the original recordings? Differences, maybe, but errors—no. Calum Macleod cautioned Helen that the Scottish scholars might have their daggers out for them: "I am not too concerned about the reviews we may receive from Scotland as there is only one Celtic Scholar there now who knows what is available .... I have every suspicion, however, that when the School of Scottish Studies, Edinburgh University, see our collection, they will make haste to send a professional collector over here. This, in my opinion, would be rather unfortunate."[33]

Helen took it relatively easy in 1965. She continued her work on her beliefs and superstitions manuscript, but was again frustrated when her Museum salary failed to appear on time. In May she wrote a cynical letter to Carmen Roy: "Years ago I taught school for six months in Mexico and at the end of every month I had to take a large square cloth to school for my money which was paid in silver dollars. Perhaps that is how my two months salary is coming from the Museum, for it hasn't appeared yet. Hope springs eternal, and perhaps the mail will have it on Monday."[34]

In fairness, it was likely that the delay in Helen's funding was due to her own indecision over her next research project. Things had changed drastically since the days of ad hoc administration, when Helen would be paid to go out in the field and collect whatever caught her fancy. The Museum now required a formal proposal with a definite design. Helen did say that she wanted to work with the Museum to develop the "Men of the Deeps", a new chorus composed of working, or retired, miners from Cape Breton. Earlier in the year Nina Cohen had approached Helen for her assistance in getting the project off the ground. The chorus was created in association with The Glace Bay Miners' Museum, Cape Breton's contribution to Canada's upcoming

*Helen Creighton filming Lady of the Legends for CBC Telescope at Evergreen, 1967.*

centennial celebrations. Helen had a good selection of coal mining songs to offer the chorus, and submitted this as her Museum project. Carmen was less than enthused: "As far as your project ... is concerned, I am not enthusiastic at all. Furthermore, I do not understand why you change your mind so often. I told you in my last letter that I needed as soon as possible a straight project to put it in my estimates. I cannot leave for the field unless these estimates are finished. You hold me at my desk in not answering clearly."[35] Eventually Helen would help to make the "Men of the Deeps" a reality, but not with funding from the National Museum.

In the spring of 1966 she received a telephone call from CBC Toronto producer Glen Sarty, who offered her an exciting new project. Originally from Nova Scotia, he had conceived an idea for filming excerpts from *Bluenose Ghosts*. He wanted to use the original storytellers wherever possible, or at least to film in those areas where the stories originated. He asked Helen to weave the stories together on camera. The film would be part of the CBC "Telescope" series and be called *Lady of the Legends.*

This was just pick-me-up Helen needed. She would be able to visit several of her former collecting areas and get reacquainted with a few of her old informants. The early summer found her and the film crew visiting Eastern Passage, where the Hartlen property had been turned into a golf course. They went to Devil's Island and Helen's old memories came rushing back. So much had changed over the years, but nevertheless there was a comforting familiarity about it all. But there were also surprises.

On their first day of shooting they travelled to Petpeswick to film Freeman Young, one of Helen's original informants for "The Nova Scotia Song." The director set Freeman up in the door of a fish shed and filmed him singing the song he had first sung for Helen some 30 years earlier. But he added a new twist. Traditional singers never repeated the last line of a song; they might speak the last few words, but never added a coda. Freeman surprised Helen by singing the last line twice. After filming was over she said to him, "Now Free, you didn't sing it like that when I was here years ago." Freeman answered, "No, but that's the way I heard 'Cathleen' McKinnon sing it on the television, so it must be right."[36] Catherine McKinnon had been closing every "Singalong Jubilee" program with the song and it had become Nova Scotia's unofficial anthem.[37] People everywhere, including Freeman, were singing it the new way. Helen later commented: "Freeman at ninety could still acquire new tricks."[38]

And at age 66, Helen too could acquire new tricks—or at least new recognitions. She was delighted when the Dartmouth Kiwanis Club invited her to be their Citizen of the Year. This was an especially sweet honour, as it came from her birthplace.

Aside from her work on the film, most of Helen's time was spent on preparing her book on the supernatural. There was no shortage of material. She had always collected examples of supernatural experiences and popular beliefs, but since the publication of *Bluenose Ghosts*, people were even more willing to share their stories. In assembling the thousands of items in her collection, Helen included several experiences of her own. Carmen Roy wanted her to exclude these. Current methodology of folklore analysis frowned upon inclusion of the collector's personal data on the grounds of objectivity. But Helen fought to keep them in:

Here now we come to what I consider one of the most important features of this book. I am not writing of them, the People from Nova Scotia, but US, We People of Nova Scotia, and I think Wayland must have had this in mind when he extended his invitation. After all, I am 6th generation on both sides of my family, and the beliefs I give as my own are not made up by me, but are part of my inheritance as a native of this province. This, I feel, takes this out of the realm of being just another compilation of beliefs and superstitions, but part of life shared by the collector. Why can I not serve the dual role of collector and informant when I have so much to offer? And why should my traditional beliefs not have their place as well as those of any other inhabitant?

They cannot possibly distract from the book's scholarship and they certainly add to its authenticity and worth. That, at least, is my impression. Otherwise anybody could write the book providing they had a file of index cards. Take that away and you remove the soul.[39]

Carmen was only trying to get Helen to work according to accepted scholarly standards. Helen realized this and over the course of the year came around to a closer understanding of what should be included in the finished manuscript. By September she was able to write to Carmen, "It wasn't easy for you to point out all the defects in my manuscript last spring, but I can see now how right you were."[40] She still included some of her own personal items, but placed less emphasis on their importance in the collection as a whole. However, the conflict over the manuscript wasn't finished yet.

Helen still wanted to have an outside publisher handle the book. She presented her argument for outside publication to Carmen in December. "When we discussed with Dr. Glover ... the writing of this book [we] also talked about a commercial publisher for it. ... [Publishing] ... with the Queen's Printer leaves much to be desired ... of course there are no royalties. Song books published with the melody don't make much money. Bluenose Ghosts on the other hand is still doing well and sold 600 copies in the last six months.... I am probably more surprised than anybody, and the royalties have made it possible for me to enjoy things that my Museum salary would never permit."[41]

It was becoming obvious to all parties that Helen's relationship with the National Museum was on shaky ground. Carmen had never liked the fact that for a number of years Helen had been given special privileges over other field researchers. In turn, Helen was uncomfortable being attached to an institution that kept going through administrative turmoil. Moreover, the ongoing struggles over her funding had caused her considerable financial anxiety for the past several years. The money she did receive for a season amounted to less that $3,000. She was especially discouraged when she discovered that she was earning less than the janitor at the Museum.[42]

However, her overall financial situation had improved in recent times. She was receiving small royalties from several publications; fees to speaking engagements were becoming more common; she had signed a contract for her book on beliefs and superstitions; and in 1965 the National Old Age Security Act lowered the pension eligibility from 70 to 65, qualifying Helen for a monthly cheque of $75. It was time to sever the ties of two decades. On 31 January 1967 Helen wrote to her friend Carmen Roy, "Today brings me to the end of twenty years with the Museum."[43]

# CHAPTER SEVENTEEN

### ✳ ✳ ✳

H elen couldn't have chosen a better time to make a new start. If she thought she might be left floundering after 20 years with the National Museum, the events of the following 12 months would certainly prove otherwise. In 1967 Canada was celebrating 100 years as a nation and the entire country was caught up in centennial fervour. It was a time for new beginnings. There was a tremendous buzz of optimism in the air. Canadians might be marking their past, but their eyes were firmly fixed on the future. The World's Fair at Expo '67 in Montreal attracted global attention. All over the country people and organizations were holding their own celebratory events and Helen was involved—directly or indirectly—with quite a number of them. She began in February by telling the graduating students at Queen Elizabeth High School in Halifax, "I place Canada's future in your hands."[1] Later in the year another group of students, this time from Dartmouth High School, would take a production of the *The Broken Ring* to Expo '67.

In May Helen returned to the University of King's College, where she had served as Dean of Women from 1939 to 1941. She was now receiving an honorary Doctorate of Civil Law. She also accepted a two-year position on the college's board of governors. Later in the year she was the first woman to be honoured as a fellow of King's Haliburton Society, Canada's oldest literary group.

In June she flew to Vancouver to chair a conference of the Canadian Folk Music Society. To commemorate Canada's centennial the Society sponsored an International Workshop on Ethnomusicology at the University of British Columbia. As the Society's vice-president, Helen chaired the conference in addition to presenting a paper on her work with Nova Scotia's Mi'kmaq music. As the chair of the Society's scholarly committee, she was also able to instigate an important research project. She secured a grant enabling social worker and folk song interpreter Marvin Burke to collect material from African-Nova Scotian informants. Mr. Burke's perhaps most significant recordings were made at the final Easter Sunday Sunrise Service held on 21 May at the Seaview United Baptist Church in Africville, a black community just outside of Halifax. Several months later the church was bulldozed into the ground and the community's inhabitants were relocated, marking one of Canada's most blatant incidents of institutionalized racism.[2]

In the summer Helen found herself once more in front of the television cameras. The producer of her last television film, Glen Sarty, was now in charge of "Take Thirty," a national afternoon show hosted by Paul Soles. Glen had extra footage left over from *Lady of the Legends* and considered that this surplus stock, supplemented by a few new scenes between Paul and Helen, would make a good program. The additional scenes were shot at Evergreen and at Eastern Passage, where she had begun her "path of destiny" almost 40 years earlier.

Helen continued her involvement with Centennial Year by making a November speaking tour to the Universities of Saskatchewan, Alberta, Winnipeg, and Manitoba. The tour was sponsored by Canada's Centennial Commission and the Association of Universities and Colleges in Canada. The year ended with a bang when in December she received the Centennial Medal, a special one-time honour given to Canadians who had made significant contributions to their country. Her first year away from the National Museum had been full and rewarding, but her contributions to the study of Canadian folklore were far from over.

In 1968 Helen's book on popular beliefs and superstitions was published. She had won her final debate with the National Museum, and her manuscript was published by Ryerson Press. They had worked closely with her in their efforts to come up with a catchy title that would appeal more to a general readership than simply folklore scholars. Since *Bluenose Ghosts* was still a good seller, they decided to piggyback on its popularity and call the new book *Bluenose Magic: Popular Beliefs and Superstitions in Nova Scotia.*[3] Although it contained many stories of ghosts and supernatural happenings, it was really a listing of beliefs and superstitions and didn't have the popular appeal of Helen's previous "Bluenose" book. Still, the reviews were favourable; the *Montreal Star* praised it as "a substantial contribution to the serious literature of folklore ... For the casual reader with a taste for the unusual and different, it should be rewarding."[4]

Although she didn't identify them as such, Helen did incorporate some of her own family lore about superstitions, remedies, and folk sayings in *Bluenose Magic*. Her personal interest and attachment to paranormal activities increased as the years went on. She frequently looked for signs that might give her direction when faced with a new venture. But her leanings towards believing in the paranormal were always based on the principles she grew up with under the teachings of the Christian church. For example, in 1956 she received a premonition of a friend's death: "Heard 3 death knocks which agitated me greatly, much more than 3 unexplained knocks should. Happened at 5 to 12, the time Cecil Sircom died. He must have been trying to get through to me.... Don't know when I've been so disturbed. As Rev. Martell said, 'That proves there is an affinity between this world and the next'."[5] A few years later she saw the image of her late friend, Stanley Walker, standing at the foot of her bed and she noted, "His presence brought no sensation of fear."[6]

Over the years she had acquired a reputation for her interest in the unexplained, and even the scientific and religious communities had looked to her for advice. There were several instances where members of the clergy consulted her regarding an alleged haunted house or poltergeist appearance: "Evening call from Rev. Edgar Bull, Toronto, who has to rid a house of a poltergeist the following night and wanted some advice about procedure."[7] In 1959 a group of psychiatrists at Camp Hill Hospital in Halifax invited Helen to give a lecture on folkways and cures in order to better understand those patients who subscribed to these beliefs.

Helen herself[8] had some communication with organizations involved with the study of the paranormal. In 1965 she wrote to Eileen Garrett, President of the Parapsychology Foundation in New York, for advice about a poltergeist case. And she was most intrigued when Duke University was investigating the possibility of establishing an Institute of Parapsychology and offered her a position on the advisory board. The project never came about, but she did share her interest in it with Carmen Roy: "What a new door of interest it opens up, particularly as I am continually having experiences myself."[9]

One of Helen's "experiences" occurred in 1968, when Lilian was dying in the local hospital. As a rule, whenever Helen was concerned about her sister she would feel the presence of her parents, which brought her great comfort. But sitting at Lilian's bedside praying with Reverend James Fraser, Helen instead felt their absence. Lilian died during the priest's prayer for Helen and it was then that Helen experienced a sensation unlike anything she had felt before. She described it as "an inflow of strength so vigorous"[10] that it lifted her like a benediction, giving her such a feeling of power it was almost akin to ecstasy.

She later learned that some clergy refer to this feeling as divine regeneration—the gift of grace. It brought Helen great comfort. She had long been responsible for Lilian's care and didn't want to harbour any feelings of relief from this burden being lifted by her sister's death. Instead, she felt sustained and was able to look back on her relationship with Lilian with love and renewed peace.

Helen would have to draw upon whatever reserves of calm she had to help sustain her through her next endeavour. Although her tenure as contract researcher was over, she still continued a working relationship with the National Museum. She had assembled many of the songs she collected in New Brunswick into a manuscript, and it was currently going through the editing process with a Museum staff editor. While it is common for editors and authors to disagree on various points when developing a manuscript for publication, this particular editor caused Helen endless frustration. A working document in one of Helen's files

*Nova Scotia Folk Singers on Citadel Hill, Halifax, c. 1967. L-R: Eunice Sircom, Kaye Dimock/Pottie, Gregory Servant, Susan Baker, Carolyn Baker, Helen Creighton.*

at the Public Archives of Nova Scotia illustrates the level of her frustration. The editor, Miss Shoemaker, had sent a detailed list of changes she had made to the manuscript. Helen went through each item individually—and her written comments demonstrate how little the editor knew about folklore:

> If you are going to use quotation marks, you can't change a scholar's quote.... If you are uncertain about "old time songs" as an expression, they could be put in quotes. This is what they were always called.... Give me strength! You've even re-done my bibliography, as though I've never done one in my life.... Why have you felt such a compulsion to change everything that I have written?... If I wish to stress that a song is on a certain theme, why should you pencil it out? I always make a point of stressing a song that has the broken ring theme because there are so many and it links them together. If I make an observation about a song it is there for a purpose....Oh my blood pressure. Again you are so factual that you've taken the human interest out of the note. Would you expect a fisherman to weep when singing a touching story? No, I'm sure you wouldn't. But it happens and this man actually broke down and couldn't go on.... Will you please put back my full description of Annie Kempton. My patience has run out for telling you why ...

Your note is no improvement and I have torn it up. Mine says what I want to say.... Surely that isn't a pencil note I see through his note. Oh no, it can't be. That would be too silly.... There is nothing wrong with your rewriting, but there is nothing wrong with my writing of this note either. I happen to prefer my own way of saying it. It's my book, or at least it was.[11]

Helen did give Miss Shoemaker credit when she found legitimate mistakes in the manuscript, but it was obvious they couldn't work together, and the Museum assigned a new editor to the project. Dorothy Burke and Helen knew each other from Helen's previous visits to the Museum. Hoping for a better relationship, Helen wrote to Dorothy in March, saying that she would keep on with her own corrections until she heard back from her. Dorothy made an attempt to smooth the waters when she responded towards the end of the month, but she also castigated Helen with "would you please rewrite your notes in as concise a form as possible, omitting the personal remarks, which are unnecessary. Let's keep our work at the proper level."[12]

In April, Helen wrote back with an apology for her remarks, adding:

It would be so much easier if I hadn't met you and liked you so much because I hate to hurt you, but if I acquiesced in all that has been done to my manuscript I would severely damage my own reputation and you would also suffer as editor.... Sorry my notes got personal, but I did try in the beginning to be patient and explain why things were wrong. To rewrite without explaining would serve no purpose since Miss Shoemaker showed herself to be unfamiliar with the subject from the start. After she changed my meaning time and again by substituting words of her own and I realized the vast amount of work she was making for me, my patience ran out.[13]

The two women eventually arrived at a reasonable working relationship, but it must have been frustrating for both parties. Helen certainly had a valid argument. She shouldn't have had to give her editor a lesson in folklore. After all, an editor on contract with the National Museum should have had more sensitivity to the genre. When the manuscript was finally completed, Helen breathed a sigh of relief. It was released in 1971 under the title *Folksongs from Southern New Brunswick*.[14] Helen was adamant about placing the word "Southern" in the title because she didn't want to be seen as infringing on the territory of her friend, Louise Manny, who worked primarily in northern New Brunswick and, two years previously, had brought out her own book of folk songs.[15] Indeed, most of the songs in Helen's new book did come from southern New Brunswick—and from one primary informant. As Helen wrote in the introduction, "This volume might have been called "The Angelo Dornan Book of Songs" because the lyrics and melodies of one singer are pre-eminent."[16] Of the 118 songs in the book, 70 were taken from the prodigious repertoire of Mr. Dornan. Like Ben Henneberry before him, Angelo Dornan had proven himself a formidable inform-ant and Helen was delighted to bring his songs to public attention.

The next year, 1971, began on a tragic note for Helen. In February her brother Terry was injured in an automobile accident in Halifax and died three weeks later in hospital. He was two years older than Helen and they had been very close. She had only two brothers remaining. Mac lived in London and Syd in Montreal, so she had no immediate family left nearby. But she had a close bond with her nieces and, fortu-nately, she had wonderful friends who lived with her at Evergreen.

Cora Greenaway and her husband lived in a small apartment down-stairs. They first met in 1963 when Helen was appointed to the board of governors of the Dartmouth Academy, a private school for boys where Cora taught. Cora had a particular interest in painted decoration found on Nova Scotian interiors. She was fluent in French, besides her native Dutch, and she worked with Helen on some of the translations of her Acadian material. They also shared a personal bond, as Cora had a brother whose mental capacity, like Lilian's, had not progressed. It was com-forting for Helen to have a friend in whom she could confide. The other tenants at Evergreen who became like family to Helen were the Olives. Nesta and David Olive occupied one of the upstairs apartments. Originally from Wales, they were jolly and full of fun, but also ready to offer sound advice when it was requested.

Helen was fortunate in the relationships she maintained with many of her other tenants. For the most part they went on to become friends. When Susan and Roy Portchmouth lived at Evergreen in the 1950s, they even invited Helen to be their son's honorary grandmother. By the1970s the house was occupied solely by adults, albeit adults with a keen sense of fun. At Christmas, a great tree was erected in the down-stairs hall and local carollers were always invited in. On Halloween, Helen loved to travel about the neighbourhood dressed as a witch, and when children came to the door, she invited them in for treats and a scary tale from the author of *Bluenose Ghosts*.

She had always enjoyed the company of young people and in 1971 she formed a performance troop to help illustrate her songs when she lectured. To lead the group, she chose a young music teacher who had been a protégé of her friend Betty Murray. Kaye Dimock was a talented soprano who would eventually go on to head the music department for the City of Halifax. Helen's accompanist and arranger was her former Evergreen tenant, Eunice Sircom, a graduate of Acadia University with a music degree in piano. Other members of the troop included Finvola

Redden, sisters Carolyn and Susan Baker, and the lone male, tenor Gregory Servant, who later alternated with James Farmer. Eunice and Kaye were both married, while the others were still in their teens or early twenties.

In July Helen travelled with her group to perform a concert series in Ottawa, beginning with a show for Canada Day on Parliament Hill. Her diary account of some of the events on the trip gives an interesting perspective on her impressions of the new fashions and protocol: "Met at airport by representative of Secty. of State expected somebody in impeccable dress. Instead met by Mr. Shapiro with fuzzy head and most casual dress but lovely smile. Girls too wore shorts or dresses with hot pants."[17] For an afternoon concert in the presence of the Governor General's party, Helen considered wearing a long dress, but was told it was an informal gathering so opted for a rose-coloured day suit with silver threads (and still worried that she was underdressed). However, she was willing to get caught up in the fun and move with the times. After the performance they all boarded a bus, and "going home was great fun. The bus was full of young people, all in a merry mood with their jobs well done ... they were all singing at the tops of their voices as the bus roared through Ottawa at 12:30 midnight, and there was I at 71, a show biz personality for the nonce, and having the time of my life. I thought of friends siting at home waiting for a stroke to carry them off. I may go first, but I'll have a much better time getting there."[18]

By this point, Helen had become the grand dame of Canadian folklore and many people vied for her attention. She was asked to sit on a number of boards, including the Encyclopaedia of Music in Canada. She was frequently interviewed on topics dealing with the supernatural, and anyone wanting to get a foot in the door with traditional music in the Maritimes paid homage to her and her work. In early June in 1972 she did an interview at Evergreen with CBC national radio host Peter Gzowski. Years earlier she had corresponded with Peter when he was managing editor of *Maclean's*. He had written a piece saying that he preferred modern voices to those of traditional singers. Helen responded with a letter outlining the value of both. Peter was appreciative but not convinced, writing back, "I believe your work has made it possible for all of us to enjoy Canadian folk music .... But I enjoy listening to Ian and Sylvia more than creaky old voices."[19] Peter is a charming man and he must have worked his magic with Helen in June, because when he left she noted in her diary, "Peter very easy to talk to, perhaps too easy because I rattled on."[20]

She may have rattled on, but Helen was an excellent interviewee. Her years as a storyteller and journalist gave her a knack for the dramatic and she knew how to take a story to its height and then drop the ball just at the climax. Her speaking voice was refined and charming, pitched in a lower register, and she used it as an instrument, lending cadence and lilt to her narratives. She was an interviewer's dream. They came in and asked a question—and she was off. Still, she didn't click with everyone. One of Canada's most respected radio and television journalists was Barbara Frum. She once interviewed Helen for the national radio program "As It Happens," but Helen wasn't pleased with the results. She later wrote: "She has evidently heard so much about me that she was nervous attempting an interview. And she asked some stupid questions. For instance she couldn't get it (this was edited from the tape) when I said that if I'd gone to a man and asked for a bawdy song I would have lost his respect. And when she asked if the people knew their own background I felt like replying that they are intelligent, but refrained."[21] Others fared much better. "Ryan's Fancy is Irish singing group, unknown to me until Dennis Ryan 'phoned to say he would like to meet me. Liked his voice on 'phone so made appointment for him to come to house. Bearded young man, but clean, and likeable personality.... He went away walking on air."[22]

In May of 1973 Helen was back in Ottawa, invited by Carmen Roy to act as co-host for a National Museum reception where a bust of Marius Barbeau was being unveiled. It was a grand affair and offered Helen the opportunity to see some of the many changes that had been implemented at the Museum. She later noted in her diary, "I believe Dr. Barbeau and I are looked on as pioneers. From three collectors when I first joined the Museum, they are now sending thirty into the field this summer."[23]

The spring and summer were busy for Helen because she found herself involved with another television program. The CBC was filming a television special with renowned string bassist Gary Karr, who lived and worked out of Halifax. Musical guests were Kaye Dimock and Jim Bennet, and Helen was involved in several location scenes. Gary and Helen developed an instant bond. She recognized him for the gifted artist he is and he appreciated her for the work she had done collecting and saving folk songs. In many of his concerts throughout the world he performed an encore with an arrangement of a beautiful song that Helen had collected from Angelo Dornan, "When I Wake In The Morning."[24] After the television show taping they began a correspondence that continued for years, and Helen enjoyed receiving Gary's notes from various locales around the globe.

The spring also brought two other interesting events. The Canadian Music Council was having its annual meeting in Halifax, and Kaye Dimock and Richard Johnston had been doing some behind-the-scenes planning that brought Helen another honour. On May 3 she took part in a panel discussion on Maritime folk music and attended a concert by the increasingly popular miners' chorus, "The Men of the Deeps." In the evening she was "surprised" (she had actually been tipped off, but swore her messenger to secrecy) with the presentation of the Canadian Music Council Medal of Honour. It was an especially gratifying tribute because it came from musicians and music educators who used Helen's collection in their own work. Helen was also pleased to share the evening with her house guest, Dr. Roxanne Carlisle, who had recently been appointed Head Ethnomusicologist at the National Museum. She was gratified to see that Roxanne, who was young and new to the Museum, could gain an impression of the body of work she had produced.

Helen spent most of the next day in bed. She was conserving her energy for that evening, when she would be the guest of honour at a gala dinner hosted by the Government of Nova Scotia. At the dinner she was feted with speeches and musical tributes, and was presented with the province's Award of Recognition. To cap the event, she took home a carved wooden replica of the famous Nova Scotia schooner *Bluenose*.

Perhaps it was all too exhausting. Shortly after the dual tributes she developed pneumonia. After three weeks in hospital she rested for an additional six weeks in a nursing home. Her friends rallied around to offer cheer, and one of the brightest moments came when she received a bouquet of roses from the "Men of the Deeps" and their director John O'Donnell—one rose for every miner in the chorus. Returning home, she continued with the work she had begun before her illness— writing her autobiography. She worked on it throughout the fall and was able to relax during the winter months. However, she did take on a few interviews and appointments.

One appointment, which she noted in her diary on 10 March 1975, is especially interesting to me:

Clary Croft had 'phoned that he was making a record about the eastern shore and would like to talk to me. Also wanted to learn how to pronounce words of Oran Cheap Bretainn. Came with his wife and I enjoyed them. He had sung with Singalong Jubilee .... Now sings 6 days a week at Sherbrooke Village in season. Nice young man, anxious to improve skills and repertoire, and wanted to hear original tapes. Played some I had here. He would like to go through the whole collection, not realizing the months that would take him. His wife works in crafts. Will probably hear from them again.[25]

No words were ever more prophetic....

# CHAPTER EIGHTEEN

### ✳ ✳ ✳

There are times when one realizes that an event of great significance has occurred, but one can't yet discern why. That's how I felt after my first meeting with Helen.

Coming from a musical family—my great grandfather, Edward Burns, made and played his own fiddle—my childhood was steeped in traditional songs as well as country, religious, and popular music. By the late sixties I had developed a respectable folk music career, singing with a Halifax chorus called "The Privateers," travelling across Canada and the United States, and representing my country at the 1970 World's Fair at Osaka, Japan. In the fall of 1970 I joined the cast of "Singalong Jubilee" and later toured with "The Musical Friends," the program's house band.

Then in the summer of 1973 I began working at the Historic Sherbrooke Village Restoration, singing folk songs and talking to tourists about local history. I knew a few local traditional songs, but I wanted to increase my repertoire. After consulting Helen Creighton's books I decided to approach her in person, hoping she might offer a few suggestions. She said she had many more unpublished songs from the Sherbrooke area around and promptly invited me and my wife, Sharon, to Evergreen for tea.

For a folk song enthusiast, an invitation to visit Helen Creighton was a big event. She was a gracious hostess. Sharon and I sat in her parlour where she served tea from two pots, samovar style—a sterling urn containing steeped tea and a brass kettle filled with hot water to dilute the strong brew. She reminisced about her collecting days in and around Sherbrooke and played us some audio tapes from her collection. When we rose to leave, thanking her for the tea and talk, she looked me square in the face and asked, "Well, aren't you going to sing for me?" This was the test. Aside from my childhood recollections, I wasn't well versed in traditional folkways. However, I knew enough not to worry that I hadn't brought my guitar, as most folk singers sang unaccompanied. And so I stood in the middle of her parlour and sang "Cape Breton Lullaby," a verse by Nova Scotia poet Kenneth Leslie set to the music of a traditional pipe tune from Cape Breton. Knowing that Helen had collected variants of it over the years, I figured it was a safe bet. I was right. When I finished singing, she walked over to me, took both my hands in hers and said, "You'll do just fine."

Like Denis Ryan of Ryan's Fancy, I went away walking on air. Helen had offered to go through her archive of published and unpublished material and give me a detailed listing of songs from the Sherbrooke area. She would also let me listen to her original field recordings so that I could better understand traditional singing styles and vocal techniques. And, best of all, she invited me to keep in touch. It was a warm and generous reception, but little did I realize that I had met the person who would become my mentor and dear friend.

I continued my job at Sherbrooke Village as a "wandering troubadour," and in the fall I began performing at a Halifax restaurant called the Clipper Cay. I was also working on my first album and, with Helen's permission, recorded several songs from her collection.[1] My career was in full swing, but Helen and I kept in touch as much as we could.

Helen was trying to slow down her own social and professional life, but in early May she travelled to Antigonish to accept an honorary degree from St. Francis Xavier University, and three days later she gave a speech at the King's College alumni dinner in Halifax. Her weekend in Antigonish had been exhilarating and, although she was well prepared for her address at King's, she found herself exhausted afterwards. She made a conscious decision to accept fewer invitations for public appearances. Naturally, she made exceptions. Her intentions to ease up on work were waylaid by the many exciting things that kept coming her way. In August she attended a reception given by the Mayor of Dartmouth, where she was presented with a special Citizenship Medal, and October saw the release of her autobiography. Once again she found herself in the limelight. She spent most of the fall giving interviews and attending book signings in Dartmouth and Halifax.

She called her life story, appropriately enough, *A Life in Folklore*.[2] Her friends enthused over it. Helène Baillargeon, now retired from singing folk songs and recently appointed a judge of the Citizenship Court in Montreal, telephoned with her congratulations. Maude Karpeles wrote with her love and congratulations saying, "you are a wonder and I am filled with admiration."[3] Gary Karr wrote Helen while on tour: "Dearest Friend, Your book has become my favourite companion ... it is being carried to the furthest points of North America."[4] Informants and their families were happy to see their names mentioned in print and to be recognized for the contribution they'd made to Helen's collection. Helen was particularly pleased to hear from the great grandson of Dennis Smith. He took the book to show his relatives in Chezzetcook, who were delighted to read her accounts of collecting from Dennis and his wife some 40 years earlier. The popular press was kind, if not enthusiastic. *Chatelaine* called it a "simple and unpretentious narrative that breaches none of the writer's personal privacy; it's nonetheless a very pleasant read."[5] The reviewer for *The North Bay Nugget* in Ontario wrote, "Miss Creighton is a clever, ingenious and warm-hearted pioneer in her field, who should have had a better biographer than herself."[6] But it was the academics who were least kind. Gordon MacLennan, writing for *Archivaria*, said that he liked the autobiography for its own sake, but added, "there is little in this book which throws light on the subject of folklore or could be of much assistance to students."[7]

Helen had attempted the impossible—and failed. She had revealed little of her personal life and made every attempt to protect the privacy and integrity of her informants. Her detractors wanted more dirt, more gossip, more in-depth analysis of her own life and those of the people from whom she'd collected. However, that wasn't Helen's style. She had grown up in an era when one kept one's personal life just that—personal. Having earned her informants' trust, she was always guarded about the intimate details of their lives. But in her discretion she also left out much that her readers had anticipated. *A Life in Folklore* told how and when, but it rarely revealed why. It remains an interesting account of her career and a fascinating entry in social history, but in many ways it was a reflection of her work—long on documentation and short on analysis. What her autobiography did reveal, however, was an amazingly rich life. And it was far from over.

Helen had many years and honours yet to come—and 1976 would prove exceptional. It began in January with a press release from the office of the Governor General of Canada. Helen was being made a Member of the Order of Canada, the highest civilian honour in the nation. In April she and her niece, Barbara Miller, went to Ottawa for the presentation ceremony. Receiving her decoration from Governor General Jules Leger was one of the crowning glories in her life and she proudly displayed two photographs of the event in her home. It was a busy spring for recognitions. The Halifax School Music Department mounted a tribute to Helen. Almost 200 young string players assembled to present selections from her collection. Shortly after, the Writer's Federation of Nova Scotia made her an honorary member and St. Mary's University, in Halifax, presented her with her fifth honorary degree.

In July she attended a banquet for Queen Elizabeth and Prince Phillip, who were visiting Halifax. A staunch monarchist, Helen was thrilled to be seated near the head table, but she would have an even closer encounter with royalty. When the Queen visits a Commonwealth country she wears that nation's highest civilian order. Helen, likewise, was wearing her Order of Canada. When the Queen spied it as she walked by the reception line, she stopped to speak to her. Helen later recounted that when the Queen enquired as to the origins of her OC, the first thought that entered her head was, "For my work in folklore your Majesty, and why did you get yours?"[8] Naturally, however, she explained about her work with Canadian folklore, whereupon the Queen surprised her further by asking about "Farewell to Nova Scotia," which she had heard throughout the province. Their brief exchange was the major highlight of Helen's year.

More honours marked the following year, which would also have moments of deep sadness. Bernie Mills telephoned Helen in the spring to tell her that Alan had been diagnosed with terminal cancer:

Realizing my distress she and Alan talked to me a few weeks later, keeping it all very cheerful and Alan joking about his loss of hair. It was a sort of game we played, but it was so much appreciated. Wrote Helene Baillargeon for real situation and her prompt answer saddened me greatly. Then on evening of 16th Bernie 'phoned again to say Alan had slipped away peacefully on Tuesday morning and that I mustn't grieve. Must think of him as on an extended tour, and that she was at peace with herself and I must be too. My frequent letters and cards seemed to have helped them both and Bernie was full of love and concern. Alan was first to make my songs known over network. Very dear friends.[9]

That same week, Calum MacLeod died of a heart attack. Calum had been a friend and co-author; Alan was a soul mate. Throughout their relationship Helen and Alan kept up a vigorous correspondence. She shared confidences with him rarely offered to others. Helen appreciated Alan's direct approach and admired his integrity as a performer. She also valued his opinion on professional matters. She had sought his counsel when the situation with Carmen Roy grew difficult. Alan's advice was both reassuring and sound: "I think you've analysed Carmen perfectly; there's obviously a basic jealousy and fear of security there, and nothing you can do about it (short of resigning from the Museum) will put her at rest, and I'm sure that's neither right nor logical, so don't let it bother you."[10] He, in return, held Helen in high regard. Although he shared some resemblance to Burl Ives, who had an international hit with Alan's song "I Know An Old Lady Who Swallowed A Fly,"[11] he resented the frequent comparison. When Helen wrote to Alan that she had "swooned" to receive a letter from the American folk singer, Alan quickly replied, "As for "swooning" when Ives writes to you, f'gosshakes gal, you've got the wrong slant on the picture ... YOU'RE the guy HE *wants* to contact, not the other way around!"[12] His response was tempered with a little professional jealousy, perhaps, but Helen could always count on Alan for a straight reply.

A month after Alan's death, Helen attended a Kodaly Symposium at Acadia University. Zoltan Kodaly was a Hungarian composer and folk song collector. Helen's work was taught in Hungary alongside his to introduce music to schoolchildren. The Kodaly method was being incorporated into music programs throughout North America, including

*Helen Creighton, Joleen Gordon, Peter Barss at opening of exhibit Older Ways, 1977.*

Nova Scotia. Many topics were surveyed, but Helen's work and collection were emphasized and she was feted as the guest of honour during the three-day seminar.

She returned to Ottawa in October as a guest of the Canadian government at a command performance for Queen Elizabeth at the National Arts Centre. The Canadian Museum of Civilization had replaced the old National Museum of Man in both structure and name, and Helen was pleased to see her own collection safely housed in new steel cabinets.

The release of two more books—*Eight Ethnic Folk Songs for Young Children and Nine Ethnic Folk Songs*[13]—capped off 1977. She and Eunice Sircom had put together the pair of small songbooks, which were designed especially for children. With the emphasis placed on her work in school music departments—especially in Halifax and Dartmouth—and her elevated public profile, Helen's work was garnering more and more attention. Her former collecting work was also being recognized by her peers. In February 1978 she was asked to write the foreword for a new monograph on Lunenburg folklore prepared for the National Museum by Laurie Lacey. He re-examined many of the beliefs and folkways Helen had explored more than 40 years earlier, and was able to bring new elements to his research that were of great interest to her.[14]

I was also beginning to work more closely with Helen. She would take me to her collection at the Public Archives and play me examples of traditional music, pointing out different singing styles and sharing stories about each song and how she had collected it. I had considered moving to Newfoundland to begin a degree in folklore at Memorial University, but several people working in the field advised me otherwise. If Helen were willing to be my mentor, I should stay and work with her. So, for the time being, I enrolled in a folklore class at St. Mary's University and continued exploring Helen's personal source material. I couldn't have been more fortunate. Helen was very interested in my studies and when I suggested she accompany me to class one evening, she eagerly accepted:

Clary ... took me to his house for dinner and then to Dr. Gillian Thomas's English class where he sang maritime (mostly Nova Scotian) folk songs for a good 2 hrs. Was a lovely evening in lounge and a large and interested class. After most of the songs I told something of the singer or gave a short story of how or where the song was collected. This was quite spontaneous and seemed to be appreciated. What opportunities Singalong Jubilee missed in ignoring these songs that Clary sings to such good effect, and makes a good living on.[15]

In May Helen made a major lifestyle change. She sold Evergreen and moved into an apartment in Dartmouth. It was not a decision made in haste. As early as 1961 she had given serious consideration to selling her family home. It had been recently repainted grey with white trim edged in black, and with its red doors and roof it was an attractive residence. Unfortunately, it was also huge. There were no takers. She put it back on the market in 1970 and had several interested buyers, but again, no serious bids. In 1975 the City of Dartmouth designated Evergreen as an historic residence, which added to the property's interest value, but also made it more difficult to sell, as heritage buildings have restrictions with regard to remodelling and exterior alterations. Helen was finding the house overwhelming. It cost a fortune to heat and she no longer wanted to be responsible for tenants, regardless of how well they got along. So, when the Dartmouth Heritage Museum offered to buy her home to refurbish as a museum site, including a display devoted to Helen's life and work, she was delighted. It was an ideal solution. She did think about moving into a cooperative known as Habitat, in Wolfville, which was owned by friends in the arts and cultural fields. However, in the end Helen opted to remain closer to her family and friends in Dartmouth.

Her new, two-bedroom apartment overlooked Lake Banook, where Helen and her family had spent many summers. It was bright and airy, with a balcony looking out through the trees down to the lake. But it wasn't Evergreen. Helen had lived there almost all of her adult life and she had difficulties making the adjustment to a small apartment. She was feeling rather lonely and melancholic when an invitation arrived from her former neighbours, Claire and Charles Hubley, who were now living in England. Visiting people who knew her from early days at Evergreen was just what she needed. The vacation would also give her the opportunity to visit with Mac and his family. She toured the English countryside, spent a week at Ascot, and met several folklore colleagues. She was also pleased to see her brother still working vigorously in his medical practice. He was, at 87, 10 years Helen's senior.

On her return to Nova Scotia Helen attended the launch of a new book by Peter Barrs and Joleen Gordon.[16] Peter is a gifted photographer who lived and worked in Lunenburg County, photographing traditional craftspeople and recording their own comments about their work. He asked Helen to write an introduction for the book, which she happily did. This was a new kind of folklore collecting. When the photographs were married to the informants' commentary, and craft notes were added by Nova Scotia Museum Research Associate, Joleen Gordon, the whole package was a valuable addition to the study of traditional folkways.

The 1970s came to a close with more honours and recognition for Helen. I continued to represent her collection in concerts and on CBC radio, and we began to conduct interviews together, with Helen talking about her life's work and I illustrating songs from her collection. It was an opportunity for both of us to earn money—and, for me, a chance to work with Helen and learn about her collection first-hand. I would gladly have paid for the privilege.

Helen's work was showcased in May at an exhibit mounted at Dalhousie University Art Gallery in conjunction with the 1979 Carl Orff National Convention. As with the Kodaly method, the Carl Orff method emphasized the use of folk melodies in children's musical training. Kaye Dimock and Valda Kemp organized the largest and most comprehensive collection of Helen Creighton memorabilia ever assembled for display. Titled after her autobiography, the exhibit was called "Helen Creighton—A Life in Folklore." With items from Helen's personal collection and many examples of her work from the Public Archives of Nova Scotia, it was an amazing tribute to a life devoted to Maritime folklore. A banquet and performance series were scheduled, with Helen taking centre stage at them all. Along with others, I performed after the banquet and Helen paid me an especially nice compliment in her diary: "A concert followed when the Hfx. Schools orchestra played the Atlantic Suite composed by Alec Tilley. Then Clary Croft sang as I had never heard him, all but the last from my collection. He made a tremendous impression."[17] Whatever impression I made was due, in no small part, to Helen's influence on my presentation of her music. She frequently offered advice about repertoire and, once we got to know each other better, critiques on my performances. A year earlier I had presented a concert in Halifax that included the Acadian lullaby Helen had collected from Laura Irene McNeil. A few days later Helen asked me to accompany her to the Public Archives to hear the original. She didn't have to say anything—the recording she played showed me that I had been singing it much too fast. She was perfectly comfortable with me bringing a personal interpretation to folk music, but when I presented a song in the style of a traditional singer, she wanted to make sure I got it right.

In 1979 Nova Scotia hosted the International Gathering of the Clans. Clan members from around the world, and especially Scotland, converged on New Scotland for meetings, concerts, family reunions, and a multitude of celebrations. Helen was delighted to be invited to attend a state banquet in Halifax held in honour of Queen Elizabeth, the Queen Mother. Later, related to the Gathering of the Clans events, Helen travelled to Pugwash to participate in the world-famous Thinkers' Conference.[18] She was no longer comfortable driving long distances, so requested a volunteer chauffeur. The organizers asked Dr. Graham Whitehead to accompany her to and from the conference. He was an English scholar, actor, and playwright who later went on to develop scripts using material from Helen's collection. She took an instant liking to Graham and wrote in her diary, "I felt I had made another friend."[19] Actually, she was to make two new friends. Graham also spoke to Helen of the work being done by his wife, Ruth Holmes Whitehead. She was a researcher of Mi'kmaq history and folklore, working in association with the Nova Scotia Museum. Helen made arrangements to have copies of her Mi'kmaq material made for Ruth, a valuable contribution to the culture's study. Knowing that she herself didn't have the knowledge-base to pursue Mi'kmaq studies, she added a note to her diary that read, "besides the good company it was good to see her excited over the material. Am glad to know that it will be well used."[20] It was important to Helen that her work was of value to other researchers. She willingly gave up her personal collection to those she felt were qualified to use it for further study. And she continued to be surprised by where her work turned up.

That July she had her good friends, Tom and Mavis Kines, staying as house guests. Tom worked for the Canadian Red Cross, but he was also a respected folk recording artist. Showing them around Halifax's historic waterfront, Helen came upon a couple of street musicians:

After lunch went over to speak to singer at sea wall and asked him where he had found the song he'd just sung. Was one of mine, so I sat beside him while the Kines finished shopping which must have been half an hour. Another young man arrived with violin and played with him and many people dropped pieces of silver in the open guitar case. All their songs were traditional and well sung. It was lovely sitting with them in the sun.[21]

From concert stages around the world ... to a pair of waterfront buskers, Helen witnessed her work being kept alive. She was able to pass on her knowledge in many ways—and to many people: to me as her protegé, to researchers such as Ruth Whitehead, and to thousands of school-children through the efforts of music teachers throughout the province. Her life in folklore had been described in her autobiography and documented in the exhibit at the Dalhousie University Art Gallery. It would soon be turned into a musical stage production. In the early spring, her friend Mary Sparling, who was the director of the Mount St. Vincent University Art Gallery, telephoned Helen with an interesting proposition. Helen noted Mary's proposal in her diary: "She had been in the Montreal airport and a fellow passenger was John Brown who had composed a musical biography about Alexander Graham Bell. Why not do one on me? So they came and talked it over.... It will be interesting to see how it works out."[22]

# CHAPTER NINETEEN

### ✳ ✳ ✳

Helen was thrilled with John Brown's musical interpretation of her life as a collector. He sought her advice throughout the writing and rehearsal process, and by the time the show was mounted at Seton Hall, at Mount St. Vincent University, she was able to write in her diary, "Everybody has been most kind and helpful and any change I suggest is immediately put into practice."[1] It was primarily an amateur, community-based production, with the participation of several professional singers and musicians, including me. John wisely decided not to attempt to tell Helen's life story, concentrating instead on her years of field research. He called his play *The Collector*.

It ran for three performances and, at the end, Helen had much to say about it:

Everything that happens seems to be the ultimate. Surely *The Collector* has been. The house was full for the three performances and all the hard work showed in how smoothly everything went. It was a happy show, and without one profanity or one obscenity! The young Helen had just the right attitude. In a rehearsal she had taken Enos Hartlan's arm as they walked away, but I told her she was young and living dangerously and the thing was to be friendly but reserved.... The older Helen too was very good. More dignified of course befitting her age.... They wanted everything to be authentic and accepted my suggestions gratefully. Actually I didn't make many. They had studied my books and knew my attitudes and philosophy.... There were some wonderful and imaginative bits.... Jim Farmer was an excellent Lukie [singing "Lukie's Boat Is Painted Green"] looking so sorrowful when he saw that his wife was dead because the blinds were down, and then gradually realizing he was free.... The Hartlan scene with its ghost stories and Jim Muise and Mr. Hartlan sparring at one another, and Mrs. Hartlan getting her word in so well was a good sample of what happened when I collected. The Boutilier scene was perhaps funnier.... Best of all in that scene was Clary Croft who made himself up as an old man in a rocking chair. No sir, he wasn't going to sing in that thing (the tape recorder) and he pretended not to hear when Lloyd was singing but sat looking straight ahead toward the audience, his fingers giving him away as he kept time. Finally after listening to John Smith his old friend, and the collector saying she would put the machine away he suddenly told her

*Cast of* The Collector *with Sister Margaret Young, Helen Creighton and John Frederick Brown, 1980.*

not to be so fast and said I had a way would charm the devil. Then he turned his rocking chair and sang I Dyed My Petticoat Red, racing it as fast as he could and looking delighted with himself. He wore a moustache and glasses and kept time with his feet when he sang, and this was probably the funniest thing in the show. Let's hope he will be available whenever they put it on again. Someone told me that when Mrs. Thomas sang the Cherry Tree Carol that I'd taken down from her grandfather, they had a lump in their throat.[2]

The theatre was not the only artistic forum in which Helen was being portrayed. In 1978 she had sat for a pastel portrait by Mary Moore. In 1980 Mrs. Moore used her initial studies to create a life-sized bust in bronze. On 10 August the Mayor of Dartmouth, Daniel Brownlow, unveiled the statue in the entrance hall at Evergreen. Helen was present and removed her glasses so that people could see how well the artist had captured her likeness, later writing, "The bust is quite impressive & looks well enough executed to last forever as busts are supposed to do."[3]

Both her consultations over *The Collector* and the unveiling of her bust at Evergreen were entertaining diversions for Helen. Most of her time was spent working on her collection of Acadian songs. The National Museum had contracted her in 1978 to assemble and annotate her French songs for future publication.[4] By June of 1980 she had begun working on the music with Eunice Sircom. For the scholarly notes, she had engaged Ronald Labelle, a graduate of the folklore program at Laval University, who was working at the University of Moncton's Centre d'Études Acadiennes. Cora Greenaway also assisted in assembling the songs, and by 6 October Helen was able to note in her diary, "Happy day. Had been working to limit of strength for some weeks to finish book. Ronald Labelle had brought his contribution ... and it was good, just what I wanted.... Had wondered if I would be able to finish the book or the book would finish me ... I will miss visits from my wonderful helpers."[5]

In the new year Helen drove to Florida with Marie Nightingale. Marie's best-selling cookbook, *Out of Old Nova Scotian Kitchens*,[6] contained many examples of the types of food lore Helen had collected all her life. She and Helen had been longtime friends and Marie invited Helen to stay at her family's condominium in Florida. Helen seized the opportunity to get away from her apartment and enjoy a three-week holiday in a warm climate. The Nightingales' condominium was also close to the winter vacation retreat of Helen's niece, Lois Harnish, and her family. Helen enjoyed long hours on the beach and described her vacation as "a perfect (and much needed) holiday."[7]

At the end of her vacation she flew home, rested and ready for a busy spring. In early May she was awarded the first honorary membership in the Atlantic Canadian Composers' Association. Later that month she attended the Annual General Meeting of the Folklore Studies Association of Canada. Most of the events were held in Halifax, but they had arranged to have the banquet in the Parish Hall at Chezzetcook. It was at this banquet, held in the community where she had collected some of her earliest material, that Helen was designated the Association's "Distinguished Canadian Folklorist." She later wrote, "Considering the quality of scholarship in this assoc., I felt I had received an honour, indeed.... Wished mother and father had witnessed it after the faith they always had that this research of mine would someday prove worth while."[8]

Although I was still living in Sherbrooke during the summers, I had stopped performing at the restored village. My wife, Sharon, was now head of the Costume Department at Sherbrooke Village Restoration and I spent my time collecting folklore. We invited Helen to join us in August for a holiday at our family homestead.

The drive from Dartmouth to Sherbrooke takes approximately two and a half hours. Nova Scotia's eastern shore is dotted with hundreds of tiny coves and inlets and dozens of small communities. Helen had visited every one of them, and as we drove along she regaled us with stories of her early collecting experiences. As we passed through any given community, she would recollect a song collected there and charge me to sing it. Driving anywhere in the Maritimes with Helen was a magical experience, but I'll always remember those drives to and from Sherbrooke. For Helen they were nostalgic journeys; for Sharon and me, they were an education. The birthday following our visit, she wrote us a lovely note: "Many thanks for my happy visit and the privilege of sharing your home in Sherbrooke. I keep recalling incidents that go back to the thirties and must see if I can find a diary or note book that covers that period. I didn't keep such a full collecting diary then, not realizing that collecting would be my life for so many years.... Today marks the beginning of a new year for me, and I hope it will approach the last year which has been full and interesting.... Love to you both. Helen."[9]

*Clary Croft and Helen Creighton, Evergreen, c. 1984. Publicity photo for the back of the author's recording* **False Knight Upon the Road: Songs from the collection of Dr. Helen Creighton.**

Indeed, her year continued to be both full and interesting. With her manuscript of Acadian songs sent off to the National Museum, Helen turned her attentions to her folktales. In October she received a visit from her friend Herbert Halpert, a folklorist from Memorial University in Newfoundland. Her diary entry shows her excitement over the meeting: "Red letter day. Herbert stopped over on way from Nfld ... He had looked over my folk tales and said if I would write note about how and where collected, he would do rest.... Was wonderful to talk over collecting experiences with such an expert in the field. Could have talked for hrs. more.... A memorable day."[10] Helen had been trying to get work done on her folk tales for years. Not feeling qualified to annotate them herself, she was overjoyed when Herbert offered his assistance. He encouraged her to write about the storytellers and give her personal perspectives on their narrative styles, saying, "*Bluenose Ghosts* is one of the most scholarly books we have on the subject in North America because it's human.... It isn't type and motif numbers and annotations that make a book truly scholarly, but the approach."[11] She eagerly began writing notes about her informants and asked me to help her with the typing.

We worked throughout the fall on her manuscript and also did another television show together. Jim Bennet was scripting a television series for CBC Halifax called "22 Hazelwood," featuring Helen's friend Joan Gregson as the matriarch of a musical family. The storylines were woven around music sung by the family and guests, and in November Helen and I were written into an episode about folk songs. She almost didn't do the show. As she wrote in her diary, she "at first declined, thinking one should know at what age to stop. Then recalled had gone on Ben Wicks program and hadn't looked too badly, and it would be nice to be in the swim again."[12] Then she almost didn't make the taping session. The day before her scheduled taping, she began to see flashing lights in her left eye. Her physician arranged a hospital appointment for the following day. However, always game, she taped the show, stopping off on the way for a brief examination with her eye doctor. Fortunately, her role was a walk-on cameo, so didn't take long. She was finished and off to her hospital appointment in good time. Her eye was fine, and no damage done. She later wrote in her diary, "I call this little adventure Helen's Caper.... I didn't blink when I signed the cost sheet, but felt pretty happy because my fee was $300.00, very welcome just before Christmas."[13]

With her manuscript of Acadian songs in the hands of the National Museum, and her collection of folk tales sent off to Herbert Halpert, Helen had more free time in 1982. It was time much needed. Always mindful of her need to be well rested, Helen now found she had to spend some days relaxing before an event and then take considerable time afterwards to recoup her energies. She began to curtail some of her commitments to organizations and societies—and was pleasantly surprised to find that even retirement can bring its rewards. When she resigned from Zonta International, citing old age, they responded by making her an honorary member. Despite her resolution to guard her energies, she did make the time for a photographic session at Evergreen. I was releasing my second album and wanted a picture of Helen and me for the back of the record jacket. All the songs were from Helen's collection, and I called it, *False Knight Upon the Road: Songs from the Collection of Dr. Helen Creighton.*[14]

In May Helen channelled all her energy towards accepting her sixth honorary degree. Mount St. Vincent University, in Halifax, presented her with an honorary Doctor of Humane Letters. Her friend, Mary Sparling, read the citation, and I was asked to represent her work with a song. Helen was worried that she wouldn't have the stamina required for the ceremony, but her diary entry after the event shows how accommodating her hosts were: "Mary [Sparling] had arranged that I wouldn't have to stand while she read my citation ... Clary Croft sang Farewell to Nova Scotia, and everybody joined in. It was the hit of the morning. He and Sharon, and my guests Richard and Eunice Sircom and Simmie, and Phyllis Blakeley and Shirley, and Cora Greenaway were sitting where I could see them all the time."[15]

Helen rested for the following three weeks, preparing herself for the next honour to come her way. On 30 May she attended a banquet in Halifax, where the Choral Federation of Nova Scotia had arranged for her to receive Nova Scotia's Cultural Life Award. Receiving an honorary degree and being granted her province's highest cultural

*Helen Creighton Fonds, PANS Binder 19: 1270. Photographer: Graham Lavers*

*Helen Creighton, Clary Croft and Mary Sparling at a reception following Helen's honorary degree from Mount Saint Vincent University, May 9, 1982.*

award were heady events indeed, but she was to receive an even greater tribute in June. This time it would come as a complete surprise.

Helen had been invited by her old friend, Sandy Ives, to attend the Annual Meeting of the Northeast Folklore Society, being held that year at the University of Orono in Maine. Since she rarely drove anymore, and certainly not for any distance, she asked two friends to accompany her. Helen had arranged for Cora Greenaway to present a paper on her research into decorative painted motifs found in Nova Scotian interiors, and also invited Wendy Scott, whom she had recently befriended after being interviewed by her for CBC radio.

Helen had no reason to suspect that she would be presented with any special recognition at this meeting. She had already received the highest tribute her American colleagues could pay when she was made a fellow of the American Folklore Society in 1969. She thought that the meeting would be perhaps her last opportunity to be amongst the leading folklorists of her day, and a happy occasion to renew a longstanding relationship with Sandy Ives and his wife Bobby. So the events that unfolded at the banquet came as a complete surprise:

Sandy made a short speech and said something about a lot of letters and presented me with a black folder at which point the whole assembly rose and clapped and clapped.... It wasn't until I said goodbye to Sandy and dear Bobby and was back in the apartment [provided on campus] that I looked inside the black book. I couldn't believe it. The letters were all written to me. I didn't dare read them then or I knew I wouldn't sleep.... In the car I read them to Cora and Wendy as we drove along ... They were full of personal affection and scholarly appreciation. ... I have thumbed that book through more than any I have ever owned.... God bless you, dear Sandy and Bobby.[16]

Of the hundreds of tributes Helen received over her lifetime, the Book of Letters from her American colleagues stood out as a personal highlight. It demonstrated the depth of feeling many held for her and, for those who didn't know her personally, it told of the influence her work had played. For Helen, whose work *was* her life, these tributes marked an acknowledgement of her years of struggle and an appreciation of the work she had done. A sampling of the comments contained in the letters illustrates the range of tributes paid to her: George Carey, of the University of Massachusetts and a student of her friend, Richard Dorson, wrote: "You don't have one hokey idea in hell who I am. But I know who you are. You're famous, and I hope by now, rich. You deserve to be both.... As for your contribution to folklore: well, my God woman, just take a look at the score sheet. They had you in the hall of fame when I was just a pup"; Pete Seeger noted that "Basic research is rarely well-paid for. But I hope you know that it will go down in history, when us 'popularizers' are forgot. We both have our roles, I guess. But there's no doubt in my mind which comes first"; and Horace Beck wrote that "Perhaps your most important achievement is that you have done something which no one else has been able to do in North America. You have brought folklore to national and public attention and given it a status in Canada it has never achieved in the United States. This you have done almost singlehandedly and for this all folklorists must be forever grateful."[17]

Helen never took lightly the tributes paid her. It must have been rewarding to look back on her early days of collecting, a period when even she couldn't have dreamed of what her efforts would eventually bring. The Book of Letters was tangible evidence that her work was appreciated by both established and up-and-coming American folklorists, and the recognition from her peers was most touching. That acknowledgement was made bittersweet when she received a letter informing her of Doreen Senior's death. She and Doreen had shared the early years. They had cut their professional teeth on song collecting. Although they had drifted apart over the years, their mutual history had formed a bond that time and differences of opinion couldn't alter. And now Doreen was dead. She had, in fact, died in December of 1981, but Helen didn't find out until October, when Robert Aitken wrote. He told Helen how he and his wife had known Doreen when she lived in Dorset. The lone offspring of parents who were themselves single children, Doreen had no surviving relatives, and the Aitkens were the closest to family she'd had. She had retired in the early 1970s as Music Advisor to the County of Exeter, and since 1972 had failed both physically and mentally. In 1979 she was placed in a nursing home, where she died two years later.[18]

Helen's memories were stirred again in March of 1983, when she was invited to Ottawa to attend special celebrations in honour of the centenary of the birth of her friend Marius Barbeau. He had died in 1969, and many of his colleagues were gathering to remember the man who had had a resounding influence on their professional lives. Helen

renewed acquaintances with long-time friends such as Kenneth Peacock and Carmen Roy. Edith Fowke, Helen's old adversary, colleague,
and friend, was not present. She and Helen had kept up their friendship and soon would be drawn into another conflict—but this time
they would find themselves on the same side.

A Newfoundlander named J. Anthony Stephenson had begun a campaign against the use of a song he considered to be solely of Newfoundland origin. He took great exception to a version of "Lukey's
Boat" that Edith and Richard Johnston had published in *Folk Songs of
Canada*. The argument he presented was that although the authors
had correctly attributed the song to Newfoundland, they had used a
melody from Nova Scotia, a melody from Helen's *Songs and Ballads
from Nova Scotia*. She had collected it as "Loakie's Boat" from Mr. and
Mrs. Edward Hartley in Dartmouth, sometime before 1930.[19] Mr. Stephenson
launched an attack on Edith and Helen, accusing them of stealing the
song from Newfoundland. He appeared at the Canadian Folk Music
Society's Conference—wearing a "Lukey's Boat Fund" button—and
lobbied Society members to join his fight. Helen was more amused
than anything, as she noted in her diary:

Letter from John C. Bird of Gordon V. Thompson firm enclosing
letter written about the folk song Lukey's Boat. Pretty crazy. Must have
been only recently that he heard I had published it and he was irate.
Didn't call me by name but bemoaned fact that it was in several music
books but with my tune, and not the one from NFLD. Called it a misrepresentation, false, a fraud, and a crime, all in one letter. I started
then to look through old papers and found that I had taken it down
between 1929 & 30.... How then did the Edward Hartleys know it
before ... 1930. Called Allan Hartley to find out if Edward Hartley had
and Nfld. connections. No they hadn't. Then had idea and asked Allan
if his father knew this song. Yes had sung it to him often. When? In
1926 & 7. Knew date because went away just after that. So that was
another proof of public domain. What will Nfld's Mr. Stephenson make
of this? It was fun digging these details and renewing thoughts of those
productive and happy years.[20]

Edith, however, was outraged at the perceived affront to her work as
a scholar, and took a far less passive approach. While most people didn't
take him very seriously, some—including Society member Tim Johnston—
had sided with Mr. Stephenson, suggesting that it was an unwitting
mistake. Edith sent Helen a copy of her rebuttal to Tim Johnston, in
which she wrote, "I can't let your statement stand that 'Clearly a scholarly
mistake was made' in Folk Songs of Canada."[21] She explained how the
song had been published with clear indications to provenance and signed

her letter, "Yours in scholarly rage."[22]

As Helen had proven to herself that she had done nothing wrong about the song, she decided to leave it at that. In any case, she had more productive things to do with her time. Throughout the summer she had been assembling copies of audio tapes, photographs, and books concerning her work with African Nova Scotians. By 1 September she was able to offer this compilation to Henry Bishop at the Black Cultural Centre of Nova Scotia. And in November the Public Archives of Nova Scotia arranged an evening devoted to her songs and films; although she didn't intend to speak, she found "there was so much to share that [she] bobbed up a good many times"[23] to offer reminiscences and explanations.

In February 1984 Helen had another of what she called her "Red Letter Days." She received a letter from the Queen[24] in response to a detailed report that Helen had sent outlining recent research that confirmed the Queen's suggestion that "Farewell to Nova Scotia" had its origins in Scotland.[25] Helen was thrilled with the letter and promptly had it framed and hung on her dining-room wall. In March she added yet another honour to her already impressive and ever-growing resumé, when the Canadian Authors Association made her their honorary National President.

The summer of 1984 was remembered by many Nova Scotians for the visit of the Tall Ships of the World. Sailing vessels from around the globe converged on Halifax, and the entire city exploded in a spirit of celebration and nautical fervour. After a concert I gave at The Public Archives featuring sea songs from Helen's collection, she graciously noted that it was a "beautiful job and had large appreciative audience."[26] What she failed to mention was that during the concert she occasionally would offer some tidbit about how a particular song was collected. Another guest at the concert was my friend, Claude Darrach,[27] an original crew member on the *Bluenose*, who was able to offer insights on a primary source. Together they helped to make the evening memorable for both performer and audience.

Helen ended the year with a warm greeting and an admission that time was catching up with her. The handmade Christmas card she sent to her friends read:

I'm 85
That's awfully old
But I just slow down as the years unfold
So let us sing most joyfully
'Cause CHRISTMAS is here
and so are WE
HAPPY CHRISTMAS![28]

Helen Creighton Fonds, PANS Binder 19:1301. Photographer: unknown

*Christmas party at the home of Alice (Creighton) and David Nicholl, 1980s. Not including spouses, all but Mrs. Nicholl Sr. and Helen Creighton are descendants of Paul and Leda Creighton.*

She spent a pleasant holiday season with family and friends, but began to be troubled by disturbing dreams. On 22 January 1985, she wrote in her diary, "For a month or more have been having dreams of deceased members of family. Mother used to see deceased members of her family around her bed before she died. The dreams don't make much sense and seem to come just before awakening. Why? Is there something I should be doing?"[29] She felt that she had her answer when on 10 March she received a telephone call from her sister-in-law Betty Creighton. Helen's beloved brother Mac had died peacefully in his sleep in London.

Two days later she attended the unveiling of her portrait at King's College. In mourning for Mac, she was reluctant to go, but she was also loath to disappoint her friends and supporters. It was "so soon after Mac's death, but Kings had been so kind in arranging this and it would mean so much to artist Gillian, that I couldn't call it off."[30] Helen had grown fond of her portraitist, Gillian MacCullough. When Gillian finished the painting the previous October, Helen had noted her impressions of both the portrait and the artist in her diary: "Had worked 14 months on it, and she is pleased. Me too though I am no expert on painting. We made it quite an occasion. Both had enjoyed the sittings. Very charming and always thoughtful and considerate...."

The painting was her idea and I agreed mainly because she was young ... and I hoped it would help her career."[31]

The portrait, painted in oils, shows Helen at her desk in the bay window at Evergreen, with the busy Halifax Harbour in the background. In the foreground, on the desk, Gillian painted several items that would be familiar to anyone who knew Helen. There is a piece of music manuscript, various papers, and a cup given to Helen by the Rayner sisters, whom she had taken to meet Dennis Smith so long before. Anyone who ever visited Helen and was served coffee would remember those cups. Also on the desk, standing in a simple water glass, was a bouquet of forget-me-nots, Helen's favourite wild flowers.

The unveiling party at King's was a great success. "Wore new blue dress created by Sharon Croft.... Guests arrived early and it turned out to be one of the warmest and most friendly receptions most had ever known.... President John Godfrey said a few nice words ... and then Raylene Rankin ... thanked me for saving heritage and then sang unaccompanied The Happy Island in Gaelic. A Lovely voice."[32]

By 1985 Sharon was designing and making all of Helen's good clothes. She had graduated from the Costume Studies program at Dalhousie University in 1978 and we had started a design firm called Croft Designs. In the fall of 1984 I enrolled in the same program to pursue my own interest in costume and textile design and to be able to help more with the business. Away from class I continued to sing and work part-time at the Public Archives of Nova Scotia. Helen supported my non-folkloric pursuits. She was declining speaking engagements and most interviews and frequently passed them on to me. I also became her unofficial correspondence secretary. We developed a good working relationship, and with Sharon and Helen spending time working on fittings and fabric selections, we were frequently together. It was during this period that Helen began to call me "her boy."

Sharon and I had become part of the extended family that looked out for Helen. We were growing increasingly concerned about her health. Although in April she had undergone extensive medical tests that turned up benign results, in May and June she began to noticeably fail. She suffered from painful arthritis and high blood pressure and had recently fallen three times in her apartment. Then, during a bath, she felt unable to move, and had to drain the water from the tub and remain there for over an hour before she gathered her strength to get out. Still, she bravely moved forward.

In August she met with representatives from Nimbus Publishing, in Halifax, to discuss the publication of her collection of children's stories in a small book called *With a Heigh- heigh-ho*.[33] Her diary reveals that she didn't "think it will set the world on fire, but it is something to look forward to and came at a time when very weak from falls etc.

and was a real boost.... Had gone downhill quickly ... I called it my woes and misery summer."[34] Most of the stories and poems had been written for her nieces and nephews in the 1920s and 1930s. As she wrote in the introduction, "those nephews and nieces who helped me in a way to write these stories have asked me many times over the years to have them published. First I just shook my head. I wondered if children today would like stories written so long ago when our lives were so different. Now we shall see!"[35] It was a nice little book, with charming line drawings by Bill Johnson, but Helen's instincts were correct; it didn't have much in the way of mass appeal for children in the 1980s.

Helen planned to make 1986 a year of rest. She was feeling somewhat better and her strength was beginning to return. In May she attended a concert put on in her honour by the Dartmouth Choral Society. Kaye Dimock (now Pottie) and I were soloists, and at the end of the concert the Nova Scotia Department of Culture, Recreation, and Fitness presented Helen with a beautiful silver-wire sculpture by noted Dartmouth artist, Dawn McNutt.

That spring I completed the Costume Studies program and was immediately rehired by the Provincial Archives to care for their artifact collection. In October I signed a contract with them to begin my most important work to date. I was asked to create an archival arrangement and description of the Helen Creighton Collection. My position came about because of my years of part-time employment at the Archives, and because Helen was determined to have someone whom she knew and trusted to work on her collection. In 1981 she had signed documents leaving her entire collection to the Public Archives, and now I had the task of working with her to catalogue the collection currently held at the Pubic Archives and to transfer folklore material from her home to permanent archival storage. Most of the funding for the project came from the National Archives Arrangement and Description Backlog Program, with the Province of Nova Scotia making up the balance.

It was my dream job. I would have to go through every piece of paper, every reel of audio tape, and every photograph and field journal in Helen's collection. Few archivists have the luxury of working directly with the progenitor of a collection, but I would be able to tap into Helen's amazing memory and gain insights directly from the collector herself. Helen, too, understood the opportunity this relationship represented. In a letter to her friend Mabel Laine, at the Encyclopaedia of Music in Canada, she wrote, "They are making the most of me while my memory is good and I am only too glad of the opportunity."[36] So began a two-year working relationship that brought us even closer together.

# CHAPTER TWENTY

## ✳ ✳ ✳

lthough working together on an almost daily basis was a pleasant and rewarding experience, it was not without its tensions. My job was to identify and catalogue every item in Helen's inventory of folklore-related material. The bulk of that collection had already been transferred to the Public Archives of Nova Scotia; Helen had stored much of her collection there for decades. However, during the first three months of my contract I spent at least three days each week with Helen, cataloguing the material she had at home and preparing it for shipment to the archival vaults. I was working on a two-year contract and trying to expedite the transfer. Helen had spent a lifetime collecting the material and was trying to hold on to it. She knew the material had to be moved but hated to see me carry it out the door. I understood completely. Nonetheless, as I wrote in my journal, by the end of January we had reached a stalemate:

A very difficult day today. I finished the inventory and began to pack up the records Helen said I could take over to the Archives. I had room in one of the boxes—so I asked if I could put some of the photographs in it and take them over as well. She appeared confused and I had her come into the storage room to see what I meant. She said, 'All my precious family photos,' as if we had never discussed their transfer. Then she saw all the [record] albums packed up and said, 'Are you taking *all* those? I haven't had a chance to listen to half of them yet!' I guess this was coming—so I said we should go into the living room and talk. I explained how painful it was for me to break down the collection like this—but my time was limited. She, of course, understood—but until today—would not face the fact that most of the collection needed to be moved. I then suggested that we photocopy any files she wished to keep at her house—and she said that would work—also she didn't need to keep very much. I will leave her alone over the weekend—I know she will give this matter a good deal of thought. So for the rest of the afternoon we just talked—she didn't want to face it—and I felt it best to just chatter about anything.[1]

I went over to her apartment four days later. She told me she understood my need to work as quickly as possible and from then on, our work together went smoothly. The Public Archives didn't take any of her personal or family papers and I made photocopies of her later diaries and current files.

The previous evening we had gone together to see a remount of *The Collector* at the Citadel Hill Dinner Theatre. John Brown had brought in a different director, and the show was presented with a new—and much smaller—cast. Helen was delighted with the production: "Glen Walton is the director. I had never seen him in this role. He knows exactly what he is doing.... I came home feeling humble. So many wonderful people spending so much time, thought and talent upon what I have done. Yes dear father and mother, the time and money are being justified as you forecast."[2]

Although Helen had never seen Glen Walton in the role of theatre director, she did know him as a filmmaker. In 1985 he had approached Helen about giving an on-camera interview about her life and career. He wanted the film to give particular emphasis to the circumstances surrounding the collection of "The Nova Scotia Song." After the filming session at Evergreen she wrote in her diary, "Liked that idea .... Questions well prepared and Clary asked them which presented pleasant atmosphere. Sat at round table in sitting room window. Hope I was not too relaxed. Didn't realize how ancient equipment was or how amateur the operator and girl assisting him were. So what the quality will be, time will tell."[3]

Two years later, on 19 February 1987, the film had its premier at the National Film Board's theatre in Halifax. Helen's subsequent diary entry was very enthusiastic:

I had seen it in the making and realized it was going to be my best effort to date.... This gala evening would show the National Film Board's 1957 film, *Songs of Nova Scotia*, and then the new one entitled *The Nova Scotia Song*.... I did everything to keep well so I could enjoy the evening, and wouldn't even eat a nut in case I broke a tooth. Consequently I felt well and was prepared for a good evening.... The hall was packed and some had to sit on the floor.... Not having taken it seriously, and knowing Clary well I relaxed and there were a few humorous touches.... Catherine McKinnon had come especially for the occasion, having been the singer who had made the Nova Scotia song famous. She was most gracious and was evidently enjoying it, but kept in background until Glen presented her and she sang the N.S. Song. Then Clary sang and that was a good final touch.[4]

Having conducted the interview and been otherwise involved with the film, it's difficult for me to be objective about its outcome. Still, I believe that Helen was right about it being her most successful effort. Glen was a relatively inexperienced filmmaker at the time, and his crew came from the local film cooperative, but it was the very lack of slick production techniques that caused Helen to be so relaxed during filming. She gave the most animated, witty, and natural presentation of any of her on-camera appearances.

In May I escorted Helen to a birthday party for one of her informants from Devil's Island. Clarence Henneberry was turning 100, and his family invited Helen to attend the celebrations being held at the Buffalo Club in Eastern Passage. Helen couldn't go alone, so asked me to take her. When we walked through the door of the club, we were greeted by the centenarian himself, who was seated at a decorated card table bearing a huge birthday cake. Beside his elbow was a water tumbler of dark rum. When his relatives asked Clarence if he recognized his guest, he replied, "'My God, Helen Creighton—you're a [hell of] a lot older than me!' They talked of the old days and Helen said, 'Remember the times we rowed to the Island?' 'I did all the rowing,' said Clarence, 'you sat on your stern!'" Helen was applauded at the party and I was asked to speak on her behalf. She later told me she was very pleased to have me there— she said it was part of my training."[5]

Helen participated in another gala celebration of her work that June. The Canadian Authors Association was meeting in Halifax and Kaye Pottie organized a concert similar to the previous year's presentation by the Dartmouth Choral Society. This time Helen provided tape-recorded introductions to the songs being sung. She was thrilled to reacquaint herself with long-established friends, and it was also an opportunity for the Association to present her with a diamond pin in recognition of her years of service.

The day before the concert I received a telephone call from Janet Smith, a producer with CBC television. She had been negotiating with the network to produce a documentary film focusing on Helen's folklore legacy and my work with her collection. Janet hoped to film a number of upcoming celebrations honouring Helen's work. She also wanted to capture some elements of the work being done with Helen's music in the schools and arranged to speak with music educators and follow me to a classroom session with elementary schoolchildren. It was an ambitious project and shooting would take place over several months. Helen declined to appear on film, but gave the project her blessing. I stayed out of negotiations between Helen and the CBC, but suggested to Janet that once Helen developed a working relationship with the television crew, she would eventually come around to being comfortable in front of the camera. On the evening of the Canadian Authors Association concert, the CBC film crew arrived to get some background shots, and Helen promptly gave them an on-camera interview. From then on, she was happy to appear on camera.

Helen's initial reluctance to appear before the television camera was simple. She told me that she was "afraid of appearing too old and forgetful and [didn't] want her last days on film to be something to be pitied later on."[6] She was trying to cope with her declining health and quite naturally didn't want to appear doddery or vague. Fortunately, she was neither, but needed to be reassured that she could still present herself in a dignified manner.

Later that summer she began to consider a possible future when she could no longer care for herself. She asked Cora Greenaway and Nesta Olive to accompany her on a visit to a local nursing home. They had been encouraging her to explore her options before the time when a hasty decision might need to be made. When I asked her if she had gone to the nursing home just to appease them, she replied that she realized she would have to face that situation at some point, but meanwhile hoped for the alternative of having someone live with her.

Helen celebrated her eighty-eighth birthday at the Citadel Hill Dinner Theatre. Sharon and I went with her as guests of her cousin, Robin Creighton and his wife, Martha. The cast presented a show featuring songs from World War I. Helen was in great spirits and sang along with many of the songs. Sharon brought a birthday cake and the cast and audience serenaded Helen with "Happy Birthday." Shortly after this celebration, Helen granted an interview to Diane Tye on behalf of the Folklore Institute of Indiana University. The topic was "Women in the Discipline of Folklore." Helen had never met Diane Tye, but was satisfied with the day's events:

Pleased to find her a very pleasant, intelligent young woman, easy to talk to.... Had arranged for Clary to be here at 12 in case I got too tired and also because she wants to see Archives collection. He was a great help although I managed whole interview alone. I broke two resolutions, one that I was through giving interviews and two that I would not attempt to feed anyone who came on business because it would be too fatiguing. However I put ingredients on kitchen counter, and Clary prepared delicious meal. Felt I must make use of this opportunity as would not want to be left out on such a study, and wished to speak for self. Enjoyed every minute, but was exhausted for days.[7]

Every effort she made now brought on exhaustion and, moreover, her voice was giving out. A few days after the interview, she consulted a throat specialist, who told her that there were no growths, but advised her to talk as little as possible. She was also suffering with chest and abdominal pains, experiencing dizzy spells, and was nerv-

*After Symphony Nova Scotia's "Tribute to Helen Creighton," November 20, 1987.*
*L-R: Walter Kemp, Mary Kelly, Scott Macmillan, Helen Creighton, Clary Croft.*

Photographer: George Georgakakos. Author's collection.

ous of being alone at night. In October she contacted a representative of the Dartmouth Senior Citizen's Bureau to enquire about having a live-in companion. By 3 November she felt so ill that her physician advised tests. I took her to Dartmouth General Hospital and stayed with her throughout the day. They kept her overnight and conducted more tests the following morning. It turned out that she had an infection that manifested itself in symptoms similar to a gall bladder attack. With medication and rest, she was feeling better in a matter of days. She returned to her apartment, where she arranged for a caregiver to spend the night. Friends and family brought in meals and did whatever they could to help. Helen obeyed every directive from her physician. She was doing everything she could to rally enough strength for an upcoming concert by Symphony Nova Scotia. On the way to the hospital she had said, "Clary, no matter what happens to me the concert must go on!"[8] It was an event that she definitely didn't want to miss.

The concert, held on 20 November at the Rebecca Cohn Auditorium in Halifax, was Symphony Nova Scotia's "Tribute to Dr. Helen Creighton." The musical arrangements were by a brilliant local composer named Scott Macmillan. I doubled as host and one of the soloists, along with Halifax singer Mary Kelly. Dr. Walter Kemp conducted the orchestra and the Dalhousie Chorale, and the CBC television crew that had been working with us for months filmed the concert, which was also broadcast over the CBC radio network. Helen was elated:

As I entered the auditorium I faced the piper who was to pipe me to my seat ... I was nearly overwhelmed. It was an emotional evening, even for those who knew me only by reputation. Much was due to Scott Macmillan's arrangements. He had wisely gone to the Archives and listened to tapes of the folk who gave me the songs, and in this he grasped the deep feeling of the singers for the songs they loved.[9]

In her diary, she added, "From the first loved every minute of it ... Scott's ... new setting of N.S. Song a magnificent finale.... And at the reception Scott held on to my hand as though he wanted to share his triumph with me.... Surely this was the ultimate and especially gratifying to me since music was my greatest interest. All other items were incidental.... As each number was presented I was taken back to the home where I had found it. If only father and mother could have shared the evening!"[10] She told me that it was the highlight of her career, coming as it did from her home turf,[11] and that she felt humbled to have been the one entrusted with saving much of the traditional music of the Maritimes. A later diary note about the concert confirms her sense of responsibility: "As I listened and realized that I was the catalyst I felt proud to have been given that trust [re: collecting music] ... Scott felt the same way about his part. And I'm sure Clary must too."[12]

Helen barely had time to recuperate from the Symphony Nova Scotia concert before she was in the spotlight again. Janet Smith and the CBC crew came to her apartment to film the final segments for *The Legacy of Helen Creighton*. Helen was probably working on adrenaline from the concert and was in fine form, relaxed and full of fun. Janet had been trying to get Helen to sing a few bars of one of the folk songs she had collected. Never much of a singer, Helen steadfastly refused. But, as her diary entry shows, her singing voice was captured for posterity: "At the end they played a trick on me. Clary had been here for the 2 days and they had tried to get me to sing which I flatly refused. But at the end he sang a verse of The Kangaroo and then asked me what the next line was. I thought that strange as he never forgets, and without realizing it, I sang the line. How they laughed. Both sessions had quite a lot of laughs ... Janet is so interested and she treated me like a goddess, or something similar. Enough to turns ones head."[13]

Helen's high spirits and increased energy may have been due, in part, to the excitement of the concert and the television tapings, but credit must also go to the attentions provided by her overnight caregiver. She tried several people before settling on Edla Owen, a charming senior whose personality and wit suited Helen to a tee. By the end of the year it was obvious that Edla was providing the care that Helen needed. She stayed with her during the night, helped her with her morning bath,

*At the launch of* La Fleur du Rosier, *Public Archives of Nova Scotia, May 28, 1989. L-R: back row: John Frederick Brown, Ronald Labelle, Glen Walton, Clary Croft, Scott Macmillan, Mary Kelly, Walter Kemp. Front row: Marie Catherine Saulnier (daughter of Laura Irene McNeil), Helen Creighton, Margaret Tse Perron.*

and served her breakfast in bed. Helen was delighted with Edla and told me, "this is a far more satisfactory arrangement than a nursing home."[14]

I continued to work with Helen throughout that fall and early winter. We had established a very satisfactory routine. I worked at the Archives most of the time, but if I needed any information, Helen was just a telephone call away. Her memory for detail was phenomenal. I remember one day in particular, when I was listening to tapes of Chief William Paul from the Shuebenacadie Reserve in Nova Scotia. There was another, unidentified male voice on the tape and I called Helen to see if she knew who it might be. She immediately said, "Oh yes, that's Staff Sergeant Larsen." Then she rhymed off the date of the taping and mentioned the contents of the information in Mr. Paul's narratives. No hesitation—just instant recall. At least two afternoons each week were devoted to working with Helen at her apartment. I usually arrived after lunch, when we would work for a couple of hours before I made tea. It was primarily during these tea breaks that she would share her personal opinions and insights and took the opportunity to speak candidly—not to her archivist, but to her friend.

In January 1988 Helen suffered another great loss. Her last surviving brother, Syd, died in Montreal. She wrote that "[he] was a good brother

*Photographer: Clary Croft. Author's collection*

***Eunice Sircom, Sharon Croft, Helen Creighton, at Helen's apartment in Dartmouth the day Helen first saw her collection of Acadian songs,* La Fleur du Rosier, *1989.***

to me. Now I am alone."[15] The youngest of six children, because of her weak heart and delicate condition, Helen had not been considered as strong as her siblings. Yet here she was, approaching her ninetieth decade, the last surviving member of her immediate family. It was difficult for her to realize that most of the people who remembered her childhood were gone. Combined with the breaking up of her life's collection and its removal to another place, it was a traumatic transition period. However, Helen seemed to be handling it very well. She knew about moving forward and her outlook made my job—and our personal relationship—very enjoyable. We had become like family.

A new Helen Creighton book was launched in May. Her friend, Rosemary Bauchman, had been working for almost two years selecting excerpts from Helen's various books for a publication she called *The Best of Helen Creighton*.[16] The launch party was held at the Public Archives and many of Helen's friends and family members were present. One of the invited guests Helen was especially pleased to see was Donald Gallagher, son of her dear friend Catherine. She hadn't seen him in years and took great delight in reminiscing with him about his mother and those early years at the lighthouse at Chebucto Head.

Helen returned to the Archives in July. I was coming to the end of my contract and wanted her to see the work that had been done. She described the visit in her diary: "Although Clary had been working on my collection for two years I had never been over to see what he has done. He had kept me well informed, but it was time I saw for myself. It was quite overwhelming, and again I realized how fortunate I am to have had anyone with such interest and dedication to be given this employment."[17]

She had every reason to be impressed, not necessarily because of my work, but for the sheer magnitude of her collection assembled under one roof. It includes 20 metres of manuscript material, made up of research notes, field journals, publication drafts and proofs, and more than 5,000 file cards. In addition, there are over 1,800 individual correspondence files; upward of 2,700 still images (photographs and artwork), and a sound and moving-image archive that ranges from wax cylinders to video film. It took me 40 weeks of 8-hour days just to listen to, and catalogue, the material on audio tape. The archive is considered by many, including Edith Fowke, to be the largest individually assembled collection of folklore in Canada.[18] Helen donated the collection to the Province of Nova Scotia. In return, she received a tax receipt for $128,153—and it would have been considerably more if the original audio discs were not with the Library of Congress in Washington and the original audio tapes with the National Museum in Ottawa.[19]

During the summer Helen's health began to fail again. She tired very easily and started using a cane to support herself around the apartment. She was also becoming increasingly hard of hearing. She commented on her condition in a diary entry made after a pleasant visit from her Ottawa friends, Tom and Mavis Kines. Several of us helped her to host a tea party for the Kines and, when they came by the next day to bid Helen farewell, she noted "that sad look in [their] eyes wondering if this was a final farewell."[20]

She spent a quiet Christmas, but since Mrs. Owen was in hospital with the flu, Helen had to rely on friends to act as her overnight caregivers. Cora Greenaway stayed over a few evenings. Jackie Dale spent Christmas Eve and Joleen Gordon stayed for New Years. Richard Sircom set up a special alarm system in case she needed attention in an emergency. Friends and family provided food, but most of her meals were now being supplied by Meals on Wheels. Through it all, she maintained a sense of humour and a will to go on that was both admirable and inspiring. By spring she had regained some of her former strength, especially after Edla Owen came back in April. Helen referred to her overnight caregivers as her "bye-lo ladies," but saved her most affectionate endearment for Edla—she was Helen's "lullaby lady."

In May Helen underwent a full physical examination. The report, prepared by her family physician, Anthony Lamplugh, noted her failed health over the previous 12 months. Helen knew all too well the truth in the report, but told me she found it hard to see it in print. Still, she struggled to keep whatever good health she had. She was determined to be strong. She wanted to fight.

She mustered her energy to attend a special ceremony at the Canadian Music Educators Association Conference held in Halifax on 6 May, where she received their Jubilate Award of Merit. In reading the citation, Vernon Ellis, an Acadia University music professor and her good friend, paid special tribute to Helen's informants, saying, "she

*Helen Creighton blowing out the candles on her 90th Birthday cake,*
*September 5, 1989. L-R: Lois Harnish, Barbara Miller, Helen Creighton, Alice Nicholl.*

appreciated and helped to bring honour to the singers ... To her these people were never just the source of a song, but were people of character possessing admirable abilities."[21]

Kaye Pottie later told me how moving the ceremony was for all those who knew Helen. When her name was called, Helen moved slowly towards the stage, using two canes. Reaching the top of the stairs, she handed her canes to a friend and strode onto the stage, where a group of elementary-school children was performing several singing games from her collection. When the children finished their last song, "There'll Be Peace in that Land Where I'm Bound," they sprinted off one side of the stage, while Helen carefully and slowly walked the other way. It was a poignant image that brought tears to the eyes of many of Helen's friends.

In June Helen attended the launch of *La Fleur du Rosier: Acadian Folksongs.*[22] She had been waiting a long time—since October 1980, when she sent her manuscript off to the National Museum, until June 1989, when I delivered the first copy into her hands. The National Museum had not been successful in their attempts to find a co-publisher for the manuscript; 17 publishers declined, although two regretted the decision given Helen's reputation. Helen had all but given up on the project until I suggested the manuscript to Robert Morgan, the archivist for the Beaton Institute attached to the University College of Cape Breton. He put the wheels in motion and, together with Tim Belliveau of the UCCB Press, and the Canadian Museum of Civilization, a co-publication agreement was reached. I was especially honoured when Helen inscribed my copy, "For Clary, discoverer of the publisher of this beautiful book."

The book launch was held at the Public Archives. Her family and friends were all quite concerned about Helen's delicate condition. Would the excitement of the party be too much for her? On the contrary, Helen handled the situation with her usual panache, making the best of a difficult situation. We had arranged to have a wheelchair present if needed, but were not quite certain whether she would use it. However, when her niece, Alice Nicholl, and Alice's husband David, drove her up to the door, Helen herself made the decision to sit in the chair. She told everyone that she had been suffering from an upset stomach and didn't want to faint and frighten the children present.

It was a glorious party. Helen absolutely glowed with delight. She basked in the attentions of her proud family and close friends. Instrumental music was provided by The Chaddock Family, a talented young ensemble who played Eunice Sircom's arrangements of Acadian melodies. A selection of songs from the new book was presented by the French Immersion students from St. Catherine's School in Halifax, under the direction of Margaret Tse Perron, who had long been a champion of Helen's work. A special guest was Marie Catherine Saulnier, the daughter of Laura Irene McNeil. When Marie told Helen how she had passed her mother's songs on to her own children, Helen was deeply gratified. She wanted the songs to live— not just in books, but with the people who initially shared them with her.

In August I received a telephone call from folk singer Ed McCurdy. He and his wife Beryl had retired in Halifax and renewed their longstanding relationship with Helen. Ed had been promoting Helen's work for more than 50 years and came up with yet another way to celebrate her legacy. He suggested a festival in her honour and invited me to join him in making it a reality. In September we met with Mayor John Savage. Dr. Savage thought a festival was a wonderful idea. The City of Dartmouth had been looking for a way to recognize Helen's forthcoming ninetieth birthday; a folklore festival would both pay tribute to Helen's work and provide a sense of celebration. He would announce the inauguration of the first annual Helen Creighton Folklore Festival of Dartmouth[23] at Helen's birthday party at Evergreen.

Thanks to the efforts of her family and friends, Helen's ninetieth birthday party at Evergreen was a great success. Her nephew, Jake Creighton, acted as master of ceremonies and read congratulatory messages from across the nation. Helen had been consulted on the formation of the festival and felt it was a wonderful idea. When John Savage made the announcement she beamed with delight. She was back home, surrounded by those who loved her. It was an afternoon filled with laughter, music, and a celebration of her long and productive life. And, I believe, it was the beginning of the end.

On 24 September Edla took Helen to the hospital. She had experienced several small strokes. Three days later Sharon and I visited her in the hospital. She was alert but experiencing pains through her neck. Her speech was slurred and she was very weak. However, by Thanksgiving Day she was feeling better. A local magazine had recently published an article about me in which I'd mentioned the strong bond I had with Helen.[24] Having read it, she telephoned and said, "I'm glad to know we're still getting along." I said, "Yes, if they only knew we fought like cats and dogs," to which she replied, "You put me in the hospital."[25]

She was able to maintain her old sense of humour, but also saw the pathos of her situation. The day before, she'd had an experience that moved her deeply. Her hospital roommate was a young woman in a wheelchair. Helen said she had the most extraordinary brown eyes and when they met hers they formed an instant bond. The young woman asked Helen how she coped with her situation and if she had faith. Helen told her that it was faith that sustained her through her difficulties, a reply that seemed to bring her young friend a sense of peace. Helen told me the story with great humility, adding, "Isn't it wonderful that even a 90 year old woman can be useful in giving someone comfort—I broke down twice just telling Dr. Lamplugh about it."[26]

Helen was getting stronger every day and by 16 October had returned to her apartment. However, she was weak enough to require 24-hour care and had to get extra support for Edla—and her improved condition didn't last long. By the end of the month she was back in hospital after suffering another stroke. She no longer spoke of returning to her apartment. On 9 November she was moved to Oakwood Manor, a nursing home in Dartmouth.

I visited as often as I could. On 12 November Helen greeted me on my thirty-ninth birthday with her usual telephone call to sing "Happy Birthday." She wished me many long years of happiness. When I replied that I would like to live as long as she, her reply was, "No Clary, don't wish for that unless you have your health—I am ready to go."[27] When I visited her later that day, I noticed that although her spirits were high, her speech had become even more slurred since the morning. She told me that she had explained to her nephew Jake, who was appointed the executor of her estate, why there were so many cancelled cheques made out to Eunice Sircom and me. We had been running all sorts of little errands over the past year and she didn't want Jake to think that we were taking money from her. Jake already knew the score. He had been very supportive of my relationship with Helen. Still, I was very touched that, even in her own suffering, she was looking out for others.

Helen struggled on at Oakwood Manor for several more weeks. Her family and friends came often, realizing the end was near. Cora Greenaway and Nesta Olive were two of the last people to visit her in the nursing home. Cora later told me, "the last time I saw her she was in Oakwood ... so cold in November ... and Nesta and I came over ... and she was sharing a room with a lady who was blind … we stayed for a while and then had to go, and on impulse I turned back, the door to the room was open … and all at once those big blue eyes, those stars, they came open and I waved to her, up came the hand … the day after she had a stroke."[28]

Helen was brought to Camp Hill Hospital in Halifax. She was still unconscious when I went in to visit her. She looked so small in the hospital bed. I stood beside her and held her hand. Then I offered her one last gift—one I knew she would appreciate even if she couldn't hear me. I sang "The Cherry Tree Carol"—the beautiful song she had first collected from William Riley many years before. She didn't even know I was there. Then again, perhaps she did. It didn't matter. I knew.

The next day, 12 December, Jake called me at home. Helen was dead.

I had no sooner hung up the telephone when it rang again. It continued to ring almost nonstop for the next three days. I had a public relationship with Helen, so I was the contact person for both the media and for her friends and colleagues around the world. Her family were absorbed by their own grief and I was pleased to be able to help. Between performances at Neptune Theatre, I threw myself into taking care of whatever details I could to make things easier for Jake and the family. I reminded Jake that Helen had requested her caul be cremated with her, so Eunice Sircom was dispatched to the apartment to retrieve it. Jake asked me to write the obituary and kindly invited Sharon and me to attend the funeral services in the company of the family. He asked my advice about music for the service and I consulted with Kaye Pottie. She suggested, aside from Helen's favourite hymns, that the entire congregation be invited to sing a song that Helen herself had set to music from an old Gaelic melody. It is called "The Hills and Glens": 'Tis Nova Scotia is my home / I love it as no other / Where man is free to ply his trade / And each to each his brother."[29]

The memorial service for Mary Helen Creighton was held on Saturday afternoon, 16 December, at Christ Church in Dartmouth during one of the worse snowstorms of the winter. The service was conducted by the Reverend Peter MacDonald and the church was filled to capacity. At the internment, Barry Shears stood in the raging storm and played "The Nova Scotia Song" on his pipes: "Farewell to Nova Scotia the seabound coast / Let your mountains dark and dreary be / For when I am far away on the briny ocean tossed / Will you ever heave a sigh and a wish for me."[30]

On 29 December 1989, I made the last entry for the decade in my journal: "This is a new year and a new start. Nimbus has already called & asked me to do the biography. I feel it is my job to do it—so I'm sure I will take it on."[31]

# CHAPTER TWENTY-ONE

### ✳ ✳ ✳

*"I will always remember you while my memory lasts"[1]*

I believe that Helen chose to die. She struggled valiantly to maintain strength until her book of Acadian songs came out; from then on her decline was steady and swift. She told me she was ready to go and did so with as much dignity as she could muster. Many of her friends and colleagues agree. Thomas Raddall later told me of the last Christmas card he received from Helen, "the phraseology she used, 'Goodbye old friend, not till we meet again, or something like that, simply goodbye.'"[2]

Tributes and expressions of condolence came pouring in after her death. Naturally, most of the personal expressions of sympathy went to Helen's immediate family, but because I had so long represented Helen in the public arena, I received dozens of telegrams, cards, telephone calls, and letters. The staff at the Canadian Museum of Civilization wrote, "Her important collection in our holdings is a testimony to her relentless work and to the many years of fruitful collaboration with the Canadian Centre for Folk Culture Studies. Please accept our heartfelt condolences."[3] The director of the Museum, Dr. George MacDonald, sent his own personal condolences, adding, "As a pioneer in Canadian folklore, she leaves a heritage for this museum and for all Canadians to share. She will be remembered as the gracious lady that she was."[4] And in the House of Commons, Dartmouth MP Ron MacDonald paid her a glowing tribute: "Mr. Speaker, I rise today to pay tribute to the late Dr. Helen Creighton ... one of the most outstanding Nova Scotians of her generation.... Today, on behalf of all Nova Scotians, I say farewell to her. Our generation and future generations will enjoy her remarkable legacy of music and folklore for she has truly given us a record of our history."[5]

Her legacy continued to be recognized long after her death. In the spring of 1990 the Aeolian Singers presented a concert at the Rebecca Cohn Auditorium in Halifax. The all-female choir featured the premiere of *Songs and Sayings*, a collage of Maritime musical and verbal expressions for women's chorus, cello, and piano, commissioned from Alasdair MacLean by CBC Radio. The choir had performed many songs from Helen's collection during its previous 14 seasons. This new work had been conceived as a tribute to Helen, but ended up as a memorial.

A two-part radio program, "Rock Meets Bone," produced by Denny Blouin and Brian MacKay, and featuring interviews with Helen and me interspersed with original field recordings from Helen's collection, was broadcast on CBC Radio.

The Province of Nova Scotia wanted to honour Helen's legacy by establishing a not-for-profit Foundation. Originally administered through the University of King's College, but now the grants-in-aid component of the Helen Creighton Folklore Society, the Dr. Helen Creighton Memorial Foundation was established in June 1990 with an initial contribution of $50,000 from Nova Scotia's Department of Tourism and Culture. Later that year, during the month of September, the first Helen Creighton Folklore Festival of Dartmouth was held.

In 1991 the East Coast Music Association changed the name of their Lifetime Achievement Award to the Dr. Helen Creighton Lifetime Achievement Award. Accepting the honour in Helen's memory, I offered homage to her informants as well, reminding the audience that "by honouring the memory of Helen Creighton with this award tonight, you are also honouring all those wonderful singers and musicians who contributed to her collection. And you are also honouring those who will come after—those who will sing songs about our lives."[6]

In February the Dr. Helen Creighton Memorial Foundation sponsored what they hoped would be the first of a series of papers devoted to folk culture in the Maritimes. Helen's long-time friend and colleague, Sandy Ives, was invited to present the first paper. He gave an overview of the state of folklore studies and activities, "The World of Maritimes Folklore," which was later published by the Foundation.[7] Ed McCurdy and I sang songs from Helen's collection, and Edith Fowke attended as a special guest.

Others continued to be influenced by Helen's legacy. In 1985 Eric Walker, a Nova Scotian graphic artist, created a folk-style collage work entitled "Helen Creighton, a Legacy for All of Us." Works of art frequently receive renewed interest after the artist's death, but in this case the attention was spurred by the subject's passing. *Arts Atlantic* magazine featured the work in 1994, writing, "This work implicitly links Walker's own artistic project with the work of the pioneer Nova Scotian folklorist."[8] Other works created in the 1990s looked to Helen's legacy for inspiration. *The Collector*, by John Brown, was remounted in 1993 and again in 1998.[9] Actor/playwright Carol Sinclair created a work centred around Helen's collection of witchcraft lore. Called *Put Witch in Bottle*, Carole asked me to perform with her in both the stage adaptation and the subsequent remounting for CBC radio. Several publications also examined Helen's legacy. These included a songbook, *Folksongs of the Maritimes*;[10] made up almost entirely of songs from her collection and assembled and annotated by her colleagues Kaye Pottie and Vernon Ellis. There was a short biography written by Hilary Sircom.[11] I contributed an examination of Helen's collection of songs from the Nova Scotia Home for Coloured Children for Charles Saunders's book, *Share and Care*,[12] and in 1997 I produced the archival segment of a double compact disc featuring recordings from African Nova Scotians.[13] Twenty-eight songs from Helen's field recordings were included, some of which may be the earliest extant sound recordings from African Canadians.

Helen's legend continued to grow. As journalist Michael Tutton wrote in a 1994 article for *The Chronicle Herald*, "Creighton [was] a folklorist who has become folklore herself."[14] Therein lay the inherent danger. Sometimes she was heralded as the quintessential folklore researcher; other times she was criticized. Either way, when the individual becomes more famous than his or her accomplishments, both praise and criticism frequently become directed towards the person rather than the work. Helen had become a public persona.

During her lifetime she had faced several challenges and criticisms of her folklore methodology, but the most critical analysis of her work began in 1993 with an article by Ian McKay in *New Maritimes*. An Associate Professor of History at Queen's University, Ian McKay's reputation for meticulous research has earned him national recognition. His penchant for controversy has brought him both kudos and brickbats. In the early 1990s he turned his attentions to Helen.

His first critique, "He is More Picturesque in His Oilskins": Helen Creighton and the Art of Being Nova Scotian," labelled Helen as "an anti-modernist intellectual entrepreneur."[15] He titled his article after a quote from a letter that Helen wrote to the Nova Scotia Bureau of Information accompanying photographs of Ben Henneberry from Devil's Island. She explained that Ben had been photographed at Evergreen fitted out in a collar and tie, but that he looked more picturesque when dressed in his oilskins. Ian used this statement to suggest that Helen was more interested in creating an image of "The Folk" than in portraying the true nature of the informants from whom she was collecting. He called Helen an anti-modernist, someone who places everything in an idealized past; an intellectual entrepreneur, suggesting that she used her education and social position and "developed a field and sought to exert property rights over it";[16] and he added, "If we take Creighton seriously and focus closely on her political and social ideals, we do this remarkable woman far greater justice than do all the warm-hearted human interest stories full of patronizing male chivalry."[17] He continued his examination of Helen's work and personal life in two further publications: "Helen Creighton and the Politics of Antimodernism," published in *Myth & Milieu: Atlantic Literature and Culture 1918–1939*, and in his book, *The Quest of the Folk: Antimodernism and Cultural Selection in Twentieth- Century Nova Scotia.*[18]

His book examines the careers of Helen Creighton and Mary Black. Mary Black was a friend of Helen's who began the occupational therapy movement in Nova Scotia. Through her work in developing the arts and crafts movement as an adjunct to occupational therapy, she became a world-renowned weaving instructor and author.[19] Helen's association with Mary Black came about through the Canadian Authors Association. When Helen was elected to the presidency of that organization in 1962, Mary wrote to her, "Always remember that your Nova Scotia friends stand behind you ready to help whenever they can and please believe me when I say I am one of these. With my best love, Mary."[20] Ian accused both women of manipulating culture and using their own power for personal gain, calling them cultural producers:

Shaped by ideologies and social processes of which they were not fully aware, such cultural producers [as Helen] did not conspire to falsify the past. Their sincerity and good intentions are not at issue. What is at issue is the conservative essentialism they installed as a way of seeing their society.... This book is not intended as an exercise in revisionism for its own sake, but rather an attempt to contribute to the opening up of debate and to the questioning of the ways in which a politics of cultural selection has made certain debatable assumptions seem like "natural" commonsense.[21]

Of Helen, specifically, he wrote, "Creighton thus exemplified the common and painful dilemma of modernizing antimodernism: in resisting the modern world so vigorously, in struggling to protect her imagined Folk from radicalism, she inevitably politicized the very sphere she wished to purify of modern politics."[22]

In short, Ian MacKay charged Helen with using her own moral and political beliefs—especially her firm anticommunist stance—to hold back the truth about Nova Scotia's material and folk culture. He suggested that she painted a picture of a pastoral, rural atmosphere not rooted in the reality of twentieth-century labour unrest and political turmoil. He maintained that Helen was patronizing towards her informants and used their shared information for her own personal gain. And he accused Helen of assuming the role of cultural arbitrator when giving advice to government officials interested in promoting tourism and cultural elements in Nova Scotia.

Reactions to Ian McKay's writings about Helen have been varied, but always passionate. In "Who Owns History Anyway? Reinventing Atlantic Canada for Pleasure and Profit," Delphin Muise noted that Ian's first article "provoked defenders of Creighton's traditional methods of gathering folk wisdom and her central place in the iconography of the province to raise a cry against McKay's revisionist intrusion."[23] Mr. Muise sides with Ian McKay, claiming that he "expose[d] her driving ambition and illuminates her public career with discussion of the somewhat narrowly defined—both geographically and ideologically—precondition she held for accepting or rejecting what was worthy about cultural production/transmission by the 'Folk'."[24]

But Helen had her defenders. *The Globe and Mail*'s columnist Bronwyn Drainie wrote:

> Given the cultural climate, it was only a matter of time before the revisionists would be out for Creighton's blood. A heavy-duty salvo against her life, her politics and her work was fired ... by Ian McKay .... The first thing one is tempted to say to people like McKay is: lighten up a little.... This attack on Helen Creighton is the old Canadian no-star system raising its envious little head again.... McKay seems to be convinced that all Nova Scotians automatically bought the Creightonian portrait of themselves .... But he has no evidence of this, only the cultural theory he's flogging.[25]

In the past I have refused comment on this matter, primarily because I felt there was more to the story than can be found in Helen's published work. I knew there were comments in her diaries that would better illustrate her personal opinions. Access to material from those diaries was denied Ian when requested it in 1989.[26] Now that they are open to public scrutiny I feel free to speak.

Helen did have strong moral and political beliefs. She was vehemently anticommunist. She did try to portray the inhabitants of the Maritime Provinces as happy people. She was protective of her informants. She did receive personal remuneration for material she collected from informants and she did her best to promote as many good things about her region as she could. All of these things are true. But what revisionist historical perspectives fail to do is to place an individual's work in historical context. Attitudes and opinions change over time, and to judge a person by current moral and political values discredits not only the individual under judgment, but the reader as well. Helen was not an ogre; nor do I believe that Ian McKay's intentions were malevolent. In a 1997 interview with Halifax's *The Daily News*, he responded that he was not trying to destroy Helen's reputation, but was tired of the homespun image he claimed she helped to create.[27] On the other hand, a strong pro-socialist attitude is manifest throughout his work, a philosophy that is the antithesis of much of Helen's belief system and way of working.

Did Helen use her own moral and political beliefs to decide what to collect—and what to publish? Of course she did. She had to be true to her own convictions and to those of many of her informants. As Bronwyn Drainie wrote in her defense of Helen's working style, "She had to walk a fine line through prudish communities, demurring when it came to recording bawdy material. Later ethnomusicologists have criticized her for this omission, but a single woman in those days coaxing ribald songs out of a Nova Scotia fisherman would have found herself quickly ostracized by his family and village."[28] Helen knew the score. Of bawdy songs, she once said, "They usually have the best music.... I remember one time asking a man ... if he could sing me some chanties, and he looked at me in disgust. He said, 'We don't sing those songs to ladies.' I was just put in my place."[29] The singers themselves did the initial editing. Both Fred Redden and Ben Henneberry had bawdy songs in their repertoires, but they wouldn't have considered singing them for Helen. Fred told me so himself.

Another tricky issue was offering informants liquor as incentive to sing and to perhaps loosen their inhibitions. Many collectors took liquor into the collecting field as a matter of course. The great American cowboy song collector, John Lomax, said of his informants, "Not one song did I ever get from them except through the influence of generous amounts of whiskey, raw and straight from the bottle or jug."[30] That method would have failed miserably for Helen. As she explained in her autobiography, "The men kept hinting that I should have brought something along to loosen their throats, but I had concluded early that if a young woman couldn't get a man to sing without bribing him with drink she wasn't worth her salt. Those who drink will take all the free liquor you supply, and then their singing gets muddled. The secret is to make your singer want to sing. A male collector might use liquor effectively, but he should have a limited amount; a woman, particularly a young one, would forfeit respect."[31]

Helen wasn't against liquor. If the informant had their own, she didn't stop collecting from them if they imbibed. And, like the bawdy song issue, the informants themselves, frequently decided when and where to have a drink. During the time Helen was collecting in the Maritime provinces, it was not unusual for many households to appear to be temperate, while the men maintained a bottle in one of the outsheds. Not everyone was comfortable with the public consumption of liquor. An example of this is shown in a letter Helen received from Angelo Dornan, who wrote to her explaining why he didn't accept her invitation for a drive into town. He initially had told her he had to go to the local post office to replace lost registration papers for his cow. That was true, but there was more to his reason for not going with Helen. He wrote, "That was not the real reason for going down, however. I wanted to go to the Vendor's before six o'clock to get a pint of 'scotch.' I could not allow you to drive me to such a place, when you had no other business. I don't think you would have relished parking your car and waiting for a 'miscreant' while he made a purchase of such a nature."[32]

Helen realized that she had a reputation to uphold. If she had brought liquor into a community she would have incurred the wrath of many people, most notably the wives of the men from whom she was collecting. She also had to avoid gaining a reputation of someone who collected and then disseminated what her society would have perceived as vulgar material. Moreover, Helen's personal convictions didn't permit vulgar material to be represented in her work. She knew she was missing out on certain aspects of folklore, but she made a conscious decision not to collect what she felt was morally incorrect. On one occasion she even pulled her work from a television program that featured some vulgar stories.

Helen wasn't a prude, but she was naive. Thomas Raddall once told me, "Well, as you know, Helen was a very plain person. And, of course, going around to the various villages she'd invariably come up against a village idiot who would assume that she was making advances to him. And she was full of tales about approaches that had been made to her sexually by these village idiots.... And she got rather hipped on the subject, because Helen was no beauty herself. She had a crushing smile, but she made no attempts at makeup or anything like that, never."[33]

Although Thomas Raddall's use of the term "village idiot" is harsh and incorrect, he does illustrate how Helen sometimes perceived an attraction that might not have been there. Then again, there were a number of real attempts from informants who tried to spark a romantic interest. Helen told of a visit to a widower and his family near Dartmouth, where she asked him to accompany her to another house to see a singer. He hesitated, so his mother-in-law said, "Why don't you go with Miss Creighton, Alex? Maybe people will think she's your financy, but that don't make no difference."[34] But, as Helen herself said, "I didn't invite attentions and that is probably why I got off with so little trouble, just enough to add a little spice to life."[35]

Helen was born and raised in the Edwardian age. It was a time of innocence, especially for many young women who were taught little, if nothing, about sex. Helen learned to flirt, but many times didn't understand when certain advances were being made. Once, when a female colleague made sexual overtures to her, she didn't understand them well enough to know how to properly handle the situation. She rebuked the advances but was so disturbed by the incident that she consulted two of her close friends, Richard Johnston and Alan Mills. They were both surprised to learn of Helen's ignorance of their mutual colleague's sexual orientation, and when they explained the situation to Helen she had to look up the word "lesbian" in the dictionary.[36]

Helen was always less interested in offering insight into her personal life than having her work in folklore examined under a microscope. Although Ian McKay's opinions of Helen's work would have wounded her deeply, they wouldn't have been completely without precedence. She'd faced many forms of criticism during her lifetime. It all hurt. The constructive criticisms wounded, but she learned from their bruises. The malicious attempts to discredit her cut deep.

Some criticisms bordered on the ridiculous. One such review of Helen's Folkways record, *Folk Music of Nova Scotia*, and Edith Fowke's companion album, *Folk Songs of Ontario*,[37] was written by Arthur Hammond in *The Tamarack Review* in 1959.[38] It was senseless and vitriolic, but nevertheless hurtful to the collectors and their informants. Mr. Hammond said the recordings "lack both the qualifications of ethnic value and that of lyrical interest."[39]

The songs aren't worth singing (I challenge anyone to sit through "Captain Conrod" in the Nova Scotia record, for instance, without actual pain) ... We also learn in the course of this record that some people in Nova Scotia play fiddle, the mouth organ, and the bagpipes (the last badly and only on isolated farms). We even hear one man making moose and bear calls through a roll of wallpaper, from which we must conclude, I suppose, that any noise made by a Canadian is of permanent preservation. Thus, at the end of so much suffering, we have learned nothing that a child in public school could not know about Nova Scotia. This is ethnography gone bad, folknoise recording reduced to the absurd.[40]

Arthur Hammond clearly demonstrated that he knew nothing about original field recordings. The real misfortune of such reviews is that they become a public gauntlet thrown before the collectors, who can elect to become embroiled in a long and convoluted dispute with the author and publisher, or recognize (and ignore) the critic's ignorance. In most cases, Helen chose to do the latter. However, there were times when she couldn't let certain statements go unchallenged.

On 4 June 1986 Bob Arlidge, an undergraduate in ethnomusicology at York University in Toronto, read a paper at the annual meeting of the Folklore Studies Association of Canada, called "An Evaluation of the early Collecting of Helen Creighton."[41] Helen heard about his paper and acquired a copy through her friend Neil Rosenberg, at Newfoundland's Memorial University.

Mr. Arlidge's primary thesis was that Helen should have used recording devices much earlier in her collecting experiences, thus avoiding many of the early mistakes she made in transcription. He stressed the fact that Helen was not a trained academic folklorist and told his audience, "It is interesting to consider here, in closing, that Helen Creighton, a woman initially in search of literary material, would take up a career not writing about folkmusic or folksong collection, or even being actively involved with song texts but rather, would involve herself primarily with that which she was least prepared to deal with."[42] Helen wrote to Neil Rosenberg and asked him to forward a copy of her letter to Mr. Arlidge.

If he has spent as much time looking over my later publications as he did on the first, he would have realized that I had learned the lessons he deplores I didn't know when I started. .... Would he have had me turn my back on the treasure trove at my door, or face a challenge and learn the hard way?... The generation gap is evident in this paper.... It was not until the early 30s when all work had been done on Songs and Ballads that Dr. Barbeau, through the National Museum, loaned me a wire recorder. To suggest that recordings should have been part of that early publication shows how far removed he is from those early days. Would that it had been possible.... He must have worked hard on his research, for he did it thoroughly. And in the end he gives me a pat on the back. Thanks Bob.[43]

It's easy to point a finger when you don't take the time to learn about your subject. Helen was aware of early recording machines, she just didn't have access to them. She wasn't alone. Even as late as 1956, Edith Fowke wrote Helen seeking advice: "What kind of tape machine do you use?... And what would you advise me to look for in a machine?"[44] Twenty years later Helen was interviewed at Evergreen and noted her awareness (and envy) of the latest technology: "Young man named Sutcliff had asked for an interview for term paper and a possible article.... Had brought a small tape recorder that just plugged in and has no microphone."[45] We tend to forget the field of folklore was in its infancy when she first began collecting. She didn't have access to the technologies and libraries we have today. When Linda Craig's research on the Scottish origins of "The Nova Scotia Song" became public, one man even wrote a letter to the editor of the London (Ontario) *Free Press*, exclaiming, "I find it hard to believe that Creighton or Catherine McKinnon didn't know this when they popularized it."[46] Did the letter writer really think that Helen would have held back that kind of information if she'd known it? She had been in active contact with folklorists around the world. Nobody came up with the tie to the song's Scottish origins until Linda Craig began investigating Scottish poetry and its transmigration to the New World.

Perhaps the harshest criticisms of Helen's work came from those who labelled her a popularizer. In 1979 folklorist Richard Tallman wrote in his review of Helen's autobiography:

Her perseverance in an area of scholarly research that is still largely ignored in Canadian academe is to be applauded; yet, her contributions are quantitative rather than qualitative.... To the professional folklorist, the extent to which Creighton emphasizes the adaptation and exploitation of her collected works to other media is alarming, not because folklore should never be used in this manner but because popularizing tends to misrepresent the folk culture to the general public.[47]

The majority of Helen's informants wanted to be identified. They were pleased to have their folklore preserved. They recognized the work being done by Helen and most were delighted to be included in her publications. William Gilkie of Sambro once said to Catherine Gallagher, "If it wasn't for Miss Creighton these songs would all die out."[48] In 1955 Laura Irene McNeil wrote to Helen thanking her for the compliment Helen paid her for working so hard on transcribing Acadian folk tales. She felt Helen was the "real worker" and wrote, "You are wonderful, and the credit should go to you more ... than to any of us, really."[49] Helen highly valued the respect and friendship of her informants. It brought her great joy to get letters like the one she received from Mary Doyle, the daughter of Grace and Sadie Clergy. Helen had written a note of sympathy when Sadie died and Mary responded by writing, "She always spoke of you as a very good friend and talked about your visits with my Dad so often."[50] Helen realized that without her informants she would have no collection. In 1979 she made the following entry in her diary. "Attended golden wedding anniversary reception for the Allan Hartleys, he being one of the last of my folk singers still living. As different of their family came up and recalled their memories of my visits, I thought what a lot I owe to that family, for they were my first contacts and it was from them I learned what folk songs are. A lovely friendly evening full of pleasant nostalgia."[51]

Occasionally an informant did request anonymity, as in the case of a man who wrote Helen in 1957 and told her about his personal supernatural experiences, ending his letter with, "Noting that you do not mention the living in your book I trust you will find no occasion to commit mine to print."[52] Helen tried very hard to honour the wishes of her informants. Singers were almost always identified, but those who shared folk beliefs sometimes asked to remain unnamed. Helen offered a reason in the introduction to *Folklore of Lunenburg County*: "because the informants were well over middle age and had never lived outside the county, and mainly because they prefer it, names of those who provided material are not given."[53]And unlike tales of phantom ships or forerunners, few people admit to a first hand knowledge of witchcraft. If they do, they most often choose to remain anonymous. Helen always tried to maintain the confidentiality of her informants, but one incident, caused by the slip of the tongue, could have brought her more trouble than she bargained for.

In August 1947 she visited a Mi'kmaq couple, Louis and Evangeline Pictou, at their home in Bear River, Nova Scotia. Evangeline told Helen that her father was a witch. Helen recounted this information in an off-the-record conversation with a Halifax journalist, who later printed the story in the newspaper. Helen was mortified. She was afraid the Pictous would be wounded by her unintended slip. She rushed back to confront her informants with the truth. She described the outcome in her autobiography: "As I turned in to their camping ground they raised their hands in greeting and I said, "I see we're still friends." "Why wouldn't we be?" so I told them and Evangeline said her father would be proud to be called a witch in the paper, and she would be too, to know she had that power. Louis was soon off on another tale but I could see they were thinking this over. Finally she said, "I know what we'll say if they mention it. We'll say, "Of course we told her that stuff; she gave us money.""[54] Helen recorded her relief in her diary: "I was so thankful I had got to them before anybody else, and now I hope the matter is ended. Such a nice couple they are."[55]

With the exception of the unfortunate intrusion at the Mi'kmaq funeral in Cape Breton, where she was given the impression by a village elder and the local priest that her presence would not be disturbing, Helen tried to maintain a respectful attitude toward her informants. In 1949 she wrote in her diary, "Cape Sable Island ... funeral ... I nearly went, but couldn't feel right about intruding upon other people's grief for curiosity."[56] However, she did arrive at informants' doors without making appointments. In the early years this made sense. Few people had telephones and Helen often didn't find her informants until she knocked on a door to enquire about songs and stories. When I once asked her if she tried to get in touch by letter or telephone once those modes of communication became common she replied, "[No, it's] usually better just to turn up at the door."[57]

The sudden appearance of a woman standing on the doorstep making enquiries about old-time songs and ghost stories must have raised a few eyebrows. Rural people in the Maritime provinces were accustomed to family and friends dropping by unannounced, but Helen was, in most cases, a complete stranger. However, her friendly manner soon won them over and they frequently developed a warm relationship. It may have taken take years for them to graduate to a first-name basis, but that was common to the social mentality of the day. It was a courtesy extended not only between collector and informant. Sandy Ives' first letter to Helen, in 1957, is addressed to "Miss Creighton"; it isn't until 1962 that he begins to use the salutation "Helen."[58]

Helen has been censured for not including personal remarks about her informants' lifestyles and habits. From a purely folkloric point of view, these observations are valuable resources to better understand the context within which the material is collected. That works if the collector enters an area, records what she wants—and never plans to revisit the area after she has published her findings. Helen could rarely do that. She was almost always welcomed back. Her visits had become highlights for many of her informants. A diary entry for 1937 illustrates the point: "Visited Mr. Tom Conrod. Poor old man looked quite miserable and not at all fit to sing so I told him I would come again. He looked at me quite pathetically and said, "You *will* come again, won't you?"[59] Louis Boutilier wrote to her, "How are you getting along with your songs? Do they sing as good as me?... come down and see me an don't for get for I would like to see you."[60] And in 1950 Maggie (Mrs. "Wentie") Boutilier wrote, "If you are still interested in recording music perhaps you would call on us some evening.... Trust I'm not being too presumptuous in writing you."[61] But perhaps the finest compliment any Maritimer can pay another is an offer of food, as Jim Apt, at Victoria Beach, did: "Don't ever go by the house hungry, there's always something here for you to eat."[62]

Did any of Helen's informants feel she was taking advantage of them? Some might have hinted about possible remuneration, or told her it was a bad time for her to collect, and a few refused outright to be interviewed. But once Helen established a relationship with an informant their mutual respect seemed to come easily. If she overstepped her professional boundaries it was out of enthusiasm and not malice. She tried very hard to give credit where it was due. Her major regret over her autobiography was leaving out any mention of Angelo Dornan. She told me that she proofread the manuscript many times over, but it was just an unfortunate memory lapse.[63]

Over the past decade since Helen's death, I have been able to interview several of her informants and/or their family members. I asked them if they felt that Helen had taken advantage of them by using their material for her publications. Not a single one expressed any such notion. Hilda Chiasson, grand-daughter of Peter Chiasson, told me that on the contrary, her family felt there was meaning in what her grandfather had shared with Helen and that it was nice for somebody to have taken notice of his work.[64]

Mr. and Mrs. Richard, on Prince Edward Island (the last two informants from whom Helen collected) remembered her with fondness. I took a copy of *La Fleur du Rosier* with me to give to them. When I pointed out their songs, Madame Richard said, "Well God Bless, isn't that something!"[65]

Should Helen have offered to pay her informants? That is a classic question that has been debated by collectors for years. Helen took the position that what she collected and published was public property. Her informants had no more rights to material passed on through the oral transmission process than she did. However, since she collected and published the material, she felt justified in receiving royalties from her publications. In essence, she didn't own the intellectual rights to the material, but she did have the right to request payment for publications containing that material. On the few occasions when she received additional funds for use of her collection, she tried to pass it on. Only in rare circumstances did she offer money for songs or stories. She offered no specific criteria in making those decisions; it was more of a gut reaction. In her autobiography she commented on such a circumstance: "It was generally considered bad policy to pay for material. Yet when I called on Louis and Evangeline Pictou, an Indian couple, my inner voice told me to break the rule. This was easy money for Louis because he could relate stories learned from his grandmother and continue basket-making at the same time."[66]

Ian McKay suggested that Helen was condescending to her informants by offering them gifts in lieu of remuneration. "Her gift-giving strategy was classic paternalism. Often Creighton would present her informant with a photograph, a gift that was 'more personal' than money, and that invoked a gift-giving relationship of mutual reciprocity and personal understanding. Not everyone was delighted with the photographs: 'Too bad your wasting good money having them developed. Please burn the negative,' wrote Angelo Dornan, a critical and important informant."[67]

Ian McKay represented Angel Dornan's statement out of context. Mr. Dornan was writing to thank Helen for copies of the photographs and, as people often do when presented with a portrait of themselves, he made a tongue-in-cheek response, which was not intended as a slight or rebuff for not being paid. Most of Helen's informants didn't expect remuneration, but were flattered, and perhaps a bit embarrassed, when a gift was offered. Helen's diary entry for a day in 1951 when she was collecting from Freeman and Bernard Young at East Petpeswick illustrates the point: "When I give Bernard his tobacco he takes it quickly as though he doesn't want any one to see, but when I gave it to Freeman, he said, 'Miss C. there isn't any need of you doin' this. I'm glad to accommodate you.'"[68] Helen tried to repay her informants in other ways. When she asked Arthur White of Kennetcook if she could buy him dinner at the local hotel, he replied, "No, that's too classy. Too much manners. Too much manners isn't good."[69]

Writing about her relationship with her informants in an article titled "Folk-Singers of Nova Scotia" in *The Canadian Forum*, Helen said, "If I write possessively about my singers it is because I feel that way.

These fishermen and farmers have been contributing to my collection of folk songs in Nova Scotia for over twenty years, and I look upon them as my friends. And besides, they speak possessively of me."[70]

There were, of course, relationships that didn't work out. Family members belonging to certain fundamentalist religious organizations sometimes objected to having Helen collect from their relatives. And the unfortunate circumstances surrounding Helen's collecting experiences with the William Riley family stand out as a weak point in her otherwise strong history of developing good relationships with informants. Because of that one incident, Helen stopped collecting from African Nova Scotians in the Preston area. In a letter to folklorist Kenneth Goldstein in 1978, she offered this explanation: "The reason my work especially in the Preston area was limited was because it was definitely unsafe for me to collect there alone, or indeed even with a companion. I didn't want to state this in the article, but it was very evident. Also this community lived too close to my home and if they were insisting on money which I didn't have, it could have been difficult."[71]

This was an example of how Helen brought her societal bias to the collecting field. Mr. Riley's daughter, Rose Mann, had every right to be concerned about her father. His son, George, had every right to ask for money—it was his privilege as an informant. Helen could either accede to their requests or leave. She chose the latter. Still, the incident didn't stop her from collecting from other African Nova Scotians. For example, in the 1950s she made several trips to Bridgetown to collect the repertoire of centenarian Charles Owens and his family.

Along with relationships with her informants, Helen developed associations and friendships with many of the leading folklore scholars and researchers of her day. She frequently offered assistance where she could. In 1941 the New England folk song collector, Carrie Grover, sought Helen's advice about collecting and assembling her folk song collection.[72] In the late 1970s she supported linguist Lewis Poteet's application for funding from the Canada Council to conduct research into the folk speech of Nova Scotia's south shore.[73]

She often received unsolicited encouragement and support from colleagues working in similar disciplines. In 1957 Sam Gesser of Folkways Records wrote to her responding to critics who suggested that Helen wasn't a trained folklore scholar: "I'm so sick of so-called Folk-lore authorities claiming to be the salvation and sole reason for making the folklore of this country available to the world, that it was like a breath of fresh air to see a person like yourself speak in humility and give credit when credit was due. Although, if anyone can claim a rightful place in the gathering and making the folk material available to all, you can."[74] That same year, Thomas Raddall wrote with his praise—and opinion on the current state of popular music in Nova Scotia: "In your quiet way you have worked valiantly and successfully to preserve what was real in this twanging age of imported hill-billy songs and phony Texas accents, and some day our rustic musicians will see the point and (I hope) bless your name."[75]

Helen also had a good working relationship with other folklore researchers working directly in her area. She respected their territory and hoped the courtesy would be returned. In fact, she refused to collect in Newfoundland because of her friendships with Kenneth Peacock and Maude Karpeles. She did little collecting on Prince Edward Island because she felt it was Sandy Ives' territory. And she only collected in Louise Manny's area of the Miramichi in New Brunswick at her invitation. Sandy Ives knew both women well, and when I asked him about their relationship, he responded, "I don't know what to say ... it was fine, wonderful ... Louise was always tremendously admiring of Helen."[76] When asked about his personal relationship with Helen, Sandy said, "I was very proud to have her as a friend ... something of an ancestor figure for me ... her name was coequal with Mackenzie and Greenleaf ... Helen Harkless Flanders ... all that first wave of collectors."[77]

Others were less kind. I asked Sandy if Helen was considered an academic folklorist by her peers:

No she was not. As a matter of fact, Dick Dorson ... who was my mentor and also my friend ... [said] "You know ... she'd always been sort of an embarrassment." I said, "What do you mean, Dick?" He said, "Well, she's not a folklorist, you know." I said, "Well, I never heard her say she was." ... Dick was very, very hipped on making the profession professional. And people like Helen didn't fit, but yet at the same time he asked her out there [Indiana University] ... had her lecture and had her talk to his classes ... so even there it's a mixed bag.[78]

However, whatever private feelings they may have harboured about Helen's professionalism, many folklore scholars applauded her efforts in their correspondence with her. Alan Lomax wrote to her in 1956 saying, "Recently I have gone over all your books carefully and have rejoiced to see how many treasures of tradition you have saved from oblivion."[79] Bertrand Bronson wrote in response to Helen's gift of her *Folksongs from Southern New Brunswick*, "What glorious fun you've had bringing your books into being! I envy you the social i.e. human—satisfactions of your work. I'm not minimizing the effort, the disappointments, the discomforts. But mine, compared to yours, has been a bloodless performance."[80] And in 1974 Wayland Hand, who knew Helen from their days together at Indiana University, wrote, "My dear, I do rejoice in your wonderful career, and I count myself lucky to know you as a close friend and colleague."[81]

Closer to home, Helen was fortunate to have developed a relationship

*Helen Creighton working at her desk at Evergreen, 1958. I inherited this desk and used it when writing this book.*

with Dr. W. Roy Mackenzie, the man whose work inspired her career. In 1949 Helen had written him to see if she might come and record any of his informants still living. He wrote back expressing his regrets: "I wish I could say it would be worth your while to visit this region, and if I could hear some records from my old friends who are now singing in paradise I should be a happy man indeed."[82] In the early 1950s Helen and Dr. Mackenzie visited the one living Mackenzie informant. By then an elderly woman, she had been only a girl when she sang for him and she'd learned her repertoire from an old lumberman who rarely spoke to others but taught her his songs.[83] Helen was later shocked and disappointed to learn that Dr. Mackenzie had destroyed all his research notes and working manuscripts.[84]

Another role model for Helen's professional career was Marius Barbeau. He offered her great support throughout his tenure at the National Museum. In a letter written in 1956, he assured her, "You will be sure to remain one of the chief pillars of folklore in Canada."[85] His words were prophetic. Helen was one of the primary contributors to the field of folklore collection. But it is her colleague, Edith Fowke, who is remembered as more academically astute. When Edith died in 1996, Phil Thomas wrote a tribute to her in the *Canadian Folk Music Bulletin*, saying, "In Canada, Edith Fowke now stands beside Marius Barbeau, who has been Canada's most noteworthy folklorist.... Helen Creighton's work left us wondering what songs her informants loved she rejected; Edith's approach to folk song collection was considerably more inclusive. Creighton believed in ghosts; Edith believed in people."[86] While I agree that Edith's collection of folk songs was more inclusive than Helen's, I disagree with Phil Thomas's latter statement. Helen did believe in ghosts. She also believed in the integrity of her informants. Edith collected bawdy songs; Helen didn't. Edith had less interest for people's beliefs in the supernatural, so she collected little in that genre. Each conducted their own form of self-editing. Their work will continue to be compared and one will be pitted against the other. To give them both their due, I quote from Canadian entertainment columnist and broadcaster Clyde Gilmour's 1982 statement in *The Toronto Star*. "Edith Fowke is one of the two leading authorities on English-language folksongs in Canada. The other is her old friend Dr. Helen Creighton .... Each speaks warmly of the other's knowledge and achievements. Both are high priestesses in the same secular religion."[87]

Can there ever be two "high priestesses"? Were Edith and Helen rivals? Sandy Ives told me that "there was sort of a competition ... between them as to who was Canada's leading folk song collector."[88] They certainly locked horns over some major issues—such as Edith's publication of labour songs—but they also had a strong bond that eventually surmounted all their differences. However, each woman tried to establish her place in the pecking order for recognition as Canada's leading folk song collector. Edith worked to establish hers as a scholar and researcher; Helen hoped to be recognized as a pioneer and collector. Helen told me of a casual conversation between them that illustrates to me their early attempts to establish their own spot in the Canadian folklore hierarchy. During the early stages of their friendship, Edith and Helen were walking together and Edith said, "When Dr. Barbeau goes—who will succeed him?" Helen thought, "Why I should of course," but didn't say anything. She remarked that perhaps she should have said something then, as it might have saved some tension between them later on.[89]

That tension came about primarily because of their opposing views on Edith's work with socialist causes and her interest in material from the labour movements. Helen disliked political dissension. She feared the violence and turmoil that sometimes accompanied labour unrest, yet she remained somewhat naive in her ideas about a solution to the social problems of the day.

Helen was strongest in her opinions of union songs. While collecting from Angelo Dornan in New Brunswick in 1954, she tuned in to Edith Fowke's radio broadcast and later noted in her diary, "... listened to Edith's program, but mostly labour songs and I don't like them."[90] She wasn't pleased that Edith continued to pormote songs from the labour movement and was even less pleased to see American political activists receive air time with similar material. A diary note for August, 1961 reads, "In eve...listened to New Party convention. Edith's labour songs much in fore here, with Joe Gleazer leading the singing; an American who writes songs of social protests at a Canadian political gathering. Not my idea."[91]

Helen was clearly conservative in her politics and lifestyle. Yet, she acknowledged that her own personal beliefs did not always align themselves with what might have been expected of her. In her early thirties, she struggled with the standard notion of sin, as represented by her clergy. "I went to church. Too much about sin and penance at heart. I don't feel as inclined as the prayer book makes me say. I know I make mistakes, but they are mistakes of ignorance, not of the heart. I know I'm not perfect, but I do honestly try ... every day. So why grovel in the dust? I think there is too much of that sort of religion and too little worshipping of God and rejoicing in His goodness.[92] She sought that goodness in others and sometimes feared that "radical" political thought and dissention among her contemporaries could bring about more harm than good. Edith's work with union songs and the popular rise of songs of conscience during the 1960s were a case in point.

But whatever disagreements Edith and Helen had with respect to politics and professional issues, they also held a deep personal regard for each other. Helen appreciated Edith's scholarly approach and Edith recognized that Helen had been working with Canadian folklore for almost 30 years before she first accompanied Helen on her inaugural fieldtrip on Nova Scotia's eastern shore. After the death of their mutual friend, John Robins, who had offered both women invaluable advice in their formative days as folk song collectors, Edith wrote to Helen, "Apart from the personal loss of a very good friend, I find myself feeling very much up in the air without him to turn to for advice."[93] And as late as 1985, Edith wrote saying, "I've always tried to include something from you i[n] each of my books because I wanted to pay tribute to you as our best collector."[94]

In 1991 I visited Edith at her home in Toronto and enquired about her relationship with Helen. She told me that she never felt there was rivalry between them and didn't think Helen was intimidated by Edith's greater recognition as a scholar: "Helen was not intimidated by anyone."[95] When asked about Helen's collecting techniques and whether she was correct in making her own decisions about what to collect, Edith replied, "I think Helen was right."[96] And when queried about their disagreements, Edith told me she considered Helen a friend—and friends could agree to disagree on many subjects.[97]

Both women made an indelible mark on the face of Canadian folklore studies. Both were strong-willed and tenacious and, I believe, in the end, both had the best interests of Canadian folklore studies at heart. They shared many confidences, rejoiced in the other's honours, and empathized with each other when they were labelled popularizers. The following column, by Val Ross, appeared in *The Globe and Mail*:

Where her colleague, folklorist Marius Barbeau, was motivated by Quebec nationalism, and Maritime folklorist Helen Creighton by a deeply conservative reverence for the past, Ms. Fowke's inspiration sprang in part from prairie socialism .... By the late 1940s, after visiting Helen Creighton, Ms. Fowke began scouting ... Central Ontario .... When Mr. Barbeau, Ms. Creighton and Ms. Fowke first ventured into folklore, they set their own rules, editing or rewording material to make it more accessible. For this they were criticized by later purists. "What a lot of nonsense!" Ms. Fowke told The Globe and Mail. "I am criticized because I am a popularizer, which is apparently a bad thing. But I feel, if I collect from the folk, I should return it to the folk."[98]

Edith and Helen thought alike on that subject. Neither wanted to see their collections used only by academics. Helen regarded herself more as a custodian than owner of the material she assembled. When she donated her entire collection to the Public Archives of Nova Scotia, she told me, "The Province has given so much to me, the people sharing what to them is a very great treasure, that I'm very glad to give it back to the Province."[99]

I have been left with my own personal legacy from Helen. In her will, she left me $5,000 and her desk. I used the money to produce another recording featuring some of the songs from her collection.[100] I use the desk every day. But I don't need a tangible reminder of Helen in my life. She is with me constantly. Her work has become my work. I have been fortunate in having a mentor who was also my dear friend. And once you had Helen Creighton as a friend, you had a friend for life. Cora Greenaway told me she feels the same way:

I can't even speak about her in the past tense ... she's with me and she looks over my shoulder ... although she was deeply devote, she liked to poke fun ... her legacy of such integrity, her research was always meticulous .... she was open to everything that was new, she was vain, no she wasn't vain, she was just like a woman, she liked to look her best.... she used to be much duller [in her dress], but then when Sharon came along the colours brightened!... she was a bit of an actress, of course too ... she'd look small and a little tired and then she'd come into a room or into the Rebecca Cohn, whatever it might have been. And her back would straighten and her chin would go up, and a big smile on her face, Helen was ready to face the world. [101]

# ENDNOTES

**\* \* \***

## INTRODUCTION

1. Tye, Diane. "'A Very Lone Worker': Woman- Centred Thoughts on Helen Creighton's Career as a Folklorist," *Journal of the Canadian Folklore Studies Association*, Volume 15, Number 2, 1993, 107.

2. Tye, 'A Very Lone Worker', 106.

3. Sandy Ives, audio-taped interview, 12 February, 1992.

4. Holt, David. "Folklore: endless in its variety," *Atlantic Insight*, Volume 9, Number 6, June 1987.

5. Horace Beck to Helen Creighton, 26 May, 1982, Helen Creighton Fonds, PANS MG1 Volume 2791 #19.

6. Greenhill, Pauline. "Lots of Stories: Maritime Narratives from the Creighton Collection" Ottawa: National Museums of Canada; Canadian Centre for Folk Culture Studies, Mercury Series, Number 57, 1985, 224.

7. Pedersen, Stephen. "Creighton's Legacy" *Mail Star* 16 December, 1989.

8. See: Brundvand, Jan Harold. Folklore: *A Study and Research Guide* 9.

9. See: Kizuk, Alexander. "Molly Beresford and the Song Fishermen of Halifax: Cultural Production, Canon and Desire in 1920s Canadian Poetry," *Myth & Milieu: Atlantic Literature and Culture 1918-1939,* ed. Gwendolyn Davies, Fredericton, Acadiensis, 1993, 180-181.

10. Shaw, Beatrice M. Hay. "The Vanishing Folklore of Nova Scotia," *The Dalhousie Review*, Volume 3, Number 3, October, 1923.

11. *Folklore* Volume 2, Number 1, Winter, 1951. Nova Scotia Folkschool Club Newsletter, Issued quarterly through the Adult Education Division, Department of Education, Halifax. PANS has Volume 3, Number 2,1952; and Volume 4, Number 2, 1953.

12. *Indiana Daily Student*, 29 July, 1942.

13. Foster, Ann. "She Tracks Down Canada's Folk Songs," *Star Weekly*, 31 May, 1958.

14. Mariposa Folk Festival Newsletter, #11, 1990.

15. Marius Barbeau in an interview given to Carolyn Willett, Halifax *Chronicle-Herald*, 26 October, 1956.

16. See: Gregory, E. David. "A.L. Lloyd and the English Folk Song Revival, 1934-44" *Canadian Journal for Traditional Music*, Volume 25, 1997.

17. See: Lloyd, A.L. *Folk Song in England* London: Lawrence and Wishart, 1967.

18. Robbins, James. "Lessons Learned, Questions Raised: Writing a History of Ethnomusicology in Canada" *Canadian Folk Music Journal*, Volume 20, 1992.

19. Diary, 11 August, 1937, Helen Creighton Fonds, PANS MG1 Volume 2830 #1.

20. Diary, 17 July, 1937, Helen Creighton Fonds, PANS MG1 Volume 2830 #1.

21. See: Sable Island Song, Creighton, *Songs and Ballads from Nova Scotia*, New York: Dover, 1966, 310.

22. Creighton, *Songs and Ballads from Nova Scotia*, 313.

23. Edith Fowke, review of *Traditional Songs from Nova Scotia* in *The Canadian Forum*, January, 1951.

24. Helen Creighton, personal interview, 24 Nov. 1986, Clary Croft Journal.

25. Helen Creighton, personal interview, 16 June 1988, Clary Croft Journal.

26. John D. Robins to Helen Creighton, 30 April 1948, Helen Creighton Fonds, PANS MG1 Volume 2817 #60.

# CHAPTER ONE

1. Now called Lake Banook.

2. Creighton, *A Life in Folklore*. Toronto: McGraw-Hill Ryerson, 1975, 3.

3. In 1924, it was incorporated as Creightons Limited. Charles continued as president until is death in 1943 and his son Paul carried on until his death in 1954. Paul's son, C.J. "Jake" Creighton took over the business until his retirement in 1991; in 1992 the company sold to long time employee, Ralph Sams, but continues to operate as Creightons Limited.

4. Creighton, *A Life in Folklore*, 8.

5. C.E. Creighton & Company leger. Jacob Creighton Fonds PANS MG1 Volume 3532 #16a.

6. *Canadian Grocer*, MacLean Hunter, February 1975.

7. Creighton, *A Life in Folklore*, 12.

8. Helen Creighton, audio-taped interview conducted by Clary Croft for PANS, 17 March, 1987, PANS AC1619.

9. Creighton, *A Life in Folklore*, 17.

10. Creighton, *A Life in Folklore*, 21.

11. Halifax Ladies College opened in 1887 and is currently known as Armbrae Academy.

12. Creighton, *A Life in Folklore*, 21.

13. Helen Creighton to Charles Creighton, [n/d], Helen Creighton Fonds, PANS MG1 Volume 2790 #1.

14. Helen Creighton Fonds, PANS MG1 Volume 2793 #2.

15. Helen Creighton, personal interview, 5 November, 1986, Clary Croft Journal.

16. Creighton, *A Life in Folklore*, 20.

17. Diary, [n/d], Helen Creighton Fonds, PANS MG1 Volume 2790 #8.

18. Creighton, *A Life in Folklore*, 22.

19. See: diary, Helen Creighton Fonds, PANS MG1 Volume 2790 #8.

20. Helen Creighton, Personal interview, 20 January, 1989, Clary Croft Journal.

21. Helen Creighton, Personal interview, 14 April, 1987, Clary Croft Journal.

22. Creighton, *A Life in Folklore*, 30.

23. For a detailed account of the events and the rescue efforts see: Kitz, Janet F. *Shattered City: The Halifax Explosion and the Road to Recovery*. Halifax: Nimbus Publishing Ltd., 1989.

24. For a copy of the poem printed as a broadsheet see: Helen Creighton Fonds, PANS MG1 Volume 2790 #5.

25. Helen Creighton, Personal interview, 12 February, 1987, Clary Croft Journal.

## CHAPTER 2

1. Helen Creighton to Charles Creighton, 11 November, 1918, Helen Creighton Fonds, PANS MG1 Volume 2811 #162.

2. See: certificate, 11 December, 1918, Helen Creighton Fonds, PANS MG1 Volume 2827 #1.

3. Helen Creighton to the Officer Commanding, Mechanical Transport Section, Royal Air Force, 13 December, 1918, Helen Creighton Fonds, PANS MG1 Volume 2827 #1.

4. Jacob Creighton Fonds, PANS MG1 Volume 3530 #1.40.

5. Diary, [n/d], Helen Creighton Fonds, PANS MG1 Volume 2827 #1.

6. Diary, 11 August [n/d], Helen Creighton Fonds, PANS MG1 Volume 2827 #1.

7. Creighton, *A Life in Folklore*, 37.

8. Bauchman, "A Profile of Helen Creighton."

9. Diary, [n/d], Helen Creighton Fonds, PANS MG1 Volume 2827 #1.

10. Creighton, *A Life in Folklore*, 39.

11. MacAllum Grant to Miss A.G. McGregor, Department of Social Service, Toronto University, 23 September, 1920, Helen Creighton Fonds, PANS MG1 Volume 2813 #70.

12. See: "My feeling ... is that you probably met Boyle's son, Joseph Whiteside Boyle Jr., who went overseas in 1920, and visited his father in Bucharest. Contemporary sources pinpoint Boyle very precisely in Romania during that period." William Rodney, Professor and Head History Department, Royal Roads Military College, Victoria, BC to Helen Creighton, 12 January, 1974, Helen Creighton Fonds, PANS MG1 Volume 2817 #68.

13. Creighton, *A Life in Folklore*, 41.

14. Helen Creighton, personal interview, 30 April, 1987, Clary Croft Journal.

15. Helen Creighton, personal interview, 30 April, 1987, Clary Croft Journal.

16. Creighton, *A Life in Folklore*, 44.

17. Helen Creighton, personal interview, 14 October, 1987, Clary Croft Journal.

18. Helen Creighton, personal interview, 30 April, 1987, Clary Croft Journal.

19. Helen Creighton, personal interview, 13 October, 1987, Clary Croft Journal.

20. Letter to editor of *Macleans Magazine* attached to original manuscript in possession of Alice and David Nicholl.

21. Original manuscript in possession of Alice and David Nicholl.

22. Letter to editor of *Macleans Magazine* attached to original manuscript in possession of Alice and David Nicholl.

23. Upton, Bertha (Hudson) 1849-1912—American author of children's books ... best known for writing a series of books that feature the adventures of a fantastic character named the Golliwogg. Along with Peg, Meg, Sara Jane, and Midget—the Golliwogg travels to a desert island, to war, to the African jungle, and elsewhere in Upton's lively verse tales.

24. The author's daughter Florence Upton illustrated the books and modelled her drawings of the character after actual Victorian-era dolls.

25. For example: in 1902, Claude Debussy published *The Golliwog's Cakewalk*. See illustrations in: Upton, Florence and Bertha Upton. *The Golliwogg's Bicycle Club*.

26. Helen Creighton Fonds, PANS MG1 Volume 2793 #8.

27. Creighton, "Unseasonable Golf."

28. Helen Creighton Fonds, PANS MG1 Volume 2793 #6.

29. Helen Creighton Fonds, PANS MG1 Volume 3514 # 3.

30. Creighton, *A Life in Folklore,* 44.

31. See: Gerson, "The Literary Culture of Atlantic Women Between the Wars," 62.

32. Charles Creighton to Helen Creighton, 25 July, 1927, Helen Creighton Fonds, PANS MG1 Volume 2811 #158.

33. Charles Creighton to Helen Creighton, 15 September, 1927, Helen Creighton Fonds, PANS MG1 Volume 2811 #158.

34. See: Vogan, "Music Education in the Maritimes Between the Wars: a Period of Transition," 85.

35. Richard S. Lambert, School Broadcasting in Canada, Toronto, 1963, p.19; as quoted in: Vogan, "Music Education in the Maritimes Between the Wars: a Period of Transition," 86.

36. Mackenzie, W. Roy. *Ballads and Sea Songs from Nova Scotia.* W. Roy MacKenzie (1883-1957) was born at River John, Nova Scotia. He was a specialist in Shakespeare and Old English philology and his mentor, G.L. Kitteridge, had studied under the great ballad scholar, Francis James Child. It was Kitteridge who encouraged him to return to River John and collects ballads.

37. Creighton, *A Life in Folklore,* 49.

38. Creighton, *A Life in Folklore,* 49.

# CHAPTER 3

1. J. Murray Gibbon's Canadian Folk Songs. Gibbon, *Canadian Folk Songs.*

2. Creighton, "Are We Truly Musical?"

3. Creighton, *A Life in Folklore,* 50.

4. Creighton, *A Life in Folklore,* 50.

5. When Helen began documenting informant names in 1928, most married women were addressed by their status as Mrs.—followed by the surname of their husband. This practice continued to be common in rural Nova Scotia well into the 1960s.

6. Creighton, *A Life in Folklore,* 50- 51.

7. This was an old German belief brought to Nova Scotia in the 18th century. Helen later found other variants of this belief when she collected folklore in Lunenburg County. There, the letters were frequently written backwards.

8. Creighton, *A Life in Folklore,* 52.

9. Creighton, *Songs and Ballads from Nova Scotia,* 101.

10. Helen Creighton, personal interview, 26 January, 1987, Clary Croft Journal.

11. Creighton, *A Life in Folklore,* 53.

12. When she went back to visit some of the early informants and recollect their songs with recording machines, she was to discover than much of her melodic notation was correct, but her time signatures and rhythmic notation needed revision.

13. Creighton, *A Life in Folklore,* 54.

14. Helen Creighton to Clary Croft, [n/d] , personal conversation.

15. Graphology, the study of handwriting for character analysis, was popular in the 1920s and 1930s.

16. Helen had "sex" penciled out and wrote in "love." Analyses of Helen's handwriting by F Oland, 14 February, 1928, Helen Creighton Fonds, PANS MG1 Volume 2816 #93.

17. Analyses of Helen's handwriting by F Oland, 14 February, 1928, Helen Creighton Fonds, PANS MG1 Volume 2816 #93.

18. In 1999, Devil's Island was the only large privately owned island in Halifax Harbour. In 1995, it was listed for sale with the asking price of $375,000. The listing also mentioned "Offers invited: for sale/lease/joint venture/treasure rights considered." Real Estate Home Guide, Volume 3, Issue 23.

19. Creighton, *A Life in Folklore,* 56.

20. Meagher's Children. See: Creighton, *Songs and Ballads from Nova Scotia,* 292.

21. Helen Creighton to Rosemary Bauchman, 30 January, 1988, Helen Creighton Fonds, PANS MG1 Volume 3511 #39. As early as 1930, the press was capitalizing on the image too. In an article about Helen's song collecting published in the *Ottawa Evening Citizen,* 2 July, 1930, the header reads: "Former Ottawa Writer Collects Native Nova Scotia Folk Songs: Miss Helen Creighton Finds Dictaphone Invaluable Ally—Pushed Hand Melodeon on Wheelbarrow at First...."

22. The festival lasted from 1927 to 1929.

23. Helen Creighton to Murray Gibbon, 13 July, 1929, Helen Creighton Fonds, PANS MG1 Volume 2811 #162.

24. John Murray Gibbon to Helen Creighton, July 22, 1929, Helen Creighton Fonds, PANS MG1 Volume 2813 #21.

25. Helen Creighton Fonds, PANS MG1 Volume 3387 #5.

26. Peryl Daly, audio-taped interview, 1992.

27. Maud Karpeles to Helen Creighton, 29 September, 1930, Helen Creighton Fonds, PANS MG1 Volume 2814 #50.

28. John D. Robins, writing in the 1932 preface of: Creighton, Helen. *Songs and Ballads from Nova Scotia,* p. viii.

29. By 18 October, 1933, she still owed J.M. Dent & Sons $244.45. See: letter from Henry Button, Canadian Agent, J.M. Dent & Sons to Helen Creighton, 21 March, 1938, Helen Creighton Fonds, PANS MG1 Volume 2811 #34. Helen continued to make payments to bring the account down, and eventually the company waived the remainder of the balance owed.

# CHAPTER 4

1. *Church Work*, February, 1931

2. Helen Creighton Fonds, PANS MG1 Volume 2793 #12.

3. Charles C. Rand to Helen Creighton, 19 November, 1932, Helen Creighton Fonds, PANS MG1 Volume 2817 #4.

4. Helen Creighton Fonds, PANS MG1 Volume 2793 #7.

5. Helen Creighton, personal interview, 1986, Clary Croft Journal.

6. Helen Creighton to W.A. Irwin, Assistant editor *Maclean's Magazine,* 10 December, 1931, Helen Creighton Fonds, PANS MG1 Volume 2811 #162.

7. In 1932, Nova Scotian educators had yet to see the value in their own traditional songs and dances. Doreen Senior was an Anglophile and considered British songs and dances superior to those which might have been found in Canada. She also introduced Morris Dancing to the curriculum—a form of dance not traditionally found in the Nova Scotia.

8. Begun in 1898 as the Folk Song Society and amalgamating with the English Dance Society in 1932, the English Folk Dance and Song Society emphasised the music component of its mandate. Its members became the unofficial arbitrators for judging the quality and value of English folk songs throughout the world.

9. Helen Creighton to Marius Barbeau, 1 August,1932, Helen Creighton Fonds, PANS MG1 Volume 2811 #162.

10. John D. Robins to Helen Creighton, 3 October, 1932, Helen Creighton Fonds, PANS MG1 Volume 2817 #60.

11. Helen Creighton to C.J. Eustace, J.M. Dent & Sons, 24 September, 1932, Helen Creighton Fonds, PANS MG1 Volume 2811 #162. See: *Hanstead Boys;* Creighton, *Songs and Ballads from Nova Scotia,* 261.

12. Helen Creighton to Marius Barbeau, 28 September, 1932, Helen Creighton Fonds, PANS MG1 Volume 2811 #162.

13. Diary, Helen Creighton Fonds, PANS MG1 Volume 2830 #8. In her autobiography, *A Life in Folklore,* page 62, Helen mistakenly writes 11 February, 1932 as the release date for *Songs and Ballads from Nova Scotia.* However, her diary for 11 February, 1933 and subsequent entries confirm the 1933 date to be correct.

14. Creighton, *A Life in Folklore,* 63.

15. Reginald L. Knowles end-papers, filled with knights and sailors and ships and shepherdesses and doves and devils and drummer-boys and all the motley company who gallop through these ... songs." Creighton, *A Life in Folklore,* 63.

16. Crampton, W.J. "Songs from Devil's Island Make Unique New Volume."

17. Diary, 26 March, 1933, Helen Creighton Fonds, PANS MG1 Volume 2830 #8.

18. Diary, 28 March, 1933, Helen Creighton Fonds, PANS MG1 Volume 2830 #8.

19. Diary, 16 April, 1933, Helen Creighton Fonds, PANS MG1 Volume 2830 #8.

20. Diary, 20 April, 1933, Helen Creighton Fonds, PANS MG1 Volume 2830 #8.

21. As quoted from Dora Baker writing in the Annual Report of the Department of Education of the Province of Nova Scotia, 1934, "The most ambitious musical program yet attempted in the schools of the province was the Music and Folk-dance festival held at Kentville on June 2nd, [1933] as the opening feature of Nova Scotia's first Apple-Blossom Festival." Vogan, Nancy F. "Music Education in the Maritimes Between the Wars: a Period of Transition" 81.

22. Diary, 31 June, 1933, Helen Creighton Fonds, PANS MG1 Volume 2830 #9.

23. Diary, 2 July, 1933, Helen Creighton Fonds, PANS MG1 Volume 2830 #9.

24. Years later, "after the coronation of King George VI, the chair the Earl had occupied during the ceremony (I presume it was the same one) would be given by him to my brother Mac, who shipped it home to mother." Creighton, *A Life in Folklore,* 75. Helen kept the chair in her home for the rest of her life.

25. Creighton, *A Life in Folklore,* 76.

26. Diary, 10 July, 1933, Helen Creighton Fonds, PANS MG1 Volume 2830 #9.

27. Creighton, *A Life in Folklore,* 82.

28. Creighton, *A Life in Folklore,* 86.

29. For the origin, history, and contemporary use of the song see: Croft, Clary. *Chocolates, Tattoos and Mayflowers: Mainstreet Memorabilia from Clary Croft.* Halifax: Nimbus Publishing Ltd, 1995, 101-105.

30. Creighton, *A Life in Folklore,* 86.

31. In fact they both continued to educate themselves in the field of folk song research. On the ship home to England that September, Doreen wrote Helen a letter saying, "Between your researches into the words & mine into tunes we ought to be quite learned soon!" Doreen Senor to Helen Creighton, 10 September, 1933, Helen Creighton Fonds, PANS MG1 Volume 2817 #146.

32. Diary, 5 March, 1934, Helen Creighton Fonds, PANS MG1 Volume 2830 #8.

# CHAPTER 5

1. Diary, 23 March, 1934, Helen Creighton Fonds, PANS MG1 Volume 2830 #8.

2. Diary, 18 June, 1935, Helen Creighton Fonds, PANS MG1 Volume 2830 #8.

3. Diary, 27 December, 1935, Helen Creighton Fonds, PANS MG1 Volume 2830 #8.

4. Diary, 15 & 22 February, 1936, Helen Creighton Fonds, PANS MG1 Volume 2830 #8.

5. Diary, 14 August, 1936, Helen Creighton Fonds, PANS MG1 Volume 2830 #8.

6. Diary, 1 September, 1936, Helen Creighton Fonds, PANS MG1 Volume 2830 #8.

7. Diary, 28 October, 1936, Helen Creighton Fonds, PANS MG1 Volume 2830 #8.

8. "If you realized that our appreciation of your fine work was essentially in giving it a wider public, then you will see why the question of fees had not been stressed in seeking contacts for you. Personally, we have no business connection in this planning whatever, but look upon your visit as an opportunity to introduce you." Rosalind F. Rieman to Helen Creighton, 31 October, 1936, Helen Creighton Fonds, PANS MG1 Volume 2817 #40.

9. Creighton, *A Life in Folklore,* 89.

10. Creighton, *A Life in Folklore,* 89.

11. Helen Creighton to Charles Creighton, 6 December, 1936, Helen Creighton Fonds, PANS MG1 Volume 2830 #9.

12. Creighton, *A Life in Folklore,* 91.

13. Diary, 10 December, 1936, Helen Creighton Fonds, PANS MG1 Volume 2830 #9.

14. See: Creighton, *Folklore of Lunenburg County, Nova Scotia.*

15. Bluenose, a two-masted schooner, captained by Angus Walters, was the undefeated champion of the North Atlantic fishing fleet and the winner of four international schooner races. Her image is depicted on the reverse of the Canadian ten cent coin and her replica namesake, *Bluenose II,* launched in 1963, is currently maintained by the Nova Scotia government for tourist promotion.

16. Diary, [February 1937], Helen Creighton Fonds, PANS MG1 Volume 2830 #1.

17. Germany built the Hindenburg, the world's largest dirigible airship, in 1936. Its northern route to North America frequently took it over Nova Scotia. On May 6, 1937 the Hindenburg burst into flames while trying to dock at Lakehurst, New Jersey.

18. Diary, 4 July, 1936, Helen Creighton Fonds, PANS MG1 Volume 2830 #8.

19. Diary, 11 March, 1937, Helen Creighton Fonds, PANS MG1 Volume 2830 #9.

20. Diary, 14 March, 1937, Helen Creighton Fonds, PANS MG1 Volume 2830 #9.

21. Given Helen's strong leanings towards patriotism, it is doubtful whether she sympathized with the German sentiment, but perhaps the mere fact that she had written an article about their visit caused her embarrassment. Her diary of 25 April, 1938, records her cleaning house and destroying some published and unpublished articles. It is most likely that this article was among them. See: Diary, 25 April, 1938, Helen Creighton Fonds, PANS MG1 Volume 2830 #9.

22. Helen's voice lessons report from the Halifax Conservatory of Music, June 1937. "Splendid progress made in such a short time. Try now to develop more head resonance and sweetness of tone." Helen Creighton Fonds, PANS MG1 Volume 2816 #34.

23. Diary, 30 March, 1937, Helen Creighton Fonds, PANS MG1 Volume 2830 #9.

24. Diary, [n/d], Helen Creighton Fonds, PANS MG1 Volume 2830 #9.

25. Diary, 25 April, 1937, Helen Creighton Fonds, PANS MG1 Volume 2830 #1.

26. Diary, 25 April, 1937, Helen Creighton Fonds, PANS MG1 Volume 2830 #1. Helen used this term several times in her diary entries and her autobiography. The term "idiot" had been common nomenclature for describing someone with a mental handicap. As late as 1902, official forms for admission to the Halifax County Poor House termed inmates "idiotic or insane." RG35, Series C, Overseers of the Poor Papers, 1901-1902, PANS. Public use of a term generally survives long after official change, but as late as 1930, the provincial government was using the terms "insane and defective" in their reports. See: Journal of the House of Assembly, Province of Nova Scotia, Halifax: King's Printer, 1930, 6.

27. Diary, 5&6 May, 1937, Helen Creighton Fonds, PANS MG1 Volume 2830 #1.

28. Diary, 31 May, 1937, Helen Creighton Fonds, PANS MG1 Volume 2830 #1.

29. Diary, [June] 1937, Helen Creighton Fonds, PANS MG1 Volume 2830 #9.

30. Helen Creighton, personal interview, 11 February, 1987, Clary Croft Journal.

31. Helen Creighton, personal interview, 12 February, 1987, Clary Croft Journal.

32. Diary, 13 July, 1937, Helen Creighton Fonds, PANS MG1 Volume 2830 #1.

33. Creighton, *A Life in Folklore*, 96.

34. Creighton, *A Life in Folklore*, 99.

35. Diary, 18 July, 1937, Helen Creighton Fonds, PANS MG1 Volume 2830 #1.

36. Doreen Senior to Helen Creighton, 11 February, 1974, Helen Creighton Fonds, PANS MG1 Volume 2817 #146.

37. Creighton, *A Life in Folklore*, 100. In 1966, Helen returned to Devil's Island to film a television program. The light keeper, Mr. MacDonald, "spoke about the lighthouse. "There's something there," he declared. "There's one thing I won't tell anybody until I leave the island, but when you go up to the light a depression comes over you and stays with you till you come down again. I've kept other lights and never felt anything like this in any one of them." Creighton, *A Life in Folklore*, 234.

38. Diary, 30 July, 1937, Helen Creighton Fonds, PANS MG1 Volume 2830 #1.

39. Diary, 3 August, 1937, Helen Creighton Fonds, PANS MG1 Volume 2830 #1.

40. Diary, 7 August, 1937, Helen Creighton Fonds, PANS MG1 Volume 2830 #1.

41. Diary, 7 August, 1937, Helen Creighton Fonds, PANS MG1 Volume 2830 #1.

42. Diary, 26 August, 1937, Helen Creighton Fonds, PANS MG1 Volume 2830 #1.

43. Creighton, *A Life in Folklore*, 108.

## CHAPTER 6

1. Diary, January 1938, Helen Creighton Fonds, PANS MG1 Volume 2830 #1.

2. Helen also received advice from Frank Willis and from John D. Robins. "I have read your most interesting broadcasts, and I think you have done a remarkable job of combining popular interest and sound information, in a fascinatingly intimate manner." John D. Robins to Helen Creighton, 12 March, 1938, Helen Creighton Fonds, PANS MG1 Volume 2817 #60.

3. Edmund Henneberry was asked to sing in his father's place because, at the time, it was thought Ben Henneberry's facial deformity made his diction unsuitable for radio broadcasts. A contemporary of Ben Henneberry's told Helen that Ben's face was damaged below the eye from a cancer operation. Diary, 20 June, 1938, Helen Creighton Fonds, PANS MG1 Volume 2830 #1.

4. Alice Henneberry to Helen Creighton, [c.1938], Helen Creighton Fonds, PANS MG1 Volume 2813 #172.

5. Creighton, *A Life in Folklore,* 112.

6. Diary, 26 February, 1938, Helen Creighton Fonds, PANS MG1 Volume 2830 #9.

7. Creighton, *A Life in Folklore* 111. Helen was to offer Walter further help in 1940. "Heard of job for janitor at Thorndyke Hotel, Dartmouth, and immediately thought of Walter Roast knowing how he has to pinch to make living on farm. Just the thing for him. He is delighted. Sensitive about withered arm, and hates to ask for jobs himself. Curiously enough I didn't know he wanted one as subject had never been mentioned, but just before he heard he thought to himself one day, Miss C. Is going to get me a job." He came to house to see me. Gratitude very touching."Diary, 17 October, 1940, Helen Creighton Fonds, PANS MG1 Volume 2830 #2.

8. Diary, June 19, 1938, PANS MG1 Volume 2830 #9.

9. Two years later, Nina Bartley Finn, the professional singer who worked with Helen on the second radio series offered these comments: "So many people here have heard your programme and were very interested in it. The only thing they balked at were the folk singers, and if you *have* the programme again, I wouldn't have them—because people who don't know—the public can't put them in the picture—they are out of their element—All they hear is a queer sounding voice—they can't see the look of delight, & at giving all they have on the part of the singer. I have explained it 20 times if once." Nina Bartley Finn to Helen Creighton, 6 May, 1940, Helen Creighton Fonds, PANS MG1 Volume 2812 #132.

10. Helen went on to collect many other examples of this regional naming style, especially in Cape Breton. For examples from her collection see: Helen Creighton Fonds, PANS MG1 Volume 2806 #6. See also: Creighton, Helen. "Cape Breton Nicknames and Tales."

11. Rental for Dict. Sept. 28-Oct.18, $6.25. Three cylinders 2.10. Very reasonable, I should think." Diary, 24 October, 1938, Helen Creighton Fonds, PANS MG1 Volume 2830 #2.

12. Diary, 4 September [1938], Helen Creighton Fonds, PANS MG1 Volume 2830 #1.

13. Creighton, *A Life in Folklore,* 116.

14. Diary, 7 September [1938], Helen Creighton Fonds, PANS MG1 Volume 2830 #1.

15. In 1941, Helen had some of the participants recreate the wedding party for a National Film Board production, directed by Laura Bolton, titled *New Scotland.* Years later some of those participants would remember Helen's visit to the wedding and the subsequent film production. "The film was showed to local men who served in the war when they were in Europe ... The celebration took place at the farm of William MacIntosh, Argyle, Guysborough Co. The "groom" was John Sullivan and the "bride" was his sister, Betty. The "best man" was John Francis McNeil (these people were all from Giant's Lake because she wanted her film to reflect the reception she attended there earlier). No one can remember who the bride's maid was. The reason the MacIntosh farm was selected was because they had electricity so they could operate the camera equipment. Filming was done by National Film Board, Ottawa. The singers were:

Angus "Ridge" MacDonald, John MacNeil, John MacGregor and Fred Kennedy. Angus "Ridge" MacDonald was the piper and also played the fiddle for dancing. Mary MacGregor danced the "Sailor's Hornpipe." [sic] Jessie Kennedy to Clary Croft, 1997.

16. "Think it was incidental music that spoiled it. N.S. Song was cut off in middle, Alphabet Song hadn't enough rhythm, and Mary L. MacKay hadn't the life Edmund Henneberry gives it." Diary, 23 October, 1938, Helen Creighton Fonds, PANS MG1 Volume 2830 #2.

17. Creighton, *A Life in Folklore,* 120.

18. Diary, 26 November, 1938, Helen Creighton Fonds, PANS MG1 Volume 2830 #2.

19. Diary, 21 April, 1939, Helen Creighton Fonds, PANS MG1 Volume 2830 #2.

20. Doreen Senior to Helen Creighton, 13 March, 1939, Helen Creighton Fonds, PANS MG1 Volume 2817 #146.

21. For some examples see: Alexander, *The Story of Our Language.*

22. Diary, 21 April, 1939, Helen Creighton Fonds, PANS MG1 Volume 2830 #2.

23. Nina Bartley Finn eventually moved to Ottawa to pursue her singing career and adopted the stage name Emma Caslor.

24. The Rayners became well known in Australia and in 1948 founded the Australian Children's Theatre. See: Clark, *Strolling Players: Joan & Betty Raynor.*

25. Diary, 13 June, 1939, Helen Creighton Fonds, PANS MG1 Volume 2830 #2. Helen was beginning to establish a pattern of protectionism for her collecting territory which would become one of the sore points among folk lore collectors. She felt that once a territory was staked out, it was off limits to another collector. She herself, adopted this rule and abided by it, later refusing to collect in Newfoundland because of the work being done there by her friend Maude Karpeles; in northern New Brunswick by Louise Manny; and in Prince Edward Island by Edward (Sandy) D. Ives.

26. Diary, 25 June, 1939, Helen Creighton Fonds, PANS MG1 Volume 2830 #2.

27. Child, *The English and Scottish Popular Ballads.* Helen was to eventually find variants of 43 Child Ballads.

28. Creighton, *A Life in Folklore,* 126. The song was: *Little Musgrave and Lady Bernard*, sung by Stanley Williams, Ostrea Lake, see: Creighton, Helen and Doreen H. Senior. *Traditional Songs from Nova Scotia,* 47.

29. Doreen Senior to Helen Creighton, [25 August], 1939, Helen Creighton Fonds, PANS MG1 Volume 2817 #146.

# CHAPTER 7

1. King's college was founded at Windsor, Nova Scotia in 1789 and granted a Royal Charter in 1802. It is the oldest degree-conferring institution in the British Commonwealth, outside Great Britain. After a fire destroyed the original complex at Windsor in 1920, the College moved to the Dalhousie University Campus in 1923.

2. See: Creighton, *A Life in Folklore,* 128.

3. Helen Creighton, personal interview, 11 March, 1987, Clary Croft Journal. Helen didn't keep copies of these reports in her personal files. However, a diary entry does show that she lobbied strongly to allow the Ajax Club (a social club for service personnel) to remain open and serve beer in a relaxed, controlled atmosphere. Diary, [n/d], Helen Creighton Fonds, PANS MG1 Volume 2815 #173.

4. Diary, 4 January, 1940, Helen Creighton Fonds, PANS MG1 Volume 2830 #11.

5. Diary, 17 July, 1940, Helen Creighton Fonds, PANS MG1 Volume 2830 #2.

6. Diary, 27 July, 1940, Helen Creighton Fonds, PANS MG1 Volume 2830 #2.

7. See: Creighton, Helen and Doreen H. Senior. *Traditional Songs from Nova Scotia,* 70.

8. "I shall never forget that day at Chebecto Head with Mrs. Gallagher ... and the convoy with all the masts sticking out of the mist. ... My little ballad class listened pop-eyes (as my U.S.A. friends say) the other day when I told them about this experience with you." Anna J. Mill to Helen Creighton, 13 October, 1940, Helen Creighton Fonds, PANS MG1 Volume 2815 #180.

9. Diary, 10 August, 1940, Helen Creighton Fonds, PANS MG1 Volume 2830 #11.

10. Diary, 23 September, 1940, Helen Creighton Fonds, PANS MG1 Volume 2830 #11.

11. Helen gave complimentary copies to friends and informants whose songs were used in the book. "New book arrived ... Took copy to Walter Roast at Thorndyke. He was very grateful ... Sent complimentary copies to; Gallagher, Henneberry, Dennis Smith, Tom Youngs, Walkers, Sircoms, Hubleys, Jean, Walter Roast, Olga, Nina, Munro, Father, Emerson, Barbeau." Diary, 6 January, 1941, Helen Creighton Fonds, PANS MG1 Volume 2830 #2.

12. Creighton, Helen, and Doreen Senior. *Twelve Folk Songs from Nova Scotia.* London: Novello, 1940.

13. Doreen Senior to Helen Creighton, 25 February, [c.1940], Helen Creighton Fonds, PANS MG1 Volume 2817 #146.

14. Ten years later, Helen would offer her criticisms to Lorne Pierce, editor at Ryerson Press. She felt Doreen's editing of her notes, "quite spoiled the book." Helen Creighton to Lorne Pierce, 20 November 1950, Pierce Papers, Box 19, f.2, item 29, QUA; as cited in McKay, Ian. *The Quest of the Folk: Antimodernism and Cultural Selection in Twentieth-Century Nova Scotia,* 82. Helen would eventually treat Doreen similarly in the preparation of their second joint publication, *Traditional Songs from Nova Scotia.*

15. Review by Frank Howes, English Dance and Song, February 1941.

16. Alice Creighton died 31 May, 1941, aged 82.

17. Diary, [n/d] May, 1941, Helen Creighton Fonds, PANS MG1 Volume 2830 #10.

18. Creighton, *A Life in Folklore,* 128.

19. The terms in Alice Creighton's will, dated 7 June, 1938, gave Evergreen to her husband Charles. Helen received all her jewellery, clothing and personal belongings, with some exceptions. Lilian received $100. Jacob Creighton Fonds, PANS MG1 Volume 3530 #1.50.

20. Helen Creighton to Clary Croft, [n/d] , personal conversation.

21. Marius Barbeau to Helen Creighton, 5 September, 1941, Helen Creighton Fonds, PANS MG1 Volume 2810 #74.

22. Diary, 21 September, 1941, Helen Creighton Fonds, PANS MG1 Volume 2830 #2.

23. See Endnote #14, Chapter Six.

24. Diary, 2 October, 1941, Helen Creighton Fonds, PANS MG1 Volume 2830 #2.

25. Diary, 4 October, 1941, Helen Creighton Fonds, PANS MG1 Volume 2830 #2.

26. Diary, 7 October, 1941, Helen Creighton Fonds, PANS MG1 Volume 2830 #2.

27. Diary, 6 October, 1941, Helen Creighton Fonds, PANS MG1 Volume 2830 #2.

28. Diary, 8 October, 1941, Helen Creighton Fonds, PANS MG1 Volume 2830 #2.

29. Diary, 10 October, 1941, Helen Creighton Fonds, PANS MG1 Volume 2830 #2.

30. Diary, 11 October, 1941, Helen Creighton Fonds, PANS MG1 Volume 2830 #2.

31. Judy Crawley to Helen Creighton, 12 November, 1941, Helen Creighton Fonds, PANS MG1 Volume 2811 #150. In 1987 Dr. Robert Macmillan wrote to Helen seeking information for research he was conducting concerning Laura Bolton. He told Helen that Laura: "passed away in 1980. ... The New York Times obituary curiously refers to her Doctoral degree from the university of Chicago. ... My research ... indicates that she did not receive such a degree ... Bolton's correspondence with Dr. Barbeau consists mainly of a series of requests for favors. Yet, I cannot see that he ever asked her for help or assistance of any kind." Robert Macmillan to Helen Creighton, 1 January, 1987, Helen Creighton Fonds, PANS MG1 Volume 3512 #7. Helen's response was gracious: "I find it so difficult to reply to your letter because there is so little I can say in favour of the lady in question. But if the world is divided between givers and takers, she would not be found in the former category, at least in my experience. ... I don't like writing unpleasant things about a person who has died. We attended an International Folk Music Council meeting in Rumania in 1959 and bowed politely to each other." Helen Creighton to Robert Macmillan, 10 January, 1987, Helen Creighton Fonds, PANS MG1 Volume 3512 #7. Helen makes no clear mention of Laura Bolton in her autobiography. Her only reference to the experience is: ".. shortly before, someone had come to my province and had attempted to take for herself on disc all the songs I had collected so labouriously, at the same time insinuating that only someone with a massive brain could operate a machine so intricate. If I've guarded my material jealously ever since, it has been because of this unfortunate encounter." Creighton, *A Life in Folklore*, 131. See also: Bolton, Laura. *The Music Hunter: The Autobiography of a Career* Garden City, New York: Doubleday, 1969.

# CHAPTER 8

1. Diary, May 1942, Helen Creighton Fonds, PANS MG1 Volume 2830 #2.

2. Creighton, *A Life in Folklore*, 129.

3. Diary, 26-29 August, 1942, Helen Creighton Fonds, PANS MG1 Volume 2830 #2.

4. Creighton, *A Life in Folklore*, 131.

5. Diary, n/d, Helen Creighton Fonds, PANS MG1 Volume 3387 #2.

6. Helen Creighton to Charles Creighton, n/d, 1942, Helen Creighton Fonds, PANS MG1 Volume 3387 #2.

7. *Indiana Daily Student* 29 July, 1942.

8. Helen Creighton to Charles Creighton, n/d, 1942, Helen Creighton Fonds, PANS MG1 Volume 3387 #2. Confirmed by transcript also in this file.

9. Helen Creighton Fonds, PANS MG1 Volume 3387 #2.

10. Helen Creighton Fonds, PANS MG1 Volume 3387 #2.

11. From 1942 to 1946, Helen received several Rockefeller Foundation grants. "Overall, the foundation's support for Creighton in the 1940s appears to have been in the rage of $2,450." McKay, *The Quest of the Folk*, endnote 106, 321.

12. Helen Creighton to Alan Lomax, 8 October, 1942, Helen Creighton Fonds, PANS MG1 Volume 2811 #162.

13. Diary, 4 October, 1942, Helen Creighton Fonds, PANS MG1 Volume 2830 #2.

14. Helen Creighton to John Marshall, 3 October, 1942, Helen Creighton Fonds, PANS MG1 Volume 2811 #162. In the eighteenth and nineteenth centuries, Nova Scotia had the largest indigenous African- Canadian population in Canada.

15. Helen Creighton to Alan Lomax, 8 October, 1942, Helen Creighton Fonds, PANS MG1 Volume 2811 #162.

16. Diary, 8 October, 1942, Helen Creighton Fonds, PANS MG1 Volume 2830 #2. She would record Mr. Tynes's version of *When the Saints Go Marching In*, on 6 August, 1943.

17. Fauset, Arthur Huff. *Folklore from Nova Scotia.* American Folklore Society, Volume 24, 1931. In 1947, Helen met a hotel owner near Annapolis Royal who met Arthur Fauset when he stayed at her hotel. ."... chat with Mrs. Crosby ... Only Nova Scotian I've ever met who knew Mr. Fauset. He had stayed here. Was light negro and told them he planned never to marry as did not want children of his to go through what he had regarding race. Hoped to devote life and raise status of coloured people. Was horrified to find how little they had progressed in N.S." Diary, 9 June, 1947, Helen Creighton Fonds, PANS MG1 Volume 2830 #3.

18. Diary, [n/d] October, 1942, Helen Creighton Fonds, PANS MG1 Volume 2830 #2.

19. Diary, 4 November, 1942, Helen Creighton Fonds, PANS MG1 Volume 2830 #2.

20. Helen Creighton Fonds, MG1 Volume 2804 #22. "To justify the Library of Congress in sending out recording equipment in wartime, I had to do some work among the Service personnel. I had heard that they often made up their own songs, but when I mentioned them they looked horrified, for few were of the parlour variety. One or two whose words I didn't understand I sent to Alan Lomax and later, when I learned their meaning, my blushes could be felt from here to Washington." Creighton, *A Life in Folklore,* 135.

21. Helen Creighton, personal interview, 26 November, 1986, Clary Croft Journal.

22. Diary, 8 July, 1943, Helen Creighton Fonds, PANS MG1 Volume 2830 #2.

23. Diary, 9 July, 1943, Helen Creighton Fonds, PANS MG1 Volume 2830 #2.

24. Diary, 23 July, 1943, Helen Creighton Fonds, PANS MG1 Volume 2830 #2. In 1997, technicians at CBC Halifax were transferring some of the recordings Helen made at this period from magnetic tape to digital audio tape. They were so impressed with the quality of the recordings she made at the time they awarded her an honorary "sound technician group 6" category—a high listing indeed. Pat Martin, telephone interview, 18, February 1999.

25. Diary, 12 August, 1943, Helen Creighton Fonds, PANS MG1 Volume 2830 #2.

26. Diary, 24 July, 1943, Helen Creighton Fonds, PANS MG1 Volume 2830 #2.

27. Diary, 7 September, 1943, Helen Creighton Fonds. PANS MG1 Volume 2830 #2. After her experience in Cherry Brook, Helen was uncomfortable collecting material from informants living directly in the African-Nova Scotian communities. But she did make several visits to the Nova Scotia Home for Coloured Children where, as early as 1942, she had heard of songs which might be of interest to her. The Nova Scotia Home for Coloured Children was opened in 1921 to serve the needs of African-Nova Scotian orphans and children placed there by social authorities. The children were involved in many community activities, the most visible of which was the annual radio (and eventually, television) broadcasts to raise funds for the Home. It continues to operate, using its original name. For a detailed history of the Home, see: Saunders, *Share and Care:The Story of the Nova Scotia Home for Colored Children.* On March 17, 1944, she took her Presto recorder to the home and recorded singing games and songs from fifteen children.

28. Diary, 25 August, 1943, Helen Creighton Fonds, PANS MG1 Volume 2830 #2.

29. Fifty-four years later, Rose Mann, now 100 years old, remembered Helen's visits with fondness and spoke of her father's affection for her. "He loved her. She was a wonderful woman." Rose Mann, videotaped interview, 9 April, 1997. Mrs. Mann lived in New York, but came home to visit her father every summer. She was one of twelve children and died in 1998 at the age of one hundred and one.

30. Helen Creighton, personal interview, 26 November, 1986, Clary Croft Journal.

31. Diary, 7 October, 1943, Helen Creighton Fonds, PANS MG1 Volume 2830 #2. In 1980, a new version of *Meet the Navy* was being mounted. Helen heard a radio interview with Alan Lund, one of the original members who was directing the show. He said he had forgotten some parts of the show, so she sent him a copy of her 1943 original.

# CHAPTER 9

1. Charles Creighton will, 10 January, 1942, Jacob Creighton Fonds, PANS MG1 Volume 3530 #1.52

2. Helen Creighton, personal interview, 11 March, 1987, Clary Croft Journal.

3. Alice Creighton Nicholl, audio-taped interview, 16 September, 1995.

4. Diary, 22 November, 1943, Helen Creighton Fonds, PANS MG1 Volume 2830 #2.

5. Diary, 10 December, 1943, Helen Creighton Fonds, PANS MG1 Volume 2830 #2.

6. Diary, 12 December, 1943, Helen Creighton Fonds, PANS MG1 Volume 2830 #2. Portia never did get back to record for Helen.

7. Diary, 14 December, 1943, Helen Creighton Fonds, PANS MG1 Volume 2830 #2.

8. Years later, after official papers were declassified, it was established that the *St. Roch* was also doing reconnaissance work in Greenland to investigate the possibility of establishing an Allied military presence there.

9. Creighton, *A Life in Folklore*, 141.

10. Henry Larsen, like most people upon hearing their recorded voice for the first time, was amazed to discover he didn't sound as he thought he would. "I enjoyed the trip, I don't think I want any of my records anyway but every time I hear Mortimer Snerd I'll think of them." Henry Larsen to Helen Creighton, 27 November, 1945, Helen Creighton Fonds, PANS MG1 Volume 2814 #124.

11. Diary, 25 March, 1944, Helen Creighton Fonds, PANS MG1 Volume 2830 #2.

12. Kluskap (Glooscap) has become the primary character in Mi'kmaq tales. European references to him were first recorded about 1850. "He goes from being one of many Persons in the traditional Micmac world, to a central position as the Micmac spirit-helper." Whitehead, *Stories from the Six Worlds: Micmac Legends* 220. The first non-native to assemble Mi'kmaq lore was missionary Silas Rand, see: Rand, Silas T. *Legends of the Micmacs*.

13. Diary, 30 April, 1944, Helen Creighton Fonds, PANS MG1 Volume 2830 #2.

14. Creighton, *A Life in Folklore*, 147.

15. Whycocogmagh is now commonly denoted as being two communities. The Mi'kmaq reserve, established in 1833, is today known by its traditional name of Waycobah.

16. Diary, 10 June, 1944, Helen Creighton Fonds, PANS MG1 Volume 2830 #2. For more of Helen's perspective on this incident see: Diary, 8 June, 1944, Helen Creighton Fonds, PANS MG1 Volume 2830 #2; and Creighton, *A Life in Folklore*, 147-8.

17. "Her description of interrupting a wake—with the priest's assistance—to collect" songs is perhaps the most insensitive passage found anywhere in her accounts of collecting. Tye, *'A Very Lone Worker': Woman-Centred Thoughts on Helen Creighton's Career as a Folklorist*, 112-113.

18. "I am glad to hear of the possibility of your getting started on a project of your own. Unfortunately, recording machines cannot be had for love or money. We ourselves have been trying to buy one without success." B.A. Botkin, Assistant in Charge, Archive of American Folk Song, Library of Congress, Washington, to Helen Creighton, 1 June, 1944, Helen Creighton Fonds, PANS MG1 Volume 2810 #151.

19. Diary, 7 May, 1944, Helen Creighton Fonds, PANS MG1 Volume 2830 #2. "Had to interrupt work to go to Hfx. to see Mr. Campbell of the Publicity Dept. and convince him that the gov't. should finance my work. Must have done my work badly because although he gave me nearly an hour, he could not see his way to support it. ... Doesn't seem to realize that I want to do something for the province and not for myself. Oh well." Diary, 3 November, 1944, Helen Creighton Fonds, PANS MG1 Volume 2830 #2. Helen also applied unsuccessfully to the government of Prince Edward Island for funds to allow her to collect there.

20. Helen Creighton, audio- taped interview conducted by Clary Croft for PANS, 17 March, 1987, PANS AC1619.

21. H. M. Estall, Wartime Information Board to Helen Creighton, 14 September, 1945, Helen Creighton Fonds, PANS MG1 Volume 2812 #106.

22. Marius Barbeau to Duncan Emrich, Library of Congress, 14 February, 1947, Helen Creighton Fonds, PANS MG1 Volume 2810 #74. (copy)

23. Marius Barbeau to Helen Creighton, 7 May, 1947, Helen Creighton Fonds, PANS MG1 Volume 2810 #75.

# CHAPTER 10

1. Several communities make up the area known colloquially as "The Pubnicos." Pubnico, East Pubnico, Lower East Pubnico, West Pubnico, Middle West Pubnico, Lower West Pubnico. The area was settled in 1653, making it the oldest Acadian settlement in Nova Scotia.

2. Diary, 27 May, 1947, Helen Creighton Fonds, PANS MG1 Volume 2830 #3. Aside from the diary entry citing Mrs. McNeil, there is no proof of Juliette Gauthier's statement to Mrs. McNeil. I would like to thank Benoit Theriault, archivist for the Canadian Museum of Civilization for the following information. Juliette Gaultier also used the artistic name: Juliette Gaultier de la Vérendrye. The Canadian Museum of Civilization has two files pertaining to her work: Canadian Museum of Civilization, CCFCS Records, " Juliette Gaultier de la Vérendrye " Collection Ms: GAV-A to E. (Documents re: French Canadian folklore), and Canadian Museum of Civilization, Ethnology Records, " Juliette Gaultier de la Vérendrye " Collection Ms: I-A-160M. (Documents re: Indian folklore & material culture). Neither contain material collected from Laura Irene McNeil.

3. Helen Creighton, personal interview, 17 June, 1987, Clary Croft Journal. At the end of her first session for the National Museum, Helen wrote a report for Marius Barbeau. "At first I found a little hesitation on the part of both Mrs. McNeil and the editor, Mr. D'Eon, about parting with their material. Confidently, Miss Gauthier has taken a lot from Mrs. McNeil, some of which has been published as, for instance, a "Berceuse" which is a Victor record 22311. I don't know whether that is the very beautiful lullaby she gave her, or whether it is some other piece. Also it is possible that Miss Gauthier has never made any money out of anything taken from Pubnico, and therefore was in no position to share with Mrs, McNeil. Still, there is a feeling, and that is why I have been most particular to give credit lines with every story which is, I suppose, as much as we can ever hope to do." Helen Creighton to Marius Barbeau, 17 October, 1947, Helen Creighton Fonds, Canadian Museum of Civilization (CMC), CR-K-1.1.

4. American writer, Martha Banning Thomas., spent several summers at Victoria Beach before taking up permanent residence there. She wrote short stories and poems with Canadian themes and published in several of the leading magazines of the day.

5. Creighton, *A Life in Folklore,* 153.

6. During the 1940s, Thomas Head Raddall was considered one of Canada's primary authors. He wrote a number of popular historical novels and a major nonfiction work *Halifax, Warden of the North.* In 1990, Acadia University in Wolfville established an annual symposium on Atlantic Canadian literature, named in his honour. For a discussion of Thomas Raddall's use of folklore

in his work see: Croft, Clary. "The Use of Folklore in Selected Works of Thomas H. Raddall" *Time and Place: The Life and Works of Thomas H. Raddall*, ed. Alan R. Young, Fredericton: Acadiensis, 1991.

7. Thomas Raddall, audio-taped interview, 1990.

8. For the complete story see: Creighton, *Bluenose Magic*, 23-25.

9. Creighton, *Bluenose Magic*, 25.

10. Diary, 21 June, 1947, Helen Creighton Fonds, PANS MG1 Volume 2830 #3.

11. Diary, 8 July, 1947, Helen Creighton Fonds, PANS MG1 Volume 2830 #3.

12. Diary, 30 August, 1947, Helen Creighton Fonds, PANS MG1 Volume 2830 #3.

13. Diary 1 September, 1947, Helen Creighton Fonds, PANS MG1 Volume 2830 #3.

14. Diary, 13 September, 1947, Helen Creighton Fonds, PANS MG1 Volume 2830 #3.

15. Diary, 14 September, 1947, Helen Creighton Fonds, PANS MG1 Volume 2830 #3.

16. Diary, 26 June, 1948, Helen Creighton Fonds, PANS MG1 Volume 2830 #3. In a note attached to the section on folk dances accompanying her report for the National Museum Helen acknowledged Joe's contribution to their collection, but is careful to note the songs were collected by her alone: "These are a few of the square dance notes; others will follow in due time. This is a new field to me, so I had no idea how to write the dances down, but it is a speciality with Mr. Raben who typed them out for me. In the songs which he helped me find, I have added his name with mine in the footnote, "collected by." It doesn't mean anything but a gesture of courtesy." Canadian Museum of Civilization, CR-C-4.1.

17. Diary, 3 June 1948, Helen Creighton Fonds, PANS MG1 Volume 2830 #3. By 1948, Helen's hair had begun to turn grey, and the pronounced grey streak which ran from her brow added to her more mature appearance.

18. For an audio recording see: "Folk Music from Nova Scotia," Folkways record, FM4006. "I do remember Dr. Creighton coming to our home in Eastern Passage on several occasions; especially on Sunday afternoons. It was on one such occasion when I was 15 or 16 that I sang "The Gay Spanish Maid" with my father. I was a bit shy at first, but felt very privileged to be asked to sing with my Dad." Sadie Henneberry to Clary Croft, 14 February, 1994. Sadie entered the Sisters of Charity in 1948.

19. Diary, 6 August, 1948, Helen Creighton Fonds, PANS MG1 Volume 2830 #3.

20. In the contract for *Traditional Songs from Nova Scotia* with The Ryerson Press dated 2 August, 1949, their standard royalties of 10% were divided as 66 2/3 % to Helen and 33 1/3 % to Doreen. Helen Creighton Fonds, MG1 Volume 2794 #8.

21. "When Dr. Alcock read over the manuscript, he found several items by which people of delicate sensibilities might be offended, and he marked these "omit."" Douglas Leechman, National Museum, to Helen Creighton, 27 January, 1949, Helen Creighton Fonds, PANS MG1 Volume 2814 #137. These included stories from informants concerning supposed ignorance of "niggers"; the identification of a man reputed to be a witch and semi-bawdy anecdotes. See: Helen Creighton Collection, Canadian Museum of Civilization, CR-C-2 Part 1-.1 to .174 and Part 2-.175 to .300.

22. Wintemberg, J.M. *Folklore of Waterloo County, Ontario*.

23. Helen Creighton to Clary Croft, [n/d] , personal conversation.

24. Diary, 21 June, 1949, Helen Creighton Fonds, PANS MG1 Volume 2830 #3.

25. Cape Sable Island is home to the famous Cape Sable Island boat. The first model was built at Clark's Harbour by Ephriam Atkinson in 1907.

26. Maida Parlow French was a writer of homey stories which appealed to Helen, although she did have an adventurous side as well. Soon after their shared visit to Bon Portage Island, Maida left to go on a trip to write about travel aboard a tramp steamer, even though several of her friends, including Evelyn Richardson, advised her against it. "Had been told many times she would be raped if she went on a tramp steamer; Mrs. Richardson agreed to this and said 'men get notions.'" Diary, 19 July, 1949, Helen Creighton Fonds, PANS MG1 Volume 2830 #3.

27. Richardson, *We Keep a Light*.

28. Creighton, *A Life in Folklore*, 160.

29. Diary, 26 July, 1949, Helen Creighton Fonds, PANS MG1 Volume 2830 #3.

30. Helen Creighton Fonds, PANS MG1 Volume 3516 #2.

31. Diary, 18 June, 1947, Helen Creighton Fonds, PANS MG1 Volume 2830 #3.

32. Diary, 11 August, 1949, Helen Creighton Fonds, PANS MG1 Volume 2830 #3.

33. Diary, 26 August, 1949, Helen Creighton Fonds, PANS MG1 Volume 2830 #3.

34. Diary, 3 September, 1949, Helen Creighton Fonds, PANS MG1 Volume 2830 #3.

35. Diary, 5 September, 1949, Helen Creighton Fonds, PANS MG1 Volume 2830 #3.

36. The Baffled Knight. Creighton, and Senior. *Traditional Songs from Nova Scotia*, 64.

37. Creighton, *A Life in Folklore*, 162.

38. Creighton, *A Life in Folklore*, 162. Helen continued to worry about what people would perceive as unladylike behaviour. On a collecting trip to Terence Bay, outside Halifax she noted: .".. was careful about smoking in some of these places, but here was one place we needn't worry. All the women smoked .. We shared ours which they took gratefully." Diary, 25 September, 1949, Helen Creighton Fonds, PANS MG1 Volume 2830 #3.

# CHAPTER 11

1. In the 1950s, Halifax musicians, such as Bill Reid, popularized the fad for Hawaiian guitar and costumes, but they played the popular music of the day. Several music teachers in Halifax offered guitar lessons in the Hawaiian style where the guitar was held horizontally on the lap and chorded using a metal bar on the frets.

2. Raben, Review, *Hoosier Folklore*. Helen's work as a scholar was being further recognized with the publication of her major article on Victoria Beach in the Journal of American Folklore. See: Creighton, "Folklore of Victoria Beach."

3. Diary, 23 July, 1950, Helen Creighton Fonds, PANS MG1 Volume 2830 #3. In the 1920s, Helen had used another home-training method to try and improve her memory. The Pelman Course was a method of memory training which used cards to improve the recall of facts, figures and faces. Refereed to as Pelmanism it was almost a fad in the late 1920s.

4. Diary, 28 July, 1950, Helen Creighton Fonds, PANS MG1 Volume 2830 #3.

5. Creighton, *A Life in Folklore*, 163.

6. *Eight Famous Fishermen*, composed and sung by Edward Deal, August 1950. Creighton, *Maritime Folk Songs*, 193.

7. Diary, 14 September, 1950, Helen Creighton Fonds, PANS MG1 Volume 2830 #3.

8. Diary, 9 September, 1950, Helen Creighton Fonds, PANS MG1 Volume 2830 #3.

9. Creighton, Helen and Doreen H. Senior. *Traditional Songs from Nova Scotia*. Toronto: Ryerson, 1950.

10. Diary, 7 October, 1950, Helen Creighton Fonds, PANS MG1 Volume 2830 #3.

11. Diary, 16 October, 1950, Helen Creighton Fonds, PANS MG1 Volume 2830 #3.

12. Senior, and Creighton. "Folk Songs Collected in the Province of Nova Scotia, Canada."

13. John D. Robins, preface, Creighton, and Senior, *Traditional Songs from Nova Scotia*, vii.

14. *Globe and Mail* 2 December, 1950.

15. *Family Herald and Weekly Star* 11 January, 1951. Helen recognized the importance of such a high recommendation from The Family Herald. "Oh, The Family Herald, was probably the only reading matter that many people had in those days. And they always had contributions of songs from—a very popular magazine in the Maritime provinces. You'd see it everywhere." Helen Creighton, audio-taped interview conducted by Clary Croft for PANS, 11 August, 1987, PANS AC1620.

16. Diary, 6 June, 1951, Helen Creighton Fonds, PANS MG1 Volume 2830 #3.

17. Diary, 16 July, 1951, Helen Creighton Fonds, PANS MG1 Volume 2830 #3.

18. Helen Creighton to Clary Croft, [n/d] , personal conversation.

19. Diary, 17 July, 1951, Helen Creighton Fonds, PANS MG1 Volume 2830 #3.

20. Diary, 27 July, 1951, Helen Creighton Fonds, PANS MG1 Volume 2830 #3.

21. Edith Fowke was born in 1913 in Saskatchewan. Her work in Canadian folklore made her the preeminent female folklore scholar in the nation. She was a brilliant scholar and a feisty advocate for the general cause of Canadian folklore studies. She received the Order of Canada in 1978 and was made an Honorary Life member of the Canadian Folk Music Society in 1984. She died in 1996.

22. Diary, 6-8 August, 1951, Helen Creighton Fonds, PANS MG1 Volume 2830 #3.

23. Diary, 1 September, 1951, Helen Creighton Fonds, PANS MG1 Volume 2830 #3.

24. Creighton, *A Life in Folklore,* 170.

25. Creighton, *A Life in Folklore,* 165.

26. Diary, 13 October, 1951, Helen Creighton Fonds, PANS MG1 Volume 2830 #3.

27. Diary, 15 June, 1951, Helen Creighton Fonds, PANS MG1 Volume 2830 #3.

28. Report of field work for National Museum, June to October 1947, Helen Creighton Fonds, PANS MG1 Volume 2806 #1.

29. Creighton, *A Life in Folklore,* 172.

30. Creighton, *A Life in Folklore,* 172.

31. Diary, 22 May, 1952, Helen Creighton Fonds, PANS MG1 Volume 2830 #3.

32. Diary, 29 May, 1952, Helen Creighton Fonds, PANS MG1 Volume 2830 #3.

33. Helen Creighton, audio-taped interview conducted by Clary Croft for PANS, 11 August, 1987, PANS AC1620.

34. Diary, 30 May, 1952, Helen Creighton Fonds, PANS MG1 Volume 2830 #3.

35. Diary, 4 June, 1952, Helen Creighton Fonds, PANS MG1 Volume 2830 #3.

36. Diary, 5 June, 1952, Helen Creighton Fonds, PANS MG1 Volume 2830 #3.

37. Diary, 10 June, 1952, Helen Creighton Fonds, PANS MG1 Volume 2830 #3.

38. Diary, 11 June, 1952, Helen Creighton Fonds, PANS MG1 Volume 2830 #3.

39. This form of song writing was fairly common. For an interesting study of one well-known "dunner" from Prince Edward Island see: Ives, Edward D. *Larry Gorman: The Man Who Made the Songs.* Bloomington: Indiana University Press, 1964.

40. Diary, 12 June, 1952, Helen Creighton Fonds, PANS MG1 Volume 2830 #3.

41. Diary, 17 August, 1952, Helen Creighton Fonds, PANS MG1 Volume 2830 #3.

42. Creighton, *A Life in Folklore,* 167- 168.

43. Diary, 17 August, 1952, Helen Creighton Fonds, PANS MG1 Volume 2830 #3.

44. Sclanders, Ian. "She's Collecting Long Lost Songs" *Maclean's* 15 September, 1952.

45. Diary, 14 September, 1952, Helen Creighton Fonds, PANS MG1 Volume 2830 #3.

46. Diary, 18 September, 1952, Helen Creighton Fonds, PANS MG1 Volume 2830 #3.

47. Diary, 19 September, 1952, Helen Creighton Fonds, PANS MG1 Volume 2830 #3.

48. Diary, 21 September, 1952, Helen Creighton Fonds, PANS MG1 Volume 2830 #3. Joseph Scull began his career in radio and eventually worked in stage, screen and television, specializing in Canadian history. After his Navy service in WWII, he was commissioned by the Minister of National Defence to write the official account of Canadian Naval operations—*The Far Distant Ships.* He had a sister Helen and eventually married a woman named Hélène.

# CHAPTER 12

1. Joseph Schull to Helen Creighton, 2 October, 1953, Helen Creighton Fonds, PANS MG1 Volume 2817 #131.

2. Diary, 17 May, 1952, Helen Creighton Fonds, PANS MG1 Volume 2830 #3.

3. In 1956, CBC Radio broadcast the full opera and in 1967 students from Dartmouth High School took it to Expo '67 as part of Nova Scotia's contributions to Canada's centennial celebrations.

4. Diary, 3 July, 1954, Helen Creighton Fonds, PANS MG 1 Volume 2830 #4.

5. Diary, 18 August, 1954, Helen Creighton Fonds, PANS MG1 Volume 2830 #4.

6. Harris, Carol E. *A Sense of Themselves: Elizabeth Murray's Leadership in School and Community.* Halifax: Fernwood, 1998.

7. Angelo Dornan to Helen Creighton, 11 September, 1952, Helen Creighton Fonds, PANS MG1 Volume 2812 #52.

8. Creighton, *Folksongs from Southern New Brunswick,* 1.

9. Diary, 1 September, 1954, Helen Creighton Fonds, PANS MG1 Volume 2830 #4.

10. Diary, 11 September, 1954, Helen Creighton Fonds, PANS MG1 Volume 2830 #4.

11. Diary, 10 September, 1954, Helen Creighton Fonds, PANS MG1 Volume 2830 #4.

12. Diary, 26 September, 1954, Helen Creighton Fonds, PANS MG1 Volume 2830 #4.

13. Diary, 9 November, 1954, Helen Creighton Fonds, PANS MG1 Volume 2830 #4.

14. Diary, 30, September, 1954, Helen Creighton Fonds, PANS MG1 Volume 2830 #4.

15. Report of field work for the National Museum, 1947-1954, Helen Creighton Fonds, PANS MG1 Volume 2806 #1.

16. Hélène Baillargeon Coté was a Quebec singer and actress who worked extensively with Alan Mills. She became best known in Canada as the host of a popular children's television show, Chez Hélène. She and Helen took an instant liking to each other. "It was charming meeting you ... You came up exactly as I had thought you would be: genuine, refined and simple." Hélène (neé Baillargeon) Coté to Helen Creighton, 15 September, 1955, Helen Creighton Fonds, PANS MG1 Volume 2810 #52.

17. Diary, 7 August, 1955, Helen Creighton Fonds, PANS MG1 Volume 2830 #4.

18. Finvola Redden was named after the heroine in one of her father's favourite songs, *Finvola the Gem of the Roe.*

19. Diary, 30 August, 1955, Helen Creighton Fonds, PANS MG1 Volume 2830 #4.

20. Diary, 16 October, 1955, Helen Creighton Fonds, MG1 Volume 2830 #4.

21. Diary, 28 September, 1955, Helen Creighton Fonds, PANS MG1 Volume 2830 #4.

22. Diary, 29 December, 1955, Helen Creighton Fonds, PANS MG1 Volume 2830 #4.

23. Diary, 29 December, 1955, Helen Creighton Fonds, PANS MG1 Volume 2830 #4.

24. Diary, 10 June, 1954, Helen Creighton Fonds, PANS MG1 Volume 2830 #4.

25. Gertrude Innes to Helen Creighton, 19 March, 1955, Helen Creighton Fonds, PANS MG1 Volume 2813 #239.

26. Diary, February, 1956, Helen Creighton Fonds, PANS MG1 Volume 2830 #4.

27. Diary 18 March, 1956, Helen Creighton Fonds, PANS MG1 Volume 2830 #4.

28. Diary, 17 March, 1956, Helen Creighton Fonds, PANS MG1 Volume 2830 #4.

29. Diary 18 March, 1956, Helen Creighton Fonds, PANS MG1 Volume 2830 #4.

30. Diary, 2 June, 1956, Helen Creighton Fonds, PANS MG1, Volume 2830 #5.

31. Creighton, *A Life in Folklore,* 177.

*32.* See: Creighton, *Maritime Folk Songs* 176. Helen gives Mr. Sellick's name as Ernest, but his daughter confirmed it as Edward. Fanny [Sellick] Burtram, personal interview, 21 July, 1992.

33. Diary, 28 September, 1956, Helen Creighton Fonds, PANS MG1, Volume 2830 #5.

34. Diary, 29 September, 1956, Helen Creighton Fonds, PANS MG1, Volume 2830 #5.

35. Diary, 29 September, 1956, Helen Creighton Fonds, PANS MG1, Volume 2830 #5. Catherine Gallagher's first letter extant to Helen in 1938 begins with "Dear Miss Creighton"; by 1956, she wrote, "My Dear Friend." Catherine Gallagher to Helen Creighton, 27 March 27, 1938 and 9 March 9, 1956, Helen Creighton Fonds, PANS MG1 Volume 2813 #2. Catherine's son, Donald told the author that his mother considered Helen to be her best friend. Donald Gallagher, telephone interview, March, 1998.

36. *Folk Music from Nova Scotia,* Folkways FM4006.

37. Oxner, Diane. Traditional Folksongs of Nova Scotia Canadian Cavalcade CCLP 2011: Rodeo Records RB1142.

38. Creighton, *A Life in Folklore,* 180.

# CHAPTER 13

1. Diary, 7 January, 1957, Helen Creighton Fonds, PANS MG1, Volume 2830 #5.

2. Diary, 23 March, 1957, Helen Creighton Fonds, PANS MG1, Volume 2830 #5.

3. Selected from Convocation address: 14 May, 1957, Helen Creighton Fonds, PANS MG1 Volume 2791 #15.

4. Catharine Gallagher's manuscript is found in PANS MG1 Volume 2798 #2-3.

5. Diary, 14 June, 1957, Helen Creighton Fonds, PANS MG1, Volume 2830 #5.

6. Diary, 29 August, 1957, Helen Creighton Fonds, PANS MG1, Volume 2830 #5.

7. Diary, 30 August, 1957, Helen Creighton Fonds, PANS MG1, Volume 2830 #5.

8. Born in the United States, Ed McCurdy became known to Canadian radio audiences beginning in 1947 with his 15 minute broadcasts from Vancouver, *Ed McCurdy Sings*. He retired to Nova Scotia in the 1980s.

9. Catherine Gallagher to Helen Creighton, 27 February, 1956, Helen Creighton Fonds, PANS MG1 Volume 2813 #2.

10. Helen Creighton to Clary Croft, [n/d] , personal conversation.

11. Diary, 26 August, 1957, Helen Creighton Fonds, PANS MG1, Volume 2830 #5.

12. Sadie Redden, telephone interview, 23 February, 1999.

13. Diary, 25 August, 1957, Helen Creighton Fonds, PANS MG1, Volume 2830 #5.

14. Belliveau, J.E. "Tales of Phantoms" *Star Weekly*, 2 July, 1957.

15. *Maclean's Magazine*, 9 November, 1957.

16. Diary, 25 September, 1957, Helen Creighton Fonds, PANS MG1, Volume 2830 #5.

17. Creighton, Helen. *Bluenose Ghosts* Toronto: Ryerson, 1957.

18. Creighton, *A Life in Folklore,* 190.

19. Beck, Horace. Review of *Bluenose Ghosts* in *Northeast Folklore*, Northeast Folklore Society, University of Maine, Volume 3, Number 1, 1960.

20. "We give our entire support to Miss Creighton who has been doing splendid work for us during the past many years." Marius Barbeau and Carmen Roy to A.W. Trueman, The Canada Council, 2 October, 1957, Helen Creighton Collection, CMC CR-K-1.8.

21. Helen Creighton, audio-taped interview conducted by Clary Croft for PANS, 17 March, 1987, PANS AC1619.In January 1959, Helen received a further Canada Council grant of $3000. Diary, 31 January, 1959, Helen Creighton Fonds, PANS MG1, Volume 2830 #5.

22. Creighton, *A Life in Folklore,* 192.

23. Diary, 7 December, 1957, Helen Creighton Fonds, PANS MG1, Volume 2830 #5.

# CHAPTER 14

1. Sadie Redden to Helen Creighton, 9 February, 1958, Helen Creighton Fonds, PANS MG1 Volume 2817 #17.

2. Diary, 27 May, 1958, Helen Creighton Fonds, PANS MG1, Volume 2830 #5.

3. Louise Manny to Helen Creighton, 18 January, 1951, Helen Creighton Fonds, PANS MG1 Volume 2815 #85.

4. The Miramichi Folk Song Festival survives today as the oldest continuing festival of its kind in Canada.

5. Helen Creighton to Carmen Roy, 13 November, 1958, CMC CR-K-1.9.

6. "Helen Creighton is unquestionably Canada's most distinguished active collector of folk material." George, Graham. "Folk Singing or Just Folks", *Saturday Night*, 30 September, 1961.

7. Diary, 31 January, 1959, Helen Creighton Fonds, PANS MG1, Volume 2830 #5.

8. *Ottawa Citizen*, 17 March, 1959.

9. The William McCauley Choir. *Canadian Folk Songs* Columbia FL226.

10. Helen Creighton to Carmen Roy, 3 January, 1959, Helen Creighton Collection, CMC CR-K-1.10.

11. Richard Johnstone to Helen Creighton, 6 January, 1959, Helen Creighton Fonds, PANS MG1 Volume 2814 #28.

12. Helen Creighton to Carmen Roy, 8 January, 1959, Helen Creighton Collection, CMC CR-K-1.10.

13. Helen Creighton to Carmen Roy, 29 April, 1959, Helen Creighton Collection, CMC CR-K-1.10.

14. Diary 16-18 April, 1959, Helen Creighton Fonds, PANS MG1, Volume 2830 #5.

15. Creighton, *A Life in Folklore,* 204.

16. Creighton, *A Life in Folklore,* 209.

17. Creighton, *A Life in Folklore,* 214.

18. Creighton, *A Life in Folklore,* 215.

19. Helen had never worked with Luc Lacourcière, but they had attended various conferences together and in 1948, Marius Barbeau had written to Helen with an idea to publish her Acadian folk tales through the Museum. He advised her he would also send them to M. Lacourcière, the present editor of des Archives de Folklore. See: Marius Barbeau to Helen Creighton, 31 May, 1948, Helen Creighton Fonds, PANS MG1 Vol. 2810 #74. In 1961, M. Lacourcière published a study of French folk tales in Canada, but omitted any reference to Helen's collection. See: Lacourcière, Luc. "The Present State of French-Canadian Folklore Studies," *Journal of American Folklore*, Volume 74, Number 294, 1961.

20. Diary, 31 August, 1959, Helen Creighton Fonds, PANS MG1, Volume 2830 #6.

21. Diary, 23 October, 1959, Helen Creighton Fonds, PANS MG1, Volume 2830 #5.

22. Helen Creighton to Marius Barbeau, 12 March, 1960, Helen Creighton Collection, CMC CR-K-1.22.

23. Luc Lacourcière to Helen Creighton, 9 April, 1960, Helen Creighton Fonds, PANS MG1 Vol. 2814 #105.

24. Fowke, Edith & Joe Glazer. *Songs of Work and Protest.* New York: Dover, 1973.

25. Helen Creighton to Carmen Roy, 27 March, 1960, Helen Creighton Collection, CMC CR-K-1.11.

26. Helen Creighton to Edith Fowke, 29 March, 1960, PANS MG1 Volume 2811 #162.

27. Edith Fowke to Helen Creighton, 1 April, 1960, PANS MG1 Volume 2812 #159.

28. Edith Fowke to Helen Creighton, 16 April, 1960, PANS MG1 Volume 2812 #159.

29. Pete Seeger was questioned by McCarthy's committee investigating communist infiltration into the United States. He refused to answer questions and incriminate others and was black-listed. He didn't perform again on American television until his appearance in 1967 on the Smothers Brothers Comedy Hour. In 1963, he was being considered as the host for a new CBC television series out of Halifax titled, *Sing-a-long Jubilee*. The producer of the show, and the

man who took over hosting responsibilities told the author that Mr. Seeger was all set to begin work, when it was discovered he might not be able to get back into the United States if he left to work in Canada. Bill Langstroth, personal interview, 19 September, 1998.

30. Helen Creighton to Carmen Roy, 2 April, 1960, Helen Creighton Collection, CMC CR-K-1.11.

31. Carmen Roy to Helen Creighton, 5 April, 1960. PANS MG1 Volume 2817 #86.

32. Helen Creighton to Clary Croft, [n/d] , personal conversation. In August 1980, Helen received a visit from Pete Seeger and his wife. Pete had come to Nova Scotia to sing at the Atlantic Folk Festival and had written to Helen requesting a meeting. She invited him and Toshi for dinner and I joined them later in the evening. It was a pleasant, relaxed evening and, as far as I could tell, Helen never brought up her former concerns about Pete's politics.

33. O'Donnell, John C. "Contribution of American Folklorists to Research on Canadian Coal-Mining Songs," *Work, Ethnicity, and Oral History*, ed. Dorothy E. Moore and James H. Morrison, Halifax: International Education Centre, 1988, 226.

34. O' Donnell, "Contribution of American Folklorists to Resrerach on Canadian Coal-Mining Songs," 233.

35. Diary, 7 August, 1943, Helen Creighton Fonds, PANS MG1 Volume 2830 #2.

36. Pete Seeger to Helen Creighton, 19 January, 1963, Helen Creighton Fonds, PANS MG1 Volume 2817 #142. Pete Seeger got in touch with Louise Manny in New Brunswick offering to come and perform at the Miramichi Folk Song Festival. Louise replied that she would be delighted to have him attend, but he couldn't sing . She didn't want professional singers influencing the tradition bearers who were the backbone of the festival. See: Creighton, *A Life in Folklore*, 202.

37. Creighton, *A Life in Folklore*, 173-174.

38. Carmen Roy to Helen Creighton, 22 February, 1960, Helen Creighton Collection, CMC CR-K-1.11.

39. Carmen Roy to Helen Creighton, 22 February, 1960, Helen Creighton Collection, CMC CR-K-1.11.

40. Lee, Jerry, review of *Land of the Old Songs, Winnipeg Free Press*, 3 August, 1960.

41. "In eve, heard beautiful program on radio with Joyce Sullivan singing folk songs. Wrote and told her she is the best woman singer I know. "Diary 1 September, 1958, Helen Creighton Fonds, PANS MG!, Volume 2830 #5.

42. Bernard Diamant to Helen Creighton, 5 March, 1960. Helen Creighton Fonds, PANS MG1 Volume 2812 #42.

43. Finvola Redden to Helen Creighton, 7 April, 1960, Helen Creighton Fonds, PANS MG1 Volume 2817 #14.

# CHAPTER 15

1. Creighton, *A Life in Folklore*, 219.

2. Creighton, *A Life in Folklore*, 220.

3. Creighton, *A Life in Folklore*, 220. Singalong Jubilee was first telecast as a summer series in 1961. It began a full season in 1969 and was cancelled in 1974. Pete Seeger was cast as the original host, but was replaced by the producer, Bill Langstroth and singer/host Jim Bennet.

4. For more information on Rory MacKinnon and samples of his music, see: Shears, Barry W. *The Cape Breton Collection of Bagpipe Music* Halifax: Taigh a' Chiuil, 1995.

5. Helen Creighton to Carmen Roy, 10 May, 1958, Helen Creighton Collection, CMC CR-K-1.9.

6. Diary 22 July, 1961, Helen Creighton Fonds, PANS MG1, Volume 2830 #5.

7. Diary, 10 July, 1961, Helen Creighton Fonds, PANS MG1, Volume 2830 #5.

8. Helen Creighton, audio-taped interview conducted by Clary Croft for PANS, 17 March, 1987, PANS AC1619.

9. Manny Pittson to Helen Creighton, 14 September, 1963, Helen Creighton Fonds, PANS MG1 Volume 2816 #158.

10. Diary, 15 August, 1961, Helen Creighton Fonds, PANS MG1, Volume 2830 #5.

11. Diary, 15 August, 1961, Helen Creighton Fonds, PANS MG1, Volume 2830 #5.

12. Creighton, *A Life in Folklore*, 221.

13. Creighton, Helen. *Maritime Folk Songs* Toronto: Ryerson Press, 1961.

14. Creighton, *Maritime Folk Songs*, xii.

15. Morrison, James. review of *Maritime Folk Songs* by Helen Creighton, *Fredericton Gleaner*, 3 March, 1962.

16. Hull, Raymond review of *Maritime Folk Songs* by Helen Creighton, *Vancouver Sun*, 11 April, 1962.

17. Creighton, Helen. *Maritime Folk Songs* Folkways FE4307, 1962.

18. Creighton, Helen and Edward D. Ives. *Eight Folk Tales from Miramichi* Orono: Northeast Folklore, Volume 4, 1962.

19. A film based on two stories from the book and also titled Bluenose Ghosts was produced by the Nova Scotia Department of Tourism. It won a first prize at the Columbus Ohio Film Festival. The Canadian Tourist Association's Maple Leaf Award was presented on 4 November, 1963 to Margaret Perry, supervisor of motion pictures for the Nova Scotia Information Services for Nova Scotia By-Ways. An edited version of the book, Bluenose Ghosts was serialized in the Free Press Weekly Prairie Farmer (Winnipeg) in 1964.

20. Mrs. Hector Richard, audio-taped interview, 24 July, 1992.

21. Creighton, *A Folk Tale Journey Through the Maritimes* 175-176.

22. Mrs. Hector Richard, audio-taped interview, 24 July, 1992.

23. Helen Creighton, personal interview, 4 February, 1989, Clary Croft Journal.

# CHAPTER 16

1. *Ottawa Citizen*, 26 June, 1963.

2. *Victoria Daily Times*, 2 May, 1963, 8.

3. *Globe and Mail* (Toronto) 6 & 7 December, 1963.

4. Helen Creighton, *Globe and Mail* (Toronto) 12 December, 1963.

5. Irene J. Alexander, President of the Alexander Muir Old Girls Association to The Canadian Authors Association, 4 March, 1964, PANS MG1 Volume 2810 #13.

6. Diary, February, 1964, Helen Creighton Fonds, PANS MG1 Volume 3510 #29.

7. Helen Creighton to Carmen Roy, 27 November, 1963, Helen Creighton Collection, CMC CR-K-1.14.

8. Helen Creighton to Jeanne Monette, 13 September, 1963, Helen Creighton Collection, CMC CR-K-1.14.

9. Helen Creighton to Carmen Roy, 1 October, 1963, Helen Creighton Collection, CMCCR-K-1.14.

10. Helen Creighton to Carmen Roy, 27 November, 1963, Helen Creighton Collection, CMC CR-K-1.14

11. *Ottawa Citizen*, 7 September, 1963.

12. Carmen Roy to Helen Creighton, 21 November, 1963, Helen Creighton Fonds, PANS MG1 Volume 2817 #86.

13. L.S. Russell to Helen Creighton, 22 August, 1961, as quoted in Helen Creighton to Carmen Roy, 27 November, 1963, Helen Creighton Collection, CMC CR-K-1.14.

14. Helen Creighton to Carmen Roy, 27 November, 1963, Helen Creighton Collection, CMC CR-K-1.14.

15. Carmen Roy to Helen Creighton, 10 April, 1964, Helen Creighton Collection, CMC CR-K-1.15.

16. Creighton, *A Life in Folklore,* 227.

17. Creighton, *A Life in Folklore,* 231.

18. Diary, 24 May, 1952, Helen Creighton Fonds, PANS MG1 Volume 2830 #3.

19. Creighton, *A Life in Folklore,* 175.

20. Diary, 19 August, 1956, Helen Creighton Fonds, PANS MG1, Volume 2830 #5.

21. Helen Creighton, personal interview, 24 November, 1986, Clary Croft Journal. The Woods' daughter, Sharon, went on to become one of the first Canadians to climb Mount Everest.

22. Helen Creighton to Carmen Roy, 2 April 1960, Creighton Collection CR-K-1.11, CMC.

23. Terry Harnish, audio-taped interveiw, 8 March, 1995.

24. Helen Creighton, personal interview, 24 November, 1986, Clary Croft Journal.

25. Helen Creighton to The National Museum: B/49.5 CR.A-6.4.

26. Creighton, *A Life in Folklore,* 232. In 1966 Helen saw her doppelganger again. This time she was walking away from herself and one shoulder was drooped, as in old age. She was comforted because fishermen had told her to see yourself walking away meant a long life.

27. H. Terry Creighton to Jeanne Monette, 20 July, 1964, Helen Creighton Collection, CMC CR-K-1.15.

28. Carmen Roy to Helen Creighton, 28 September, 1964, Helen Creighton Fonds, PANS MG1 Volume 2817 #86.

29. Helen Creighton to Carmen Roy, 30 September, 1964, Helen Creighton Collection, CMC CR-K-1.15.

30. Creighton, Helen and Calum MacLeod. *Gaelic Songs in Nova Scotia* Ottawa: National Museum Bulletin 117, 1964.

31. *Canadian Poetry*, Canadian Authors Association, Volume 18, Number 3, 1965.

32. Bassin, Ethel. Review of *Gaelic Songs in Nova Scotia, Folk Music Journal*, The English Folk Dance and Song Society, 1966.

33. Calum MacLeod to Helen Creighton, 2 January, 1965, Helen Creighton Fonds, PANS MG1 Volume 2815 #50. For Calum MacLeod's detailed opinions on his negative reviews see: Calum MacLeod to Helen Creighton, 3 June, 1965, Helen Creighton Fonds, PANS MG1 Volume 2815 #50.

34. Helen Creighton to Carmen Roy, 7 May, 1965, Helen Creighton Collection, CMC CR-K-1.16.

35. Carmen Roy to Helen Creighton, 11 May, 1965, Helen Creighton Collection, CMC CR-K-1.16.

36. Helen Creighton to Clary Croft, [n/d] , personal conversation.

37. In 1972 the provincial government entered a float in the Rose Bowl parade at Pasadena, featuring a floral interpretation of the famous schooner Bluenose. It featured Nova Scotia born, internationally famous singer, Anne Murray, singing a revised version of Farewell to Nova Scotia, called Hello from Nova Scotia, with permission to change the lyrics from Helen. It won the Ambassador's Award.

38. Creighton, *A Life in Folklore*, 233. Helen later recalled that Freeman Young was not the shy singer portrayed in the film where he sings Farewell to NS. He would sing at the drop of a hat. He sang with a very gentle voice while his cousin Bernard sang very loudly—so loudly in fact that the veins would stick out in his neck. One day they were singing together for Helen and Bernard said, "You don't sing very loud, Free!" Freeman pointed to Helen's tape recorder and said, "You don't have to—that does it for me!" Helen Creighton, personal interview, 5 November, 1986, Clary Croft Journal.

39. Helen Creighton to Carmen Roy, 16 February, 1966, Helen Creighton Collection, CMC CR-D-2.1.

40. Helen Creighton to Carmen Roy, 29 September, 1966, Helen Creighton Collection, CMC CR-K-1.17.

41. Helen Creighton to Carmen Roy, 2 December, 1966, Helen Creighton Collection, CMC CR-K-1.17. R.G. Glover became the director of the National Museum in 1964.

42. Helen Creighton, personal interview, 11 February, 1987, Clary Croft Journal.

43. Helen Creighton to Carmen Roy, 31 January, 1967, Helen Creighton Collection, CMC CR-K-1.18.

# CHAPTER 17

1. As cited by Stephen Kimber, *Daily News*, 7 Feb. 1993 2.

2. Africville was situated at the northern end of Halifax on the shores of the Bedford Basin. Halifax City Council made the decision to remove the inhabitants and use their land for civic purposes. The former inhabitants are still fighting for justice. See: African Genealogy Society, editors, with contributions by Donald Clairmont, Stephen Kimber, Bridglal Pachai and Charles Saunders. *The Spirit of Africville*. Halifax: Formac, 1992.

3. Creighton, Helen. *Bluenose Magic: Popular Beliefs and Superstitions in Nova Scotia* Toronto: Ryerson, 1968.

4. Reinke, W.C. Review of *Bluenose Magic: Popular Beliefs and Superstitions in Nova Scotia, Montreal Star,* 9 Nov. 1968.

5. Diary, 10 April 1956, Helen Creighton Fonds, PANS MG1 Volume 2830 #4.

6. Creighton, *A Life in Folklore*, 217.

7. Diary, 18 June 1976, Helen Creighton Fonds, PANS MG1 Volume 3510 #29. In July of that year, Reverend Bull visited Helen at Evergreen. He reported the person he had helped lived in an apartment and felt she was possessed. He said the Lord's Prayer and the three highest words in the Bible (Father, Son and Holy Ghost), and blessed the cross she was wearing. When he left there was a feeling of peace in the apartment. See: Diary, 1&6 July 1976, Helen Creighton Fonds, PANS MG1 Volume 3510 #29.

8. See: Eileen J. Garrett, President , Parapsychology Foundation, New York, to Helen Creighton, 29 Jan. 1965, Helen Creighton Fonds, PANS MG1 Volume 2813 #7.

9. Helen Creighton to Carmen Roy, 16 April 1962, Creighton Collection, CMC CR-K-1.13, as cited in: McKay, Ian. *The Quest of the Folk*, 95.

10. Creighton, *A Life in Folklore*, 239.

11. Helen Creighton Fonds, PANS MG1 Volume 2795 #5.

12. Dorothy Burke to Helen Creighton, 31 March 1969, Helen Creighton Fonds, PANS MG1 Volume 2811 #17.

13. Helen Creighton to Dorothy Burke, Helen Creighton Fonds, PANS MG1 Volume 2811 #162.

14. Creighton, Helen. *Folksongs from Southern New Brunswick* Ottawa: Canadian Centre for Folk Culture Studies, National Museum of Man, 1971.

15. See: Manny, Louise and James Reginald Wilson. *Songs of Miramichi* Fredericton: New Brunswick Press, 1968.

16. Creighton, Helen. *Folksongs from Southern New Brunswick*, 1.

17. Diary, June 1971, Helen Creighton Fonds, PANS MG1 Volume 3510 #29.

18. Diary, June 1971, Helen Creighton Fonds, PANS MG1 Volume 3510 #29.

19. Peter Gzowski to Helen Creighton, 10 Oct. 1963, Helen Creighton Fonds, PANS MG1 Volume 2813 #96. Ian and Sylvia Tyson are major Canadian folk artists and had an international hit with *Four Strong Winds*.

20. Diary, 2 June 1972, Helen Creighton Fonds, PANS MG1 Volume 3510 #29.

21. Diary, 17 Jan. 1973, Helen Creighton Fonds, PANS MG1 Volume 3510 #29.

22. Diary, 16 Oct. 1972, Helen Creighton Fonds, PANS MG1 Volume 3510 #29.

23. Diary, 16 May 1973, Helen Creighton Fonds, PANS MG1 Volume 3510 #29.

24. Creighton, *Maritime Folk Songs*, 91.

25. Diary, 10 March 1975, Helen Creighton Fonds, PANS MG1 Volume 3510 #29.

# CHAPTER 18

1. Croft, Clary. *Sun, Moon and Stars* Fiddlehead FA-101, 1976.

2. Creighton, Helen. *A Life in Folklore* Toronto: McGraw-Hill Ryerson, 1975.

3. Maud Karpeles to Helen Creighton, 19 October, 1975, Helen Creighton Fonds, PANS MG1 Volume 2814 #50.

4. Gary Karr to Helen Creighton, 15 January, 1976, Helen Creighton Fonds, PANS MG1 Volume 2814 #51.

5. *Chatelaine*, October 1975.

6. *North Bay Nugget* (Ontario), 14 November, 1974.

7. MacLennan, Gordon. Review of *A Life in Folklore*, *Archivaria*, Summer 1977.

8. Helen Creighton to Clary Croft, [n/d] , personal conversation.

9. Diary, 14 June, 1977, Helen Creighton Fonds, PANS MG1 Volume 3510 #29.

10. Alan Mills to Helen Creighton, 15 September, 19[?], Helen Creighton Fonds, PANS MG1 Volume 2816 #1. Alan's correspondence with Helen was frequently written on file cards or any other paper he had at hand and contains few full dates.

11. *I Know An Old Lady Who Swallowed A Fly*, words and music by Alan Mills and Rose Bonne.

12. Alan Mills to Helen Creighton, [n/d], Helen Creighton Fonds, PANS MG1 Volume 2816 #1.

13. Creighton, Helen and Eunice Sircom. *Eight Ethnic Folk Songs for Young Children* Toronto: Gordon V. Thompson, 1977. Creighton, Helen and Eunice Sircom. *Nine Ethnic Folk Songs* Toronto: Gordon V. Thompson, 1977.

14. Lacey, Laurie. *Lunenburg County Folklore and Oral History: Project 77* Ottawa: National Museums of Canada, 1979.

15. Diary, 9&13 February, 1978, Helen Creighton Fonds, PANS MG1 Volume 3510 #29.

16. Barss, Peter and Joleen Gordon. *Older Ways: Traditional Nova Scotian Craftsmen*. Toronto: Van Nostrand Reinhold, 1980.

17. Diary, 18-20 May, 1979, Helen Creighton Fonds, PANS MG1 Volume 3510 #29.

18. Industrialist, Cyrus Eaton, held annual meetings of influential thinkers from around the world. The Thinkers' Conferences inspired the Pugwash Movement which, along with Joseph Rotblat, was awarded the 1995 Nobel Peace Prize.

19. Diary, 28 June, 1979, Helen Creighton Fonds, PANS MG1 Volume 3510 #29.

20. Diary 17&24 July, 1979, Helen Creighton Fonds, PANS MG1 Volume 3510 #29.

21. Diary 9 July, 1979, Helen Creighton Fonds, PANS MG1 Volume 3510 #29.

22. Diary, 22 May, 1979, Helen Creighton Fonds, PANS MG1 Volume 3510 #29.

# CHAPTER 19

1. Diary, 16 March, 1980, Helen Creighton Fonds, PANS MG1 Volume 3510 #29.

2. Diary, 3 April, 1980, Helen Creighton Fonds, PANS MG1 Volume 3510 #29. Carolyn Thomas led a choir from Preston. They sang several African Nova Scotian songs from Helen's collection, including *The Cherry Tree Carol*, which Helen had collected from Carolyn's grandfather, William Riley.

3. Diary, 7&10 August, 1980, Helen Creighton Fonds, PANS MG1 Volume 3510 #29.

4. "...my contract for Acadian songs has gone through, but for ten, not fifteen thousand. However, if it isn't finished in a year, I can apply for the remaining five thousand. Diary, 17 February, 1978, Helen Creighton Fonds, PANS MG1 Volume 3510 #29.

5. Diary, 6 October, 1980, Helen Creighton Fonds, PANS MG1 Volume 3510 #29.

6. Nightingale, Marie. *Out of Old Nova Scotian Kitchens*. Halifax: Petheric Press, 1970.

7. Diary, 6-25 February, 1981, Helen Creighton Fonds, PANS MG1 Volume 3510 #29.

8. Diary, 23 May, 1981, Helen Creighton Fonds, PANS MG1 Volume 3510 #29.

9. Helen Creighton to Sharon and Clary Croft, 5 September, 1981. Clary Croft Collection.

10. Diary, 19 October, 1981, Helen Creighton Fonds, PANS MG1 Volume 3510 #29.

11. Herbert Halpert to Helen Creighton, 5 March, 1982, Helen Creighton Fonds, PANS MG1 Volume 3514 # 9. Because of personal and professional commitments, Herbert Halpert never did finish his work on the folk tales. After Helen's death, Ron Caplan, publisher of *Cape Breton's Magazine* and owner of Breton Books, got in touch with me concerning their status. He eventually published the manuscript, with scholarly notes by Michael Taft. See: Creighton, Helen. *A Folk Tale Journey Through the Maritimes* ed. Michael Taft and Ronald Caplan, Wreck Cove, Breton Books, 1993.

12. Diary, 20 November, 1981, Helen Creighton Fonds, PANS MG1 Volume 3510 #29. Several months earlier, she had taped a segment of an interview show for Canadian Cartoonist and television personality, Ben Wicks.

13. Diary, 20 November, 1981, Helen Creighton Fonds, PANS MG1 Volume 3510 #29.

14. Croft, Clary. *False Knight Upon the Road: Songs from the collection of Dr. Helen Creighton* WRCI- 2015, 1986. *False Knight Upon the Road* is a song Helen collected from Ben Henneberry. See: Creighton, *Songs and Ballads from Nova Scotia*, 1.

15. Diary, 8&9 May, 1982, Helen Creighton Fonds, PANS MG1 Volume 3510 #29. Phyllis Blakeley and her sister, Shirley, were long time friends of Helen's. Phyllis worked at the Public Archives of Nova Scotia and supported Helen's storage of her collection there for decades. In 1982, she was appointed Provincial Archivist.

16. Diary, 12 June, 1982, Helen Creighton Fonds, PANS MG1 Volume 3510 #29.

17. Helen Creighton Fonds, PANS MG1 Volume 2791 #15.

18. See: Robert Aitken to Helen Creighton, 3 October, 1982, Helen Creighton Fonds, PANS MG1 Volume 2817 #146.

19. Songs and Ballads from Nova Scotia. See: Loakie's Boat, Creighton, Songs and Ballads from Nova Scotia 274.

20. Diary, May, 1983, Helen Creighton Fonds, PANS MG1 Volume 3510 #29.

21. Edith Fowke to Tim Johnston, January, 1985, (copy) Helen Creighton Fonds, PANS MG1 Volume 2812 #159.

22. Edith Fowke to Tim Johnston, January, 1985, (copy) Helen Creighton Fonds, PANS MG1 Volume 2812 #159.

23. Diary, 30 November, 1983, Helen Creighton Fonds, PANS MG1 Volume 3510 #29.

24. Actually, unless correspondence is from the Queen personally, it is always, like Helen's letter, signed on her behalf by a lady-in-waiting.

25. "...thank you for the very considerable amount of trouble you have taken in following up Her Majesty's enquiry made during your meeting in Nova Scotia eight years ago." Elizabeth II to Helen Creighton, 1 February, 1984, Helen Creighton Fonds, PANS MG1 Volume 2812 #88. See: Craig, Linda. "The Scottish origin of Farewell to Nova Scotia," *Dalhousie Review,* Volume 58, Number 3, 1978.

26. Diary, 12 June, 1984, Helen Creighton Fonds, PANS MG1 Volume 3510 #29.

27. Mr. Darrach is also an author who wrote of his experiences at sea along Nova Scotia's coast. See: Darrach, Claude. *From A Coastal Schooner's Log* Halifax: Nova Scotia Museum, 1979.

28. Christmas Card. Helen Creighton to Sharon and Clary Croft, December 1984, Clary Croft Collection.

29. Diary, 22 January, 1985, Helen Creighton Fonds, PANS MG1 Volume 3510 #29.

30. Diary, 13 March, 1985, Helen Creighton Fonds, PANS MG1 Volume 3510 #29.

31. Diary, 25 October, 1984, Helen Creighton Fonds, PANS MG1 Volume 3510 #29.

32. Diary, 13 March, 1985, Helen Creighton Fonds, PANS MG1 Volume 3510 #29. Raylene Rankin later became a member of the family musical group, The Rankins, and gained international fame as a singer.

33. Creighton, Helen. *With a heigh-heigh-ho*. Halifax: Nimbus Publishing Ltd., 1986.

34. Diary, 28 August, 1985, Helen Creighton Fonds, PANS MG1 Volume 3510 #29.

35. Creighton, *With a heigh-heigh-ho*, 4.

36. Helen Creighton to Mabel Laine, 10 July 10, 1987, (copy), Clary Croft Collection.

# CHAPTER 20

1. 29 January 1987, Clary Croft Journal. The family photograph albums were ones Helen had earlier suggested be kept with her collection at the Archives. In order for Helen to receive a tax credit for her donation, her entire collection had to be on site at the Public Archives of Nova Scotia. I tried to stress the point that she might find the total loss of her entire library too unnerving, and asked the provincial archivist, Carmen Carroll if there was anything we could do. Subsequently we made far more photocopies of items than we originally had intended.

2. Diary, 20 January, 1987, Helen Creighton Fonds, PANS MG1 Volume 3510 #29. I had been invited to join the cast, but was too busy at the Archives.

3. Diary 23 February, 1985, Helen Creighton Fonds, PANS MG1 Volume 3510 #29.

4. Diary, 20 February, 1987, Helen Creighton Fonds, PANS MG1 Volume 3510 #29.

5. 21 May, 1987, Clary Croft Journal.

6. 29 June, 1987, Clary Croft Journal.

7. Diary 16 September, 1987, Helen Creighton Fonds, PANS MG1 Volume 3510 #29.

8. Helen Creighton to Clary Croft, 4 November, 1987, personal conversation.

9. Note attached to newspaper clipping about the concert; photocopy in collection of author.

10. Diary, 20 November, 1987, Helen Creighton Fonds, PANS MG1 Volume 3510 #29.

11. Helen Creighton, personal interview, 27 November, 1987, Clary Croft Journal.

12. Diary, 22 November, 1987, Helen Creighton Fonds, PANS MG1 Volume 3510 #29.

13. Diary, 12 December, 1987, Helen Creighton Collection, PANS MG1 Volume 3510 #29. *The Legacy of Helen Creighton* aired on 13 September, 1988.

14. Helen Creighton, personal interview, 27 November, 1987, Clary Croft Journal.

15. Diary, 30 May, 1988, Helen Creighton Fonds, PANS MG1 Volume 3510 #29.

16. Bauchman, Rosemary. *The Best of Helen Creighton* Hantsport: Lancelot Press, 1988.

17. Diary, 7 July, 1988, Helen Creighton Fonds, PANS MG1 Volume 3510 #29.

18. Edith Fowke, [n/d], personal conversation.

19. See: Helen Creighton to Michael Koener, Encyclopaedia of Music in Canada, 25 November, 1988, Helen Creighton Fonds, PANS MG1 Volume 3387 #3.

20. Diary 26, 27 & 28 July, 1988, Helen Creighton

21. Citation for the Jubilate Award to Dr. Helen Creighton" *Canadian Music Educator* Volume 31 Number 2, September 1989.

22. Creighton, Helen and Ronald Labelle. *La Fleur du Rosier: Acadian Folksongs* Sydney: University College of Cape Breton Press and Ottawa: Canadian Museum of Civilization, 1988.

23. The festival eventually move to Halifax and in 1997 was discontinued. However, the organization responsible for the initial festival operates as The Helen Creighton Folklore Society. It promotes the appreciation and awareness of folklore in the Maritimes through concerts, sponsorship of writing contests, awards at music festivals and annual grants.

24. See: Benjamin, Craig. "Cups of Tea," *Cities Magazine* Volume 3, Number 6, October, 1989.

25. Helen Creighton to Clary Croft, 9 October, 1989, Clary Croft Journal.

26. Helen Creighton to Clary Croft, 9 October, 1989, Clary Croft Journal.

27. Helen Creighton, 12 November, 1989, personal conversation.

28. Cora Greenaway, 14 October, 1992, audio-taped interview.

29. Creighton, *Maritime Folk Songs,* 210.

30. Creighton, and Senior, *Traditional Songs from Nova Scotia,* 265.

31. 29 December, 1989, Clary Croft Journal.

# CHAPTER 21

1. Sarah Clergy to Helen Creighton, n/d, PANS MG1 Volume 2811 #100. Grace Clergy's wife Sarah (Sadie) wrote Helen several warm letters fondly remembering their time together.

2. Thomas Raddall, 1990, audio-taped interview.

3. Staff of the Canadian Centre for Folk Culture Studies, Canadian Museum of Civilization, to Clary Croft, 13 December, 1989.

4. Dr. George MacDonald, Museum of Civilization to Clary Croft, 13 December, 1989.

5. Mr. Ron MacDonald, MP Dartmouth, *House of Commons Debates,* Volume 131, Number 115, 2nd Session, 34th Parliament, Wednesday, 20 December, 1989.

6. Excerpt from citation read at ECMA ceremonies, 1991, Clary Croft.

7. Ives, Edward D. *The World of Maritimes Folklore* Halifax: The Helen Creighton Foundation, 1992. The lecture series didn't continue.

8. *Arts Atlantic*, Volume 13, Number 2, 1994, 36.

9. August 1993: The Collector at Chrichton Community Centre, presented by Drimmindown Entertainment, John Brown's company. *The Collector,* 1998, Weston Nova Scotia, Downstage Centre Productions, John Brown, dinner theatre. July and August. "Celebrating the 65th anniversary of Dr. Helen Creighton's finding of Farewell to Nova Scotia".

10. Pottie, Kaye and Vernon Ellis. *Folksongs of the Maritimes* Halifax: Formac, 1992.

11. Sircom, Hilary. *Helen Creighton* Tantallon, Four East Publications, 1993.

12. Croft, Clary. "What Band That Sunday Morning?". Afterword: Charles Saunders. *Share and Care:The Story of the Nova Scotia Home for Colored Children*. Halifax: Nimbus Publishing, 1994.

*13. Lord You Brought Me A Mighty Long Way: An African Nova Scotian Musical Journey* Contemporary CD Produced by Karl Falkenham; Archival Showcase CD produced by Clary Croft, CBC and The Black Cultural Centre of Nova Scotia, 1997.

14. Tutton, Michael. "Creighton's bequest" *Chronicle-Herald*, 28 January, 1994.

15. McKay, Ian. "He is More Picturesque in His Oilskins": Helen Creighton and the Art of Being Nova Scotian, *New Maritimes*, Issue 92, Volume 12 #1, September/October, 1993.

16. McKay, "He is More Picturesque in His Oilskins": Helen Creighton and the Art of Being Nova Scotian, 15.

17. McKay, "He is More Picturesque in His Oilskins": Helen Creighton and the Art of Being Nova Scotian, 15.

18. McKay, Ian. "Helen Creighton and the Politics of Antimodernism" *Myth & Milieu: Atlantic Literature and Culture 1918-1939*, ed. Gwendolyn Davies. Fredericton: Acadiensis, 1993. McKay, Ian. *The Quest of the Folk: Antimodernism and Cultural Selection in Twentieth-Century Nova Scotia* Montreal: McGill-Queen's University Press, 1994.

19. Black, Mary. *The New Key to Weaving: A Textbook of Hand Weaving for the Beginner Weaver*. Reprinted New York: Macmillan, 1980.

20. Mary Black to Helen Creighton, 8 July, 1962, Helen Creighton Fonds, PANS MG1 Volume 2810 #135. A note of interest: I was the Contract Archivist for the Helen Creighton Fonds at the Public Archives of Nova Scotia. Several years later, I was Archivist for a substantial portion of Mary Black's collection at the same repository.

21. McKay, Ian. *The Quest of the Folk*, 40.

22. McKay, Ian. "Helen Creighton and the Politics of Antimodernism," 16.

23. Muise, D.A. "Who Owns History Anyway? Reinventing Atlantic Canada for Pleasure and Profit" *Acadiensis* Volume 27, Number 2, spring 1998, 129.

24. Muise, D.A. "Who Owns History Anyway? Reinventing Atlantic Canada for Pleasure and Profit" *Acadiensis* Volume 27, Number 2, spring 1998, 129.

25. Drainie, Bronwyn. "Folklorist brings out the worst of the spoilsports" *Globe and Mail*, 5 February, 1994.

26. Ian McKay to Helen Creighton, 16 August, 1989, Helen Creighton Fonds, PANS MG1 Volume 3511 #16.

27. MacDonald, Andrea. "A False Note", *The Daily News*, 29 September, 1997, 21.

28. Drainie, Bronwyn, "A Passion for Tall Tales and Sad Refrains" *Globe and Mail* 23 December, 1989.

29. Helen Creighton, audio-taped interview conducted by Clary Croft for PANS, 17 March, 1987, PANS AC1619.

30. Brundvand, Jan Harold. Folklore: *A Study and Research Guide*, New York: St. Martin's Press, 1976, 39.

31. Creighton, *A Life in Folklore*, 102-103.

32. Angelo Dornan to Helen Creighton, [n/d], Helen Creighton Fonds, PANS MG1 Volume 2812 #52.

33. Thomas Raddall, audio- taped interview, 1990.

34. Creighton, *A Life in Folklore*, 72.

35. Creighton, *A Life in Folklore*, 70.

36. Helen told me the story in detail, but since the other party is still living, I have chosen to keep her identity private. Helen Creighton, personal interview, 11 February, 1987, Clary Croft Journal.

37. Fowke, Edith. *Folk Songs of Ontario* Folkways records, FM4005.

38. Hammond, Arthur. "The Unquiet Groove" *The Tamarack Review* Issue 13, 1959 116-121.

39. Hammond, "The Unquiet Groove," 116-121.

40. Hammond, "The Unquiet Groove," 116-121.

41. A synopsis of the paper was published in the Bulletin of the Folklore Studies Association of Canada, Volume 10, Numbers 1-2, May 1986.

42. Arlidge, Bob. *An Evaluation of the Early Collecting of Helen Creighton*, n/d. copy of paper sent to Nova Scotia Provincial Archivist, Carman Carroll by Neil Rosenberg, 1986, Helen Creighton Fonds, PANS MG1 Volume 3512 # 11.

43. [copy] Helen Creighton to Neil Rosenberg, 29 January, 1987, Helen Creighton Fonds, PANS MG1 Volume 3512 #11.

44. Edith Fowke to Helen Creighton, 21 July, 1956, Helen Creighton Fonds, PANS MG1 Volume 2812 #159.

45. Diary, 16 February, 1976, Helen Creighton Fonds, PANS MG1 Volume 3510 #29.

46. Brown, Lance G. "Folk song has its roots in Scotland"[letter to editor] *London Free Press*, 5 January, 1990.

47. Tallman, Richard S. "Folklore research in Atlantic Canada: An Overview," *Acadiensis*, University of New Brunswick, Spring 1979.

48. Diary, 26 September, 1951, Helen Creighton Fonds, PANS MG1 Volume 2830 #3.

49. Laura Irene MacNeil to Helen Creighton, 11 November, 1955, Helen Creighton Fonds, PANS MG1 Volume 3513 # 1.

50. Mary Doyle to Helen Creighton, [n/d], Helen Creighton Fonds, PANS MG1 Volume 2812 #59.

51. Diary 21 August, 1979, Helen Creighton Fonds, PANS MG1 Volume 3510 #29.

52. Helen Creighton Fonds, PANS MG1 Volume 2810 #149. Marked: RESTRICTED ACCESS.

53. Creighton, *Folklore of Lunenburg County, Nova Scotia*, 2.

54. Creighton, *A Life in Folklore*, 154-155.

55. Diary, 14 August, 1947, Helen Creighton Fonds, PANS MG1 Volume 2830 #3.

56. Diary, 14 August, 1949, Helen Creighton Fonds, PANS MG1 Volume 2830 #3.

57. Helen Creighton, audio-taped interview conducted by Clary Croft for PANS, 11 August, 1987, PANS AC1620.

58. See: Edward D. Ives to Helen Creighton, 20 August, 1957 and 30 March, 1962, Helen Creighton Fonds, PANS MG1 Volume 2813 #247.

59. Diary, 4 May, 1937, Helen Creighton Fonds, PANS MG1 Volume 2830 #1.

60. Louis Boutilier to Helen Creighton, 10 October, [n/d], Helen Creighton Fonds, PANS MG1 Volume 2810 #157.

61. Maggie [Mrs. "Wentie"] Boutilier to Helen Creighton, 26 November, 1950, Helen Creighton Fonds, PANS MG1 Volume 2810 #158.

62. Helen Creighton Fonds, PANS MG1 Volume 2705 #17.

63. Helen Creighton, personal interview, 9 September, 1987, Clary Croft Journal.

64. Hilda Chiasson, tape-recorded interview, August, 1992.

65. Mrs. Hector Richard, audio-taped interview, 24 July, 1992.

66. Creighton, *A Life in Folklore,* 154-155.

67. McKay, Ian. *The Quest of the Folk*, 108.

68. Diary, 13 September, 1951, Helen Creighton Fonds, PANS MG1 Volume 2830 #3.

69. Diary, 7 July, 1952, Helen Creighton Fonds, PANS MG1 Volume 2830 #3.

70. Creighton, Helen. "Folk-Singers of Nova Scotia," *The Canadian Forum,* July 1952.

71. Helen Creighton to Kenneth Goldstein, 12 April, 1978, Helen Creighton Fonds, PANS MG1 Volume 2811 #162. Helen published a version of this story naming Mr. Riley in: Creighton, Helen. "Collecting Songs of Nova Scotia Blacks" *Folklore Studies in Honour of Herbert Halpert* ed. Kenneth Goldstein and Neil Rosenberg, St. John's: Memorial University, 1980.

72. Carrie Grover to Helen Creighton, 17 October, 1941, Helen Creighton Fonds, PANS MG1 Volume 2813 #87. See: Grover, Carrie. *A Heritage of Song* Maine [n/d], Reprint Norwood Pa.: Norwood, 1973.

73. See: Poteet, Lewis J. *The South Shore Phrase Book* Hantsport: Lancelot Press, 1983. Poteet, Lewis J. *The Second South Shore Phrase Book* Hantsport: Lancelot Press, 1985.

74. Sam Gesser to Helen Creighton, 18 June, 1957, Helen Creighton Fonds, PANS MG1 Volume 2813 #19.

75. Thomas Raddall to Helen Creighton, 12 May, 1957, Helen Creighton Fonds, PANS MG1 Volume 2817 #1.

76. Sandy Ives, audio-taped interview, 12 February, 1992.

77. Sandy Ives, audio-taped interview, 12 February, 1992. Sandy was referring to William Roy Mackenzie who collected in Nova Scotia, Elizabeth B. Greenleaf who collected in Newfoundland, and Helen Harkless Flanders who collected in New England.

78. Sandy Ives, audio-taped interview, 12 February, 1992.

79. Alan Lomax to Helen Creighton, 14 August, 1956, Helen Creighton Fonds, PANS MG1 Volume 2814 #173.

80. Bertrand Bronson to Helen Creighton, 31 December, 1971, Helen Creighton Fonds, PANS MG1 Volume 2810 #169.

81. Wayland Hand to Helen Creighton, 22 October, 1974, Helen Creighton Fonds, PANS MG1 Volume 2813 #116.

82. W. Roy Mackenzie to Helen Creighton, 11 July, 1949, Helen Creighton Fonds, PANS MG1 Volume 2815 #57.

83. See: Moore, Marion F. "Canada's First Folk Song Collector Visits Halifax". Halifax *Mail Star.* 8 January, 1955, 12.

84. See: Lovelace, Martin. "W. Roy MacKenzie As A Collector of Folksong" *Canadian Folk Music Journal* Volume 5, 1977 5-11.

85. Marius Barbeau to Helen Creighton, 8 November, 1956, Helen Creighton Fonds, PANS MG1 Volume 2810 #74.

86. Thomas, Phil. "Edith Fowke 1913-1996" *Canadian Folk Music Bulletin,* Volume 30, Number 4, 1996 23.

87. Gilmour, Clyde. "A passion for folksongs and plain English," *Toronto Star,* 30 October, 1982.

88. Sandy Ives, audio-taped interview, 12 February, 1992.

89. Helen Creighton, personal interview, 31 August, 1987, Clary Croft Journal.

90. Diary, 3 Septermber, 1954, Helen Creighton Fonds, PANS MG1 Volume 2830 #4.

91. Diary, 3 August, 1961, Helen Creighton Fonds, PANS MG1, Volume 2830 #5.

92. Diary, 1 March, 1933. Helen Creighton Fonds, PANS MG1 Volume 2830 #8.

93. Edith Fowke to Helen Creighton, 14 January, 1953, Helen Creighton Fonds, PANS MG1 Volume 2812 #159.

94. Edith Fowke to Helen Creighton, 12 December, 1985, Helen Creighton Fonds, PANS MG1 Volume 2812 #159.

95. Edith Fowke, personal interview, 18 May, 1991.

96. Edith Fowke, personal interview, 18 May, 1991.

97. Edith Fowke, personal interview, 18 May, 1991.

98. Ross, Val. "Lives Lived" Edith Fowke Toronto *Globe and Mail,* 3 April, 1996.

99. Helen Creighton, audio-taped interview conducted by Clary Croft for PANS, 17 March, 1987, PANS AC1619.

100. Croft, Clary. *Live from the Lunenburg Folk Harbour Festival,* Telltale Productions, 1990.

101. Cora Greenaway, audio-taped interview, 14 October, 1992.

# BIBLIOGRAPHY

✳ ✳ ✳

## UNPUBLISHED SOURCES

Helen Creighton Collection, Canadian Museum of Civilization. [CMC]
Helen Creighton Fonds, Public Archives of Nova Scotia. [PANS]
Jacob Creighton Fonds, Public Archives of Nova Scotia. [PANS]
Clary Croft Journal.
Fischer, Jerome E. *Acadian Folk Music of Nova Scotia* 1975 Thesis (MA) Hunter College, City University of New York.
Alice and David Nicholl personal collection.

## NEWSPAPERS AND PERIODICALS

*Acadiensis*
*American Anthropologist*
*American Girl*
*Atlantic Advocate*
*Atlantic Insight*
*Atlantic Province Book Review*
*Archivaria*
*Arts Atlantic*
*Canadian Author and Bookman*
*Canadian Composer*
*Canadian Folk Music Journal*
*Canadian Folk Music Society (newsletter)*
*Canadian Forum*
*Canadian Geographic Journal*
*Canadian Grocer*
*Canadian Journal for Traditional Music*
*Canadian Music Educator*
*Canadian Poetry*
*Chatelaine*
*Chorus*
*Church Work*
*Chronicle-Herald* (Halifax)
*Cities*
*Daily News* (Halifax)
*Dalhousie Review*
*Ethnomusicology*
*Family Herald and Weekly Star*
*Folklore*
*Folklore Studies Association of Canada, Journal*
*Fredericton Gleaner*
*German-Canadian Yearbook*
*Globe and Mail* (Toronto)
*Halifax*
*Homes and Gardens*
*Hoosier Folklore*

*Indiana Daily Student*
*Journal of American Folklore*
*Journal of Education* (Province of Nova Scotia)
*Journal of the House of Assembly*
*London Free Press (Ontario)*
*Maclean's*
*Mail Star* (Halifax)
*Mariposa Folk Festival Newsletter*
*Montreal Star*
*Music Across Canada*
*New Maritimes*
*North Bay Nugget* (Ontario)
*Northeast Folklore*
*Nova Scotia*
*Onward*
*Ottawa Citizen*
*Port and Province*
*Readers' Digest*
*Real Estate Home Guide*
*Saturday Night*
*Sing Out! The Folk Song Magazine*
*Sojourn*
*Star Weekly*
*Sunday Leader*
*Tamarack Reviews*
*Toronto Star*
*Vancouver Sun*
*Victoria Daily Times*
*Weekend Magazine*
*Western Folklore*
*Winnipeg Free Press*

## INTERVIEWS CONDUCTED BY THE AUTHOR

Bennett, James L., telephone interview, 2 October, 1997.
Bower, Finvola, telephone interview, 23 February, 1999.
Burtram, Fanny [Sellick], personal interview, 21 July, 1992.
Chiasson, Hilda, audio-taped interview, August,1992.
Creighton, Helen, audio-taped interview, 12 March, 1987 and 11 August, 1987.
Daly, Peryl, audio-taped interview, 1997.
Fowke, Edith, personal interview, 18 May, 1991.
Gallagher, Donald, telephone interview, March, 1998.
Gordon, Joleen, audio-taped interview, 3 November, 1997.
Greenaway, Cora, 14 October, 1992.
Harnish, Terry, audio-taped interview, 8 March, 1995.
Ives, Edward D. (Sandy), audio-taped interview, 12 February, 1992.
Langstroth, Bill, personal interview, 19 September, 1998.
Martin, Pat, telephone interview, 18, February 1999.
Nicholl, Alice (Creighton), audio-taped interview, 16 September, 1995.
Orenstein, Henry, personal interview, 6 December, 1994.
Raddall, Thomas, audio-taped interview, 1990.
Redden, Sadie, telephone interview, 23 February, 1999.
Mr. and Mrs. Hector Richard, 24 July, 1992.
Ernest Sellick, audio-taped interview, 21 February, 1992.
Sircom, Eunice, telephone interview, 21 February, 1999.

# AUDIO RECORDINGS

Creighton, Helen. *Folk Music from Nova Scotia* Folkways FM4006, 1956.
Creighton, Helen. *Maritime Folk Songs* Folkways FE4307, 1962.
Croft, Clary. *False Knight Upon the Road: Songs from the collection of Dr. Helen Creighton* WRCI-2015, 1986.
Croft, Clary. *Live from the Lunenburg Folk Harbour Festival*, Telltale Productions, 1990.
Croft, Clary. *Sun, Moon and Stars* Fiddlehead FA-101, 1975.
Fowke, Edith. *Folk Songs of Ontario* Folkways records, FM4005.
*Lord You Brought Me A Mighty Long Way: An African Nova Scotian Musical Journey* Contemporary CD Produced by Karl Falkenham; Archival Showcase CD produced by Clary Croft, CBC and The Black Cultural Centre of Nova Scotia, 1997.
The William McCauley Choir. *Canadian Folk Songs* Columbia FL226.
Oxner, Diane. *Traditional Folksongs of Nova Scotia*
Canadian Cavalcade CCLP 2011: Rodeo Records RB1142.

# MOVING IMAGES HELD AT PANS

"Arts and Entertainment Reports" CBC Television Collection: Various reports that appeared on *1st Edition*: The Collector.
*Bluenose Ghosts* Directed by Martin Alford for the Communications and Information Centre, Nova Scotia Department of Tourism, 1972.
*The Box* Produced by Henry Orenstein for the CBC, 1961.
*Evergreen* Directed by Penny MacAuley for ATV/ASN PANS 198741 [Interview conducted with Helen Creighton, 29 July, 1987. Sound only on video tape]
*Gary Karr and Friends* Produced by the CBC, 1973.
*Helen Creighton's 90th Birthday Party* Robert Creighton Collection, 1989.
*Lady of the Legends* Directed by Glen Sarty for the CBC, 1967.
*Land of the Old Songs* Produced by the CBC, 1960.
*The Legacy of Helen Creighton* Directed by Janet Smith for the CBC, 1988.
*Marine Highway* Produced and Directed by Margaret Perry for the Nova Scotia Department of Trade and Industry, Nova Scotia Travel Bureau, 1957.
*Nova Scotia By-Ways* Produced and Directed by Margaret Perry for the Nova Scotia Information Services, Nova Scotia Travel Bureau, 1961.
*The Nova Scotia Song* Produced and Directed by Glen Walton, 1987.
*Songs of Nova Scotia* Directed by Grant Crabtree for the National Film Board, 1958.

# PUBLISHED SOURCES

"100 Years with Creightons isn't dull." *Canadian Grocer,* MacLean Hunter, February 1975.
African Genealogy Society, editors, with contributions by Donald Clairmont, Stephen Kimber, Bridglal Pachai and Charles Saunders. *The Spirit of Africville* Halifax: Formac, 1992.
Alexander, Henry. *The Story of Our Language* Toronto: Thomas Nelson and Sons, 1940.
Arlidge, Bob. *An Evaluation of the Early Collecting of Helen Creighton*, synposis of paper published in the Bulletin of the Folklore Studies Association of Canada, Volume 10, Numbers 1-2, May 1986.
*Arts Atlantic* Volume 13, Number 2, 1994.
Barbeau, Marius and Arthur Lismer, Arthur Bourinot. *Come A-Singing!: Canadian Folk-Songs* Ottawa: National Museum of Canada Bulletin #107, Queen's Printer, 1959.
Barss, Peter and Joleen Gordon. *Older Ways: Traditional Nova Scotian Craftsmen*. Toronto: Van Nostrand Reinhold, 1980.
Bassin, Ethel. Review of *Gaelic Songs in Nova Scotia, Folk Music Journal*, The English Folk Dance and Song Society, 1966.
Bauchman, Rosemary. "A Profile of Helen Creighton" *The Atlantic Advocate*, Volume 72, Number 4, December 1981.
Bauchman, Rosemary. *The Best of Helen Creighton* Hantsport: Lancelot Press, 1988.

Bauchman, Rosemary. "Dr. Helen Creighton, C.M.: a self-legend in writing folklore" *Canadian Author and Bookman* Volume 56, Number 3, 1981.

Bauman, Richard. "Belsnickling in a Nova Scotia Community" *Western Folklore* Volume 31, 1971.

Beck, Horace. Review of *Bluenose Ghosts. Northeast Folklore*, Northeast Folklore Society, University of Maine, Volume 3, Number 1, 1960.

Beck, Jane C. "'Enough to charm the heart of a wheelbarrow and make a shovel dance'—A Portrait of Helen Creighton," *Journal of the Folklore Studies Association of Canada* Volume 7, 1985.

Belliveau, J.E. "Tales of Phantoms" *Star Weekly*, 2 July, 1957.

Belliveau, J.E. "She's working against time to preserve ballads out of the past" *Star Weekly* 7 July, 1956.

Benjamin, Craig. "Cups of Tea", *Cities Magazine* Volume 3, Number 6, October, 1989.

Black, Mary. *The New Key to Weaving: A Textbook of Hand Weaving for the Beginner Weaver* Reprinted New York: Macmillan, 1980.

Blakely, Phyllis. "Preserving our cultural heritage" *Atlantic Province Book Review* March,1976.

Bolton, Laura. *The Music Hunter: The Autobiography of a Career* Garden City, New York: Doubleday, 1969.

Brown, Lance G. "Folk song has its roots in Scotland"[letter to editor] *London Free Press* 5 January, 1990.

Brundvand, Jan Harold. *Folklore: A Study and Research Guide* New York: St. Martin's Press, 1976.

Cameron, Donald. "Thanks for the Memories" *Weekend Magazine* 28 September, 1974.

*Canadian Music Educator* "Citation for the Jubilate Award to Dr. Helen Creighton" Volume 31 Number 2, September 1989.

*Canadian Poetry*, Canadian Authors Association, Volume 18, Number 3, 1965.

Carpenter, Carole Henderson. *Many Voices: A Study of folklore Activities in Canada and Their Role in Canadian Culture* Ottawa: National Museums of Canada, Canadian Centre for Folk Culture Studies, Paper 16, 1979.

Child, Francis James. *The English and Scottish Popular Ballads* 5 Volumes, Boston, 1882-98.

*Chorus*, newsletter of the Choral Federation of Nova Scotia. Volume 14, Number 3, June 1989.

Clark, Mavis Thorpe. *Strolling Players: Joan & Betty Raynor* Melbourne: Lansdown Press, 1972.

Coleman, Thomas. "Keep that bawdy song, sailor boy, for the saviour of Maritime folklore", Toronto *Globe & Mail*, 3 April, 1976.

Craig, Linda. "The Scottish origin of Farewell to Nova Scotia", *Dalhousie Review,* Volume 58, Number 3, 1978.

Crampton, W.J. "Songs from Devil's Island Make Unique New Volume," *Port and Province*, April 1933.

Creighton, Helen. *A Folk Tale Journey Through the Maritimes* ed. Michael Taft and Ronald Caplan, Wreck Cove, Breton Books, 1993.

Creighton, Helen. *A Life in Folklore* Toronto: McGraw-Hill Ryerson, 1975.

Creighton, Helen. "Are We Truly Musical?", *Onward*, 14 January, 1928.

Creighton, Helen. *Bluenose Ghosts* Toronto: Ryerson, 1957.

Creighton, Helen. *Bluenose Magic: Popular Beliefs and Superstitions in Nova Scotia* Toronto: Ryerson, 1968.

Creighton, Helen. "Cape Breton Nicknames and Tales" *Folklore In Action: Essays for Discussion in Honor of MacEdward Leach,* edited by Horace P. Beck. American Folklore Society, Volume 14, 1962.

Creighton, Helen. "Collecting Songs of Nova Scotia Blacks" *Folklore Studies in Honour of Herbert Halpert* ed. Kenneth Goldstein and Neil Rosenberg, St. John's: Memorial University, 1980.

Creighton, Helen. *Folksongs from Southern New Brunswick* Ottawa: Canadian Centre for Folk Culture Studies, National Museum of Man, 1971.

Creighton, Helen. *Folklore of Lunenburg County, Nova Scotia* Toronto: McGraw-Hill Ryerson, 1976. [reprint of the National Museum of Canada Bulletin Number 117, Anthropological Series Number 29, 1950. Authors additions to second edition]

Creighton, Helen. "Folklore of Victoria Beach", *Journal of American Folklore*, Volume 63, 1950.

Creighton, Helen. *Maritime Folk Songs* Toronto: Ryerson Press, 1961.

Creighton, Helen. "Sable Island" *Macleans Magazine* 1 December, 1931.

Creighton, Helen. *Songs and Ballads from Nova Scotia* New York: Dover, 1966. Originally published without postscript by J.M. Dent & Sons, Toronto, 1932.

Creighton, Helen. "Unseasonable Golf" *Sunday Leader,* 8 November, 1925.

Creighton, Helen. *With a heigh-heigh-ho* Halifax, Nimbus, 1986.

Creighton, Helen and Calum MacLeod. *Gaelic Songs in Nova Scotia* Ottawa: National Museum Bulletin 117, 1964.

Creighton, Helen and Doreen H. Senior. *Traditional Songs from Nova Scotia* Toronto: Ryerson, 1950.

Creighton, Helen, and Doreen Senior. *Twelve Folk Songs from Nova Scotia* London: Novello, 1940.

Creighton, Helen and Edward D. Ives. *Eight Folk Tales from Miramichi* Orono: Northeast Folklore, Volume 4, 1962.

Creighton, Helen and Eunice Sircom. *Eight Ethnic Folk Songs for Young Children* Toronto: Gordon V. Thompson, 1977.

Creighton, Helen and Eunice Sircom. *Nine Ethnic Folk Songs* Toronto: Gordon V. Thompson, 1977.

Creighton, Helen and Ronald Labelle. *La Fleur du Rosier: Acadian Folksongs* Sydney: University College of Cape Breton Press and Ottawa: Canadian Museum of Civilization, 1988.

Croft, Clary. *Chocolates, Tattoos and Mayflowers: Mainstreet Memorabilia from Clary Croft,* Halifax: Nimbus, 1995.

Croft, Clary. "The Use of Folklore in Selected Works of Thomas H. Raddall" *Time and Place: The Life and Works of Thomas H. Raddall,* ed. Alan R. Young, Fredericton: Acadiensis, 1991.

Croft, Clary. "What Band That Sunday Morning?." Afterword: Saunders, Charles. Share and Care: The Story of the Nova Scotia Home for Colored Children Halifax: Nimbus Publishing, 1994.

Darrach, Claude. *From A Coastal Schooner's Log* Halifax: Nova Scotia Museum, 1979.

Davis, Jennifer L. *World War II Collection in the Archive of Folk Culture, American Folklife Center, The Library of Congress* Washington: Library of Congress LCFAFA, Number 15, August 1995.

Davies, Gwendolyn. "The Song Fishermen: A Regional Poetry Celebration" *People and Place: Studies of Small Town Life in the Maritimes,* ed. Larry McCann, Fredericton: Acadiensis, 1987.

Doerflinger, William M. "Cruising for Ballads in Nova Scotia" *Canadian Geographic Journal* Volume 16, 1938.

Drainie, Bronwyn, "A Passion for Tall Tales and Sad Refrains" *Globe and Mail* Toronto, 23 December, 1989.

Drainie, Bronwyn. "Folklorist brings out the worst of the spoilsports" *Globe and Mail* Toronto, 5 February, 1994.

Dunn, Charles W. Highland Settler, *A Portrait of the Scottish Gael in Nova Scotia* Toronto: University of Toronto Press, 1953.

Fahs, Lois S. *Swing Your Partner: Old Time Dances of New Brunswick and Nova Scotia* [collected and arranged by author; appears to have been used as instructional book for Provincial Summer School, Saint John, New Brunswick, copyright, Canada, 1939.]

Fauset, Arthur Huff. *Folklore from Nova Scotia* American Folklore Society, Volume 24, 1931.

Flewwelling, Martin. "Profile: Dr. helen Creighton" *Atlantic Advocate* Volume 78, Number 8, April 1986.

*Folklore* Volume 2, Number 1, Winter, 1951. Nova Scotia Folkschool Club Newsletter, Issued quarterly through the Adult Education Division, Department of Education, Halifax.

Foster, Ann. "She Tracks Down Canada's Folk Songs", *Star Weekly,* 31 May, 1958.

Fowke, Edith. *Canadian Folklore: Perspectives on Canadian Culture* Toronto: Oxford University Press, 1988.

Fowke, Edith. *Folklore of Canada* Toronto: McClelland and Stewart, 1976.

Fowke, Edith. "Labor and Industrial Protest Songs in Canada" *Journal of American Folklore* Volume 82, 1969.

Fowke, Edith. *The Penguin Book of Canadian Folk Songs* London: Penguin, 1973.

Fowke, Edith. edited and annotated, *Sea Songs and ballads from ninethenth-century Nova Scotia: The William H. Smith and Fenwick Hatt manuscripts* New York: Folklorica, 1981.

Fowke, Edith and Alan Mills. *Canada's Story in Song* Toronto: Gage, 1960.

Fowke, Edith and Carole Henderson, with Judith Brooks, comp. *A Bibliography of Canadian Folklore in English*. Downsview: York University, 1976.

Fowke, Edith & Joe Glazer. *Songs of Work and Protest* New York: Dover, 1973.

Fowke, Edith and Richard Johnston. *Folk Songs of Canada* Waterloo, Ontario: Waterloo Music, 1954.

Fowke, Edith and Richard Johnston. *More Folk Songs of Canada* Waterloo, Ontario: Waterloo Music, 1967.

Fraser, Mary. *Folklore of Nova Scotia* Antigonish: Formac, 1975. (Reprint)

French, Maida Parlow. *Apples Don't Just Grow* Toronto: McClelland & Stewart, 1954.

George, Graham. "Folk Singing or Just Folks", *Saturday Night*, 30 September, 1961.

Gerson, Carole. "The Literary Culture of Atlantic Women Betweeen the Wars" *Myth & Milieu: Atlantic Literature and Culture 1918-1939*, ed. Gwendolyn Davies, Fredericton, Acadiensis, 1993.

Gibbon, J. Murray. *Canadian Folk Songs* Toronto: J.M. Dent & Sons, 1927.

Gillis, James D. *The Cape Breton Giant* Reprinted Wreck Cove: Breton Press, 1988.

Gilmour, Clyde. "A passion for folksongs and plain English," *Toronto Star*, 30 October, 1982.

Gledhill, Christopher. *Folk Songs of Prince Edward Island* Charlottetown: Square Deal Publications, c.1973.

Greenhill, Pauline. "Lots of Stories: Maritime Narratives from the Creighton Collection" Ottawa: National Museums of Canada; Canadian Centre for Folk Culture Studies, Mercury Series, Number 57, 1985.

Gregory, E. David. "A.L. Lloyd and the English Folk Song Revival, 1934-44" *Canadian Journal for Traditional Music*, Volume 25, 1997.

Grover, Carrie. *A Heritage of Song* Maine [n/d], Reprint Norwood Pa.: Norwood, 1973.

Hammond, Arthur. "The Unquiet Groove" *The Tamarack Review* Issue 13, 1959.

Harris, Carol E. *A Sense of Themselves: Elizabeth Murray's Leadership in School and Community* Halifax: Fernwood, 1998.

Henderson, M. Carole. " Folklore Scholarship and the Socio-political Milieu in Canada" *Journal of the Folklore Institute*, Volume 10, 1973.

*HerStory 1976*. A Canadian Women's Calendar, Saskatoon Women's Calendar Collective, 1975.

Holt, David. "Folklore: endless in its variety" *Atlantic Insight* Volume 9, Number 6, June 1987.

*House of Commons Debates*, Volume 131, Number 115, 2nd Session, 34th Parliament, Wednesday, 20 December, 1989.

Hull, Raymond review of *Maritime Folk Songs* by Helen Creighton, *Vancouver Sun*, 11 April, 1962.

Ives, Edward D._*Folksongs of New Brunswick* Fredericton: Goose Lane Editions, 1989.

Ives, Edward D. *Larry Gorman: The Man Who Made the Songs* Bloomington: Indiana University Press, 1964.

Ives, Edward D. "Twenty-one Folksongs from Prince Edward Island" *Northeast Folklore* Volume 5, 1963.

Ives, Edward D. *The World of Maritimes Folklore* Halifax: The Helen Creighton Foundation, 1992.

*Journal of the House of Assembly*, Province of Nova Scotia, Halifax: King's Printer, 1930.

Karpeles, Maud. An Introduction to English Folk Song London: Oxford University Press, 1973.

Karpeles, Maud. *Folk Songs from Newfoundland* London: Oxford University Press, 1934.

Karpeles, Maud. *Folk Songs from Newfoundland* London: Farber and Farber, 1971.

Kitz, Janet F. *Shattered City: The Halifax Explosion and the Road to Recovery* Halifax: Nimbus, 1989.

Kizuk, Alexander. "Molly Beresford and the Song Fishermen of Halifax: Cultural Production, Canon and Desire in 1920s Canadian Poetry" *Myth & Milieu: Atlantic Literature and Culture 1918-1939*, ed. Gwendolyn Davies, Fredericton, Acadiensis, 1993.

Lacey, Laurie. *Ethnicity and the German Descendants of Lunenburg County, Nova Scotia* Ethnic Heritage Series, Volume VII, Halifax: International Education Centre, St. Mary's University, 1982.

Lacey, Laurie. *Lunenburg County Folklore and Oral History: Project 77* Ottawa: National Museums of Canada, 1979.

Lacourciere, Luc. *Le Conte Populaire Fancais en Amerique du Nord*. Paper presented at the International Congress of Folklore, Kiel, Copenhagen, 1959.

Lacourciere, Luc. "The Present State of French Canadian Folklore Studies" *Journal of American Folklore*, Volume 74, Number 294, 1961.

Lambert, Richard S. *School Broadcasting in Canada* Toronto: University of Toronto Press, 1963.

Leach, MacEdward. "Celtic Tales from Cape Breton" *Studies in Folklore in Honor of Stith Thompson* ed. Edson Richmond. Bloomingdale: Indiana University Press, 1957.

Leach, Maria, ed. *Standard Dictionary of Folklore, Mythology, and Legend* 2 volumes, New York: Funk and Wagnalls, 1949-1950.

Lee, Jerry, review of *Land of the Old Songs, Winnipeg Free Press*, 3 August, 1960.

Lloyd, A.L. *Folk Song in England* London: Lawrence and Wishart, 1967.

Lovelace, Martin. "W. Roy MacKanzie As A Collector of Folksong" *Canadian Folk Music Journal* Volume 5, 1977.

Lutz, Pam. "Clary Croft/Ed McCurdy" *Atlantic Insight* Volume 4, Number 8, 1982.

MacDonald, Andrea. "A False Note", *Daily News* 29 September, 1997.

MacGorman, Harry R. "Lady of the legends: she collects ghosts for kicks" *Nova Scotia* Volume 1, Number 1, June 1969.

Mackenzie, W. Roy. "Ballad Singing in Nova Scotia" *Journal of American Folklore* Volume 22, 1909.

Mackenzie, W. Roy. *Ballads and Sea Songs from Nova Scotia* Cambridge: Harvard University Press, 1928.

Mackenzie, W. Roy. *The Quest of the Ballad* New Jersey, Princeton University Press, 1919.

MacNeil, Joe Neil. *Tales until Dawn: The World of a Cape Breton Gaelic Story-Teller* Kingston and Montreal: McGill-Queen's University press, 1987.

Manny, Louise and James Reginald Wilson. *Songs of Miramichi* Fredericton: New Brunswick Press, 1968.

*Mariposa Folk Festival*, [newsletter] Number 11, February/March 1990.

McCawley, Stuart. *Cape Breton Come-All-Ye* Glace Bay: Brodie, 1929.

McKay, Ian. "He is More Picturesque in His Oilskins": Helen Creighton and the Art of Being Nova Scotian, *New Maritimes*, Issue 92, Volume 12, Number 1, September/October, 1993.

McKay, Ian. "Helen Creighton and the Politics of Antimodernism" *Myth & Milieu: Atlantic Literature and Culture 1918-1939*, ed. Gwendolyn Davies, Fredericton, Acadiensis, 1993.

McKay, Ian. *The Quest of the Folk: Antimodernism and Cultural Selection in Twentieth-Century Nova Scotia* Montreal: McGill-Queen's University Press, 1994.

Manny, Louise and James Reginald Wilson. *Songs of the Miramichi* Fredericton: New Brunswick Press, 1968.

Moore, Marion F. "Canada's First Folk Song Collector Visits Halifax." *Mail Star*, 18 January, 1955.

Morrison, James. review of *Maritime Folk Songs* by Helen Creighton, *Fredericton Gleaner*, 3 March, 1962.

Muise, D.A. "Who Owns History Anyway? Reinventing Atlantic Canada for Pleasure and Profit" *Acadiensis* Volume 27, Number 2, spring 1998.

Nightingale, Marie. *Out of Old Nova Scotian Kitchens* Halifax: Petheric Press, 1970.

Nowry, Lawrence. *Man of Mana: Marius Barbeau* New Canada Publications, N.C. Press Limited.

O'Connor, Patricia J. *The Story of St. Christopher House 1912-1984* Toronto Association of Neighbourhood Serices, 1986.

O'Donnell, John C. *"And Now the fields Are Green": a collection of coal mining songs in Canada* Sydney: University College of Cape Breton Press, 1992.

O'Donnell, John C. "Contribution of American Folklorists to Research on Canadian Coal-Mining Songs" *Work, Ethnicity, and Oral History* ed. Dorothy E. Moore and James H. Morrison, Halifax: International Education Centre, 1988.

Parsons, Elsie Clew. "Micmac Folklore" *Journal of American Folklore*, Volume 38, 1925.

Parsons, Elsie Clew. "Micmac Notes" *Journal of American Folklore*, Volume 39, 1926.

Peacock, Kenneth. *A Practical Guide for Folk Music Collectors* Canadian Folk Music Society, 1966.

Pedersen, Stephen. "Creighton's Legacy" *Mail Star* 16 December 1989.

Pedersen, Stephen. "Maritime concert unforgettable" *Chronicle-Herald* 23 November, 1987.

Peyser, Joan. *The Memory of All That: The Life of George Gershwin* New York: Simon & Schuster, 1993.

Pierce, Gretchen. "School's string tribute to Helen Creighton" *Chronicle-Herald*, 21, May, 1976.

Poteet, Lewis J. *The South Shore Phrase Book* Hantsport: Lancelot Press, 1983.

Poteet, Lewis J. *The Second South Shore Phrase Book* Hantsport: Lancelot Press, 1985.

Pottie, Kaye and Vernon Ellis. *Folksongs of the Maritimes* Halifax: Formac, 1992.

Raben, Joseph. Review in *Hoosier Folklore,* Volume 9, Number 4, 1950.

Rand, Silas T. *Legends of the Micmacs.* New York and London: Longmans, Green, and Company, 1894.

*Real Estate Home Guide*, Volume 3, Issue 23, Halifax Dartmouth Real Estate Board, 15 June, 1995.

Reinke, W.C. Review of *Bluenose Magic: Popular Beliefs and Superstitions in Nova Scotia, Montreal Star*, 9 November, 1968.

Richardson, Evelyn. *We Keep a Light* Toronto: McGraw Hill Ryerson, 1945.

Robbins, James. "Lessons Learned, Questions Raised: Writing a History of Ethnomusicology in Canada" *Canadian Folk Music Journal*, Volume 20, 1992.

Robertson, Marion. *The Chestnut Pipe: Folklore of Shelburne County* Halifax: Nimbus, 1991.

Rosenberg, Neil V. "Country Music in the Maritimes: two studies" St. John's: Memorial University Department of Folklore, reprint series, Number 2, 1976.

Ross, Val. "Lives Lived" Edith Fowke *Globe and Mail*, 3 April, 1996.

Saunders, Charles. Share and Care: *The Story of the Nova Scotia Home for Colored Children* Halifax: Nimbus Publishing, 1994.

Schull, Joseph. *The Far Distant Ships: An Official Acount of Canadian Naval Operations in the Second World War* Ottawa: King's Printer, 1950.

Sclanders, Ian. "She's Collecting Long Lost Songs" *Maclean's* 15 September, 1952.

Seeger, Pete. *The Incomplete Folksinger* edited by Jo Metcalf Schwartz, New York: Simon and Schuster, 1972.

Senior, Doreen H. and Helen Creighton. "Folk Songs Collected in the Province of Nova Scotia, Canada" *Journal of the English Folk Dance and Song Society*, Volume 6, 1951.

Senn, Roma. "The Spooky World of Helen Creighton" *Atlantic Insight* Volume 5, Number 8, 1983.

Shaw, Beatrice M. Hay. "The Vanishing Folklore of Nova Scotia," *The Dalhousie Review*, Volume 3, Number 3, October, 1923.

Shears, Barry W. *The Cape Breton Collection of Bagpipe Music* Halifax: Taigh a' Chiuil, 1995.

Sircom, Hilary. *Helen Creighton* Tantallon, Four East Publications, 1993.

Staebler, Edna. "Would You Change the Lives of These People", *Maclean's*, 12 May, 1956.

Taft, Michael. "A Bibliography for Folklore Studies in Nova Scotia" *Three Atlantic Bibliographies* compiled by H.F. McGee, S.A. Davis, and Michael Taft. Halifax: St. Mary's Univesity, 1975.

Tallman, Richard S. "Folklore research in Atlantic Canada: An Overview", *Acadiensis*, University of New Brunswick, Spring 1979.

Thomas, Phil. "Edith Fowke 1913-1996" *Canadian Folk Music Bulletin*, Volume 30, Number 4, 1996.

Turcot, Marie-Rose. "In the Heart of Acadia with Juliette Gaultier", National Library of Canada, music Division, 1929-39, Harold Smith Collection.

Tutton, Michael. "Creighton's bequest" *Chronicle Herald*, 28 January, 1994.

*Twentieth Century Children's Writers* St. Martin's, 1978, 2nd edition, 1983.

Tye, Diane. "'A Very Lone Worker': Woman-Centred Thoughts on Helen Creighton's Career as a Folklorist", *Journal of the Canadian Folklore Studies Association*, Volume 15, Number 2, 1993.

Tye, Diane. "Retrospective Repertoire Analysis: The Case Study of Ben Henneberry, Ballad Singer of Devil's Island, Nova Scotia" *Journal of the Canadian Folk Music Society*, Volume 16, 1988.

Ullman, Christiane. "German Folksongs of Lunenburg County, NS" *German-Canadian Yearbook*, Volume 5, Toronto, 1979.

Upton, Florence and Bertha Upton. *The Golliwogg's Bicycle Club* London: Longmans, Green & Company, 1896.

Vogan, Nancy F. "Music Education in the Maritimes Between the Wars: a Period of Transition" *Myth & Milieu: Atlantic Literature and Culture 1918-1939*, ed. Gwendolyn Davies, Fredericton, Acadiensis, 1993.

Waller, Adrian. "These Songs Are Our Songs" *Readers' Digest*, Volume 113, Number 675, July 1978.

Whitehead, Ruth Holmes. *Stories from the Six Worlds: Micmac Legends* Halifax, Nimbus, 1988.
Wiggins, William. Review of Folklore of Lunenburg County, Nova Scotia. *American Anthropologist* Volume 75, #6, December 1973.
Wintemberg, J.M. *Folklore of Waterloo County, Ontario* Ottawa: National Museum, Bulletin 116, 1950.

# SUPPLEMENTARY HELEN CREIGHTON BIBLIOGRAPHY

Note: In addition to works cited in the text the following includes a listing of extant publications by Helen Creighton

*A Life in Folklore* Toronto: McGraw-Hill Ryerson, 1975.
"A Pioneer Business Woman" *The Business Woman* April 1928.
"Another Distinguished Native" *Port and Province* May 1932.
"Are We Truly Musical?", *Onward,* 14 January, 1928.
"As I Waited On the Corner" *East and West* 1923.
"Ballad Bagging" *The American Girl* Volume 21, Number 8, 1938.
"Ballads from Devil's Island" *Dalhousie Review* Volume 12, Number 4, 1935.
"The Birdie Game" *Toronto Evening Telegram* March 1925.
*Bluenose Ghosts* Toronto: Ryerson, 1957.
*Bluenose Magic: Popular Beliefs and Superstitions in Nova Scotia* Toronto: Ryerson, 1968.
"Canada's Maritime Provinces: An Ethnomusicological Survey" *Ethnomusicology* Volume 16, 1972.
"The Canadian Babes in the Woods" *Toronto Saturday Night* March 1928.
"Canadian Girl Witnesses Bull Fight in Mexico" *Toronto Star Weekly* c.1922-1923.
"Cape Breton Nicknames and Tales" *Folklore In Action: Essays for Discussion in Honor of MacEdward Leach*, edited by Horace P. Beck. American Folklore Society, Volume 14, 1962.
"Capturing Folklore of Tape" *Canadian Author and Bookman* Volume 46, Number 3, 1971.
"The Carillon of Ottawa" *Western Home Monthly* October 1927.
"Carols and other songs for Christmas" *Canadian Composer* Volume 45, December 1969.
"Christmas Remembered" *Halifax* Volume 2, Number 1, 1979.
"Collecting Folk Songs" *Music Across Canada* Volume 1, Number 3, April 1963.
"Collecting Songs of Nova Scotia Blacks" *Folklore Studies in Honour of Herbert Halpert* ed. Kenneth Goldstein and Neil Rosenberg, St. John's: Memorial University, 1980.[Editor's Page]
*Church Work* 1930s.
"Fiddles, Folk Songs and Fishermen's Yarns" *Canadian Geographical Journal* Volume 84, Number 3, December 1955. Reprinted, March 1972.
"Fishing for Albacore (St. Margaret's Bay, Nova Scotia)" *Canadian Geographical Journal* Volume 3, Number 1, July 1931.
"Folk Dancing" *Encyclopaedia Canadiana* c.1960.
"Folk Music" *Canada Music Week* November 1972.
"Folk-Singers of Nova Scotia", *The Canadian Forum*, July 1952.
"Folk Songs in Nova Scotia" *The Canadian Guider* October 1950.
*Folksongs from Southern New Brunswick* Ottawa: Canadian Centre for Folk Culture Studies, National Museum of Man, 1971.
*Folklore of Lunenburg County, Nova Scotia* Toronto: McGraw-Hill Ryerson, 1976. [reprint of the National Museum of Canada Bulletin Number 117, Anthropological Series Number 29, 1950. Authors additions to second edition]
"Folklore of Victoria Beach", *Journal of American Folklore*, Volume 63, 1950.
"The Haunting Past" *The Maritimes* (Imperial Oil), March 1952.
"History of the Draarouth Schools" *Greenvale Journal* c.1913-1914.
"History of the Nova Scotia Branch of the Canadian Author Association" Canadian Author and Bookman Volume 42, Number 4, 1967.
"Hooked Rugs for Color" *Chatelaine* May 1929.
"Junior Riding in Halifax" *Mayfair* May 1937.
"La Quemada" *East and West* 1923.
"Linen Two Centuries Ago" *Toronto Saturday Night* October 1927.

"The Little White Hen With the Yellow Feather" *Chatelaine* May 1929.
"Lois and A Potato" *Picture Book Paper* November 1927.
"Looking back on a satisfying career" *Canadian Composer* Number 120, April 1977.
"Love Making in Mexico" *Toronto Saturday Night* November 1927.
"Madam Tussard Has A Rival" *Toronto Star Weekly* August 1928.
[Maritime Letter] *Mayfair Magazine* c.1930-1943
*Maritime Folk Songs* Toronto: Ryerson Press, 1961.
"Maritime Woman Wins" *Toronto Star Weekly* December 1932.
"The Mayflower" *Toronto Saturday Night* June 1928.
"Miss Elizabeth Smellie, V.O.N." *Toronto Saturday Night* February 1928.
"Miss Marjorie Price (carilloneur)" *Toronto Saturday Night* September 1927.
"Mr. Squidgy Squoogy" *Chatelaine* August 1928.
"Music in Ottawa" *Musical America* New York, 1928.
"The Mystery of Margaret Floyer" *Toronto Saturday Night* February 1928.
"Nathan Hatt of Nova Scotia" *Sing Out! The Folk Song Magazine* Volume 13, Number 1, February-March 1963.
"Nova Scotia Folk Songs" *Journal of Education* March 1937.
"Old Christmas Customs in Nova Scotia" *Canadian Geographical Journal* Volume 68, Number 6, 1961.
"Onions,eels and peppermint tea" *Sojourn* Issue 1, March 1975.
"Pieces of Eight" *The Maritimes* (Imperial Oil), December 1951.
"Preserving the Art of a Vanishing People" *Homes and Gardens* Volume 6, Number 8, August 1929.
"Roly the Frog" *Western Home Monthly* May 1928.
"Rudyard Kipling and the Halifax Doctor" *Atlantic Advocate* Volume 55, Number 10, June 1965.
"Sable Island" *Maclean's Magazine* 1 December, 1931.
"She Helps Children Appreciate Art" *Toronto Saturday Night* June 1928.
"The Songs of Nathan Hatt" *Dalhousie Review* Volume 32,Number 4, Winter 1953.
"Song Singers" *Maclean's Magazine* December 1937.
*Songs and Ballads from Nova Scotia* New York: Dover, 1966. Originally published without postscript by J.M. Dent & Sons, Toronto, 1932.
"Songs for Christmas" *Atlantic Advocate* Volume 50, Number 4, 1959.
"Songs from Nova Scotia" *International Folk Music Journal* Volume 12, 1960.
"Squid Oh!" *Forest and Outdoors,* October 1929.
"The Sparow's Wicked Deed" *Toronto Evening Telegram* February 1925.
"Telling the Children Stories Over the Air" *Toronto Weekly Star* September 1927.
"Teachers as Folklorists" *Journal of Education* Series 4, Volume 14, Number 7, 1943.
"They Nurse 3000 Patients Every Day, V.O.N." *Maclean's Magazine* November 1928.
"Twilight and Evening Star" *Toronto Star Weekly* November 1928.
"Unseasonable Golf" *Sunday Leader,* 8 November, 1925.
"W. Roy Mackenzie, Pioneer" *Newsletter of the Canadian Folk Music Society* Volume 2, July 1967.
"Young People in Love With the Museum" *Toronto Star Weekly* 1928.
Creighton, Helen and Calum MacLeod. *Gaelic Songs in Nova Scotia* Ottawa: National Museum Bulletin 117, 1964.
Creighton, Helen and Doreen H. Senior. *Traditional Songs from Nova Scotia* Toronto: Ryerson, 1950.
Creighton, Helen, and Doreen Senior. *Twelve Folk Songs from Nova Scotia.* London: Novello, 1940.
Creighton, Helen and Edward D. Ives. *Eight Folk Tales from Miramichi* Orono: Northeast Folklore, Volume 4, 1962.
Creighton, Helen and Eunice Sircom. *Eight Ethnic Folk Songs for Young Children* Toronto: Gordon V. Thompson, 1977.
Creighton, Helen and Eunice Sircom. *Nine Ethnic Folk Songs* Toronto: Gordon V. Thompson, 1977.
Creighton, Helen and Ronald Labelle. *La Fleur du Rosier: Acadian Folksongs* Sydney: University College of Cape Breton Press and Ottawa: Canadian Museum of Civilization, 1988.

# INDEX

✳ ✳ ✳